Going IT Alone:
The Handbook for
Freelance and Contract
Software Developers

A detailed guide to self-employment for software and web developers—from identifying your target market, through to managing your time, finances, and client behavior

Leon Brown

Impackt Publishing

We Mean Business

Going IT Alone: The Handbook for Freelance and Contract Software Developers

First published: November 2016

Production Reference: 1041116

Published by Impackt Publishing Ltd.
Livery Place
35 Livery Street
Birmingham B3 2PB, UK.

ISBN 978-1-78300-140-8

www.packtpub.com/business

Credits

Author
Leon Brown

Reviewer
Rehan Jaffer

Acquisition Editor
Nick Falkowski

Content Development Editor
Amey Varangaonkar

Copy Editors
Pranav Kukreti
Utkarsha S. Kadam

Project Coordinator
Neha Bhatnagar

Proofreader
Safis Editing

Graphics
Abhinash Sahu
Jason Monteiro

Production Coordinator
Melwyn D'sa

Cover Work
Melwyn D'sa

About the Author

Leon Brown is a software developer and trainer from Liverpool in England. His mantra is that he practices what he preaches and preaches what he practices. With over 20 years of experience in software development, Leon has developed software for legacy and modern platforms ranging from the Amstrad CPC, ZX Spectrum, and Amiga through to the Web and smartphones.

Leon has a diverse range of commercial experience, including the delivery of Internet systems and training for household names, including UNICEF, the NHS, SAGE, and The University of Manchester to projects for small businesses, start-ups, and charities. His experience of working with such a diverse range of organizations has allowed him to understand how to approach the different types of situations affecting software development projects. His projects ranged from the creation of websites and apps to CRM and the use of AI for reporting and decision-making.

Leon regularly writes for web industry magazine *Web Designer* from *Imagine Publishing*, in which he has written feature articles and tutorials covering web development. His most notable articles for the magazine provided detailed insight into securing websites against common methods of hacking, such as session hijacking and SQL injection. These articles gained highly positive feedback from the magazine's readers in the following issues.

Acknowledgements

I would like to thank my mum, Phyllis Brown, for buying my first computer, the gift that sparked my interest in programming. I would also like to thank my friends and family for their support over the years to help me become a professional—Chinyere Brown, Christine Bobb, Norman Bobb, The Capos (Mark Smith, George Heron, Ian Kerr, Dan Inwood, Andrew Lee), Jonathan De Vaal, and Ashley Moore.

I've also been very fortunate to have come across great people in business who have provided advice and mentoring: Claire Bicknell of Catena, who provided great leadership in my first commercial project as a student and provided the advice and opportunities to gain the experience that kick-started my career; Jonathan Read of Village Software, who has provided a lot of advice on operating the business side of software development; Jeanne Hatton of Uniti, who provided the opportunity to enhance my early web design and development portfolio that led to greater opportunities; to all these people and others who have been a positive influence, thank you!

About the Reviewer

Rehan Jaffer is a London-based freelance Ruby on Rails developer with a decade of experience. His clients have ranged from renegade entrepreneurs to companies producing software used by the CEOs of FTSE 100 companies. He has co-authored a book on SQL for Tealeaf Academy and has written for numerous technology and programming blogs. His other interests include artificial intelligence, medicine, and physics.

I would like to thank my parents for their constant and unwavering faith in me; my brother Sadiq and my peers Stephen Wight, Michael Weagley, and Timmothy Lewis for their advice, both on technology and otherwise; Liz, Bart, Hazel, Keegan, Martin, Kristina, and many, many more for their friendship and support. Without all of you, none of this would have been possible.

Contents

Chapter 4: Creating a Brand   93

Chapter 5: Networking, Marketing, and Sales   113

Preface

Whether it is through a desire for better work flexibility, a way to make some extra money, redundancy, or a change in career direction, freelancing and contracting are increasingly attractive options for software developers who create anything from databases and websites through to phone apps and enterprise systems. Drawing from my time of learning lessons the hard way, this book is written and designed to inform software developers at all levels of experience about the business side of freelancing and how approaches to implementing software are as much of a business consideration as more traditional business activities, such as marketing and business planning.

For students, freelancing offers an ideal opportunity to earn and learn, with the added benefit of work-based learning being accepted by many courses as a contribution toward the final qualification. Known as APEL (Accreditation of Prior Experiential Learning), this experience can count for as much as the majority of a qualification if it can be proven that the majority of the course content is learned through experience from work. With most students being young and free of financial commitments (or at least fewer commitments), the main benefit of freelancing is to gain a better position in the job market through CV enhancement and gaining the types of experience that can be used to impress potential employers at interviews. Payment is always nice, but the primary focus for students should always be on building the type of experience that will open future opportunities.

Those who are already working in the industry are likely to find themselves at one point or another in the position where moving into a freelance career is a desire or the only option, but is nevertheless something scary. Unlike students, professionals have to earn real money to pay their bills, hence do not have the luxury of being able to accept work regardless of their budget. This means that professionals need to have more focus on getting the business aspects right to remain profitable. Unlike students, more experience of the same type of work doesn't add any strategic value when it comes to making more money in the long term.

Being successful as a freelance or contract software developer isn't just about having knowledge of standard business practices in addition to having programming skills. Freelance developers need to understand how to integrate software development methods with their chosen business model. With software technologies changing and adapting on a regular basis, freelance software developers need to keep up to date with anything emerging in their field that may affect how they implement their business strategy or risk becoming irrelevant overnight; this is ever more true when working with open source technologies, especially with recruiters for contract roles seeking people with experience of the latest *buzzword*.

With most people considering the option of going freelance coming from a background primarily of permanent employment, it is all too easy to make decisions that are highly biased toward their technical experience. Likewise, those who have a background primarily in business development can also be vulnerable to making decisions that are too biased from a traditional business perspective. Being successful in freelance software development requires the knowledge of both disciplines to be combined in order to achieve the best outcome. This allows the identification of profitable business strategies that can be implemented in ways that minimize risk.

The focus of this book is to provide an insight into freelancing and contracting, written from a freelance software developer's perspective. With chapters designed to take you from everything you will need to start your freelance business, through to best practices for software development and dealing with clients; you will learn how to avoid costly mistakes by becoming efficient in the way you develop your code, along with how to manage your clients and the people you work with. You will also learn about the strategic business side so that you can clearly identify your approach to win and deliver the type of work you want, along with developing partnerships and other resources you will need to be successful and profitable.

When establishing your freelance operation, you will need to undertake adequate preparation. The chapters of this book are arranged in a logical order that is likely to reflect the different activity stages you will need to engage as you progress. Each section describes the specific activities you will need to be aware of, allowing you to build a business plan that you can continually refer back to in order to keep focused on your goals and see how opportunities are progressing and developing.

What this book covers

Chapter 1, Introducing Freelancing, covers the main considerations to you need to bear in mind for making the move into freelance programming. It introduces the different entity options to operate under, along with considerations for running activities in the early days and the types of freelancing to match your aspirations.

Chapter 2, Positioning Yourself in the Market, covers the considerations required to find the type of work you want and are best suited to. The chapter highlights how to review the market for creating a plan that identifies opportunities for you to carve your niche to win the types of client you can be successful with on both financial and technical levels.

Chapter 3, Defining Your Business Model, covers an exploration of different business models and how they can be applied to your freelance business. You will learn how to create a business model canvas that identifies important elements of your business concept, from strategic partners to customer relationships and key activities.

Chapter 4, Creating a Brand, delivers an introduction to the concept of branding and how it can be applied to all parts of your freelancing, from the creation of your business model through to marketing and project delivery.

Chapter 5, Networking, Marketing, and Sales, presents the options for marketing programming services to your target audience. You will learn the specific differences between between networking, marketing, and sales, as well as how they complement each other.

Chapter 6, An Introduction to Client Types, shows how to identify common traits of clients in order to quickly build a picture of who you are dealing with. You will learn how to use information gained from observations to your advantage when it comes to risk assessment, negotiation, pricing, and project planning.

Chapter 7, Managing Clients, covers learning how to work with clients at each stage of a project to avoid problems that can occur. Discover how risk management, complexity measurement, client analysis, and expectations management can be used to lead projects to a successful outcome.

Chapter 8, Negotiation, introduces a framework for achieving a fair conclusion in negotiations that allow both sides to win. Most importantly, this understanding of negotiation will help you to avoid costly mistakes that impact your finances and reputation.

Chapter 9, Software Development Resources, Patterns, and Strategies, presents approaches to programming that provide benefits for flexibility and coping with changing client requirements. This chapter shows how to strategically construct code to reflect the challenges you are likely to face in your freelance projects.

Chapter 10, Software Development Methodology, introduces the standard processes of software development as used in industry. This chapter compares these different approaches to identify the types of situation they are best suited to. You will learn how to take the best of everything to incorporate into your own methodology.

Chapter 11, Creating Quotes and Estimates, covers avoiding the pitfalls of using a lowest price strategy or *guestimates* when bidding for work. This chapter will show you how to use information analysis to identify a profitable price to charge for your work.

Chapter 12, Project Management, shows how to apply everything covered in the earlier chapters to projects in ways that strategically protect you. Methods to clarify communications, implement formal processes, identify the right people to allocate, and more are discussed.

Who this book is for

Going down the self-employed route in software development offers many opportunities to develop awareness and skills to enhance your career. Whether you are a student currently studying software development or a veteran software developer already in the industry, this book provides you with insights you need to avoid the pitfalls of self-employment and to succeed with software projects that are profitable and sustainable.

Conventions

In this book, you will find a number of styles of text that distinguish between different kinds of information. Here are some examples of these styles, and an explanation of their meaning.

New terms and **important words** are shown in bold.

> **Lists**
> Lists appear like this

> **Make a note**
> Warnings or important notes appear in a box like this.

Reader feedback

Feedback from our readers is always welcome. Let us know what you think about this book—what you liked or disliked. Reader feedback is important for us as it helps us develop titles that you will really get the most out of.

To send us general feedback, simply e-mail `feedback@packtpub.com`, and mention the book's title in the subject of your message.

If there is a topic that you have expertise in and you are interested in either writing or contributing to a book, see our author guide at `www.packtpub.com/authors`.

Piracy

Piracy of copyrighted material on the Internet is an ongoing problem across all media. At Packt, we take the protection of our copyright and licenses very seriously. If you come across any illegal copies of our works in any form on the Internet, please provide us with the location address or website name immediately so that we can pursue a remedy.

Please contact us at `copyright@packtpub.com` with a link to the suspected pirated material.

We appreciate your help in protecting our authors and our ability to bring you valuable content.

>1

Introducing Freelancing

Instead of jumping head first into starting your freelance activities, the first steps should be based around investigating whether freelancing is right for you. With there being many ways to engage freelancing activities to suit your ambitions and commitments, freelancing provides the flexibility to be a full time or part time supplementary occupation, both offering different levels of risk and opportunities regarding finances and your commitments to operating as a freelancer.

The freelance lifestyle

The life of the freelancer is often one that is misunderstood by those outside of the profession, the typical image of the freelancer being a guy/lady of leisure who chooses their own working hours, takes seven holidays per year, gets the opportunity to travel to luxury locations for work and gets paid lots of money.

Whereas this lifestyle can be the case for the lucky few, the reality is that the freelance lifestyle typically requires a higher level of commitment, discipline, and knowledge of business than the equivalent employed position. Most freelancers don't work 9 to 5, but more likely whenever to whenever, which usually means longer overall working hours. Holidays are usually restricted to fit with the work and cash flow situation, meaning that work will always dictate when it is best to take a holiday and not when a freelancer feels like it—and there is no holiday or sick pay either!

Not all is as tough as it may sound, especially if you enjoy your work and manage your finances well. Pay is typically significantly better than the equivalent employed position on a per hour worked basis, which can be good for your bank balance if you are able to secure the volume of work, whether it be from a longer term project or several smaller projects. A word of caution regarding evaluation of finances is that unlike being employed, the amount as a freelancer will vary each month depending on how much work you are able to secure—so make sure you have enough saved for months to cover where you have little or no work! This is especially the case when working on more demanding projects in which there will a time lapse between completion of the project and finding the next work source.

As a freelancer, expect to work in a wide range of places, from being invited to travel around the country or overseas, to more 'unique' places such as the company basement.

Providers of freelance projects will offer different levels of luxury to freelancers, the best often being the bigger well-known companies who have bigger budgets to spend—so if you're wanting to get involved with projects that take you to sunny places instead of the company basement, these are the companies that you want to freelance/contract with. The only issue is that these types of opportunities are much more difficult to win and you are likely to have to start at the bottom of the freelance work chain—building your portfolio and freelance experience with many smaller and usually less prestigious projects before you are even considered to be considered as a candidate by one of the bigger luxury organizations. In addition to your portfolio, you should consider looking at how you can build your network of contacts in the right places, allowing you to be recommended for the types of opportunities you desire, as they open.

Is freelancing for you?

It sounds like an easy question, but whether freelancing is the right option for you needs some careful consideration and answers to more detailed questions. Questions you should ask yourself are:

> ➤ Can you afford to be a freelancer?
>> ➤ If you have children or relatives who rely on your earnings, will they suffer if you develop cash flow problems?
>> ➤ Does your current financial situation give you enough margin to cope with situations where payments are delayed?
>> ➤ You don't want to be in a situation where you lose your home because a few of your clients are late paying their invoices
>> ➤ Health is an important factor to consider:
>> ➤ Are you healthy enough to invest the required effort to succeed as a freelancer?
>> ➤ Can you afford health insurance if you are not living in a country with a socialized medical system?

> ➤ Can you handle being a freelancer?
>> ➤ If you like/need a regular work pattern, then freelancing probably isn't for you. Many projects will require phases where you need to work late and work flow isn't always constant enough to ensure that you can always work set hours on the types of work you want to be doing and are getting paid for
>> ➤ Do you have a passion for the services you intend to provide? If you're in it just for the money, you would be better getting a regular job that pays a good salary. If you have skills that are in demand and difficult to find, there's no reason why you shouldn't be able to secure a job with a salary that is significantly higher than the average programmer's salary
>> ➤ If you can work well under pressure, then you will cope with many scenarios you will encounter as a freelance programmer

> ➢ Can you handle working overtime when everyone else is out enjoying the sun? Working in that company basement at the weekend on a hot day can be extra fun!

➤ Do you have good business acumen?

> ➢ By being a freelancer, you are in effect being your own business, hence the need to make good business decisions, develop good strategies, and know how to keep your services profitable. If you fail at any of these, you will get into difficulty that will cause you problems on both a professional and personal basis

➤ Do you see the bigger picture or just the next step?

> ➢ Being able to see the bigger picture of all aspects of the projects you are involved with is an important part of being successful in a freelance career, especially when it comes to programming. This isn't restricted to your technical skills, but also for how everyone else fits within projects, and management of political issues

➤ How well can you communicate?

> ➢ Success of a project will always depend on good communication. You need to be able to extract the right information from clients to get the job done efficiently and profitably, as well to do the 'right' job. You will also need to be able to adjust your communication style for different types of clients—see *Chapter 7, Managing Clients*

➤ Can you be assertive if required?

> ➢ Although not always required, it's important to know when and how to be assertive when required. It's not always good to be assertive with clients, but sometimes this is a requirement in situations where clients are taking advantage or pushing you into a situation that is unacceptable

➤ Are you confident?

> ➢ If you don't show confidence in yourself, then potential clients won't have enough confidence to hire you—and those who do will quickly lose confidence or look to take advantage

> ➢ Being able to accept rejection and persevere without being demoralized is an important quality—especially in the early days when you don't have a strong enough portfolio to stand out from the competition. An ability to accept rejection and embrace criticism will allow you to adapt and persevere until you get hired; this is ultimately a numbers game, where you increase your chances of being hired with each project/contract application—using your response to previous feedback to further increase your chances

Defining your motivations

Knowing your motivations for freelancing will help you to focus on achieving your ambitions. The following are some of the reasons that have motivated people to get into freelance software development:

Boosting employability

Keeping in mind that the purpose of freelancing doesn't have to be a permanent arrangement, freelancing to boost your employability can be a smart move in times where the jobs market has more applicants per job and fewer jobs available. Graduates often suffer the most from this dilemma, as the jobs they seek demand a level of experience that isn't gained from the lecture theatre, which puts them at a disadvantage when they are competing against people who already have several years of experience.

Freelancing to boost employability isn't primarily about getting the best payment rate, but about strategically building your employability portfolio, so make sure to keep focused on only seeking and accepting the type of work that adds value to this—anything that doesn't fit this motivation will only increase the amount of time it takes you to get to the level of employability that you require. Elements of your employability portfolio you should be aiming to improve through freelance activities should include:

A list of people who would be happy to provide you with a reference:

> ➤ People who are willing to recommend you to people they know
>
> ➤ Hands on experience of skills specified in the job adverts you plan to apply for
>
> ➤ An understanding of how businesses work
>
> ➤ Useful information to use at interviews that demonstrates both your technical and business process awareness

Not to be confused with volunteering or contributing to open source projects, freelancing to boost employability should be specific about where your involvement and responsibilities start and end. The following are some suggestions on what you should make clear to your freelance clients:

> ➤ **Payment**: Never work for free, as this risks you being perceived as free labor which can generate the perception of your time not having value
>
> ➤ **Rate**: The rate you charge for your time is a signal to clients how much you perceive yourself to be worth; setting a rate that is too low can lead to a perception that you don't value your skills to be at the same standard as people who charge a higher rate—or that what you are providing isn't worth paying a premium for. At the same time, smaller businesses are not able to afford the same types of rates that bigger businesses can afford, hence you should research the standard rate for the market segment you are targeting; standard contractor rates in northern England are in the region of £300 per day for mid-weight PHP contract roles in established higher turnover organizations, but you may struggle to get half of this rate for projects with small start-ups, simply because they don't have the cash

➤ **Time**: Specify the duration of your availability in terms of days and working times, as well as the duration of your project involvement. This avoids you getting involved in situations where clients are expecting you to provide support far beyond completion of the project and interrupting your other freelance projects or the job you eventually win

➤ **People**: Be specific about who you want to be dealing with on the project. For the purpose of boosting your employability, you want to be gaining credibility with people who are influential and are well connected, hence being in the position where they can recommend you and provide you with leads. Additionally, you want to ensure that there are specific procedures on how and who contacts you with details relating to what you are being asked to produce; the last thing you want is for people with no authority asking you to develop features that aren't authorized by key decision makers in the client's organization, which could then reflect badly on you and affect your chances of being recommended

➤ **Tasks**: Make it clear what you do and don't do. People often make assumptions about what your job role include, which can lead to clients becoming unhappy when they perceive that you have been lazy by missing out important parts of their requirement. An example of this is that a lot of people think that a web designer also does SEO (gaining high positions on Google), web development, database development, and everything else to do with websites—leading to situations where they complain that the website they have purchased isn't on page one of Google, where this wasn't part of their request. Regardless of who is right and wrong in this scenario, customer dissatisfaction will only result in you not being recommended and possibly causing negative word to spread about you, which goes against your motivation of boosting your employability. Avoid this by clearly stating what you do upfront, even if you believe that the client already knows—stating it to them, preferably also in writing for future reference, avoids any scope for confusion that is detrimental to your primary motivation

Learning new skills

Whether it's learning about organizing finances, negotiation, project management, or new software development skills, freelancing will open many opportunities for you to learn skills that you wouldn't learn in a regular job. In addition, freelancing often offers you the opportunities to learn the skills you want to learn, rather than the skills that your current employer wants you to.

Where learning is a significant motivation for freelancing, consider listing the types of skills and the reasons you wish you to learn and gain experience of them. This could be part of boosting employability, or to complement studies on a formal course, such as a degree. Whichever the reason for wanting to learned new skills, take some time to consider the order and timescales to invest in learning them so that the exercise of learning can be best applied to the purpose. For example, learning a set of skills in the wrong order for the purpose of improving results on a formal course would have little benefit if skills being learnt from freelancing were in the reverse order of the course, as early course subjects will be missed from freelance exercises and knowledge gained to be applied to later subjects in the course schedule could be forgotten.

Taking a break

The motivation to go freelance isn't always as serious as developing a career or a main source of income. Using freelancing to take a break from full time working provides a solution to the following concerns:

> **Employment gaps**: When the time comes to go back to full time employment, having a gap of employment on your CV is something that can prevent you from being invited to interviews, as employers can see this as an indication of you needing to refresh your skills in order to become productive. Doing small amounts of freelance work during your break allows you to fill this employment gap with details of the type of projects you have been involved with, which may also benefit your employability due to increased exposure to complementary skills and knowledge gained

> **Network drain**: The people you know are the most important asset you have—regardless of whether you are self-employed or employed, so it's important not to cut your connections and to be pro-active about making sure that people remember who you are and what you do. When it comes to getting back into full time employment, having people who can recommend you or who may be able to offer you a position can make the difference between having a significant advantage for getting your next role and simply not being invited to interviews. Additionally, working on freelance projects for an existing employer is a good way to keep options open to return to their employment after you've taken your break

> **Outdated skills**: Areas of software development such as front end web development and games programming for consoles have a higher than usual demand for developers to be learning new techniques and to be aware of upcoming technologies. Taking a break of anything longer than a few months introduces the risk of making your skills outdated by the time you decide to return to employment, making it difficult for you to secure your next role. Freelancing during your career break ensures that you are at least aware of new developments and can gain exposure to them to keep your skill set relevant

Increasing financial security

Going into business of any type, whether it is freelance or otherwise, is always a risk that starts with financial insecurity. The financial security from freelancing occurs over time, as you become established with the right types of clients and income sources. The following are details of factors that can combine to make long term freelancing more financially secure—if you are successful and have the right business model:

> **Multiple income sources**: Not being dependent on one employer means that if, for whatever reason, a client decides they no longer need your services, you still have the ability to generate income from other clients you deliver your services to. For this to work out, you need to make sure to have:

> ➤ The right type of clients—focus on clients who have the type of turnover (money going into their business) to be able to invest worthwhile amounts into the services you provide; building a business around lots of clients who spend small amounts is both more time consuming and higher risk

> ➤ Trust and reputation—people who spend large amounts are often motivated by buying into convenience in the sense of buying into someone they can trust to get the job done properly and not to cause unnecessary trouble

➤ **Asset ownership**: Developing assets that you own provides you with a significant advantage if you develop something of commercial value, as this provides the option to generate passive income or to sell the asset for a significant amount that would more than justify the amount of time and resources you have invested into it's creation:

> ➤ A major difference between the work you produce freelance and the work you produce under employment is ownership. Obviously, the work you create under an employer's working hours is classed as their property, but it may also be a surprise to find that an employer can own work produced by an employee outside of regular working hours if it is deemed to be within the scope of their employment—that is, if you are hired as a software developer, then software developed outside of their working hours can also be defined as within scope of their employment. This can lead to significant issues should you create something of significant commercial value in your own time while under the employment of someone else

> ➤ Most freelance projects in which you are developing tailored code to the project will have a clause in the contract to state the work you are being paid for is owned by whoever is hiring you—this is fine and to be expected, but make sure that ownership is only limited to what they are paying you to write; that is, make sure that there is no scope for clients to claim ownership of code components written outside of their project, regardless of whether it is used in their project or not

➤ **Passive income**: This type of income occurs where you invest little or no time for it to be generated, and is often as a result of the creation of an asset you have created. An example of passive income is royalties from phone apps; once you have developed the right app for which there is a demand and which supports a revenue-generating business model, the app will generate regular income once it is marketed correctly to persuade people to buy/use the app. Jake Birket is an example of a programmer who set up as indie developer Grey Alien Games (`http://www.greyaliengames.com/`) and makes a passive income by developing games that he sells through his website and online gaming portals such as Valve's Steam. Once Jake has created his games, he is not limited to how much money he can make, providing that his marketing is able to reach the types of people who want to play his games—and most importantly, pay for them

> ➤ **Knowledge**: Knowing your financial situation is an issue relevant to everyone, regardless of whether they are employed or self-employed. The advantage of self-employment in this respect is that you have full access to your financials in order to know what you can pay yourself, and of any potential financial issues that could occur. Although being in employment offers you legal protection through employment rights that are not automatically given to self-employed people, circumstances can occur in which an employer who otherwise seemed to be in good financial health goes bankrupt, leaving their employees without pay and looking for new work—something you should be protected against to a degree as a freelancer by being aware of your own finances and not being solely dependent on one source of income, like regular employees usually are

While not being initially the most secure option, with jobs no longer being for life and not necessarily offering you a share of the success your work generates for them, freelancing poses some advantages not offered by employed work—and a greater degree of security if you succeed in becoming fully established; although it should be noted that depending on freelancing as a career isn't for the faint hearted.

Generating a side income

Using freelancing as an activity to earn some money as an activity outside of full time work commitments is a good way to raise money to make purchases such as holidays and hobby interests, or even as a way to increase your savings. Without the pressure of making sure that enough money is being earned from work activities to pay the bills, freelancing to generate a side income allows you to take a much more relaxed approach to how you work and therefore provides more flexibility on which work you accept.

In addition to producing code for other people/businesses, there is the option of creating your own product. This angle has more risk due to not having any guaranteed payment and relying on having the right product features to convince people to make the purchase, but as a side income, this method doesn't risk financial problems and can earn a significant amount if it pays off.

Case study: New Star Soccer

New Star Soccer, created by Simon Read is an example of an independently developed app that achieved commercial success and even beat FIFA 13 and other high profile sports games to win a BAFTA award. The financial success of the mobile game for Android and iOS (iPad and iPhone) peaked at sales generating £7,000 in just one day, and regularly earning £1,000 per day after its release—you do the math to identify how much the game earned.

Not all was plain sailing with the game's development, which had been through several versions until it achieved major success with the breakthrough mobile version. The first version of New Star Soccer was created as a side project to Simon's day job working in IT support and earned him a few hundred pounds per month in sales, which is great to have as a supplementary income to a regular salary and emphasizes the flexibility offered by starting your self-employment on a part-time basis.

Within three years of developing the game as a side project, New Star Soccer 3 was able to generate an average income between £2,000 and £3,000 per month. The sales statistics at this point were enough to convince Simon that taking redundancy from his full time job to concentrate on his game project full time was now viable financially, and resulted in him making his side business full-time. With the project now being Simon's sole income for him and his wife, working on the project was now more serious and not just a hobby that happened to make some income—with the need to make sure that income continued to come in so that bills could be paid and food was on the table, Simon had to work 12 hour days at the expense of a social life. Despite the minor sacrifices for making the project a full-time business, Simon enjoyed a successful first year with continued sales of his game and his wife helping with the admin side.

Although the project had been successful, problems started to hit after Simon was given a £17,000 tax bill for the sales generated by New Star Soccer 3, as well as poor sales of versions 4 and 5 of New Star Soccer and an unsuccessful experiment to launch several separate games outside of the football theme; namely New Star Grand Prix and New Star Tennis. Simon's saving grace was the inclusion of his game Super Laser Race in a game bundle distributed by Valve's Steam game portal; this alone generated £14,000 in just one week and allowed Simon to pay off his debts.

Serious success in Simon's game business didn't return until the release of the mobile version of his New Star Soccer series, which has regularly generated income of £1,000 per day and as much as £7,000.

Several lessons can be learned from the case study of New Star Soccer:

➤ Starting a project part-time allows for experimentation to identify where niche demand exists for software products at minimum financial risk to yourself

➤ Income generation from developing software products requires time to grow, so don't quit too early

➤ Software projects become a lot more serious when you make them into a full time job, so be prepared to commit serious time, potentially at the expense of a social life in the early days

➤ Software products need time to mature inline with what users are willing to pay for, hence the first release is unlikely to be the one that everyone wants. Make sure to adapt your software product in response to real user feedback—not just on your own belief

➤ Making the wrong software product is costly, if not financially disastrous. Make sure to perform market research to identify what there is a demand for before you even start the design process, never mind writing the code

➤ Successful sales will never be constant, so make sure you keep savings to accommodate dips in sales and unsuccessful product launches

➤ Tax is one of the only things in life that can be guaranteed, so make sure you set aside money you make from your software product sales to cover tax bills at the end of the year

> ➤ Selling software in volume is the key to making significant income. Make sure to have your software available on portals and software stores that your target customers will be looking on to make purchases

Freedom

Freedom comes in many forms, and with being self-employed as a freelancer, the ability to choose the types of projects you work on that fit the lifestyle you want can be one of them. The following are some of the factors that dictate the level of freedom you have on projects:

> ➤ **Working times**: Projects that don't require you to work on-site often allow you to choose your own working times, which can be useful for managing your work around life commitments such as family. Flexible working times are also important for being able to manage multiple projects, making sure that you aren't dependent on only one source of income

> ➤ **Projects**: With the flexibility to pick and choose who you work for and what on, you have control over what work you get involved with. If a project or client sounds like too much trouble, you have the ability to turn down the work in order to look for something that's likely to be less hassle. Additionally, there are also your own projects that you may want to develop for sale, which an employer may not be want you to create under their employment; using freelancing to support this project, you can take full control over what you develop

> ➤ **Implementation**: Depending on the type of projects you are involved with, there is often a level of freedom for you to decide how to implement what you are being hired to create. This could be in terms of the programming languages you use, frameworks or programming patterns. For your own projects, you also have the freedom of deciding which features are to be developed as part of the product

With such levels of freedom, it's easy to become undisciplined to a point that affects your work performance. Where you have freedom to choose when you start work, it's important to make sure that the work gets done, so if you start work late, you must have the discipline to make up the time and even work extra hours where required. Where you have freedom on how to implement a project, you also need to be disciplined to make sure that the code you develop is maintainable and is a good setup for the client—not necessarily what best suits you.

Alternative to unemployment

Facing unemployment is a prospect that most people would want to avoid. For those who are already unemployed and are struggling to get back into work for whatever reason, freelance software development has several benefits:

> **Finances**: It's not difficult to secure an amount of work paying more than what the state may pay to support unemployment. With software development being a specialist skill that's in demand, securing a rate for your work that's at least double minimum wage isn't difficult—even if you have much to learn about software development. At the time of writing, typical UK freelance programmer rates start at roughly £15 per hour and rise up to £40 per hour for more experienced and established software developers

> **Employability**: As mentioned already, freelancing may not be the permanent goal, but it adds value to your work history and CV by providing you with hands on experience that you can both write and talk about, allowing you to appear more convincing to potential employers

> **Reputation**: Making contacts through your freelance activities is a useful asset to securing future work, whether it be employed or on a freelance basis. If you are good at what you do and are able to impress people with what you create, people will naturally recommend you to people, which opens opportunities for more paid work

Fun

All reasons given until this point has focused on the serious aspects relating to career and financial issues, but don't forget that work should be enjoyable. Work that pays a lot is desirable, but no work is worth being involved with if it has a detrimental effect on your life, health, and/or family.

Programming isn't the type of work people can stick with if it's not something that interests them enough to keep motivated when needing to solve tough problems, never mind tough clients. Make sure to choose freelance working for the right reasons—that is the types of projects and clients that don't turn out to be a nightmare and of which you would be proud to have as part of your portfolio.

> **Motivation**: Enjoying the work you do is a way to improve the quality of service you deliver to your clients, which therefore increases opportunities for recommendations that lead to more freelance and employment opportunities

> **Engagement**: Taking an interest in the work you do will allow you to identify how the software you create can be further improved beyond the initial specification. For client based projects, this can be used as an advantage to sell additional features of interest upon completion of the initial project. If you are developing your own software product, your engagement with the project can be used to identify additional features that may help to increase sales or open new opportunities to evolve your business model

Don't quit the day job

As tempting as it may be, it wouldn't be wise to quit your day job to go freelance full time until you have both tested the market and built relationships with a network of good quality clients and suppliers. Even if you land a project that will set you up financially for a few months, there is no security to ensure that there will be enough work to keep you going after the project ends, or even that the project will not run into some type of complication that will jeopardize what and when you are paid.

Being successful in a company employing you as a programmer and being successful as a freelance programmer are two different things that you will quickly learn as you work on freelance projects. If your background is working in agencies who provide services to their own clients, you will already be aware of how there is a need to strategically develop your code to manage on-going change requests, which is something that may be alien to you if you have only worked in organizations who are highly organized and/or have little changing requirements relating to the code you have developed for them. Using your time to experiment with freelancing will allow you to gain an insight to the situations you will encounter on freelance projects and so allow you to learn to strategically design your code for better flexibility that can handle changing specifications—especially for projects where the budget is fixed and the client has unrealistic delivery time expectations.

Instead of seeing your freelance career as an alternative to your day job, start it as an experimental hobby that complements your financial income. The hobby itself should contain both the business and technical skill elements that you want to eventually turn into a full time career. This method allows you to experiment in a way that jumping into freelancing head first wouldn't allow you to - by allowing you the flexibility to make mistakes and build your business model around your experiences. If you are good with both the business and technical aspects of what you wish to turn into a freelance career, you will be able to identify, develop, and refine aspects of your service to appeal to segments of the market that fit the types of ambitions for the projects you wish to work on. It's through this experimentation that you can closely integrate your marketing activities to build a brand and reputation that will enable you to build a stream of work from recommendations resulting from your experimentation—something that you would otherwise not have been in a position to do by jumping head first into full time freelancing.

Legal entities

There are several legal entities that you can choose to run your business under, each having their own advantages and disadvantages. The following are brief descriptions of what they are and who they may be more suitable to.

Sole trader

The most simple of legal business entities, being a sole trader means less paperwork and less hassle, with the advantage of providing you with more time to invest in the work that makes you money. As a sole trader, your only responsibilities regarding tax are to register with HMRC within three months of starting to trade and to complete a tax return each year.

As a sole trader, you pay your tax at the end of each year, unlike working as an employee where you pay tax each time you receive payment from your employer. There is also some leverage given by the tax man, as you are given from 6th April to 31st January to make your payment. This is beneficial for those who plan in advance, but can cause a bit of a problem for those who leave everything to the last minute, if there is a cash flow problem.

Partnership

Partnerships are a great way to combine the skills and assets of multiple people from different backgrounds to enable higher chances of success for a business. An example of this would be someone who has a good background in marketing and business management working with someone who has good technical expertise—allowing them to create a superior product that has the backing of a well-executed marketing strategy and business structure, of which the business wouldn't have succeeded without the contribution of both parties. Good examples of partnership successes have included Steve Jobs (the business brains) and Steve Wozniak (the technical brains) who founded Apple, while Sergey Brin and Larry Page co-founded Google.

Although there are many advantages to setting up a business through a partnership, there are also several major disadvantages:

➤ Success requires both parties to contribute their share to the partnership. Many partnerships fail because one or more parties take advantage of the other(s) by not investing the effort that is expected of them

➤ Opportunities can be missed when a decision or authorization is required by a partner who isn't available or contactable—unlike a sole trader, who makes decisions and reacts straight away

➤ Disagreements and disputes between business partners can be damaging to the business and in the worst case scenarios can lead to their destruction

To avoid such problems, planning and precautions should be put into place that protect the interests of all involved:

➤ Creation of a formal contract between all partners that details all terms of the partnership, including percentage of ownership, delegation of responsibilities and the procedure for termination of the partnership

➤ Monitoring of the partnership activities to ensure that all members are fulfilling their obligations

> ➤ A set procedure for decision making that identifies who has authority to make decisions for different types of situations and ensuring that all parties are contactable as much as realistically possible

Limited company

Unlike setting up as a sole trader or partnership, trading as a limited company requires much more effort to set up and trade—as all accounts need to be recorded in a specific format and submitted to Companies House for their approval. In short, setting up as a limited company results in much more paperwork which results in more distractions from your core business activities and higher admin/accountancy fees.

There are, however, several advantages to setting up limited company:

> ➤ The business becomes a separate entity from yourself, meaning that any debts are owned by the business. Should the business run into financial difficulties, any debts are separate to yourself—meaning that you wont be forced to sell assets like your house to settle the business debts. Keep in mind that company directors can still be held responsible for company debts should they be proven to have allowed the company to continue trading while insolvent, or for any personal guarantees given

> ➤ There are certain tax advantages to benefit from being a registered company once your profits reach a certain level. Your accountant will be able to advise you on this

Home or away?

When setting up as a freelancer, one of the first decisions you will make will be on where you deliver your services. Sometimes the nature of your work will dictate this automatically—as an example, if you will be relying mainly on agency placements, then you will be working at the office of the agency's client. Other than these few exceptions, you will need to decide whether it is best to work from home or a dedicated place of work.

The home office

Working from home certainly provides a range of advantages in convenience for the self-disciplined, but can also prove to be a detriment to productivity for those who are easily distracted by temptations.

Advantages

There are certainly some useful financial and lifestyle advantages in choosing to work from home:

➤ No travel—saves time and expenses:

    ➢ Without travel, you can start work earlier or catch up on more sleep should you wish. No travel also means that you eliminate wasted time associated with heavy traffic and cancelled trains, as well as saving your personal expenses of getting to work. This is also handy when you end up working late, meaning that you can avoid the additional hassle of traveling home

➤ Save on rent:

    ➢ By working from home, you avoid spending on additional rent, which is something that comes in handy when money is tight—especially when you are first starting out as a freelancer

➤ Tax savings:

    ➢ If you are working from home, you can claim a proportion of your costs on expenses such as home insurance, heating, lighting, water rates, council tax and general maintenance as a business expense so that the amount of tax you pay is lower

➤ Work in your pajamas:

    ➢ If you're feeling lazy or feel more comfortable working in your pajamas, then this is certainly a benefit to have

Disadvantages

Although there are a number of desirable advantages, working from home also has a few disadvantages that will affect your productivity and strategic capabilities:

➤ Many interruptions:

    ➢ Whether it's family, neighbors, pets, or friends, disruptions can ruin your productivity—especially when you are 'in the zone' when working on more intensive work requirements. It's said that such disruptions can take you up to 25 minutes to regain your mode of thought and productivity

➤ No physical location barrier to separate work and personal life:

    ➢ For people who like routine, what is considered to be home will become blurred as work. This is especially a disadvantage when under pressure at work with 'home' distractions making it harder to get into work mode, while also the opposite being true when trying to switch off from thinking of work during out of hours time

> ➤ No collaboration environment:
>> ➤ If you are working with other professionals on a regular basis, the home isn't usually a great place to foster collaboration activities
>> ➤ Lack of contact with other people can contribute to negative psychological effects, resulting in decreased morale and productivity

> ➤ Likelihood of having to give clients your home address:
>> ➤ On the whole, this shouldn't be a problem—and being an 'ethical' freelancer means that client's shouldn't have to be hunting you down. However, there are some clients who are unrealistic on their working relationships with you—sometimes going as far as to pressure you into working unrealistic hours by suggesting that they come and work with you on a Saturday morning or during the night. It's in these situations where having a real working address can avoid certain situations—what would you do if you client turned up at your house at 10am on a Saturday morning to insist that you work on their last minute requirements?

> ➤ Temptation to not work and do something social instead—like watch TV
>> ➤ At least in a separate working environment you can ensure that there are no distractions like your TV and gaming console. At home, you have access to all of your entertainment—will this pose a risk of being a distraction from doing real work perhaps?

The real office

For many people, it's certainly useful to have a separate workplace than home, but what expense does having a dedicated office for your work have?

Advantages

The main advantages of having a real office for your business activities revolve around improving your productivity. As a freelancer, the faster you turn out your work, the more you can earn in the time you have available for work.

> ➤ Work-hour structure can help you keep focused—that is, traveling to work like a regular job:
>> ➤ Working away from home avoids the possibility for you to get too comfortable working at home and to ensure that you have the same routines as you would have with a regular job where you travel to work for set times. This is good for people who are less disciplined in their time management, as having a regular work structure helps to ensure that work actually gets done rather than having work productivity suffer from home distractions and putting work off until later

➤ More likely to be viewed by clients as a professional:

 ➢ Although in reality an office is no reflection of your technical competency, in most cases having an office to invite clients to meet you will provide them with more confidence that you are a real business that they can depend upon. This is especially true for small and startup businesses who have no technical knowledge in the areas that they are hiring you to help them with

➤ Separate your home from your work more easily:

 ➢ Some people will find that living both a work and social life in the same environment difficult to live with—that is, where does work start and end? A real office gives a psychological boundary to ensure your work and social lives don't merge into one. In this case, the saying never mix business with pleasure has never been so true!

➤ More convenient if you are hiring people to work with you or if you are working in a partnership:

 ➢ For most, it will feel less comfortable to have employees and business partners working from their home. With an office, you can have others working in a real work environment to ensure that there are no home distractions and have a common workplace that fosters creativity and collaboration

Disadvantages

Having a dedicated office for your work will certainly push up your expenses and rule out some of the savings you could make by working from home. If you are the type of person who is disciplined enough not to get sidetracked by home distractions or simply don't have a big budget to begin with, using an office may be something would want to consider at a later date—if at all.

➤ Rent can be expensive

 ➢ Certainly, during the early days of setting up as self-employed, every penny counts. Whatever you spend on office rent is money that you can't spend on other aspects of your business that will lead to success and your ability to make a profit. Can you afford to rent an office?

➤ Additional costs such as business rates and insurance not covered by your home insurance:

 ➢ At least when working from home, some of your home insurance and council tax that you would otherwise be paying can be recovered

➤ Can get lonely if it's just you in the office, but not the case if you work with other people

> ➤ Requirement to invest in furniture:
>> ➤ Having an office is all very nice, but it will only be of any value when it is properly furnished. In addition to the other associated costs such as business rates, insurance, and rent, you will also have to invest in office furniture, meaning more money that is taken away from aspects like marketing that are critical to your success

Renting desk space

For those who find it difficult to be productive from home and can't afford or want to spend on the extra expenses of renting an office, there's the option of renting some desk space from an established company or a business incubator unit. This option provides a happy medium where you get all of the advantages of having an office to work from, but at a fraction of the rental cost. You also benefit from not having to directly pay many of the expenses associated with setting up your own office such as furniture, heating, lighting, and business rates, because these will be covered by the desk rent.

Co-working spaces

A new type of desk renting is referred to as co-working, where freelancers and small business owners are able to purchase desks to work from on a day to day basis. This is a step down from renting desk space, which is a more permanent arrangement and has cost saving advantages if you only need to use the desk for a couple of days per week. There are also some events arranged as co-working days where different freelancers attend to work—although these often tend to be about an opportunity to network with other freelancers and less about doing work, so don't expect to be highly productive if you attend these events.

Cafes

A popular option for many freelancers in all fields, especially freelance writers, is to work from a cafe. This has become a lot more popular since the emergence of mobile computing and with most cafes now offering free wifi Internet access. The combination of these factors means that many freelancers only need to have a laptop to access everything they need to work from an environment that separates them from the distractions of home—or even the office!

Cafes provide an ideal place to get work done, with their environments not being too noisy and the ability to access refreshments when wanted. Their open space also provide good locations to hold meetings, whether this be with clients or people your collaborate with.

Without being tied to working from a single location, you have the advantage of being able to choose different cafes to work from—whether this be through choice or convenience. Although you will be paying for your refreshments, it is likely that any costs will be lower per month than any of the other options while still providing most of the advantages.

Summary

There is no individual way to run your self-employment business. Some people may start freelancing as a part-time project that grows to a full-time occupation, some may keep their activities as a part-time activity motivated by the lack of dependency to generate a full salary, whilst other people may jump head first into launching their venture as a full-time operation. The only factors to say which method is right are the business environment and your personal circumstances. It is also these circumstances that influence how you run your business activities that are likely to define what you consider as success—a student making £1,000 per month would be considered highly successful in most cases, whereas the same sales statistics were considered disastrous when this was achieved in the release of Simon Read's New Star Soccer 4.

Almost as important as how you decide to run your business, and most likely to be highly influential in this, is the legal formation you use. The most simple structure being a sole trader, which has significant advantages in reduced admin requirements, but also leaves you personally exposed guaranteeing all debts incurred by your business activities when things don't go to plan. Partnerships provide advantages for shared responsibility and potential access to a wider range of skills that can significantly increase the success of the business, but just one bad partner can introduce problems and expenses that undermine the contributions of everyone else. Limited companies provide an amount of legal protection and the ability to raise money by selling parts of the business to investors, but also come with much more red tape requirements.

There is no need to hire expensive office space when you are able to work from home, especially when you are starting up when any money you have will be better spent on marketing and other activities used to make and complete sales delivery. For those who find it difficult to work from home due to distractions, desk space or co-working offices are an option to have a formal place of work without the full costs of a dedicated office.

$\gg 2$

Positioning Yourself
in the Market

Every industry has different groups of people you can sell to, with members of each group sharing characteristics and interests that define who they are. Being able to identify these groups will allow you to make your software, services, and marketing highly targeted to generate the type of reaction that you need to succeed.

Market segments

Whatever services and/or products your freelance business provides, you will most likely find that all clients are unique; there are characteristics shared by those who have a commonality, such as the industry they operate in, business structure, or any other factor. These shared characteristics are the ones that allow you to categorize your market into segments that identify the following:

- ➤ The different client types you can target
- ➤ The individual needs each client group
- ➤ Parts of the market that have the capability to deliver to
- ➤ The difference in profitability opportunities

These identifications and others help you to build the foundations for effective marketing and business strategy. By understanding the characteristics of the types of buyers in the market, you will be able to tailor what you offer and how you appear to match what you know appeals to them. This approach affects everything from product development and service delivery to marketing and managing your finances—simply because your target market segments combined with the business environment and your financial ambitions dictate what's possible to deliver.

Although targeting every buyer in the market may sound like the best option make the most sales, focusing your attention on a limited portion of the market will allow your business to become more appealing to those you intend to sell to. Although, specializing in specific market segments dramatically reduces the number of people you can sell to, it also opens opportunities to increase your overall sales and extend your brand exposure:

➤ Tailored marketing activities and content appeals to people who share specific characteristics and interests

Case Study: Nextpoint, based in Liverpool—England, had spent years providing generalized software development services to small businesses who didn't understand anything about what that software could be used for. This proved to be a difficult approach to sell software services because potential clients were unable to use their imagination to see how software could improve their business processes and solve problems they faced. By specializing in the creation of software specifically for education, Nextpoint was able to eliminate its reliance on buyers needing to use their imagination and instead provide specific examples of how software could be used to specific solve problems that their target market, educators, could specifically relate to.

➤ The more specific your marketing is to a specific type of person or organization, the more likely the targets are to have an interest in the marketing message

Case Study: Not only did Nextpoint focus their software products to become specific to the education market, they also further specialized in designing software to assist specific education needs such as dyslexia. This specialized focus has allowed for highly targeted marketing that appeals to people in search of help that traditional learning tools don't cater to. This focus led to marketing being able to communicate to a highly specific message that the target audience could relate to and therefore gain confidence in the product being right for what they need.

➤ Specialized products and services designed specifically for the needs of a market segment allow for **unique selling points** (**USPs**) that your competitors don't offer

Case Study: Nextpoint's change in focus led to the identification of specialized learning methods that are highly effective for learners in the target audience. The identification of these learning methods meant that software features could be produced to facilitate these learning methods that are not available in competing software products. Understanding how the needs of learners, their educators, and parents differed to each other meant that the software could be designed in a way that adapted itself to each type of user. Meanwhile, the marketing communications strategy was able to make use of this understanding to promote each unique benefit to their intended beneficiary.

➤ A specific focus makes it easier to gain interest from media organizations that can provide mass exposure to your brand and its activities

Case Study: Nextpoint's focus on delivering learning and teaching solutions for specific education needs such as dyslexia was easy to understand and relevant to emerging news stories. As a result, media attention was gained from organizations including the BBC that resulted in exposure on radio, websites and in newspapers.

➤ Refining your processes to match a specific type of client for improved productivity and profitability

Case Study: By specializing to deliver software that address common problems experienced by all members of their targeted market segment, Nextpoint were able to create a series of standard software configurations that allowed them to deliver working systems quickly without the need for major investment. Additional optimizations to time costs were made possible through the use of a centralized software system, with new clients being provided with an account to access their purchased functionality—as opposed to purchasing of a unique installation. This approach eliminated the main costs associated with previous projects, where their different requirements meant the need to develop fully bespoke features before clients could access any functionality.

Pricing yourself appropriately

A common mistake made by many new market entrants is the use of price as a selling point; with these entrants trying to undercut the competition and then falling into the trap of not being profitable enough to justify the effort, or even making a loss. Sun Tzu, a military strategist whose philosophy is studied by industry leaders, wrote:

> *"The general who wins a battle makes many calculations in his temple before the battle is fought."*

> *- Sun Tzu, The Art of War.*

Like the generals who win on the battlefield, smart people fully evaluate the field they operate within and identify the position they hold before concluding the type of pricing strategy to use. Understanding the market environment in relation to your own attributes opens opportunities to identify to target your products and services at spaces occupied by little or no competition. Described thoroughly in the book Blue Ocean Strategy, these spaces in the market are opportunities for you to establish yourself without resorting to cutthroat pricing strategy that leaves you vulnerable to exploitation and minimizes your ability to earn a decent living.

Fortunately for software developers, the cost to deliver services are minimal—a basic laptop and electricity is all you need to get started; with many of the software development tools now available for free via the Internet. The downside to this the lowered barrier for new market entrants—meaning that there will always be people who are less smart than you who resort to undercutting everyone in the market. Sun Tzu continued his writing by saying:

> *"The general who loses a battle makes but few calculations beforehand. Thus do many calculations lead to victory, and few calculations to defeat..."*

> *- Sun Tzu, The Art of War.*

It is no coincidence that most startup businesses cease operating within their first three years; mostly due to a mixture of poor management and not understanding their market. Like those generals who lose on the battlefield, people behind failed businesses have lacked the ability to thorough research their market in order to build informed plans that maximize their chances of success. Often, these are the market entrants that you will compete with who cause problems for everyone in the market; not because they are good at what they do, but due to their unrealistic and unmaintainable pricing strategy.

These market entrants are often people who have little or no business experience, with many neither having the required technical skills, who as a result resort to making sales by undercutting everyone in the market. Some of these people may not have any software development skills and simply run their business by outsourcing all of their projects to the lowest bidder. If you operate in a country with high living costs such as the UK, you can't compete on price against people living in countries where living costs are a fraction of your own. You know the pricing situation is bad when there are literally people offering database development for $1 per hour!

Market entrants who haven't done their homework and price themselves in a way that makes it impossible for them to deliver the goods are both a threat and an opportunity:

> **Threat:** Their low pricing strategy contributes to buyers in the market expecting software development to be provided at rates comparable to the amounts paid to supermarket checkout staff

> **Opportunity:** Buyers who have been burnt buy sellers who have not been able to deliver on their promises will be looking to use factors other than price to identify value in what they are buying

With so many market entrants emerging with poor pricing strategy and lack of technical skills, many buyers are subsequently being stung when choosing to hire software development at low cost. Although there will always be a market segment for low cost software development, people already stung when choosing price as the main factor in their previous hiring will be looking for other factors that guarantee better quality. This is an opportunity for you to charge a premium price through establishing yourself with reputation for reliability and being an expert in your field.

Important factors to be taken into consideration when deciding on your pricing strategy include:

> The market rate

  Knowledge of the average rates already charged in the different market segments can be used as a measure for what you should be charging. Be careful to select prices from competitors who have comparable operational attributes such as the type of product/service you are selling and geographical location you are selling in. For example, looking at freelance web development rates in London would give you a highly distorted view if you are selling these services in a less expensive city such as Liverpool.

Pricing yourself below the market rate sends a signal to people that suggests you perceive yourself as less capable than other software developers. With people often being so busy, this can lead to you being overlooked and missing opportunities to demonstrate your capabilities. At the same time, lower rates can attract the types of client who have unrealistic expectations and/or are actively looking to exploit you.

➤ Quality standards

This is a major factor that is directly dictated by your pricing strategy:

"The moment you make a mistake in pricing, you're eating into your reputation or your profits."

- Katherine Paine, founder of Delahaye Group

When aiming to offer the lowest prices, you are forced into a position where the cutting corners and rushing the job are the only options available to keep your sales profitable at a margin that's worth your time. Both of these options affect the level of quality you can deliver; while this may be acceptable for some, it will never allow you to build a reputation for delivering the type of quality that the highest paying clients seek. With this in mind, there will always be market segments where clients are willing to accept sacrifices in their purchase—that is there's a reason why people wear old clothes when painting and decorating.

At the other extreme, aiming to offer the highest quality will escalate the need to charge the highest prices. While this will price you out of the reach of the majority of the buyers in the market, the reputation you build will place you in a position where only a small number of your competitors are able to reach. With these market segments having more of an interest in the quality you provide over the price you charge, your sales strategy becomes more on focused on making high value sales more than high volume sales. In these circumstances, you may use a specialization, rare skill, guarantee or certification to boost your appeal in a way that allows you to justify extremely high value-based pricing—this being where you sell your services based on the value to the client and not as a fixed hourly rate.

When deciding on your pricing strategy, quality level(s) requirements of your target market segments should be thoroughly investigated to identify whether you are in a position to profitably provide your services and/or products. Always remember that your time has value and therefore has a cost. There's no point in charging the lowest prices to make a few sales with margins that turn out to be earning you less than minimum wage; if you are doing that, you would literally be better off flipping burgers at one of those fast food restaurants we all know!

> ➤ Available resources

The availability of resources is the other major influence of pricing strategy. Resources you can access define the options available to you for delivering your services and developing your products. Budget will also influence your ability to access resources—whether they are labor, expertise or digital assets such as code components.

Most of the time, cutting corners will impact on quality; an example of this being technical debt, where poor quality code results in higher ongoing maintenance costs. The exception to this is where you make use of ready made resources that allow you to avoid investing time in building a project's foundations. In this case, the use of ready made resources not only allows you to reduce production time, but also can lead to higher quality output from code components that have already been tried and tested.

These resources could be tools you have developed yourself, have purchased or even make use of one of the many open source projects. They can allow you to significantly reduce production time and therefore be much more competitive with price. This means that it is possible to identify a compromise that cuts out enough development time to make it possible to be profitable and competitive with price sensitive segments of the market; or to be even more profitable in market segments where price is not an issue.

An important consideration for using resources to influence your pricing model is the definition of limitations. Clients will often ask for customizations that are not available in your resources; your options will already be limited if you are buying your resource from a third party. The main risk in this situation is when you have developed your own resource—where the temptation is to agree to create the feature as part of your standard pricing. It's important to distinguish between off the shelf software features that are already available and custom software development that requires the purchase of time. Get this wrong when selling your resources and you will find yourself in a situation where it becomes impossible to satisfy the client while making a profit. It is for this reason that many providers software solutions based on existing resources will only offer minimal customizations—that is eliminating unknown risk to profitability.

> ➤ Your experience and professional value

Never undersell yourself; it limits your career prospects and will attract the type of client looking to exploit you. If you are highly experienced, you can produce work faster and at better quality than someone who has less experience so why accept being paid the same hourly rate? In this type of situation, it's only fair that you charge more for your time because the client gets a better outcome in less time. With this also translating to the possibility of them also saving money on their overall costs, you can't fairly compete on an hour for hour rate against someone offering less experience, knowledge and capability at a lower price.

If you have a skill that is rare, then you can negotiate higher prices. In software development, an example would be software development in non-mainstream languages such as Cobol; which allows you to demand as much as eight times more than a programmer doing the same job with a mainstream language like PHP.

Some situations require a certain set of skills, while others have a preference for you to meet certain criteria for red tape. Either way, having some type of specialism allows you to target market segments that has limited competition, and as such, allows you to negotiate higher rates.

Developing specialist skills is certainly something worth considering as part of your strategy if you don't already have them. An ability to negotiate higher rates and more easily secure new work can be gained simply through target market segments where there is a skills shortage. Examples of this include knowledge and experience of statistical analysis theory and AI algorithms; while there are many PHP and Javascript developers, there are not as many PHP developers who have the specialist knowledge and experience of AI algorithms—especially for projects requiring advanced use of AI such as image recognition and big data analysis. With supply and demand having a direct influence on rates being offered, buyers in the market will be willing to offer higher payments when they can't attract enough people with the skills to do the job.

Although the required learning investment to master these skills and knowledge may be high, it is a worthwhile investment because the higher entry level barrier keeps the market segment closed to the types of market entrants who are likely to attempt to undercut everyone. With those operating in the market segment also having to have invest heavily in their learning, it is much more likely that they will value their skills and therefore not be willing to undersell themselves. The limited number of suppliers in the market segment and its difficulty to become a new market entrant results in more demand than there is supply - hence keep rates higher and negotiation power in your favor.

➤ The market segments you intend to target

Although you may be providing the same services to everyone, different segments of the market will have different expectations for quality, service, and price. Small businesses tend to demand the most for their money, so dealing with this segment and remaining profitable requires an entirely different strategy to dealing with large corporate type organizations where there is often a culture of wastage in expenditure.

Market segments are not only to be defined by business sizes, but also by other factors such as their characteristics and target audiences. For example, targeting charitable organizations will require a completely different strategy to public sector services. In the same way, small businesses that have already been running for a few years have completely different needs to recent start-ups, even though they are both part of the same small business category.

Market specific influences

The going rate that you can be paid is directly affected by the markets you operate in and your position within the market. Three main factors that will affect your ability to successfully and competitively price your services are:

> ➤ The capability and willingness of the competition to lower their prices

> ➤ The skills required by the buyers—in general, the more skills required, the less competitors who are capable and so hence allows you to increase your prices

> ➤ Certification is a factor that is value by some, but not all buyers. People who tend to value certification tend to be people with an academic background or people who have inside industry knowledge and trust of the certification vendors; for example, someone who knows about PHP development and knows about the official PHP framework Zend may be more inclined to take notice of developers who are Zend certified—similarly, someone who knows about online marketing would be more confident in hiring people who were Google AdWords certified. The value of certification is being able to immediately be able to show an endorsement by a trusted organization in your skills meeting a minimum standard. However, it should be noted that it is worth investigating how your target audience perceive the value of certifications—as this would have no value if you are dealing with people who only look at your previous experience and/or who are unaware of the certification vendors and the meaning of their certifications

> ➤ Brand loyalty—if you have existing relationships with prospective clients or have been recommended to them by their trusted sources, the buyer will have more confidence that you will deliver a quality solution and not let them down

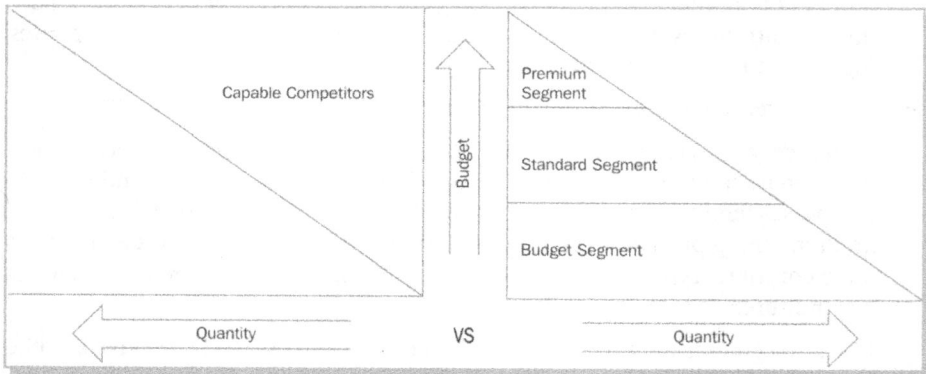

Diagram 2.1: Market volume versus price-based competitor reach.

Diagram 2.1 shows how there is a bigger market for clients with smaller budgets, but with fewer competitors capable of profitably targeting the lower end of the market. As the budgets for the client segments increase, more competitors are capable of profitably targeting the segments on a price only basis.

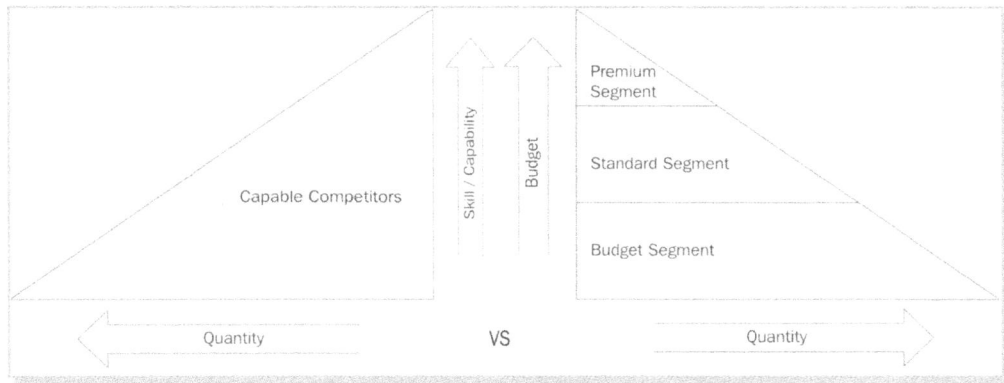

Diagram 2.2: Market volume versus skill-based competitor reach.

Diagram 2.2 shows how skill level requirements mirror the rates offered from buyers in the market. It shows how more competitors are capable of bidding for projects requiring less skill, with fewer competitors able to compete as skill requirements increase. The lack of supply to market segments requiring higher skill levels allows you to demand higher rates. Examples of clients you should expect to find in each of the project budget segments include:

➤ **Premium segment**: These are organizations with very large turnovers (total money going into the business) and are involved in large scale operations. The massive size of these organizations tends to amplify all factors, including outcome of your services offering greater value through massive exposure. Their overall expenditure is amplified to a point that any high rates they offer you is barely noticeable in the greater scheme of their operation costs. Inefficiencies and corporate culture in these organizations often lead to higher value spending decisions that are motivated more by internal politics than the desire to make a saving

➤ **Standard segment**: Typically small to medium enterprises (SME businesses) that are established and employ anywhere from 20 to 250 staff. These businesses have experience and financial exposure to allow them to understand realistic costs, but not to the extreme level as the premium segment businesses. Organizations in this segment tend to be savvier about the prices they pay—looking to pay inline with the average market rates

> ➤ **Budget segment**: These tend to be micro businesses and startups. Often one man bands who don't have experience of business and view finances in the same way as personal money; for example, £100 can go far to cover living costs, but doesn't cover much business expenses such as rent, insurance, and so on. Even where owners of these businesses have an understanding of business level finances, they are often in a situation where they have limited funds and hence unable to pay attractive rates even if they appreciate the value of your work

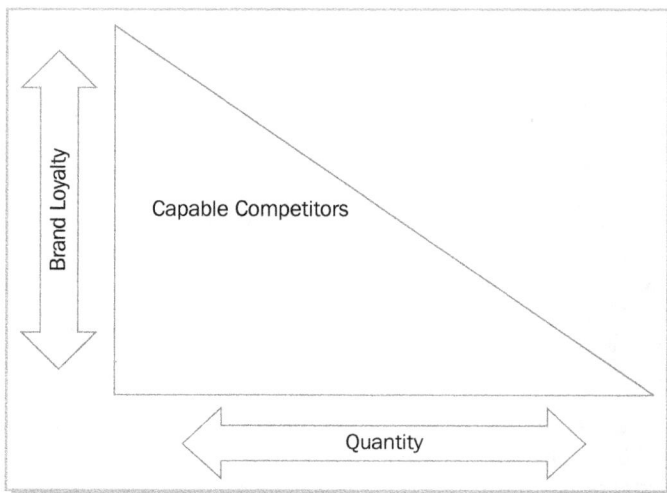

Diagram 2.3: Market volume versus brand-based competitor reach.

Diagram 2.3 shows how fewer competitors are capable to compete on brand loyalty as this factor becomes more important. This is an important factor if you or your competitors have had a successful working relationship with the prospective client or where recommendations have been given by their trusted sources.

The equilibrium price – segments and prices

Referred to as the equilibrium price, this is the compromise point that offers the best outcome between pricing yourself within reach of the largest number of buyers who are willing to spend at a rate that earns you the best profit. Identifying this price point is important because it dictates what you can deliver within the budget you have available.

While there may be market segments willing willing to pay a high price, the only segments that matter are those that you can reach. For this reason, it is also highly important to identify who your audience is. Who can you access with your marketing and what are the barriers to those you can't?

There will be more people able to pay at the lower end of the scale, but can you deliver your product or service profitably to them? If not, is there a cut down version that you can offer that still satisfies this audience and that delivers you a profit? You will never deliver a profit if you make a loss on every sale—no matter how many you sell!

For the people willing to pay a premium for your product, what additional value can you include that will persuade them to upgrade to the more expensive version? These people will not pay a premium for the same product that you offer to other people at your standard price, yet increasing your prices for everyone may cost you sales from the majority of your customers. If focusing exclusively on premium customers, will their sales cover those you lose from your mainstream customer segment?

In short, each market segment you target should have a version of your product or service that is tailored to their interests; this may not be exclusively based on price, but could also involve features that relate to other factors such as expertise, business category and size of their organization. Pricing can still be used to categorize market segments, such as:

➤ **Budget segment**: Those who need what you offer at the lowest possible price; the price is the main and possibly the only factor that will persuade these people to buy from you. In most scenarios, there will be plenty of people in this audience and so hence your earnings will need to come from volume of sales. The question is do you have the capability to produce, deliver, and market your product or service to this audience in a way that earns you enough to be worthwhile?

➢ Scalability is an approach that can be used to address budget segments of markets. This is where a one size fits all approach is taken to develop a standard solution that can be used to supply a demand—an example being a website template that can be sold to website designers for customization or directly to clients as part of a standard website creation. This approach bares the full cost of development upfront and can break even after a specified number of sales are made. These upfront development costs, known as non-repeatable engineering costs, are a once only investment; whether you sell one copy or a million, the development costs don't scale up with the sales you make. This means that there are opportunities to be highly profitable if you can sell in large volumes, but also a risk of not recovering the cost of your time investment if you don't make enough sales

➢ It's important to be very specific when selling pre-made template style systems, as this approach goes wrong when offering buyers the ability to request specific customizations; especially when you are already selling to market segments who expect the lowest prices. Many software developers operating this approach minimize their risk by limiting the level of customization they offer—if providing any at all

➤ **Standard segment**: People who know the market value of your product or service and are willing to pay a price that's fair. These people are usually better informed and will buy based on their perception of a fair deal and the need for good quality. These people recognize that prices that are too cheap are usually reflected by a reduction in quality and so therefore need your product or service to be provided at a quality standard that is equal to or better than those of the market leader

➤ **Premium segment**: Not many people fall into this tier, but those who do will usually have excess money to spend and will be happy to pay above the market rate. These people will also want some added value—a perception of prestige (brand), tailoring and fast turnaround for delivery are just a few examples of what can be offered to this segment

With the preceding insights in mind, it is important to identify which price segments you are able to successfully target with your price strategy. Often it is not possible to target both the top and bottom tiers with the same brand, as there would be a conflict in how both groups perceive you. The equilibrium price shows which market would be most profitable—if you have the marketing and production capability to profitably sell in volume, then targeting the middle and bottom tiers would fit your strategy; otherwise, making less sales with bigger profit margins justified by an increased quality of your product will be less risk and easier to produce a profit.

Building quality for market segments

Quality is a factor that everyone would like, but its delivery is often restricted by skills, time, resources and budget. The definition of quality is something that changes between different groups of people; another reason to identify market segments that share characteristics. Whether the buying criteria is based on money, time or another factor, your ability to be successful with the market segment comes down to whether you are positioned to profitably deliver the quality that its buyers expect.

Meeting customer needs

The key to delivering the right quality to market segments lies in understanding their needs. Offering a product or service with high quality on all factors may result in you pricing yourself out of the market, whereas offering a version of your product or service that has selected features of interest tailored to be appealing to defined audiences will mean that you are able to make a better impression amongst those who you target as well as increasing your sales potential. Examples of tailoring your quality to customer needs include:

> ➤ Providing an entry level version of your service or product

> This allows you to target those who are either restricted by budget or experimenting with using your offering to see how they benefit. Designing your entry level version to have all of the basic features with options to upgrade is a great way to lure customers into spending more with you as their needs and budget grow over time.

> An entry level version of your service or product should offer only the basics to meet the buyer's requirements—possibly with the ability to upgrade later.

> Example: If you are selling websites, an entry level option could be a single page website made from a pre-made template made to show basic information such as telephone number, e-mail address and description of the client's business. This option allows buyers with a low budget to have a quality solution that meets the main requirements of their project criteria. Options can be provided that allow them to upgrade their website with new pages, design alterations and other custom features once they are ready and have the budget.

➤ Versions for different sizes

Whether it is families, businesses or individuals you target, producing versions for different sizes allows you to adjust the quality and quantity of time, resources and/or materials required to deliver something that the customer is happy to pay for. If you were to sell clothes, it would be an advantage to make your business appeal to everyone by having options to suit different shapes and sizes. The reverse of this is also true; using blue ocean strategy to specialize in sizes and shapes that competitors don't offer means you can access segments of the market that will have a keen in interest in your products and services. Its difficult being 6'5" when the longest trousers sold in mainstream shops are a size or two too small—not to mention fitting into seats on public transport!

In terms of business software, you may want to investigate the influence of the organization sizes using your product/service. With the obvious difference of large organizations being the number of user accounts or installations, you may identify new requirements for features and support that impact on your production and ongoing costs. Identifying this not only allows you to differentiate versions of your product or services to catering towards different buyer sizes, but also to highlight unique costs and savings that need to be integrated into your pricing model.

Example: Online education software is often sold as a subscription on a per user basis. This allows for pricing options that can scale from the individual account needs of a parent with just one child, to potentially hundreds of accounts that a full school may need. On one hand, a school with hundreds of users will require more support than a parent with just two children, while on the other hand, the scale of school users would likely result in a lower support cost for general questions that only need answering once. For example, a teacher asking a question could apply the answer for up to thirty students in their class, while the parent would only apply it to their two children. Additionally, the school teachers may want to use the software in a way that allows them to set and manage homework—additional features that wouldn't be required by parents.

While schools should obviously pay a higher overall price compared to parents, the ability to identify efficiencies that occur when scaling up the use of software can allow you to offer discounts to high value buyers without cutting into your profit margin. Identification of additional features that are useful to how teachers use the software differently to parents opens opportunities for making the product more appealing to them in a way that can be allow for new pricing options for feature upgrades and extra services.

➤ Occupation specific versions

This is most relevant when selling to specific professions and trades, tailoring the product or service to become appealing to a specific occupation.

Example: An accountancy software package that has specific features turned on or off to make its functionality relevant to a businesses operating in a specific sector.

Example: An education software for math's could have the same content and exercises tailored for different industries, allowing it to become appealing to training organizations who need to teach math's in relation to the industry they deliver training for.

Market research

Whether it is state run, a private sector operation, charity or social enterprise, cash is the blood flow of any organization; without it, the organization cannot function and will cease to exist. In the same way, an organization with no cash flow isn't able to function properly to meet its objectives. Whether you operate purely for profit or to benefit a community, your ability to identify what people want to buy and at what prices will dictate whether you succeed or fail.

Failing to plan is planning to fail

A common mistake made by new market entrants is to basing prices entirely on what people say they will pay rather than what it costs to deliver and be profitable. This approach is both lazy and naive, exposing their business to exploitation from market buyers, while at the same time increasing risks that limit their ability to deliver quality and make a profit.

> *"If ignorant both of your enemy and yourself, you are certain to be in peril."*
>
> *- Sun Tzu, The Art of War*

The essence of good price planning is to:

➤ Gain an understand of what the market wants to pay

➤ Identify the perceived value of the product or service

➤ Identify 'who' you can sell to

➤ Calculate the costs to bring your product or service to market

➤ Identify the expected client communication and management overheads

➤ Calculate the cost to deliver your product or service to the customer

➤ Incorporate your profit margin

All of the preceding contribute to successful pricing in selling products and services when the correct information is captured, highlighting the importance of selecting reliable information sources and factoring margins for error. Some information sources will almost never give truly accurate information; an example being how most buyers will never indicate the maximum price they are willing to pay—especially if they are negotiating the best price from you. In these circumstances, you can look at verifying your data by cross-referencing against other information you capture. For example, the price that customers say they are willing to pay could be compared to their opinions of equivalent product/service prices.

Cost to market

Another mistake made by new market entrants is forgetting to factor in the cost of developing a product or service into their pricing and profit forecasting. The cost to market includes:

➤ Research and development: Inclusive of meetings, plans, and research to create the product as well as to identify what people want

➤ Cost of equipment purchases

➤ Training expenses

➤ Other costs that may also be incurred depending on your specific product or service

Depending on the country you operate from, there may also be ways for you to reduce your cost to market through:

➤ Tax credits that compensate business expenses—for example, the UK offers tax reductions to home operated businesses as well as for those operating in sectors such as computer games development

➤ Costs for professional services such as training can be used to reduce tax—as a genuine business expense, these are not included as part of any taxable profit you make; it is worth checking with an accountant about this

➤ Equipment costs can be used to reduce tax costs—although some countries such as the UK don't allow an outright tax deduction because equipment is considered as capital and therefore has value to be resold; this is treated differently in the way that the tax reduction is returned over a number of years inline with how the country views the depreciation of equipment capital. It is worth speaking to your accountant about this

Certainly in terms of services aimed at market segments that want or need a more affordable solution, there can be a higher cost to market in order to develop some type of customized component that allows for a reduction in ongoing service/product delivery expenses. Although money can be made through sales, profit is only achieved once any upfront investment for services, equipment, research and development has been recovered.

Cost of delivery

In addition to the costs for getting your product or service to a state that it can be sold in the market, there are also ongoing costs that scale up as your business grows. These include costs for hiring staff, customer support, marketing, and rent—some of these will be proportional to your sales, while others will have a staggered increase as you hit specific milestones; for example, increasing the size of office premises means higher rent. All of these costs have to be factored into pricing for recovery through each unit sale. This means that if you intend to sell at smaller volumes, your prices need to be higher so that each product/hour unit sold absorbs a bigger portion of your costs.

Calculate your profit margin

In summary, your profit is a simple calculation made from:

Profit = Total Sales Value - Cost to Market - (Unit Cost x Unit Quantity)

Don't forget that not all available units will necessarily be sold. Examples where this may happen include:

➤ Products passing their valid selling dates or relevancy—examples outside of software include sell by date for food and relevancy date for items such as newspapers and magazines

➤ Sample units distributed for marketing purposes—example samples for journalists to review

➤ Time that doesn't get booked due to lack of demand, or time spent on marketing and admin activities

Time value

Where your business is about using your skills to sell time, an easy method for identifying your daily rate could be to use the following steps:

➤ Identify how much you want to earn per year

➤ Identify how many days you can realistically work in a year

➤ Divide your target earning amount by the number of days you can work

Being overly optimistic with the number of days you expect to sell will result in you not being able to achieve your target earnings. This means that a lower estimate for your available working days reduces risk and increases the chances of you exceeding your target. You also need to incorporate any time you expect to take out for holidays, sickness and anything else that would make you unavailable work; unlike being employed, you don't get paid for these.

Realistically, aiming to earn a full salary in six months of work provides enough margin for three months of the year to be spent on holiday with an additional three month margin for anything unexpected, such as the economy becoming difficult. This means that any time you sell beyond the six month target is what allows you to earn more than the equivalent employed programmer; and rightly so, considering that you are a disposable worker that frees companies from their employment law obligations and other employee related expenses such as training and equipment costs. Smart people don't just aim to sell time, but to make the most from the least effort.

> *"Great results can be achieved with small forces."*
>
> *- Sun Tzu, The Art of War*

Earnings you make also need to be structured to cover:

➤ Difficult times

Being a disposable resource, you are not protected by employment law—meaning no redundancy pay and minimal notice for project/contract termination. As a result, freelancers and contractors are the first to feel the brunt of circumstances such as economic events like the 2008 financial crisis. Make sure you have enough savings to cover any risk of operating in difficult market conditions that.

➤ Training expenses

Demand for specific sub-skills within programming is always changing. Not long ago, Flash and Actionscript were highly sought after skills for front end web applications, with Javascript being the poor man's choice that was limited in functionality. These days, not only are Flash and Actionscript irrelevant, but Javascript has become relevant to everything from browser-based software through to server side applications development, **Internet of Things** (**IoT**) and its use in commercial products such as Sony's PlayStation 4.

An investment into training is not optional if you want to stay relevant; especially if you want to charge higher rates. There are two types of training cost—cash and time. Cash costs are associated with purchase of courses and learning materials such as books, while time is about the time you spend learning and practicing to master the skills. Even where cash costs can be eliminated, learning will always have a time cost that converts to a cash value; time spent learning is time lost from earning—hence the saying of time is money. Make sure to factor time in the year that you expect to spend on upgrading your skills; even if this is in your spare time.

➤ Equipment purchases and maintenance

Unlike programmers employed by companies, you don't have anyone who will buy you equipment and software licenses for your job. To top this, many employers don't just buy their employees entry level versions, but whatever is top of the range—with upgrades each year. This is an employment benefit that you miss out on by going the self employed route at a cost to your profitability. This is something that your clients save on by not needing to make these purchases—so make sure your rates factor in the value of equipment and software licenses you provide with your service.

Maximizing your earning potential is a big part of the game, so it makes sense to understand how you are valued within the industry. Questions you should be considering include:

➤ What is the average salary being offered for the equivalent employed role?

➤ What rates are currently being offered in the contracting market?

➤ What level of experience do you consider yourself to be at?

➤ What complementary secondary skills do you have?

➤ What type of responsibilities are you willing to accept?

➤ What type of organization are you looking to target?

➤ How much holiday time do you want?

These are all questions that have a direct impact on identifying a realistic daily rate that offers minimal risk; remember, risk management is about avoiding unnecessary risk and keeping odds in your favor, so always look to maximize your earnings to keep risk low!

With the game being about identifying ways to maximize your appeal to buyers in the market, it's important to know how to package and present your attributes in a way that convinces buyers that you're right for their job. Every buyer is different in some way, even when they share many common characteristics. This means that although you may have already identified market segments to target, your strategy for approaching them may be designed in a way that further specializes in making you appeal to buyers with more specific characteristics.

> *"He will win who knows how to handle both superior and inferior forces."*
>
> *- Sun Tzu, The Art of War*

The approach to further specialize in more specific characteristics may be taken more through circumstance than personal choice. For example:

➤ Where your programming skills and experience can't compete with other programmers in the market, look to compete by combining the use of a secondary skill, or by finding buyers who don't have the budget to attract the best programmers.

➤ Where you are confident that your skills are competitive with the standards of the market leading programmers, build your rates to reflect the highest prices offered in the contract job adverts you find in your research.

It's easy to make the assumption that buyers only need someone who can write their code, but the reality is that there are many more factors to successfully completing software projects than merely writing the code. Writing the right code to solve the right problem is more important than writing any old code. Code without the right data will never produce the required output. A project that faces interference from political agendas is unlikely to be completed to its full potential, on time or within budget. Projects designed in a way that are unrealistic to deliver within the available time or budget need specific intervention for identifying the minimum viable product. You can see the pattern of these requirements— there are opportunities in every market segment for you to stand out from the competition by emphasizing relevant secondary skills you have that many other programmers don't.

> *"He who only sees the obvious, wins his battles with difficulty; he who looks below the surface of things, wins with ease."*
>
> *- Sun Tzu, The Art of War*

While you are likely to focus on a main type of work that earns the majority of your income, such as a contract-based role, there is nothing to stop you from engaging other types of self employed work to fit around this. For example, while your day work may focus on earning money from a contract project, the time you spend traveling on the train and some evenings could be used to work on mini freelance projects such as writing, small websites, apps and provision of services such as tuition. All of this helps to top up your earnings and open potential future opportunities that allow you to evolve your business while reducing your exposure to unfavorable circumstances you can face as a disposable contract worker.

Summary

Understanding who you intend to sell to will allow you to clearly define what your business is about, who you intend to deal with, what you will offer, and how you plan to be profitable. The key to understanding your market is research, so make sure that you do this thoroughly and make use of reliable information sources.

Even when your research indicates a high demand for what you plan to offer, a clear focus should always be kept on whether your ideas are financially viable. All markets can be separated into multiple segments, categorizing buyers who share common characteristics. In terms of pricing, this often translates to the three general categories of budget, standard, and premium buyers; each needing to be tackled in a unique way to guarantee that your services or products can be delivered in a way that meets their quality expectations and is financially viable. It's important to identify what can be offered for the market segment(s) you target from the start so that you can avoid lower paying buyers negotiating extras that make your offer unprofitable.

With an understanding of factors relating to positioning yourself in the market, the next chapter will cover issues related to building a business model; a key part to identifying how your business can operate profitably with the types of people you are selling your services and products to.

3

Defining Your
Business Model

A business model defines how a business idea can be operated in a way that is profitable. All businesses are unique in some way or another, with many taking an influence from competitors using proven business models that have delivered success. Knowing what makes a business model, and how to adapt them to match the environment you operate in, can maximize your chances of being successful.

Types of business model for software

The mistake made by a lot of software developers who decide to go into business is placing too much emphasis on the technical side of software development. This mistake stems from software development's culture as a whole, which generally tends to advocate sharing of code, information, and ideas, as demonstrated by the open source movement. Although this ideology can prove effective for learning and building a reputation in software development, it shouldn't be confused as being a business model—one of many reasons why software developers find themselves underpaid or failing to make their business a commercial success.

Your business model should look at the method you intend to use for developing and distributing your software in order to define how a business can be built on your skills in software development. Some models make use of software development as the primary business, whereas other models use of software development as a component supporting other business activities. The following are the main business model categories that commercial software development fall under:

Software Development as a Service (SDaaS)

The most obvious way to make money with your software development skills is to allow businesses and individuals to hire you. This business model focuses on selling your time to produce software that meets the requirements of the people or business who are hiring you.

Advantages

This method of building a business around software development has several advantages that make it ideal for people starting out in business:

> ➤ **Lower risk of making serious mistakes**:Being paid by the hour/project means that you don't risk working for several years to create something that doesn't make enough money to justify your time investment

> ➤ **Easy to define**: The business is all about selling a service to create software for people who hire you—easy for you and your clients to understand, which therefore minimizes the risk of costly mistakes

> ➤ **Allows you to learn as you go**: Not needing to create code before making a sale means that you can learn about the buyer and their requirements in a way that allows you to refine your processes to reflect your experiences as they happen

> ➤ **Proven model**: This type of business model has a guarantee to work providing that you can generate the required sales, set the right processes, and negotiate a price that covers the cost of your time and expenses

> ➤ **Minimal startup costs**: In the age of the Internet and social media networks such as LinkedIn, it is possible to start this type of business with almost no money—a quick visit to a website such as Freelancers.net (`http://www.freelancers.net`) will reveal several projects that you can apply for if you have the skills

> ➤ **High flexibility**: The nature of software development combined with portable computing and Internet connectivity means that there is a high amount of flexibility to work at times and locations to suit what is best for you. Once established, you can also select to choose when to take on client work—and more importantly, who you will accept to work for

> ➤ **Reactive software design**: This is where you are designing software to solve a known problem with an understanding of how your chosen design needs to accommodate scope for change. Understanding what the original minimum viable product is and which features are reactive allows you to sell a service to develop both the original requirements and any ongoing alterations

Disadvantages

Not all will be rosy when running your business on the SDaaS model. The nature of this type of business attracts and causes several problems:

> ➤ **Undefined expectations**: The businesses and people who hire you to write their software will often not have a complete understanding of what they want or need from the end result. This means that your job becomes more difficult in needing to manage projects to avoid situations that can damage your profitability, client relationship and ability to complete the project. With experience, you will learn to develop skills and policies for client communications and management that result in better-defined documented specifications which avoid the type of ambiguity that cause problems later in the project; hence the sooner you learn these skills, the sooner you are able to minimize this type of risk

➤ **Unknown time cost**: Your clients often need their software developed in the minimal amount of time, or have a limited budget that affects the time available to complete their project before your profit margins are reduced. At best, the amount of time you identify for completing a project is an educated estimate; regardless of how detailed your method is to come to your identification. A solution to this dilemma is to provide estimates as a range, detailing factors that may impact the actual development time—such as the client failing to provide required content!

➤ **Changing situations**: Your clients will have many associated factors that will influence what they want from the software they hire you to develop. These factors may change over time and therefore result in changes to the software specification, hence resulting in additional time and costs that the client may not be able or willing to negotiate to pay for

➤ **Fixed price can be a profit killer**: Many clients want to know upfront what the total cost for their project will be, meaning that there is a risk of you losing money or working for almost nothing if you don't get your calculations and time estimates correct when deciding your price. Clients can also be unrealistic and tough to negotiate with when introducing changes to their original requirements—even going as far as trying to fit in extra features as part of the original specification's wording; this is how you unexpectedly lose money

➤ **Cheaper countries are a growing threat**: The nature of software development not requiring software developers to be on-site for their work, combined with Internet technologies making it easier for people to work and share their work from any location, means that companies and self-employed individuals from abroad located in countries with lower currency values and living costs are in a better position to compete against you at a lower price. This becomes a serious problem if these competitors have the same level of skill and customer service that you can deliver

This threat is often more specific to the budget end of the market, where sellers compete on providing the lowest price and buyers primarily seek to hire the lowest bidder; hence sellers located in countries with lower currencies and living costs having an outright advantage to win this type of work. At the other end of the market, buyers in the premium segments tend to judge less on price and more on factors relating to quality—whether that be customer service, knowledge, assurances, or code quality; as a result, competitors who target this segment tend to use any difference in living costs and lower currency value maximize their profitability and instead focus on competing with their skills and knowledge instead of price

> ➤ **Undermining media and technology**: The ability to charge the fee you view your time and skills to be worth is dependent on finding clients who perceive your skills to be worth the price you demand. An emerging problem for software developers is how the perception of their skills is being undermined by the media and increasing accessibility to off the shelf technology products. Examples include a certain business reality TV show giving apprentice candidates a day to create an app, news stories exaggerating the success of a five year old gaining a Microsoft Office certification, and do it yourself website creators with marketing emphasizing no need for coding skills to create websites. While all of these examples are technically correct in their specific context, they play a large role in the public's perception of software development being a child's play activity, therefore leading to incorrect assumptions on software and technology:
>
>> ➤ A very basic app could be created in one day, but something that has any meaningful use will take weeks, months, or years to develop, depending on its features
>>
>> ➤ Microsoft certifications for using software such as Word are easy to pass; they are not in the same league as software development-focused certifications such as the **Microsoft Certified Solutions Developer (MCSD)**
>>
>> ➤ Basic websites can be created without coding skills through **WYSIWYG (What You See Is What You Get)** tools such as Wix or Dreamweaver, but these are limited to any pre-made the features they offer and can produce very poor formatting code that is bad for Google search rankings. As soon as you need to do something that the website builder can't do or where you need to better optimize your content for search engines, you need to get involved in writing or editing code
>>
>> ➤ Projects of medium complexity can now be created with the use of open source systems such as WordPress with no programming knowledge—just an understanding of how to install the code to hosting. These systems can often be customized with existing templates and have functionality extended through readily available plug-ins; allowing clients who experiment with their WordPress installations to develop an incorrect preconception of software development being click to install. This leads to a justification on difficult stances such as insisting they hire you at minimum wage for features they want requiring bespoke programming and customizations

The result of this misinformation being generated and spread through misleading marketing and media is that there are segments of the market where programming skills have become devalued to a point where clients perceive they could do the job themselves with a few days of training.

Figure 3.1 : Do training courses like this damage perceptions of potential buyers by suggesting that they can learn everything required to do the job in just six weeks for £40?

Conclusion

Using the SDaaS model is a good way to get started in software development, allowing you to learn about the types of situations that and how they can be resolved. This model is also the option that has the fewest startup costs, with it being possible to start earning straight away by finding a project that pays through one of the many project-bidding websites or projects advertised through social media.

It is also possible to evolve this model into one of the independent business models that are described in the following sub-sections of this chapter. Small businesses and individuals who make a living from software development often evolve their main business model from SDaaS into one of the other models; these being **Software as a Product** (**SaaP**), **Software as a Service** (**SaaS**), or software supporting a service. In the case of Basecamp (`https://basecamp.com`), formerly 37 signals, the company was originally founded to provide website redesign services, but eventually changed their business model to SaaS selling subscriptions to their in-house developed project management system.

Software as a Product (SaaP)

At the other extreme of software development business models there's selling software as a full product—a complete contrast to simply selling the service to create software. This model relies on creating a software product that people are willing to purchase, hence making the wrong product could potentially result no money returned from the time invested. In addition to the time cost, you may also need to hire the services of other professionals, such as graphic artists, to assist with the production of content for integration within your software, hence there being a higher cost to bringing your product to market.

Advantages

Like with the previous method, there are several advantages to building a software business around your own product development:

➤ **Your own control**: You are in control of what the final product will be, meaning less chance of problems arising from changes to the project specification

➤ **Better understanding**: With the product being your own business, you in a better position to understand what the software needs—as opposed to trying to understand someone else's business

➤ **Freedom and flexibility**: You are more likely to have the type of freedom to develop features you want in your software

➤ **Financial potential**: There is scope to make a lot more money with your own software product if everything goes right—compare earnings of up to £500 per day of contractors using the SDaaS model, with the peak daily earnings of £7,000 generated by the indie game New Star Soccer. This massive difference highlights the scalability benefit provided in this model, where the time to create the product is not proportional to the amount of money it can make. In contrast, increasing profitability using the SDaaS model can only be achieved by investing more time or by finding higher-paying clients

Disadvantages

The freedom of the SaaP model comes with its own disadvantages to match its advantages:

➤ **Higher risk of failure**: Unlike selling your skills for an hourly fee, there is the possibility of making no money if you develop a software product that there's no demand for or if you don't have the right marketing strategy. You will only ever know this for sure after you have developed your software, by which time it is already too late to recover your time investment

➤ **Need for more business skills**: In order to minimize the higher risk of failure, there is a need for more skills and experience in business to make sure that the right decisions are made for your product's development and marketing. This includes the ability to perform high quality market research, design your product in line with known factors that persuade people to buy it, and also to have an understanding of how to market your software product; including routes to market and strategic partnership formation. Failure in any of these will harm the product's ability to recover the cost of its development

➤ **Less opportunity to learn as you work**: Developing software to your own specification that is unlikely to change means that you have less reason to learn software patterns that allow you to make your code flexible to accommodate future change requirements. This factor, combined with the possible urgency to continually get your products completed before their budget is depleted, could lead to a situation where you fail to develop your technical skills enough to remain employable as a software developer should there be a time when you decide to quit developing your own software and either go back to the SDaaS model or exit self-employment and return to being employed by an employer

➤ **More serious consequences for mistakes**: Mistakes that lead to your product failing to be ready for sale during a peak sales time, as well as in the previously mentioned market research and marketing activities, can result in consequences as serious as the product making no sales. In contrast, the less risky SDaaS model would just result in an unhappy client who still pays if the completion date is missed

➤ **Need for project management**: The success of your software product will depend on your ability to get the product to market. This means making sure that you can complete the project within the available budget—that is making sure it is completed on time and that you don't overspend when hiring additional help. This also means that there is a greater need for self discipline so you don't get distracted by Facebook!

➤ **Can be hit and miss**: Not all of your products will generate the amounts of money you need them to, meaning there will always be the risk of the next version failing to sell

➤ **Proactive software development**: The software being developed is at best based on an educated guess of what will make money. This means that there is no guarantee that
the time spent developing the software translating to an amount of money that makes the effort worthwhile. It is also important not to miscalculate your chances of success based on media bias; newspapers, magazines, television, and websites tend to only cover the success stories of a few developers—giving an impression that the majority of independent app developers are highly successful, when the reality is that most apps fail to make any profit

Conclusion

The SaaP model has a mixture of benefits and causes for concern, which although convenient, makes it more difficult to work with than the SDaaS model. The higher starting cost may also be a barrier to whether you are able to work with this model, as you would need to already have money to fund upfront time investment into the software development as well as needing a budget for any additional help such as for content creation like graphics.

There is some good news that can help overcome the barriers to working with this model. The most obvious would be to seek grants and investors, which would overcome the financial requirements to kick start your project. A type of investor to consider would be software publishers, who are able to support your project by providing an advance on your royalty payments in addition to taking care of the marketing side. Publishers would require you to develop the software in line with their vision, so expect to negotiate on features and make changes to your original design of the software; this in effect changes your model toward the SDaaS. Another consideration for using a publisher is that you receive a much smaller amount per unit sale, which isn't as significant as it may sound if the publisher can produce significantly more sales than you would be able to if marketing it yourself.

Speaking of kick starting your project, a more recent trend of funding this type of software development is through crowd funding. This is where software developers pitch their ideas to potential buyers in a bid to get people to contribute toward the project's funding requirements; ranging from small to reasonably large donations. The ability to succeed with this method of fund raising is based on a mixture of generating a large amount of awareness for your project and having a clear message to convince people to donate larger amounts of money, hence the total amount you generate being a mixture of small and large donations. Although you need to pitch your product idea in a way that is appealing enough for people to want to invest in it, this approach to funding provides a higher degree of flexibility compared to other funding sources, who most likely will want a significant ability to dictate features of the end product. It is certainly worth checking out online crowd funding platforms such as Kickstarter.com (`https://www.kickstarter.com`)to see whether this is something worth considering.

It is probably no coincidence that many software developers evolve their business model from SDaaS to SaaP when they eventually become confident in their understanding of both software development and the users of their software, where they are able to identify a product design that can be used to solve the problems faced by many people. This approach allows the development of a software product to be created as a side project, which although taking longer to develop, sidesteps the financial funding burden and also allows the product to be developed with real insight to the features of the software product that people need and hence are already willing to buy—as opposed to jumping into this model head first and making mistakes through assumptions.

Software as a Service (SaaS)

The emergence of mainstream access to the Internet, fast data transfer speeds, and advancements in the capabilities of web browsers, has opened opportunities for a new type of software business model in recent years; this being the output of the software that is sold as opposed to selling the software itself.

The SaaS model shares many similarities with selling SaaP—most notably the similarities in its focus on developing the software upfront and therefore the likely need to have funding for its development and any pre-requisite research to ensure that the product design matches market demand.

Advantages

SaaS provides the same types of advantages as the SaaP model, but with a twist:

> ➤ **Your own control**: Like with developing SaaP, you are in control of the software you are developing. The difference with this model is that the focus is on the type of service you are creating the software to deliver

> ➤ **Flexibility**: With software being provided as a service via the Internet, especially if it is a web-based software accessed through a web browser, it is easy for new updates to be added without complicated distribution to end users. In the case of web applications, the updated version is immediately available to users as soon as it has been installed to the web server. This means less need to develop features upfront, and therefore allowing the software service to be brought to market sooner at less cost

> ➤ **Diverse income streams**: The primary users of your software service may or may not be the people who buy the services you sell. In the case of social networks such as LinkedIn, Facebook and Twitter, the service sold is advertising, hence their paying customers being marketers. It is important to distinguish who your paying customers are so that you don't neglect to develop the features you need to make sales; in the case of Facebook, marketers are provided with powerful tools that can make their advertising highly targeted. Having a plan on monetization from the beginning also helps to avoid a situation where you have gained a user base who refuse to make enough payments for you to make a profit and who use excessive resources that increase your operation costs—especially if your software service is based on heavy data usage such as video, sound and large images

> ➤ **Financial potential**: Like with the SaaP model, there is the potential to make a lot more money without proportionately increasing time requirements. In comparison to software developers using the SDaaS model to charge up to £10,000 for 20 days of intense work, whereas an established software service with 400 subscribers paying £25 per month could match this with only casual user support as real work. This model has even more financial potential if you are able to target premium market segments wanting to buy higher value subscriptions that earn you from £12,000 to more than £20,000 per year

> ➤ **Continuous income**: Unlike the SaaP model where sales are a one off and repeat sales require extra effort to produce and market new software versions, subscribers to SaaS systems pay a continual subscription. This means that you only need to retain customers by keeping the system relevant to their needs and keeping an eye on customer satisfaction. This also means that there is scope to grow a business around your software—as opposed to the hit and miss fortunes of the SaaP model

Disadvantages

The disadvantages of the SaaS model are mainly evolutions of those from the SaaP model:

➤ **Additional costs**: With this model relying on you providing hosting for your software service, there will be additional costs for renting at least one server for your software service to be available online. Reliability of your software service's availability is important if you want people to continue subscribing, so corners shouldn't be cut to
buy cheaper hosting that doesn't provide a decent uptime guarantee. This is a concern when using shared hosting, where code of other users of the server can lead to your web application going offline

➤ **More need for cost analysis**: Unlike the SaaP model, you are also likely to require additional hosting and bandwidth capabilities as you sell more subscriptions to your software service—especially if your software features produces data or accepts uploading of documents. This leads to higher requirements to analyze the costs associated with users' usage to make sure that whatever they are paying doesn't increase your costs in a way that makes their subscription unprofitable

➤ **More risks involved**: With the potential for mistakes to be made in the cost analysis as well as other risks such as online hacking, there is scope for much more to go wrong than there is for software sold to users in a way that uses their own hardware resources

➤ **Need for project management**: In the same way that project management is required for the SaaP model and for the same reasons

➤ **Proactive software development**: The need for the services delivered via the software are at best based on an educated guess, of which there is no guarantee that enough people can be attracted pay the amounts of money needed to break even or make a profit. The outcome could be an expensive exercise to identify that there isn't enough interest for the software service to be viable as a business, hence a waste of time in developing the software

Conclusion

The SaaS model provides more freedom and much higher earning potential, but at the cost of higher risk. Unlike the SaaP model that this has evolved from, there are some additional risks and costs that grow with the success of this model. It is for this reason that there should be more time and effort invested into the business planning wherever this model is used because mistakes in identifying the costs for running the service can result in significant amounts of money being lost through unexpected expenses.

The main risks of the SaaS model revolve around its reliance on using server resources that you are responsible for maintaining and paying for. When users start to require more resources than your business plan has accommodated for, you will quickly find where the faults lie in your financial plan. No matter how well you plan the financials for your strategy based on this model, you should expect some unexpected events to occur that will reveal weaknesses in your cost structure—and therefore be able to rectify this as soon as possible.

The primary risks associated with this model makes creating a beta version of your software before its main launch more important so that threats to your financial success can be identified early and ironed out with reliable usage data from real users of your system. This avoids fixes being based on assumptions about problems causes that later turn out to be incorrect and lead to the same problems on a bigger scale. The beta version also helps to expose other types of problems aside from those relating to your financial plan, especially when it comes to issues such as data security threatening to both cripple your system's ability to deliver the services you sell and damaging customer confidence. Losing either of these can lead to your business being in a position where money is lost through legal action and a reputation that makes it impossible to attract the number of customers you need to be profitable. Launching a beta version of your software service is an effective way to protect against this type of situation by emphasizing that the software is not fully complete and therefore users accept the possibility of unexpected situations—that is users agree that usage of the system is at their own risk.

Furthermore, the architecture of the software system can be made to minimize the risks that this model poses to you. Modern advancements of web browsers allow web-based software to store data on the user's computer and also for offline access to functionality. This opens opportunities for you to design your software shift processing and data storage to the user's hardware, meaning that your server can manage more user requests by offloading data processing to the user's computer, while reducing the need to store and process user data. The result of integrating these types of features into your system's architecture will be the requirement of fewer server resources to service your user base as your business grows, hence lower operating costs and the potential to eliminate risks from unexpected usage from users who use more resources than your financial plan accommodates. The decentralization of your user data also opens possibilities for reducing the impact of data security breaches on your main server(s) by not having a single known location to attack.

Like with the SaaP model, starting with small scale ambitions will reduce the risk of develop a software service with expensive to developing features that aren't used enough to justify their development. Starting a business based on this model with a specific and simple to implement service allows this type of system to get to market sooner, so that future decisions on features can be directly influenced by user feedback, especially when it comes to identifying which features can be monetized.

Software Supporting a Service

The final software business model we look at is in complete contrast to the previous models where the business is about the output of the software, whether this is creation of the software itself or the outcomes it generates. The software supporting a service model intentionally relegates the software system to a supporting role that forms no part of the description of the service being sold. This is not to say that the software becomes irrelevant in this model; it's about the software being a mechanism to allow the delivery of service features.

This model is more often used for departments within larger organizations, especially where there's a reliance on in-house developed resources for supporting its operations. A successful mainstream example of this model in use is Uber; an Internet based taxi service whose operation is dependent on the use of their phone app to provide customers with software features to request rides. These software features are used to facilitate everything from capturing journey details and assignment of the most suitable driver, through to payment for the journey and facilitation of other information.

Advantages

The software supporting a service model is unique in the way that it allows you to make money as the software is being developed. This provides several advantages when it comes to startup costs and risk reduction:

> **Lower entry barriers**: Unlike the other software business models, you can start trading without writing any code, therefore allowing you to start your business quickly

> **Fund software development inline with services sold**: Not having to develop your software system upfront means that you can use money generated from service sales to fund the software system development. This means that you avoid the possibility of investing time into a software project that doesn't generate enough money to justify the time invested, or having your vision of the business being disrupted by the need to satisfy the demands of investors your have received money from to fund the software development costs

> **Can make unprofitable services highly profitable**: Processes that have high time costs can often be automated through the use of software, hence reducing the costs associated with providing a service in order to improve profitability to a point that would otherwise be impossible

> **Opportunities for new service categories to be delivered**: Known in business circles as Blue Ocean Strategy, the adaption of business services to deliver unique elements not offered elsewhere can be achieved through the use of software. This can result in being able to target new customers who are willing to pay a premium, making a significant impact on profit potential, especially if you are operating in a saturated market that forces you to operate on razor thin profit margins to remain competitive

➤ **Reactive software design**: The ability to sell services before designing your software allows you to identify first hand what the software needs to do in order to support your services. This could be to improve the quality of your services in order to give you a unique selling point, or more often than not, to allow you to be more efficient so that you can either increase your profit margins or be more price competitive

Disadvantages

Although software supporting a business has advantages in getting started and the types of flexibility it offers to reduce risks associated with other models, it also has several unique disadvantages such as:

➤ **Software development is a cost**: No matter how you look at its contribution to the business, every hour spent on further developing the software is a cost that needs to be funded by time spent on money making activities. This means that there is a need to justify software feature development on the basis of how it supports services being sold to become more profitable or to capture new customers

➤ **Software development is dictated by service needs**: The success of the business is dependent on the services being sold and not necessarily the software; hence the immediate needs of the services will dictate what is viable to develop as part of the software system. This isn't good if the features you want to develop can't be justified by the number of paying service clients it will benefit

➤ **Software development competes against service time**: If you are personally delivering the services that the software is designed to support, there is the scope for conflict to occur in your time management regarding how much time you dedicate to services you sell and the time you invest into the software's development. Limiting your time on the software development in order to generate income from your services will result in the software taking longer to launch for supporting your services, which may result in lost opportunities to maximize profits, to evolve services in ways that win new sales, or simply to retain existing clients through increased satisfaction and/or price competitiveness that the software system would allow through supporting the business operations

Conclusion

The software supporting a service model is possibly the easiest model to execute that doesn't require upfront investment and minimizes the risk of developing unused software features that erode profitability. With options to develop the software as the services are being delivered, it is possible to learn about the software requirements as you deliver your service, meaning that you are able to fund the research and development of your software system from selling your services before starting software development.

Success with this model requires you to fully understand the role of the software in supporting the services being sold. With the software itself not directly responsible for making money, the software features need to be strategically designed to support the business activities that generate money, which could be to produce more sales, retain customers or increase efficiency for improved profit margins. Understanding how to identify the purpose of the software in this model is the difference between your software being a critical component of a successful business or failing to provide any meaningful support that justifies the expense of the software development.

There is an importance to allocate the right amount of time between money making activities that the software supports and the development of the software. Even though the software development is an initial cost to the wider business, it is the software component that you are developing that can be used to open or take advantage of opportunities that increase your earning potential. Neglecting your software development in favor of focusing on short term money making activities can damage long term capabilities. This is of concern when opportunities only exist for a limited time, where delaying your software development leads to missing opportunities and resulting in your software having no purpose by the time it is completed.

> *"When opportunities occur through events but you are unable to respond, you are not smart."*
>
> *— Sun Tzu, The Art of War*

With this in mind, there is a need to incorporate risk assessment into your project planning, allowing you to weigh up whether the goals of the software you develop are achievable before you invest your time into developing the software.

Business Model Canvas

Once you've identified the type of business model to use, the next step is to identify a structure to operate with. The Business Model Canvas is a useful tool that can be used to identify the components of your model and to visualize their relationships in order to identify how they work.

Components

The first step in building your Business Model Canvas is identifying the different components that will make your business model. Every business is unique in some way, so whereas you may use the same general model as many other software businesses, there will always be some difference in the way you are structured to operate. Knowing in detail how your model works and what makes it unique will allow you to operate and make decisions that play to your strengths.

> *"If ignorant both of your enemy and yourself, you are certain to be in peril."*
>
> *— Sun Tzu, The Art of War*

Value proposition

Starting the design of your business model with a definition of what you provide to your customers will help to identify the requirements for each of the other components in your model. The value proposition isn't about what you do, but the reason why people buy from you; what we do as software developers is write code, but the reasons that motivate our customers and clients to buy from us is what the software does. Whether it provides a solution to boredom in the form or entertainment, addresses the need to achieve better school results or manage sales for a business, these are all values that motivate people to use software.

Understanding what your customers want will allow you to build your business model and software in a way that makes it appealing and as a result easier to market.

Key considerations include:

> What makes customers want to buy from you?
> What else do you offer that the customer will need?

Key partnerships

Key partners of your model are people and organizations who are suppliers or collaborators. You can't do everything yourself, hence key partners are vital for allowing you to execute your business plan—especially when they are able to provide their contributions to a higher quality and at a lower cost than if you were to do it yourself. Care should be taken to select key partners who can operate in a way that's compatible with your model's structure and can benefit your business.

"We cannot enter into alliances until we are acquainted with the designs of our neighbors."

– Sun Tzu, The Art of War

Key considerations:

> Who are the people you need to work with and supply you?
> What are the benefits of working with these people?

Key resources

Aside from people you need to work with or supply you, there are tools and materials you need to make use of in order to deliver your value proposition. These resources are often linked to key activities, such as your computer for programming, devices such as smart phones for testing and server for storing your online system.

Key considerations:

> ➤ What resources are required to deliver your value proposition?
> ➤ What resources are required to support?
> ➤ Customer relationships
> ➤ Revenue stream
> ➤ Distribution channels

Key activities

These are important activities your business must undertake to fulfill the value proposition that makes your customers want to buy from you. With your business being software-oriented, a lot of the key activities will be related to developing and maintaining your software. Models based on the software supporting a service are also likely to have additional money making activities listed under this category.

Key considerations:

> ➤ What are the activities required by your value proposition?
> ➤ Customer relationships
> ➤ Revenue stream
> ➤ Distribution channels

Customer relationships

The importance of defining the type of relationship to have with your customers shouldn't be underestimated. If you speak to anyone who has enough experience in business, especially marketing, the consistent message you will get about buying is that it comes down to who decision makers want to do business with. Managing your customer relationships is important because having a great product or service becomes irrelevant if people don't want to do business with you.

Customer relationships come in many forms, but from a marketing perspective, the only qualities in a customer relationship are those that persuade the customer to keep buying from you. Depending on what it is you are selling, the important factors could be trust, confidence, satisfaction, enjoyment, admiration or something else related to the customer's perception of their dealings with you. By understanding your customers, you are able to identify which factors of the customer relationship are most important to them for building brand loyalty to you.

Key considerations:

> ➤ What type of relationship is expected of you from the customer?
> ➤ How can you integrate the expected relationship into your operations?
> ➤ What is the cost of integrating the expected relationship into your operations?

Customer segments

Identifying market segments that your customers exist within allows you to be highly specific in the delivery of your service and marketing. Understanding your customer segments will allow you to match the right value proposition that uses the required cost structure and marketing message to be sent through the distribution channels needed to make targeted sales.

Key considerations:

➤ What are the customer categories you are creating value for?

➤ Which customer category is most important?

➤ Why is your most important customer category important?

  ➢ Volume

  ➢ Profit margin

  ➢ Loyalty potential

  ➢ Other reason

Distribution channels

The channels that your customers are reachable through can have a large impact on the development of your marketing strategy, message and possibly your product/service. Sales and therefore profitability are dependent on being noticed by the types of people who you want to buy your product, hence understanding how you can get your product, brand and message to them will make the difference between making the type of sales that define success or failure.

The following are the key considerations:

➤ What channels do your customers have access to?

➤ Which of the channels are most effective?

➤ What are the costs associated with each channel?

➤ Which channels offer the most value?

➤ How do you measure success with channels?

  ➢ Sales

  ➢ Engagement

  ➢ Brand awareness

➤ How do customers use the channels?

➤ How can the channels be integrated into your activities?

Cost structure

Understanding the costs involved with developing and delivering your product or service will allow you to make better pricing decisions that avoid unnecessary risk. This understanding not only allows you to identify the sales price and volume needed to break-even, but also the available options for targeting different customer segments. The outcome of the investigation results in the identification of feature/quality combinations that can be matched to customer segments; which in turn can be packaged as part of a value proposition that can be profitably delivered.

It is important to take into account that not all costs scale with your sales volume. For example, marketing relating to advertising may have a fixed cost regardless of how many sales they generate, meaning there is minimum number of sales needed to recover the upfront costs before profit is made. These factors should be taken into consideration when identifying sales targets—and whether these are realistic to achieve.

Key considerations:

> What are the costs involved in running your business?

> Which of the costs are fixed?

> Which of the costs scale with the number of sales needed?

> What are the costs for each product unit?

Revenue streams

As demonstrated by the four software business models, there are different ways that your software can be monetized depending on the model you are using. Revenue streams identify the specific features or activities of your software based product/service that produces income. It is important to identify that not every feature or activity you engage to develop or deliver produces money for your business. Being aware of the types of feature and/or activity that generate money also allows you to strategically design your product/service in a way that can target the interests of your customer segments to provide value propositions that appeal to their specific interests.

Key considerations:

> What value propositions are your customer segments willing to pay for?

> What methods do your customer segments use to pay you?

> How do you your customer segments prefer to pay you?

> What is the contribution of each revenue stream to the overall revenue?

Canvas

The canvas is a visual tool that allows all of the components to be visually listed ard related as a diagram. Where the canvas is written on a whiteboard or large poster, sticky notes can be used for the flexible addition and editing of components:

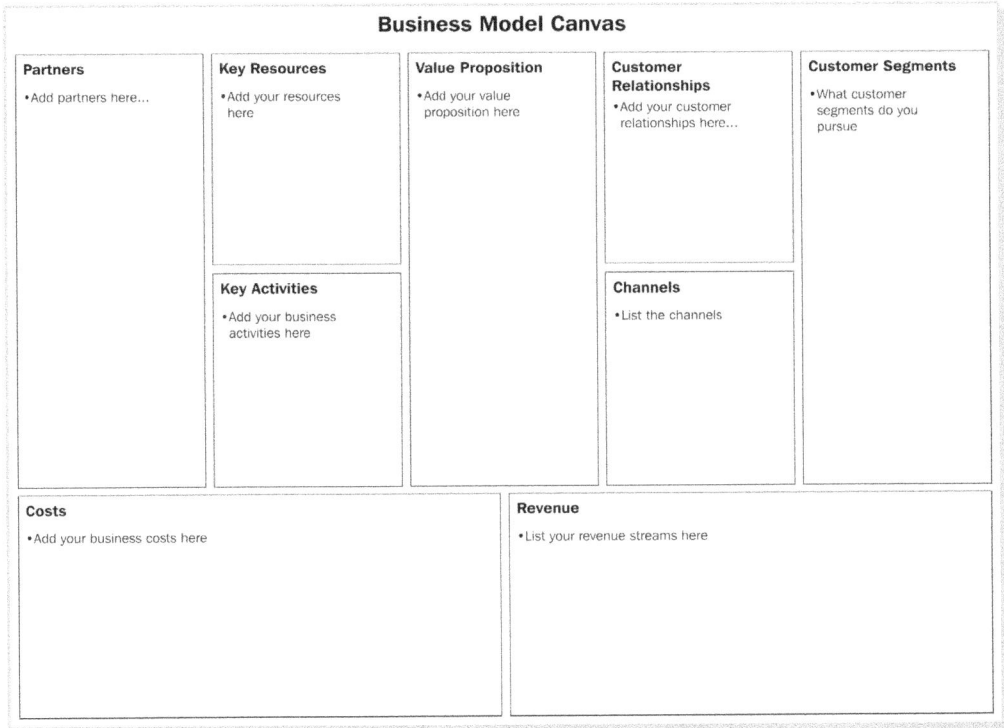

Business Model Canvas

Partners	Key Resources	Value Proposition	Customer Relationships	Customer Segments
•Add partners here...	•Add your resources here	•Add your value proposition here	•Add your customer relationships here...	•What customer segments do you pursue

Key Activities
•Add your business activities here

Channels
•List the channels

Costs
•Add your business costs here

Revenue
•List your revenue streams here

Figure 3.2: The layout of the Business Model Canvas.

Problem tools

There are additional tools you can use as part of your business model's definition. With the emphasis so far being to define the bigger picture of software business models and how define them through the Business Model Canvas, there are also other tools that you can make use of for addressing specific problems you face in business.

Product life cycle

Relevant to business models that rely on selling a product or service that can only be sold once, the product life cycle describes each stage that the product goes through, from beginning to end. Understanding these stages allows you to identify where your product is currently positioned regarding its profitability so that you can anticipate upcoming sales and prepare to take action for when sales and profit start to decline.

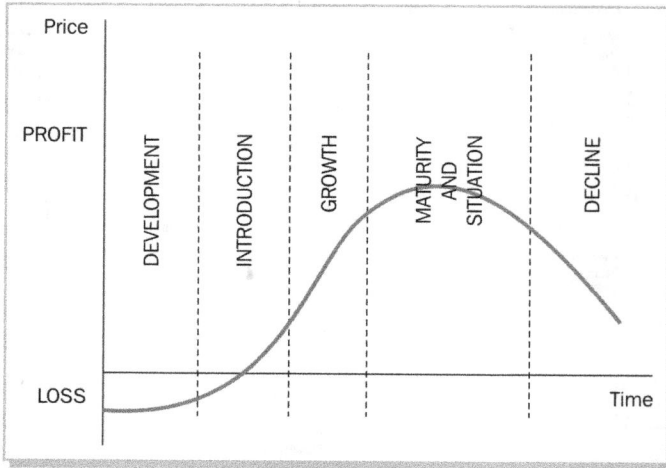

Figure 3.3: The stages of the product life cycle in relation to time, profit and loss.

Development

The first stage of the product life cycle is the development of the product. As indicated in Figure 3.3, the development phase is created at a loss. In real projects, there may be a steeper increase of losses generated by the software development before costs start to decrease toward the end of the product development.

Key trends:

➤ Increasing losses occurred through development costs

➤ Extensions to development due to missed deadlines and/or unknown factors

Introduction

The introduction stage is where the product arrives to market, ready for customers to buy the product. With the exception of high profile products, it should be anticipated for sales to start fairly low until the marketing campaign and word of mouth take effect in raising sales volume. There is a high need to generate awareness at this stage so that potential customers are aware of the product, its capabilities, and how it meets their needs and interests.

Customers who purchase a product in this phase of the product life cycle are often referred to as early adopters—the types who are wanting to have the latest in technology and willing to take a risk in their purchase not meeting its full potential or their expectations. This phase tends to have high marketing costs for generating awareness to what is often a small market.

Key trends:

> ➤ High investment in marketing promotions to inform people and raise awareness of value propositions
>
> ➤ Stimulation of demand through discount pricing
>
> ➤ Emphasis on targeted marketing activities aimed at early adopters and using them to become brand ambassadors for generating word of mouth recommendations

Growth

After your product has been introduced to the market and has gained the attention of early adopters, sales start to shift towards mainstream customers who make their purchase decisions based on the product's reputation and where its value propositions meet their core values, needs, and interests. Growing sales to reach mainstream customers requires a successful introduction phase that establishes confidence in the product, hence the need for good quality control.

Key trends:

> ➤ Advertising designed to promote awareness of the brand to more customer segments
>
> ➤ Increasing the number of distribution channels that the product is available from
>
> ➤ Use of early adopter feedback to iron out flaws and improve the value propositions

Maturity and saturation

Once the product has reached the awareness of the mass market, its ability to reach new customers becomes limited and therefore its sales growth starts to slow to a point where there are no further increases. It is also during this phase that the success of the product will have captured the attention of competitors, who will have released their own imitations of the product in order to capture a slice of the market—another factor that will reduce your sales potential.

Key trends:

> ➤ Increased competition imitating the product
> ➤ Attempts to differentiate the product from the competition through feature enhancement and distinct branding
> ➤ Profit optimization by seeking to lower production and support costs
> ➤ Establishment of collaborations with new key partners to become more competitive

Decline

The final phase of the product life cycle is when the majority of the mainstream market has bought a version of the product, whether it be your own or one of the imitations that have appeared on the market. Products that are designed as a one off purchase will not produce further sales from the same customers, hence sales will decrease. It is in this phase that there is a need to introduce innovations; either in terms of product enhancements to value propositions that entice existing customers to upgrade, or to find new customer segments that the product can be sold to.

Key trends:

> ➤ Marketing efforts to generate repeat sales from existing customers or expand sales to new customer segments
> ➤ Price reductions to increase the appeal of the product to new "price sensitive" customer segments
> ➤ Enhancement of features to support new value propositions
> ➤ Diversification of the product to appeal to new customer segments

Five Forces Analysis

This analysis identifies five forces that control the market(s) that you operate within. Central to this analysis is the rivalry of market competitors that exist to serve and react to the other four forces. Five Forces Analysis complements the identification of the product life cycle by providing the ability to see how the market may change during each phase:

> *"We are not fit to lead an army on the march unless we are familiar with the face of the country—its mountains and forests, its pitfalls and precipices, its marshes and swamps."*
>
> *– Sun Tzu, The Art of War*

from "The Five Competitive Forces That Shape Strategy" by
Michael E. Porter, Harvard Business Review, January 2008

Figure 3.4: The five forces that exist in all markets affecting the balance of negotiating power.

Rivalry among existing suppliers

The central element that allows for the existence of the other four forces is the presence in
the market of other entities competing for the same business. More competition provides
buyers (customer segments) with more bargaining power and can eventually lead to the
market becoming saturated to a point where buyers have the power to force prices to a
minimum and quality to a maximum in order to receive the best value propositions. This
eventual situation is referred to in another analysis tool, Blue Ocean Strategy, as a red ocean,
where it is necessary for businesses to operate high risk razor thin margins just to survive.

Key considerations:

➤ How fierce is the competition?

    ➢ Is it a red ocean?

➤ Who are the market leaders?

    ➢ Do they have too much influence in the market for you to compete
against?

➤ What market share does the typical business in the market capture?

    ➢ Would an equivalent market share be considered a success for
your business?

Threat of substitute products or services

The next step up from existing competitors is the availability of alternative options that your customer segments can choose to buy instead of your product or service. These are not direct competitors in the sense that they provide an equivalent product or service, but instead offer alternative solutions that match the value propositions that the market seeks to buy. Regardless of whether you sell a product or service, substitutes can come in any form—for example a service that provides the same value propositions as your product.

Key considerations:

➤ What alternative solutions are there to provide your value proposition?

    ➤ Are there specific situations in which these alternatives are viable options?

➤ What situations are substitutes for a valid option?

    ➤ It is entirely possible to put a website together with Microsoft Word, but would it be accepted by someone wanting highly optimized HTML for search engines?

Threat of new entrants

With most startups failing within their first three years, most new market entrants are not likely to pose the same level of threat as existing competitors in the market. They still pose a threat to damage your sales and ability to negotiate with buyers; especially when it comes to entrants who price themselves to make a loss—the types who later cease operating when they run their business into debt.

The more serious threat from new market entrants comes from those with significant financial clout, as well as those with the ability to disrupt the market through innovation. There is a relationship between these two factors—innovation is often made possible through financial investment. The types of market entrant who pose the most risk are those who are, or are backed by, large companies already established in other markets.

The cancelled Nintendo PlayStation project became a serious mistake for Nintendo, which led to Sony becoming a market entrant to the videogames industry—and ultimately using their financial clout to become a dominant player in the market. At the time of writing, Sony's PlayStation Network (PSN—the online gaming network for PlayStation games consoles) generates more money than Nintendo's entire business. Additionally, the anticipation of certain businesses becoming a new entrant can also be enough to lose significant sales—as happened to Sega in 2000 with their Dreamcast games console when many console buyers held off upgrading in anticipation for the launch of Sony's PlayStation 2.

A consideration that can be used to protect your business against the threat of new entrants, especially those who are inexperienced enough to introduce loss making pricing, is the requirement of skills and certification to become eligible as a player in the market. A requirement for higher skills will mean the need for more commitment from new market entrants to learn those skills, hence them likely to place a higher value on their time. Where certification is required, otherwise known as red tape, the difficulty, effort and skill required to complete the necessary paperwork can be enough to deter many of the potential market entrants.

Key considerations:

> ➤ How easy is it to provide an equivalent to your product or service?
>> ➢ For software development services, are there software service equivalents such as Wix.com, or open source projects like WordPress, that lower the skill requirements for new entrants?

> ➤ Is red tape a barrier to market entry?
>> ➢ Effort required to meet all of the requirements may deter the majority of potential market entrants, if not making it impossible.

> ➤ Does your brand recognition within the market protect you?
>> ➢ New market entrants may find it impossible to win business from customers who are already highly satisfied with your services and products.

> ➤ Are your customers willing to pay a premium price for your product or service?
>> ➢ If so, this will protect you against unproven new market entrants using aggressive pricing strategies to undercut you.

Bargaining power of suppliers

In addition to other sources of work that your suppliers target, the number of competitors and alternative suppliers in your market are likely to influence your ability to negotiate better value propositions from suppliers. Negotiation goes against you when your suppliers are in a position where there is more demand for their supplies than they can fulfill, whether it be from the market you operate in or otherwise; hence every competitor in your market who needs their services plays a role in eroding your ability to negotiate. With the exception of a market crash or where your supplier's market becomes flooded with alternatives, you will always be at your strongest negotiation position when establishing a new market category— that is, Blue Ocean Strategy.

Key considerations:

> ➤ How eager are suppliers for your business?
>> ➢ Can they afford to turn your business away?

> ➤ Do suppliers have more demand than they can fulfill?

> > ➤ Can they pick and choose who they work for?

> ➤ Are the growing number of competitors in your market affecting your ability to negotiate?

> > ➤ Are your competitors increasing demand for supplies to a point where suppliers are able to turn away your business to fulfill orders from your competitors offering suppliers a more lucrative deal?

> ➤ Are you able to gain buying power with big orders to suppliers?

> > ➤ Are you able to become classed as such an important customer that suppliers will go out of their way to retain customer loyalty?

> ➤ Are there alternative suppliers you can negotiate better deals with?

> > ➤ Are there better deals on the market that you can use to negotiate your existing supplier to give you a better deal?

Bargaining power of buyers

The buyer has the most negotiating power when a market has more suppliers than there is a demand for. Where you have a high number of competitors who offer the same solution and substitutes who also provide comparable options to your value propositions, there becomes the need to be highly efficient in your operations in order to be able to offer the highest value propositions with the most competitive prices so that you can win the sales you need. Alternatively, differentiating your services products in a way that targets less competitive or new market spaces is a viable solution to this problem.

Key considerations:

> ➤ What are buyers demanding?

> > ➤ Do they want lower price, high quality, or both?

> ➤ How achievable is it to be profitable in meeting the buyer's demands?

> > ➤ Are the demands of buyers worth your time and effort?

> ➤ What innovations can you develop to increase profit margins and meet demands?

> > ➤ Is there a way that you can become better positioned to win business and make a profit?

Seven Domains Assessment framework

One of the main risks of launching your own business idea is in failing to perform enough analysis to identify its potential for success. Seven Domains Assessment framework is a checklist tool that can be used to identify whether a business idea has potential to succeed, highlight its flaws, and help to avoid basic mistakes being made:

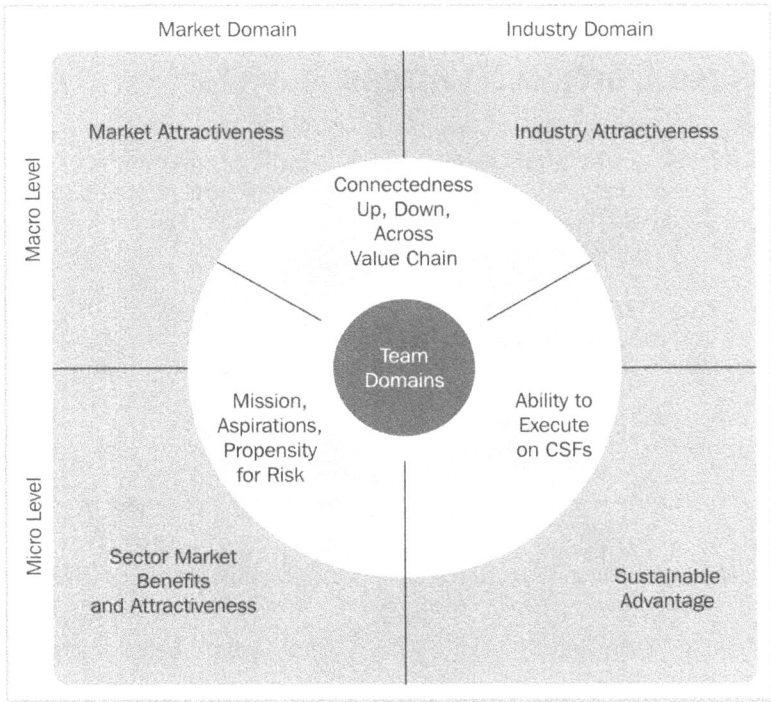

Figure 3.5: The relationships of the seven domains for validating business ideas.

Market domain/macro level – market attractiveness

This looks at the overall market's ability to provide a profit. Specific consideration is given to identifying the number of customers in the market, volume of sales, pricing segments and emerging trends. The analysis of trends in the market is important for identifying the likeliness of growth, stabilization, or decline, hence suggesting how the current market attractiveness may change.

Key considerations:

> How many customers are there in the market?

> How many sales are made to the customers?

> What are the pricing segments?

> What trends suggest potential for future growth or decline?

Market domain/micro level – market sector benefits and attractiveness

Success is likely to be limited if your product or service is designed in a way that makes it perceived to be, a jack of all trades—master of none. The market sector benefits and attractiveness analysis looks at identifying opportunities to target specific segments of the market in a way that allows you to use your unique position and strengths to your advantage in order to increase your chances for success.

Make sure to use a full range of research techniques such as questionnaires, online research, report reviews, and interviews that include both qualitative and quantitative questions to answer so that both statistical analysis and insights to unknown information can be gained.

Key considerations:

> ➤ Which customer segments in the market stand to benefit most from your value propositions?

> ➤ How is your product or service idea different to existing alternative already in the market?

> ➤ Can you grow the appeal of your value propositions to become attractive to other customer segments?

Industry domain/macro level – industry attractiveness

This stage is essentially Five Forces Analysis, looking at the feasibility of entering a market based on the difficulty to enter and operate. The first analysis looks at whether it is possible to enter the market with your skill set, certifications, and resources—the risk of entering a market where minimal or no obstacles are faced means that it will also be easy for new competitors to enter when your success captures their attention.

The other side to this stage, which is also covered in Five Forces Analysis, is the identification of difficulties to operate in the market after entry. The main difficulties revolve around existing competition, who have the potential to make it difficult to win enough sales for your business to be feasible, force prices down to a point where there is little or no profit, and/or use their market position to secure deals suppliers that disable you from being able to compete on price or deliver quickly enough. Where competitors are able to make operating this difficult, questions should be raised as to whether it is worth operating in the market. Where competitors are unable to force such difficulties to operate in the market, the analysis identifies that the business idea can be operated successfully.

Key considerations:

> ➤ Is there a high skill requirement to enter the market?

> ➤ What red tape requirements exist for you to operate in the market?

> ➤ Are there signs of existing or emerging shortcuts to bypass required skills or red tape?

> ➤ How fierce is the existing competition in the market?

> ➤ Are the smaller market players able to operate with acceptable profit?

> ➤ Do buyers and suppliers have an unfavorable negotiation power?

Industry domain/micro level – sustainable advantage

Upon completion of your research to identify the potential for rewards and problems of entering and operating in the market, you are now in a position to see how you can build unique selling points that allow you to offer value propositions for targeted customer segments that your competitors in the market are unable to match.

In terms of software development, skill itself is often an advantage, especially when you have skills in the types of advanced programming or knowledge of a specialized field that can lead to producing solutions that your competitors can't provide. For example, having advanced knowledge of artificial intelligence algorithms and a background in healthcare would place you in an ideal position to create products and bid for contracts that requires you to combine these skills and knowledge. This combination would not only allow you to write the product code, but also to understand the requirements of the target buyers/users, along with understanding how their industry operates. Using this combination to its full effect provides you with advantages in both the bidding and product development processes that your competition will find difficult to match.

The use of such specialized advantages are considered to be sustainable, as most competitors will be unable to up skill their capabilities and/or access substitutes that allow them to offer alternative solutions to meet the same value propositions. An example of how competitors can bypass skills and knowledge advantages you may have is the modern website design market. Originally, website creation required an understanding of HTML to get started, hence locking out players without these skills and keeping project rates within the region of £5,000 for a basic website.

These days, the availability of web page creation features in common software such as Microsoft Word and through online services like Wix.com (`http://www.wix.com`), has opened opportunities for new market entrants who barely have any technical skills. As a result, the market has become flooded with people offering to create websites at hardly any cost; massively disrupting how players can compete, along with distorting expectations of buyers who don't understand the difference between skilled web developers/designers and someone who exaggerates their abilities. Those days of £5,000 websites made from simple HTML are long gone; now replaced with buyer expectations to have their websites provided with full content management systems, SEO, responsive design and other expensive to implement features—for as little as £100! Unfortunately, this story is not uncommon when operating with advantages that are not sustainable.

Programming skills can also be utilized to develop a sustainable advantage in the form of your own in-house systems that increase the efficiency of your processes and/or allow you to provide new types of value proposition. This can be effective where you have levels of skill and knowledge that are unavailable to competitors in the industry—the software equivalent of the Colonel's secret recipe.

Red tape is a potential form of sustainable advantage in the form of certifications, patents, trust, and reputation, that can be difficult or discouraging for your competitors to earn when there is a cost of time and effort.

Key considerations:

> ➤ How easy is it for your competitors to copy your service or product?
> ➤ What substitutes can your competitors use to provide the same solution?
> ➤ What resources and/or skills can you access that the competition can't?
> ➤ Do you have patents that can stop competitors copying your USP's?
> ➤ Have you or can you develop in-house systems to make you more competitive?
> ➤ What do market competitors have that you don't?

Team domain – mission, aspirations, and propensity for risk

Having assessed the market environment and your ability to operate within it, the next step is to identify the level of commitment you have to making the business work. This assessment includes any other people you may be working with, or just yourself if you are working alone.

There are many factors that affect an individual or team's commitment to entering business. Motivations relating to personal interests, desired lifestyle, subject passion, and ethics can play a large part in persuading people to commit the required effort to make the business a success, whereas risks relating to finances and career progression may be barriers to commitment. Hard work is another factor that may deter people from being willing to commit to the business idea.

"One may know how to conquer without being able to do it."

–Sun Tzu, The Art of War

The importance of commitment shouldn't be underestimated. Regardless of how feasible the business idea and the opportunities that exist in the market are, a business plan can only be executed by people who are willing and able to commit to doing the job.

Key considerations:

> ➤ Are you passionate about your idea?
>
> ➤ What are your interests in the idea?
>
> ➤ What do you want to achieve with the business idea?
>
> ➤ Can you afford to take the associated financial risk?
>
> ➤ Are you willing to make the required financial commitment?
>
> ➤ How will engaging the business idea affect your career progression?
>
> ➤ Will failing affect your reputation?
>
> ➤ Are you willing to work the long hours and put the hard work required by the business?

Team domain – ability to execute on the critical success factors

Not all factors in business have the same weight in contributing to success, with some allowing you to succeed without them and others being a mandatory requirement. The factors that are mandatory for the success of the business are called critical success factors—there should be special consideration to identify whether you and your team can successfully execute them.

Key considerations:

> ➤ Which decisions can critically harm the business if you get them wrong?
>
>> ➢ Who is in the best position to make these decisions?
>>
>> ➢ What experience do they have in making similar decisions?
>>
>> ➢ What were the outcomes when they made these decisions?
>>
>> ➢ Are there key partners that you can consult to make more informed decisions?
>
> ➤ Which activities does the business idea require to be fully and successfully executed?
>
>> ➢ Who has the skills to perform these activities?
>>
>> ➢ What level of experience do they have in these activities?
>>
>> ➢ Can you access replacements if they become unavailable or leave the team?
>>
>> ➢ Are there key partners that you can collaborate with to increase the chances of successful execution?

➤ Which decisions have the potential to significantly enhance the performance of the business?

> ➢ Are you or any of your team members in a position to make these decisions?
>
> ➢ Is there a track record of making the best choice in this type of decision?
>
> ➢ Do you or your team member(s) have the ability to perform adequate levels of analysis for making these decisions?
>
> ➢ Are there key partners who can provide you with consultancy to enhance the quality of these decisions?

➤ Which activities have a significant impact on the success potential of the business?

> ➢ Do you or your team have an advanced level of skill to perform these activities?
>
> ➢ Are these activities going to distract you or your team from performing the activities that their skill set are best suited to?
>
> ➢ Is it worth outsourcing these activities to a specialist key partner who has the required level of experience to execute these activities to a higher standard?

Connectedness up and down the value chain

The saying of it not being what you know but who you know is never more true than in business. Successful business often comes down to having good connections, hence there being a need to identify whether you and your team are positioned well enough with people you know to make your business idea work.

Some situations require you to identify your connections to solve a problem, whereas other situations require you to identify what types of people you and your team know that place you in a unique position to engage business.

Key considerations:

➤ Do you know people who can supply you with the resources required by your business idea?

➤ How good are your relationships with these people?

➤ Do you have relationships with people who can distribute your product or service?

> ➢ Are they willing to become a distribution channel for your product or service?
>
> ➢ How can your relationship make them take more of an interest in understanding your product or service?

➤ Do you have relationships with people who are potentially in your customer segments?

> Can they be persuaded to advocate your product or service?

> Would they want to buy your product or service?

> Would your relationship make them want to buy from you instead of the competition?

> Why would they want to buy from you instead of the competition?

> Can you use your knowledge of these people to make your value propositions more attractive to them?

> Is their trust in you a factor that will make buying from you more appealing to them?

➤ Do you have relationships with businesses you will compete with?

> How will your business idea affect your relationship with them?

> Can these businesses be viewed as a key partner in any way?

The McKinsey 7S framework

Understanding the components you need in your business and how they link to each other is an important part of designing a successful business model. The McKinsey 7S framework can be used as a reminder to identify the components you need in your business and how they relate to each other. In essence, this framework is a simplified version of the Business Model Canvas, but with relationships already identified:

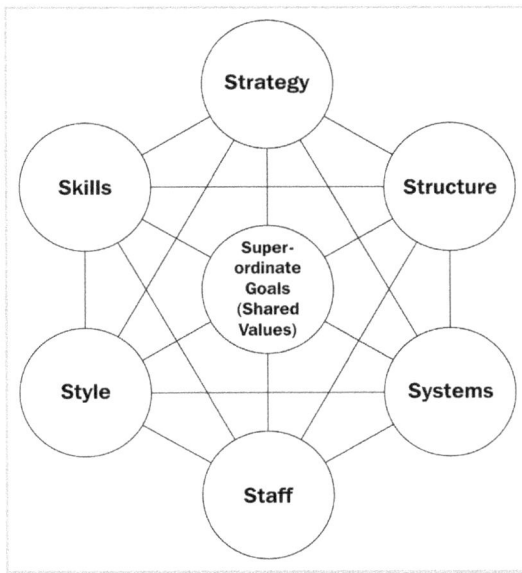

Figure 3.6: The relationships of the seven components of a business.

Goals and shared values

The central component of your business are the goals and shared values that your business exists to fulfill. For some organizations, this is simply to make a profit, whereas other organizations such as charities and social enterprises place a higher priority on their social agendas. Understanding ambitions will allow you to accurately define the requirements of each of the other components in order to fulfill them.

Strategy

Possibly more than any other component, strategy is dictated by the central element that defines the goals and shared values of the organization. There is always going to be more than one method to achieve the same goal, hence the type of strategy you use will depend on your vision, aspirations and ethics. Make sure to develop a strategy that your team are both comfortable and capable of executing to avoid failure resulting from conflicting politics and lack of experience—in other words don't be over ambitious.

Skills

A strategy has no value unless it can be executed with the skills needed for it to succeed. Ideally, the strategy should be designed to make use of the skills that you and your team already have, but there may also be the requirement for skills that you don't have—or at least not to the level required to successfully execute the strategy. There is a requirement in this type of situation to either hire new staff who have the required skills, or to identify key partners who can contribute to the strategy's execution. In the case of using key partners, this can be achieved by partnering with other freelancers, contractors, and businesses, who specialize in the skills required; although caution should be taken to make sure that the key partners you select have the right level of skills and can operate in a way compatible with the style that you and your team use to work, in order to avoid conflict.

Structure

The execution of strategy through the deployment of skills needs to be performed in a structured way that avoids problematic situations and conflict occurring through politics. This involves the use of a formal structure to identify which members of the team are able to make certain types of decisions and who is responsible for managing different staff and key partners who have been brought into the project for collaboration. Structure is all about facilitating a high quality flow of information that improves performance and decision making capabilities.

Style

The style in which you and your team engage business activities is an important factor that can avoid both technical and political conflicts. When it comes to writing your software, all team members need to be able to write code in a consistent style that other team members are able to understand; having just one person break this can introduce both technical and political conflict to the business. This highlights the need to vet skill capabilities when recruiting new staff and selecting key partners for collaboration. The same issue of execution style exists for other areas of the business aside from the technical programming implementation, hence the need to ensure there are shared styles for working across all business activities.

Systems

The performance of all other entities in the organization are enhanced by the systems you use, hence the need to make sure that you make use of the right systems that can provide both capability and efficiency. Along with skills, systems are what allow you and your staff to play a part in the strategy's execution, hence the importance of ensuring that everyone has the required levels of skills to use the systems they need to execute their part of the strategy.

Staff

This could just be yourself if you are working as a lone software developer, or more likely to involve key partners you collaborate with and people you employ. Either way, staff are an important part of your business because businesses don't run themselves. There is a need to ensure that the people in your business have a compatible style of working, skills required to execute their part of the strategy and the ability to use the systems of the business. It is also a big advantage to have staff sharing the same values of the business in order to ensure consistency and to avoid political conflicts that disrupt execution of the strategy based on differing ethics and values.

Fitting everything together

With this chapter identifying several tools that can be used to build your business model, it is now time to put this knowledge into practice. This section will look at how these tools describe two businesses who target the same customer segments, but use different software business models.

The business descriptions

The first step in our comparison is to describe the two businesses. Both target the education market, providing software based solutions for primary and secondary school learning, but using different software business models that affect how they provide their solution and hence how they operate.

IXL Learning

Based on the SaaS model, this is a web-based software service for children to learn and practice math skills required by their school curriculum. The service tackles the school curriculum requirements by providing access to a large number of math activities that children, parents, and teachers can pick and choose from. The interactive activities are made more appealing to parents and teachers by tracking the child's progress in order to provide access to reports that identify what progress has been made during the child's engagement with the online activities.

Nextpoint

Using the software supporting a service model, Nextpoint operates a traditional tuition agency style business that focuses on the same market as IXL, but with a specific focus on teaching a specific learning strategy to people who struggle with math. The business uses a software system designed to support all activities related to providing tuition services, including session booking, creation of learning plans and engagement of revision exercises. Students are provided with access to an online login account where they can access software service features relating to
the tuition services they are engaging.

Comparison: McKinsey 7S framework

Although both businesses operate in the same market, it is clear from their descriptions that there are significant differences in their approach to providing a solution that affects how their software systems are used. These differences can be summarized using the McKinsey 7S framework, which identifies their operation structure and motivations.

Goals and shared values

The shared goals and values for each of the businesses identifies the similarities and differences of the problems they aim to solve and their value proposition:

IXL Learning	Nextpoint
Focus: ■ Technology first and foremost Education: ■ Solve real world problems in education ■ Help teachers to teach and students to learn ■ Improve the learning process Technology: ■ Focus on creating technology to reshape learning and teaching for the better ■ Belief in the power of technology enhancing learning through creativity ■ Mission to innovate education	Focus: ■ Learning strategy first and foremost Education: ■ Break barriers to understanding math concepts ■ Provide an effective learning strategy for disadvantaged learners ■ Innovate teaching and learning for disadvantaged learners through strategy Technology: ■ Focus on technology to assist executing the learning strategy ■ Technology as a tool to engage learners ■ Technology as a tool for extending the learning methods ■ Belief in the power of technology to enhance decisions in teaching strategy

Strategy

The strategy adopted by each business is a complete reflection of their goals and shared values, hence their strategy having an equivalent component for each of the identified core values:

IXL Learning	Nextpoint
Focus: ■ Identify problems in teaching and learning that can be addressed with the help of software technologies Education: ■ Match software apps to their real world counterpart problem ■ Develop specific tools to improve engagement of mainstream teaching strategies ■ Help teachers and parents integrate the use of IXL Learning tools into their teaching and coaching routines ■ Provide a wide range of content to meet every area of the school curriculum Technology: ■ Build software tools to match the needs of teachers and learners ■ Integrate creativity into learning exercises ■ Enhance the execution of teaching strategy through the use of IXL.com software Sales: ■ Higher volume sales with lower sale pricing	Focus: ■ Identify the causes of problems in learning and develop learning methods to overcome them Education: ■ Develop new ways to express math concepts using non math thinking processes ■ Teach learners to think of math inline with everyday thought processes ■ Engage parents and teachers concerned about learners who are struggling with math ■ Provide a specific range of content to match the tuition programs provided Technology: ■ Build software components to match learning strategy concepts ■ Use software to increase learning engagement ■ Create software tools to influence delivery of tuition sessions ■ Build software that can make sense of learner progression for better lesson planning ■ Develop reporting tools that identify causes of problems for better decision making in teaching Sales: ■ Lower volume sales with higher sale pricing

Skills

The models used by both businesses make use of many skills, that are shared between them, to produce and raise awareness of the core software components. The differences in how the business strategies focus their delivery of learning solutions introduce two main differences in the skill sets used. With IXL Learning focusing on international high volume sales, their learning product has been made available in 11 languages and hence requires skills in language translation. In contrast, Nextpoint only sell tuition services to a local geographical area within the UK and so hence can avoid the effort and expenses of language translation, but requires teaching skills in order to provide the tuition services that are sold to their customers:

IXL Learning	Nextpoint
■ Learning content design	■ Learning content design
■ Graphic design	■ Graphic design
■ Software development	■ Software development
■ Marketing	■ Marketing
■ Project management	■ Project management
■ Customer support	■ Customer support
■ Quality assurance / testing	■ Quality assurance / testing
■ Language translation	■ Teaching

Structure

Despite both businesses being involved in the development of software that focuses on delivering solutions for learning math, the differences in their goals, values and strategy results in a completely different structure for their operations. With IXL Learning trading internationally, their organization structure has specific departments with people engaging job roles matching a specific skill set.

On the other hand, Nextpoint is a micro business that operates a highly agile structure that keeps overheads to a minimum through the use of outsourcing to key partners and engaging staff across multiple activities; in short, the Nextpoint structure could be operated as a very small team or even as an individual:

IXL Learning	Nextpoint
■ Chief Executive Officer (CEO) who defines the overall direction of the business ■ Department teams, each having a director responsible for executing their individual area of the business strategy: <ul><li>➢ Finance/accounts</li><li>➢ Sales</li><li>➢ Marketing</li><li>➢ Customer support</li></ul> ■ Product development: <ul><li>➢ Content development</li><li>➢ Software development & IT</li><li>➢ Product management</li><li>➢ Quality assurance</li></ul>	■ Director of the business who defines the overall direction of the business ■ Director, staff and key partnership collaborators/suppliers contribute to multiple areas of the business strategy: <ul><li>➢ Finance/accounts</li><li>➢ Sales</li><li>➢ Marketing</li><li>➢ Customer support</li><li>➢ System development</li><li>➢ Teaching</li></ul>

Style

The styles of business engaged by both are vastly different due to the differences in their structure and strategy. With IXL Learning being a much larger organization consisting of fixed departments that require more overhead commitments, there is a higher requirement for operations to be formal and structured so that each department can run in harmony with each other for executing the business strategy and further developing the software within targeted release schedules and budget.

With Nextpoint being a much smaller business and not making money directly from the software development, the business is able to operate in a less formal fashion. Best practices are still adhered to for ensuring the quality of software code, but with significant differences in job roles combining skills from multiple domains when required:

IXL Learning	Nextpoint
■ Structured and formal processes for co-ordination of departments ■ Emphasis on best practices for software development	■ Agile operation of business processes ■ Emphasis on best practices for software development

Systems

Despite both businesses operating different software business models in ways that are often the opposite to each other, they both share a dependence on software systems that are central to their operations. The main differences are in the customer facing systems used by each business, with IXL providing a much wider range of topics to make their subscription options more relevant and appealing, while Nextpoint only provides content and features that are related to supporting their tuition programs:

IXL Learning	Nextpoint

■ In-house developed learning software is the product sold to customers:
■ Access to learning exercises:
   ➤ Wide range of topics
   ➤ For use as revision exercises
■ Access to learning reports:
   ➤ Generated by learning exercise interactions
■ Additional systems for:
   ➤ Sales and marketing
   ➤ Accountancy management
■ Additional systems for Communications:
   ➤ Internal communications
   ➤ External communications
	■ In-house developed learning platform is the product to support and enhance the service sold to customers:
	   ➤ Ability to request tuition sessions
	   ➤ Access to tuition session history
	■ Access to tuition program learning content:
	   ➤ Specific to registered tuition programs
	   ➤ For use as revision exercises
	   ➤ For use within tuition sessions
	■ Access to learning reports:
	   ➤ Generated within tuition sessions
	   ➤ Generated via learning content interactions
	■ Additional systems for:
	   ➤ Sales and marketing
	   ➤ Accountancy management
	■ Additional systems for Communications:
	   ➤ Internal communications
	   ➤ External communications
	   ➤ Delivery of tuition services via Skype

Staff

With both businesses having a focus on using software technologies as a major part of delivering their education solutions, they share a strong emphasis for a large number of their staff and key partner collaborators to be involved in the production of the education learning content, whether this be through programming, design of graphics or concept design for software features. The key difference is in how staff of IXL Learning are hired for a very specific type of job, whereas Nextpoint as a small agile business will get staff and key partner collaborators in any area of the business that they have suitable skills to engage.

IXL Learning	Nextpoint
Shared values: ■ Interest in improving education through technology Specialist roles: ■ Sales people—Multiple specialist sales roles ■ Marketeers—Multiple specialist marketing roles ■ Accountants ■ HR ■ Product management ■ Product designers, ■ Product managers ■ User interface designers ■ Web production artists ■ Front end software developers ■ Server side software developers ■ Data analyst ■ Quality assurance	Shared values: ■ Interest in improving education through modernized learning strategy Specialist roles: ■ Accountant (Key Partnership) Semi-specialist roles: ■ Full stack software developer—one programmers takes responsibility for the full software system; with scope to expand later or develop key partnerships in this area later if required ■ Content developers—Multi-skilled content creators who have skills and experience in teaching, programming and content design ■ Tutors—Provide the tuition service directly to the customers Generalist roles: ■ Marketing and sales—Engaged by the full team where required ■ Quality assurance—Testing performed by team members and key partners to identify software issues before release

Comparison – Business Model Canvas

Another of the tools covered in this chapter that can be used to compare both businesses is the Business Model Canvas, which provides a more detailed insight to the different components of the business models. The Business Model Canvas highlights how both business models share common elements in many of their categories, with the exception of the categories for value propositions, revenue streams and customer segments. It becomes clear from these categories that although IXL Learning and Nextpoint use software to provide solutions for a similar type of problem, there are vast differences between their value propositions, revenue streams and customer segments—with the former business model designed as a solution to help people teach and the latter model being designed to deliver the teaching services. Another major difference between between the two models lies within their value propositions and target market segments. The former being designed to help with mainstream teaching and appeal to the mass market, while the latter focuses on a the smaller segment of the market that need an alternative to mainstream teaching strategy; hence why the learning method is part of the value proposition.

Even though these differences may sound small on paper, they have a large impact that cascades throughout the full structure and execution of their models. With software being key elements of both models, it is important for the software components to be designed in a way that supports their owner's business strategy. Whereas both businesses make use of software to deliver learning solutions for math, the way that the software is designed and provided to customer segments are different due how the businesses differ in their structure and operation strategy. Their software systems are designed in a way that reflects how their business operates—one has a revenue stream from selling subscriptions to use the software, while the other's revenue stream is from the services that the software creates a demand for. This identification shows how one model's software design is influenced by an agenda to reduce support in order to eliminate user costs, while the other's model benefits when its software design can create more demand for support as an opportunity to sell services.

IXL Learning

Key Partners:	Key Activities:	Value Proposition:	Customer Relationships:	Customer Segments
■ Google—AdWords ■ Education websites. ■ Web hosting suppliers. ■ Internet service provider (ISP). ■ Mobile and landline communications provider. ■ Printing companies	■ Education content design. ■ Software development. ■ Software testing. ■ System maintenance. ■ Social media marketing. ■ Customer support	■ Improve math skills. ■ Improve confidence. ■ Pass exams. ■ Motivate students to study. ■ Increase student/teacher engagement in learning. ■ Understand learning performance.	■ Monthly family subscription. ■ Annual family subscription. ■ Annual class subscription for teachers. ■ Multiple class subscriptions for schools	■ Teachers ■ Schools ■ Tutors ■ Parents
	Key Resources: ■ Software system platform. ■ Servers. ■ Education content. ■ Internet access. ■ Web hosting	■ Compare learning performance to curriculum targets. ■ Allow more informed decision making for lesson planning and teaching strategy. ■ Reduce homework marking. ■ Reduce stress. ■ Make more time available for other teaching activities. ■ Embrace technology for learning—key selling point for schools		
		Channels: ■ Online advertising. ■ Education websites. ■ Education exhibitions. ■ Tutors (recommendations to parents) ■ Social media—Facebook, Twitter, Google+ and Pinterest		

Cost Structure:	Revenue Streams:
■ Staff costs—mostly in software design and development. ■ Web hosting. ■ Advertising—especially via Google AdWords. ■ Exhibition space	■ Family—subscriptions to apps and reporting features. ■ Upgrade subscription for extra family members after the first child. ■ School—class subscriptions to apps and reporting features. ■ Upgrade class subscriptions for more than 30 children. ■ New subscriptions for each class using the system

Nextpoint

Key partners:	Key activities:	Value proposition:	Customer relationships:	Customer Segments
■ Tutor directories ■ Teachers ■ Tutors ■ Web hosting suppliers ■ Internet service provider (ISP) ■ Mobile and landline communications provider ■ Printing companies ■ Subcontractors	■ Tuition delivery ■ Learning strategy design ■ Education content design ■ Software development ■ Software testing ■ System maintenance ■ Social media marketing ■ Content marketing ■ Customer support	■ Overcome difficulties in learning math ■ Improve math skills ■ Learn math faster ■ Motivate students ■ Pass exams ■ Reduce stress ■ Develop and manage an effective learning strategy ■ Embrace new teaching strategy	■ Fixed duration tuition course ■ One off tuition ■ Day course ■ Access to learning tools for delivering learning strategy	■ Parents ■ Tutors ■ Training organizations
	Key resources: ➤ Tutors ➤ Software system platform ➤ Education content ➤ Mobile Internet access ➤ Web hosting		**Channels:** ■ Tutor directories ■ Education websites ■ Social media—Facebook, Twitter, LinkedIn ■ Learning support networks	

Cost Structure:	Revenue Streams:
■ Staff salary	■ Tuition services (parents)
■ Subcontractor fees	■ Course delivery (training organizations)
■ Web hosting	■ Commission from tuition (tutors)
■ Travel expenses	

Comparison: conclusion

Despite both business models aiming to solve the same type of problem, it becomes clear after more detailed investigation that there are significant differences in terms of their core values, how they solve the problem and how the resulting features of the software are designed and developed to become part of the business.

IXL Learning

With IXL Learning's income stream coming from subscriptions to their learning platform, its business model becomes highly focused on providing value propositions for their customer segments that justify buying subscriptions. These value propositions revolve around providing solutions that make it easier to manage learners—whether it be parents of children who may or may not understand the school curriculum requirements themselves, or teachers who are under pressure to manage large class sizes. The value propositions provided through the software platform are not only a method to help children learn more about math, but also a way to reduce the workload of teachers by reducing the need to mark homework, assist with report writing and also to make informed decisions for lesson planning. All of these are key motivations that persuade teachers to actively persuade their schools to buy subscriptions with IXL Learning.

Additionally, IXL Learning subscriptions are designed in a way that allows the business to maximize their profitability by adjusting prices to appeal to the two customer segments they target. Both pricing methods are designed to specifically appeal to their target customer segment so that the higher paying customer segment can't opt to buy the cheaper option. Furthermore, the revenue potential of each customer segment is maximized by the need to pay a small amount extra once the number of students per class or family has been exceeded. Schools are a lucrative customer segment because they have to pay per class; with class sizes reaching 40+ students, that a lot of money being paid per school!

Nextpoint

The Nextpoint business model is very much the opposite the one used by IXL Learning, despite it sharing many similarities on paper. The most obvious difference is that Nextpoint doesn't sell subscriptions to its software platform; it instead uses software as a value proposition and resource to increase efficiency in the delivery of tuition services. As a result, their learning platform exists to support the delivery of services to maximize both customer satisfaction and profitability. As far as the Nextpoint model is concerned, it is just a coincidence that software has been identified as a supporting resource used by the business strategy.

The core values of Nextpoint are based on the delivery of a specific learning strategy for math. As a result, the model's value propositions are defined around around the consistent theme of providing alternative methods for learning math. This theme reaches throughout the business model to heavily influence the design and execution of both the software and business strategy.

Unlike IXL Learning's platform which is designed to maximize income from revenue streams generated from paid subscriptions, Nextpoint's learning platform is designed to support and create demand for services that are purchased by customers. This means that in order for the software to provide value to the business model, it must play a role in maximizing profit potential from tuition services sold and open opportunities for new service sales. The software provides its best contribution to the business model when it can provide learning guidance in a way that reduces time for admin and tutors spent on paperwork and lesson preparation, while increasing the satisfaction and interest of the customer segments to a point where they want to purchase more tuition and/or complimentary services. As a result, the design of the software revolves achieving these agendas.

Summary

Advances in computing technology and their adoption by the mainstream public has opened many new opportunities for the design of software-oriented business models. The computing technology advancements that without doubt have had the most impact is the mainstream adoption of the Internet—with its sidekick, the web. Both which have allowed new ways for software to be accessed and hence new ways for software businesses to operate.

The ability to consider SaaS to be subscribed to and/or support other purchased services means that you no longer need to consider your software business to be primarily about writing software, but also about creating services. This is an attractive option to consider for your business venture when considering how software products and development skills are becoming increasingly devalued through market trends like the introduction of free to play (F2P) gaming, misleading media coverage and the availability of content authoring tools such as PowerPoint are leading to an expectation for software to be freely available and software development to be provided for near minimum wage.

For people wanting to engage the more traditional software business models that focus on creating SaaP or service, there are many opportunities to be successful where you can identify market segments where there is enough demand from people willing to pay what the product or project is worth; these primarily being businesses with financial turnovers in the millions rather than in the tens or hundreds of thousands. The good news for anyone wanting to operate in the provision of software development services is that the vast majority of IT business projects are still in the domain of custom software development. However, with the advent of cloud IT services, times are changing—with organizations being tempted to eliminate the maintenance of their bespoke systems by moving their IT infrastructure to the cloud.

Regardless of which type of model you choose to base your business on, there is a need to fully define and validate the idea in order to understand how everything fits together; and whether it's at all viable. It's for this reason that formal tools exist for you to use in designing your business model—each having their own identifications to highlight. Seven Domains Assessment framework is a tool worth considering before commencing the formal design of your business model so that the idea can be tested against basic criteria required for success. Upon confirmation that the idea can succeed, other tools such as the Business Model Canvas and McKinsey 7S framework can be used to build a description of the business model in a way that guarantees all major components and their relationships are defined.

> 4

Creating a Brand

Branding is an important factor in the success of any business, whether it be a corporation on the scale of companies like Google and Sony, or a small one-man freelance business. The mistake a lot of people make in their assumption about branding is that it is simply a design that is applied to visual marketing materials such as brochures and websites. Although these visual elements may be part of the mix that form a brand, they are not the brand. This chapter looks at what branding really is, and how you can focus on activities to build your own brand in a way that can positively affect your ability to make sales and increase profitability.

A brief definition of what branding is and isn't

A client once said to me that he had a brilliant idea for a brand to use for his new business; it would have a certain type of logo, and xyz visuals for the letterhead and his website. As nice as the client is, it was clear to me at the time that he didn't understand what branding was or how to apply it to his business strategy. With the wrong people giving advice to this client, he could have spent a lot of time and money on design services that ultimately wouldn't deliver a return on his investment—not because there would be a fault with the design, but because the design elements aren't created to support his brand. Many people not in the know would be confused at this point, because surely creating a brand is all about how people see you through your logo, business literature, and so on.?

It is this question that is the answer to why so many people have the wrong idea of what branding is about. Branding isn't about what people see of you, but what they think of you. It's true that people will make a judgment about your capabilities based on how you visually present yourself, but even this comes down to what they think about what they are seeing. The best visually designed brochure or website in the world isn't going to generate a lot of business if it is full of spelling mistakes, or written in a way that doesn't connect with the reader. A business will not generate sales with customers who have read bad reviews or who have been told bad stories of how the business operates. Visual branding plays a part of forming a perception of the business, but the exercise of branding is always going to be about making people think of you in the way that you want them to think of you.

This radically different view of what branding is about opens a wider scope for the types of activities you should be thinking about engaging to build your business brand.

> ➤ Who are you targeting?

> ➤ How do you want these people to perceive you?

> ➤ Do you want to be considered as a specialist, or do you want to be considered as more of a generalist?

> ➤ What are your **USPs** (**Unique Selling Points**) and how do you want people to recognize them?

> ➤ What values do you want people to associate you with?

These are all very important questions that you need to know the answers to in order to be successful in building a brand that is of value to how you market yourself to win new clients as well as retain existing clients, and secure more work.

Know your audience

Knowing who you are aiming to sell to is the most important question to know the answer to, not just because you need to know what they want to buy, but because the answer to this question dictates how the answers to your other branding questions are formed.

Software development is a difficult service to sell if the client doesn't know what they want or need because it's not easy for them to see the relationship between what software does and the benefits provided. Knowing about your audience gives you some advantage in the sense that it allows you to identify what benefits to focus on when you talk about what you offer. Even more so, specializing your software development in one sector or for one purpose allows you to better understand how you can benefit your target market and to be more specific in describing those benefits when you are speaking to people.

If you intend to become a generalist freelancer, you will have different types of client who buy different types of services from you—some of which may be outside the scope of programming. This is also good because it means you can fill more of your time with work that pays and allows you to reduce the risk of having no work when the demand for one type of service dries up. In terms of branding, you would want to avoid becoming known as a jack of all trades, so focusing your different services around a common theme such as marketing will allow you to be seen as an expert in this area, rather than someone who will give anything a try.

Identify perceptions required for objectives

Once you know which audiences you want to aim your services toward, the next step is to identify how you want them to think of you. As defined earlier in this chapter, branding is all about controlling how people think of you in order, and in the sense of a business, these perceptions must link to benefits for the business that help it achieve its objectives. What objectives do you have that rely on how people think of you? Some examples may include:

Objective	Perceptions required
Charge premium rates above the industry average	■ Highly experienced in the field you operate in ■ Detailed knowledge of the subject on a level that others wouldn't know ■ Ability to write the type of code to solve problems others can't ■ Able to apply experience and knowledge to deliver additional benefits relating to quality, time, and financial savings that more than cover any fee you charge
Sell lots to people with smaller budgets	■ Inexpensive to hire
Make sales to people who don't have technical knowledge	■ Approachable and willing to provide advice ■ Easy to understand
Sell to busy people	■ Known for delivering what's been promised on time and without problems ■ High amount of customer satisfaction
Get coverage in the media	■ Specialists in the area you operate ■ Reliable as a source of accurate information ■ Easy to approach when required

By making this type of list, it becomes a lot more clear what type of brand perceptions you need to build in order to help you achieve your objectives. Although branding is closely related to sales and marketing, you will also see that not all objectives are directly about making sales, such as getting media coverage, being able to charge above the industry rates, and being considered as environmentally friendly.

Specializing – becoming a domain expert

The decision to specialize in delivering a specific type of software development service may rule out the majority of the market you can sell to, but it also provides the advantage of significantly increased capability of closing sales with the people you are specializing in selling to; in some situations, you are also able to command a higher rate. This isn't because people have a preference for you to only develop the type of software they want, but the fact that you specialize in the type of software development they need gives them more confidence that you understand their requirements.

Additionally, because you specialize, you are able to create your marketing material and sales pitch to be more specific; to communicate exactly how buyers benefit from buying into you; whether it be your case studies, describing examples or the style of writing that appeals to the people you are marketing to, your specialism allows you to appear to be perceived as having already delivered what the buyer wants, hence being a lower risk for anything going wrong and more capable of turning things around if they do.

Specializing as a software developer can come in the form of only servicing a specific type of client, or only working with specific types of technologies. Both of these open opportunities to get recommended for work because you simplify the message of what you are about and what you do. The following are examples of how some software developers decide to specialize:

> Sector specialization:

>> Marketing

>> E-commerce

>> E-learning

>> Security

> Technology specialization:

>> Front-end web development

>> Server-side web development

>> PHP

>> HTML5

>> Java

>> Moodle

>> WordPress

You will notice the last examples in the list being Moodle and WordPress, both of which are systems developed with PHP. These are popular systems that a lot of people specifically request to be used in their projects, with a lot of the people hiring not knowing that there is any relationship between PHP and these systems. Whereas good PHP programmers will be more than capable of installing and modifying Moodle and WordPress because they are PHP systems, the perception of the buyer will be that someone perceived as a specialist in Moodle or WordPress is the better person to hire—even though the WordPress specialist is likely to have much less capability; it's well known that a lot of people classed as WordPress specialists are good at installing WordPress and tinkering with the code, but aren't quite programmers, similar to how users of Instagram are not often real photographers, or where someone who can create a website with Wix isn't a web developer if they don't have coding skills. Even though the PHP developer is the better candidate, the WordPress specialist will win more WordPress projects because of how they are perceived to be capable of delivering more with WordPress, hence showing the importance of defining how people perceive your capabilities.

Generalizing – targeting a wider audience

The opposite strategy to specializing is generalizing, which although has the risk of having you perceived as a jack of all trades, can also pay off if executed well. When using a generalist strategy, it's important to set yourself apart from specialists, which includes not using phrases in your marketing that suggest you are a specialist—there are few better ways to lose the trust of a knowledgeable customer by claiming to be a specialist in one subject/service, and then in the same conversation/marketing claim to offer a list of other services:

Specialists in Wedding Photography

We specialize in the provision of the best photography for your wedding day.
You only have one wedding day. No room for mistakes in your photography.

Check out our other services:

Window Cleaning

Web Design

IT Support

Figure 4.1: Would you trust an advert that claims to specialize and at the same time contradicts itself by offering unrelated services? The stakes are even higher when there is no room for mistake in what you are buying.

The main strength of being a generalist is the ability to increase your relevance to a wider range of projects, and providing that you have the level of skill that these project opportunities require, finding new work upon completion of a project is likely to be much easier because your skill set can be applied in many more ways than those of a specialist; the trick for being a generalist is to know the level of complexity you can deliver in the areas you generalize in so that you can hand pick projects that you can successfully complete without running into difficulties—not always an easy task considering that even specialists still run into problems with these issues.

As a generalist, the perception you must work hard to avoid is of being a jack of all trades, which affects your credibility and your negotiation capabilities to win higher-paying projects. Credibility is important for branding exercises because:

➤ It is an asset for generating word of mouth recommendations that lead to sales

➤ It can be used to open media exposure to get known by more people and increase credibility

➤ It is a factor taken into account by clients when selecting a supplier

➤ It can be used to boost the appeal of project tenders you make

With branding being all about managing perceptions, the way to avoid being classed as a jack of all trades and to produce a perception of higher integrity is to be selective with communications used with the people you deal with. The following are some ideas of what a generalist developer providing a wide range of software services, from games development, to web design, e-commerce, and CRM systems may want to communicate:

Target	Core subjects communicated	Optional specifics to mention
Start-up businesses	■ Internet sales and marketing	■ Websites ■ Pay per click advertising ■ Affiliate systems ■ Social media
Established businesses	■ Software for marketing ■ IT business systems ■ Internet sales and marketing	■ Phone apps ■ Viral games ■ Facebook apps ■ Internet sales and marketing ■ CRM systems ■ Invoicing systems ■ Databases ■ SEO
Entertainment journalist	■ Lifestyle and information apps ■ Games	■ Game design ■ Game programming technologies
Business journalist	■ Successes of client business systems ■ Current technology innovations and their case studies ■ Future technologies and their expected impact on business operations	■ Databases ■ Software systems ■ CRM systems ■ Internet sales and marketing
Technology journalist	■ Web systems security ■ Emerging technologies ■ Case studies of completed client projects	■ Software systems

Take note of how the proposed topics of discussion are defined as clear to understand generalized subjects, as opposed to specific skills. For example, you may have various skills in areas of web design, content writing, installation/configuration of open source software systems, and management of pay-per-click advertising such as with Google AdWords, but you will get a lot more people taking an interest in what you can do by discussing the benefits of Internet marketing in general, as opposed to talking about the technicalities of specific subjects such as what makes a good website or what how pay-per-click advertising works. This is because people wanting to hire generalists are often the types who are primarily interested in the outcome and have a specific goal of what they want to achieve—for example they want to make more sales with better profit margins.

Another reason why people hire generalists is to reduce their involvement in managing their projects. By selecting someone who can take on the responsibility of the entire project, they reduce their requirements to manage the collaboration of specialists that they would otherwise have to select. By presenting yourself as someone who can take away the need to understand the technicalities and the need to spend time managing a team of specialists, you present your services as a cost effective proposition that saves money through saved time in addition to what the service delivers—and this is the perception that you need to get across as your branding.

The following are tips for generalizing:

> Decide the generalist angle you want to communicate that doesn't involve describing everything in minute detail—for example simplify websites, affiliate marketing systems, e-commerce, and so on, to online sales and marketing systems

> Emphasize the benefits to the client in terms of time saved from selecting and managing a team of specialists—in other words you take care of the whole problem

> Emphasize how the client doesn't need to learn specifics in order to make good judgment on who to hire—that is your capability to deliver what you promise

> Build relationships with proven specialists for projects that require levels of skill outside of your capability

Case study

Mark Smith, a freelance journalist who has written for heavyweight industry publications including the Daily Mirror, has worked on numerous stories of all sizes that have required the use of opinions and facts from sources to both build the story and provide credibility. Sources have ranged from first-hand witnesses of historic events, including veterans of World War 2, through to business owners and academics. Like many journalists, Mark highly values regular contacts because they are trusted and easy to contact without spending time on researching unknown and unproven people—especially where stories can lead to legal action being taken against the newspaper on the basis of libel resulting from incorrect information.

The relevance of an information source is highly dependent on the situation and context of a story, as well as the purpose they are being used to emphasize. In the case of a local news story, someone with no industry or academic connection can still provide value by allowing the story to show an opinion that is reflective of people who live in the area that the story is being reported to.

The majority of work assignments given to Mark in his journalism career have been based on tight deadlines with a specific space to fill for newspaper publications. As a result, Mark has a list of people who are known to be knowledgeable about specific subjects so that they can be contacted immediately in order to meet tight deadlines for stories given at short notice. Although being knowledgeable on a subject is an important factor, the nature of Mark's work having such tight deadlines means that a higher importance is given to people who are known to be able to answer his phone calls, or if not, get back to him quickly; the bottom line for information sources in any story is to have the quote ready for when the story goes to print—because today's news has no value after tomorrow. Getting exposure in the media through journalists is all about becoming an asset they can use to solve their daily work dilemmas—how can you make them do their job better without causing additional problems?

Being a specialist has two notable advantages for getting onto the contact list of journalists—being simple to remember and highly specific to what you do. This means that you are more likely to be the first person a journalist thinks of when they need to get an informed opinion or facts about a story. Having an easy to describe specialism also means that your description/profile is more likely to stand out when it comes to time pressed journalists looking through their contact lists for useful information sources.

Kick starting perceptions

Getting people to perceive you in the way that best benefits your business and marketing strategies will rarely happen quickly until you have momentum behind your brand. When establishing your brand, you should consider activities that can positively influence how people perceive you and give reasons to generate discussion about you in order to create more awareness about you. In an age of social media platforms such as Twitter, LinkedIn and Facebook, there has never been an easier time for kick starting your own brand. The following are ideas for activities that can be used to kick start brand recognition and perception:

Doing a good job

Not to be dismissed as a separate activity to branding; doing a good job for clients who appreciate your work leads to recommendations and a list of people you can turn to for providing references and positive quotes to use for your marketing materials.

Unfortunately, doing a good job isn't just about doing a good job. Unlike other professions where quality can be easily judged visually, quality in programming is often about incorporating benefits such as flexibility and efficiency that can only be fully appreciated with an understanding of the consequences of a bad job. In terms of brand perception, this means that you can get yourself into a situation where clients perceive your performance as poor when you have done a good job. This risk emphasizes the importance of managing expectations and maintaining clear communications in order to ensure that the client continues to perceive that you are doing a good job. See chapters 6, 7, 8, and 12 for in-depth detail about managing this.

Limited time offers

Providing an offer that provides a significant increase in value compared to the industry standard is a good way to get the attention of potential buyers. Offers of this type come in many forms, whether it be lower price, two for one, extended support or packaging complimentary products/services with the purchase. The increased value proposition made with this type of offer is a good way to help potential buyers forget about any doubts they have about your lack of track record.

Unfortunately, providing exceptional value comes at a cost—and if that cost isn't being funded by the client, it is provided at a cost to yourself, which is unmaintainable in the long term without your sacrificing earnings or risking losing money. The other issue faced with offering exceptional value to win work is that people start to perceive this to be the standard rather than the exception, which makes it difficult for you to generate profit that's worth your time.

The time element is the most important part of the limited time offer. By emphasizing that the offer is for a limited time throughout your marketing and delivery of the service or software product, you minimize the risk of people assuming that the offer is the standard that you offer; this is important because it is difficult to raise prices/rates after you have already supplied at a lower price. This also has the advantage of persuading people to buy sooner than later and to spread the word, especially through social media platforms such as LinkedIn, Twitter and Facebook. If managed properly, this type of exposure can lead to being hired again, but at your regular rates after the time-limited offer has expired; happy clients impressed by your services will not only trust you to get the job done, but they will recommend you to other people they know.

Competitions

Similar in a sense to limited-time offers, competitions are about providing something that captures the interest of your target audience with a view to persuading them to register as well as to spread the word via social networks, e-mails, blogs and media coverage. Like with time limited offers, there is a cost for offering the prize of the competition, whether it be a time or materials cost; never consider time to not be of value, because time spent delivering a service as a prize is time not spent earning, hence there is a cost of lost opportunity to work.

The value of using competitions in your brand marketing is the amount of exposure which helps you to become recognized as well as building your marketing database. With the right type of prize aimed at the type of people you intend to sell to, combined with the right marketing, the exposure gained can cost less than the equivalent exposure generated through advertising and return a higher number of registrations.

When deciding on how to use competitions for your branding strategy, some thought must go into selecting the type of prize that contributes to influencing the perception of the service or software product you provide as well as being of interest to the audience you target. Two potential prizes in high demand for Christmas of 2013 were Sony's Playstation 4 and Sesame Street Big Hugs Elmo; offering either of these as prizes would generate a lot of interest, but neither prizes are likely to help your brand perception or marketing database if you are selling software services for factory production line management.

Appropriate competition prizes needn't be expensive. By partnering with businesses who offer complimentary services and products that aren't in direct competition with you, there is the opportunity for you to run a competition using your brand that combines part of your services or products with those you are partnering with. All parties are able to benefit through the generation of competition registrants and possibly through how the services/products can be combined in their functionality.

Branding exercises using competitions are only one part of a wider strategy. By using competitions to build a relevant marketing database, you are able to make use of social media and e-mail newsletter marketing to follow up and further engage competition registrants to become more aware of your brand and allow you to become more relevant to their interests—not to be confused with sending spam, so check out chapter 5 on marketing.

Rewarding customer loyalty

Showing recognition to your existing clients is a good way to make sure that they not only keep buying from you. As a small business, you have the advantage of being able to get to personally know all of your clients. Although it may be something you take for granted, clients/customers are impressed when you are able to show that you recognize them personally. This by itself is enough for them in return to remember you and therefore increase the chances that they return to buy from you.

The concept of this type of recognition can be taken further by rewarding regular customers—at a small cost, the customer/client can be persuaded to keep buying out of a sense of loyalty in return for the reward. A good example is of a local pizza shop I use most weeks to buy a pineapple pizza; they always know what I order and give a free can of Sprite because I'm a regular. The cost of their freebie is minimal, but the impression given from their customer service recognizing what I like to order as well as showing their appreciation with the freebie generates a sense of appreciation and loyalty that none of the other three pizza shops on the same road have gained; it would probably feel slightly embarrassing to have them see me walk past their shop with a pizza from one of the other shops who don't know me and probably couldn't care less who I was. The moral of the story is a psychological one—recognizing your customers and emphasizing your appreciation of loyalty through reward is a good way to ensure they keep coming back, potentially to a point where they feel dealing with anyone else would be unethical.

Rewarding loyalty can come in many forms from informal rewards such as the previous example, to having a loyalty reward card such as those used by companies like Tesco, Boots, and Starbucks. Depending on the type of software you provide and the type of clients and customers you deal with, the type of rewards will vary, but should always be around about the same ratio. Taking the preceding pizza example: the freebie is valued at £0.60 and the pizza value is £6, so the reward discount is 10%. In a software example, providing a reward to the value of 10% could be:

> ➤ For an iPhone game, giving a free in app purchase valued at £2 for every £20 spent

> ➤ For a bespoke software client spending £20,000 on your services, doing overtime to meet a few last minute changes, delivering additional training and/or providing other complimentary services

> ➤ Sending a box of chocolates as a Christmas present to a small business who hires you on a regular basis to make amendments to their website

The key to using customer loyalty rewards to enhance perceptions of your brand is to be selective in who and what you reward, as well as making sure that the people you are rewarding know that they are being rewarded; your brand will never benefit from rewarding clients and customers if they perceive it to be part of the standard deal. In terms of being selective of the reward, you not only want to be selective of the value of the reward you provide in comparison to how much the client/customer spends with you, but you also want to ensure that the gift is appreciated—that is there's no point in sending an expensive bottle of champagne to a client who is teetotal; which may be perceived as you not knowing much about them as a person.

Strategic partnerships

Forming partnerships with other businesses that are able to complement the software development services or product you sell can be a way to gain recognition from potential buyers who are aware of and trust the brands of your strategic partnerships. For the same reason, care should be taken when selecting strategic partners to protect your brand and customers from organizations who are discovered to have unethical business practices or have a risk of having their own PR disasters in which an association brings your reputation into disrepute.

Strategic partnerships should be a benefit to all parties involved, which includes your clients and customers. Questions to consider when selecting organizations to approach for forming strategic partnerships could include:

> ➤ What can they provide that will allow you to better serve your clients and customers?

> ➤ Why would they be interested in partnering with you?

> ➤ Do you have enough credibility for them to justify an interest in being associated with you?

It helps to be known by organizations you intend to form partnerships with, so having an active networking strategy that makes use of social networks as well as real-world networking will be of benefit.

Certifications

Getting the endorsement of organizations known by decision makers and influencers in your target audience is a useful asset to gaining a level of trust in your capabilities. Keep in mind that certifications are only as useful if they are known and trusted by the people you are marketing to; a general small business owner will be likely to be more impressed if you can you have some type of Google certification than a Zend developer certification, which they are unlikely to know exists. On the other hand, people involved with software development such as project managers looking to hire contractors may be more impressed with the Zend certification because of it being more specific to showing knowledge of good software development practices with PHP.

Influencers

Knowing who matters in influencing decisions and perceptions is important for marketing. These are the people that a large amount of success will depend upon—a good or negative opinion about you and your capabilities can make the difference in key decision makers following through to make a purchase. Whether they be looking to invest a significant amount, or many people making a small value purchase, buyers will always feel more confident in dealing with you if you have been recommended by someone whose opinion they trust.

There are many types of influencers, each of whom have the ability to influence in different ways depending upon their social status and connection to decision makers. On one scale, there are celebrity style influencers—who may be people well known in an industry for their own achievements, or who could be real celebrities. This type of influence is more about how celebrity influencers are known and trusted by the people you are marketing to and their relevance to what you are marketing. It would be great to have someone well known like Nigella Lawson to recommend your software product or services, but unless there is a connection in what they are perceived to be an expert in and what you are marketing, their recommendations would have little influence.

At the other end of the scale are the type of influencers whose importance many people forget about. These are the people known personally in one way or another by the influencer whose opinion and knowledge in related subjects are valued. This type of influencer may not have the same mass audience influence as the celebrity influencer, but they have a much more influence over the decision makers they influence because of the personal connection. Examples include personal friends, family or co-workers who have proven their loyalty and/or competency throughout the time they have been known to the individual.

As programmers, we generally tend to look at a lot of issues purely from a technical angle. It's important to remember that unless decision makers have a background in software development, the chances are that in most cases, and unfortunately for us as programmers, technical perfection is rarely valued; and it's for this reason that that the average decision maker wouldn't take your Zend certification as anything noteworthy, even if you explained what it was about. This also applies to influencers, each of whom have their own factors that they prioritize in making their opinion of you and your brand. Knowing what factors influencers prioritize highest and acting to positively influence perceptions of your qualities and capabilities in these areas is the best way to kick-start their recommendations.

Reliability

> **Punctuality** : It's not uncommon for software projects to run over-schedule, you only need to look at Government projects for evidence of this. People who are aware of this issue in the IT industry, or who identify an importance for their projects to be delivered to schedule, will be more impressed by your ability to show that they can leave you to develop their software and have it ready for when you've said it would be. Software development isn't easy to predict timescales for, so perfecting your ability to achieve this will automatically allow you to stand out from the crowd.

> **Availability** : Some people need to know that whoever they are working with can be available when they are needed. This is even more the case when the service or software you are selling is directly related to the core business process of the client, such as ensuring that their e-commerce website for making sales or for making important demo presentations to potential buyers/users of a software system the client has hired you to develop; non-availability for situations like this can lead to loss of business for the client, which could cost more than any savings they would make on hiring a part-time worker

> **Workmanship** : People hire or buy software to solve a problem. They need to know that what you offer resolves their problem and there is no need for them to worry about technical issues that take up their time. Whereas most people don't understand or know the value of good quality code, the benefits of good workmanship that translates to the ability to more quickly turn around change requests without limitations and reduced risk of bugs being introduced through the software process. People may not understand the direct benefits they get with good quality code, but they will become to rely on you and your software capabilities once they see that that hiring or buying from you doesn't cause them more problems

Personality

People ultimately buy from people, no matter what they are buying or their motivations. The perception of being approachable, positive minded, enthusiastic and genuine should never be underestimated. Having so-called soft skills significantly helps programmers to handle toxic situations that may arise with clients by knowing how to express communications in a way that persuades the client to comply without resistance; these skills are not directly related to programming software, but can make a significant difference that dictates whether a project succeeds or fails. Most people don't like to be associated with negativity or other factors that cause conflict, which is why people like to avoid office politics wherever possible. Influencers will go out of their way to make decision makers buy from you if they perceive you as a person who wont cause them problems with personality issues such as negativity, being awkward about what's delivered, and generally disrupting a team's progression by upsetting people:

> ➤ **Reputation** : A good reputation comes as a result of reliability, but is a factor that is more than just being reliable. Reputations are built on achievements and show the added value you offer. When clients say that they want a software developed, or that they want to buy your software, there is little more that will capture their interest in dealing with you if they are able to see an impressive list of what you have done for other people and what they say about you. Industry awards are also a good way of boosting your reputation, which shows that you are recognized by the industry as one of the best

> ➤ **Prestige** : For the same reason that certain people like to have expensive cars such as a BMW or Ferrari and who would feel ashamed of having a regular car such as a Ford, there are people who want to use exclusivity and scarcity as a bragging right. In the case of software, this is likely to be influenced by high spending clients who want to justify the high prices of their own products and services to their clients and customers by using the exclusivity, scarcity and/or reputation of your software or services to give the impression that what they are selling is the best in their market. An example of this would be e-commerce security features for selling to people who have concerns about making online payments:

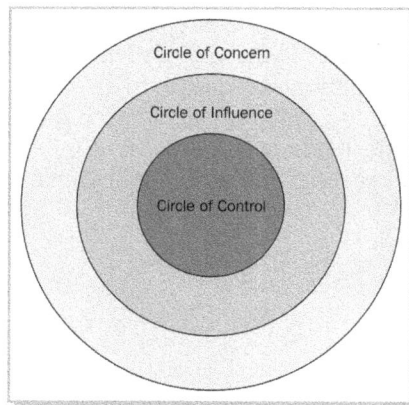

Circle of Concern

Circle of Influence

Circle of Control

Figure 4.2: The three forms of influence that affect how people perceive situations that lead to decision making.

Circles of influence will have actors who play their individual roles of persuasion:

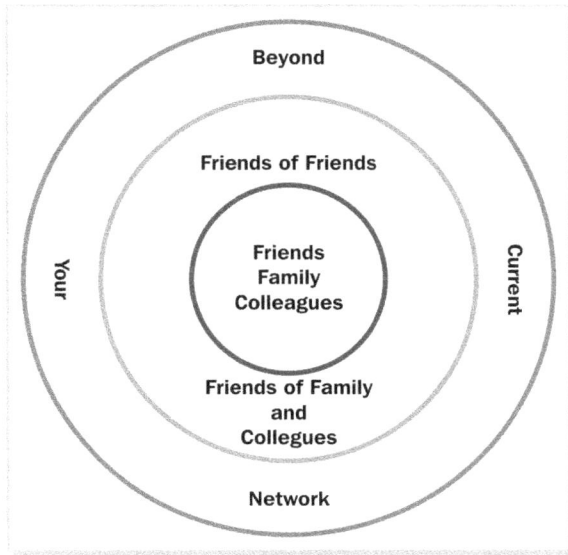

Figure 4.3: The circle of influence applied in a general context to the average working person.

As represented in Figures 4.2 and 4.3, the opinions and actions of people are affected by their inner circle of friends, family and possibly colleagues depending on the situation. Each of these people also have their own network of people who they are influenced by, meaning that your branding shouldn't just be about directly influencing the perceptions of the people you are marketing to, but also the people they trust the opinion of and the people that those trusted opinions are affected by. The dynamics of these influencers become evermore interesting with the rise of social media where the people's perceptions are also influenced by bloggers or YouTube video creators.

Media exposure

Making use of the media to generate awareness of your brand is an effective way to generate trust and credibility. Coverage in trusted websites, magazines, newspapers, radio, and TV programs that your target audience listen to and read will get you the type of attention that advertising in the same publications wouldn't achieve. This type of media isn't freely given away, so you need to consider an angle to make your software and services newsworthy—check the chapter section on writing press releases in *Chapter 5: Networking, Marketing and Sales.*

Content marketing

Developing content with a view to generating an awareness of your brand is a method that can be highly effective if you have skills in content creation. These skills can come in many forms, whether it be writing, video, animation or even app development. The most important aspect of content marketing is engagement—there is no point in making content nobody is interested in reading/watching/using, so it is important to know angles that fit your brand ambitions that are also effective in producing the types of engagement you need to justify your time investment in content marketing.

The downside to this type of marketing is that good content requires time and skill to produce. Making mistakes in identifying the right content angles, people to target, distribution strategy, or meaningful end results may be time consuming, and like any type of business activity, time also has a cost. Content creation can only be justified in a business sense where results generated can justify the cost of time invested. Where you don't have the skills yourself, it means that you have to hire someone else—which will cost both money and time, so there is a high requirement for having a clear strategy that defines how the content will play a role in supporting the overall business strategy.

Bar a few exceptions such as pay-per-click marketing, nobody likes to be presented with content that is blatantly trying to sell something. Furthermore, content that has been created primarily as a sales pitch is much harder to gain the acceptance for, publication and distribution by strategic partners and influencers (see previously in this chapter), who will be concerned about losing engagement with their audience by presenting a sales message as informative content; remember that nobody likes content that is blatantly selling to them, hence readers/viewers/users can switch off if they are provided with too much advertising.

The key to success in content marketing is creating content that people will take a genuine interest in, in a way that presents you in line with your branding objectives—as a software developer, this is likely to be as an expert and thought leader of the subject. It is also important to create content on subjects, as well as with a tone, that your readers will understand and take an interest in; hence if your target audience is the education sector, you want to be promoting issues relating to education in relation to how your software can be used, rather than talking about how you created your latest algorithm for analyzing student learning performance.

The success of your content strategy is highly dependent on your ability to build a powerful network that can add credibility, generate interest and distribute your content to large numbers of people. In today's Internet-connected age of social media, this can be fairly easy to achieve if you are able to present yourself as the type of person that people of interest would want to collaborate with and your content is produced to a required standard.

Guest blogging is an example of how this can generate good results, where you write a blog post for someone's blog who operates in the market you are targeting your content strategy towards; not only does this get your name out to the right audience, but you are able to gain instant visibility to numbers of people you don't already have access to. Combine this with the use of conversation engagement on social networks such as Twitter and you have a highly effective platform for generating rapid awareness of your brand identity, especially where engaging content can be repeatedly re-shared by people.

Who do they think you are?

When it comes to branding, it's important to remember that most people aren't interested in how the software is developed, but how what you create solves their problem. Software development principles are an important issue to understand for avoiding technicalities that lead to situations that affect how people perceive your reliability, but aren't the type of topic that should be directly communicated to the buyer unless they come from a software development related background. With branding being about persuading people to have a favorable opinion of you, the type of language you use in your communications, whether it be spoken or written, is as important as anything visual. Careful consideration should be used in all of your communications, whether it be over the telephone, face to face, e-mail, newsletter, brochure, website or media published content to make sure that the style of language used, which includes the use of any jargon, is worded in a way that makes the people you are speaking to feel comfortable in dealing with you. The type of perception you may want to create could include some consideration of:

> **Understandability**: Special care needs to be taken for people who don't have a background in software development to make sure that they understand what you are talking about. Try to refrain from using any jargon that is likely to be outside their scope of knowledge, as this can lead to them feeling out of place or inferior, both of which can lose their attention to your communication

> **Confidence**: This is for confidence in themselves as well as in your capabilities. People need to feel that they are capable of using the information you are providing, as well as having confidence that the information you are providing them with is correct and of good

> **Motivation**: The style of communications you use should motivate and inspire people to take action, especially if that action is related to you winning or completing client projects

> **Directness**: Being direct on issues of importance saves time and makes the level of importance clear. The stereotype of the British being a good example of often not being direct enough, which leads to interpretations of a message as not as high priority or important; this is an example of cultural communication bias, where at one end of the spectrum, cultures such as the Finnish are not openly expressive in their wording to a point where they are perceived to be highly, while at the other end cultures such as those of Americans tend to be highly expressive to a point where they gain a stereotype of being very talkative and loud—however correct or incorrect that may be.. The ability to effectively communicate the level of importance will earn you a level of respect and trust when clients need to feel they should have someone they can rely on to keep them updated on circumstances, but at the same time knowing how to communicate urgency without causing offence

> **Transparency**: People never like to be lied to, and even though masking the truth may not strictly be a lie, it will cause doubt and mistrust. When people learn that you are open about what and how you provide your software, which includes providing the client with the ability to retain the rights to the code you write specifically for them, they will quickly learn to value you as someone they can trust and will give you a higher preference in future work because of this. Nobody likes to deal with people who are known to add hidden costs and clauses to contracts, so avoid this to retain good ongoing client relationships

The single most identifiable reason why Apple has risen to the successes it has is because they are very specific about how they design their products to be easily accessible to people with a minimal understanding of technology. Contrary to how technology people complain that Apple products are too restricted and limited, the point to remember is that Apple don't create their products for hardcore technology enthusiasts. If Apple were to listen to what these enthusiasts wanted, they would make themselves much less appealing to their core audience and most likely lose their unique selling point (USP) that sells their products; the main USP being that because Apple tightly control what is allowed on their devices also means that their users can be assured that they are protected against the type of poorly designed apps, malware and viruses found on less restrictive platforms such as Android and Windows.

The moral of the story is that success in developing our software comes from knowing and listening to our real customers so that we can create a solution and user experience that appeals to them. Although it's good to speak and listen to other technology people, with the exception of a minority of projects and products, it's also important to remember that we are not selling our software products and/or services to technology people, hence the need to make sure that the software and development services are presented in a way that's easy to understand, see the benefits of and gain the confidence to use without causing problems of losing credibility. When people think of what you do, your brand is to make sure you are perceived as the solution that your software or development services provide, and not merely as software.

Summary

Contrary to popular belief, creating a brand is not simply about creating a few visuals for use across your marketing stationery, but is primarily based around using psychology to influence how people think of your business brand; as a freelancer, this would be yourself. Building a brand that has a business benefit requires serious thought about who you are intending to sell your software products and services to, along with understanding how these people think, who they are influenced by and what you need them to think of you in order for them to become interested in buying from you.

Visual elements are an important part of the psychology behind branding, but all falls under the category of communications; that is, you make use of visual branding as part of your communication activities in order impact how your message is perceived. Branding is all about how your message is perceived, so make sure to invest effort into communicating the right message and also that it is interpreted in the right way by the people you are aiming to target.

Not everyone you target with your branding should be the people you intend to sell to. People who are influential directly or indirectly have an impact on your brand's visibility to the people you aim to sell to, as well as their perception of the qualities you aim to promote. This is never a short-term game, but building good relationships with people you know to be influencers will pay off in the long run if you have a clear strategy for how your branding supports your marketing.

> 5

Networking, Marketing, and Sales

The old saying of it being more about who you know than what you know is certainly true when it comes to business and is often the distinguishing factor between people who achieve success and those who miss out. We all start in the world with minimal contacts, meaning that even the most connected people have been in a position where they had minimal contacts. This section focuses on the different methods and avenues you can use to build your network of contacts that can support your marketing and business strategy.

Understanding networking

Put simply, networking is about meeting people who could turn out to be useful in one way or another. These people could be immediately useful to yourself, to people you know, or even may become useful at some point in the future.

Many people make the mistake of viewing networking as an activity purely for making sales, hence their approach to networking events and other platforms such as social media being to sell to everyone. Nothing loses people's attention more than speaking to someone who is blatantly only interested in making a sales pitch; it comes across as impersonal and most likely to be of no interest. As a result, this type of approach to networking tends to have minimal impact, especially if the room is full of the same types of people who are only there to make a sales pitch.

If networking isn't about selling to people, then you are probably wondering how could it be of use to you. Networking is a useful activity to:

> **Establish a reputation**: First and foremost, people buy based on trust. If you are able to convince others that you are trustworthy and an expert in your field, they will happily recommend you to people they know who may need your services.

> ➤ **Expand your potential**: Develop key partnerships by using networking to find people you can collaborate with on projects. This allows you to target new markets and open opportunities that can make your services and products more relevant by accessing additional resources, skills and time from other professionals. An example of this could be collaborating management consultants; who in addition to being an asset for managing difficult project, could also be of use for the design of management features in any software product you are developing. Collaboration with these key value partners also opens opportunities to share market access—i.e. they can become resellers of your products and services in addition to them providing a solution to problems you may have in your projects.

> ➤ **Become informed**: Information is power; hence tapping in to the knowledge of others is a great way to obtain useful information for your business activities. This information can range from specialist information relating to your area of expertise, through to happenings in local business and insights to how other businesses operate and emerging opportunities. All of this information leads to you being in a better position to take advantage of the evolving environment, whether it's being in the right place at the right time for winning new work, or evolving your business to develop new unique selling points that will win you new business and/or increase your profitability.

> ➤ **Open sales opportunities**: Not to be confused with making a sales pitch; new opportunities to make sales is usually as a result of the preceding points, although there will be some circumstances where people you talk to at an event will have an interest in buying into your services.

Defining a networking strategy

All businesses are different and as a result there is no single networking strategy that works for everyone. A networking strategy should be designed to specifically match how you are set up in business, hence providing the highest convenience for connect with your target audience. Remember that networking isn't about making a sales pitch; it's about building your contact list, learning information and building your reputation in a way that places you in a position of strength in the market.

Networking comes in two main flavors:

> ➤ **Online networking** through forums and social media websites. These are especially handy for extending your reach to people you would never meet on a face to face basis:

>> ➤ Example: Twitter, LinkedIn, and Facebook can be used to find and engage in relevant conversations that lead to gaining new contacts of interest.

➤ **Real world networking** performed mainly at organized events and later followed up with one to one meeting:

    ➢ Example: There are many business networking events held at bars and cafes that allow people in business to speak to each other. Find out where these are and attend.

Although these are two different ways to network, they are essentially the same activity—speaking with people of interest to establish trust and credibility. Online and real-world networking aren't mutually exclusive, hence a networking strategy can combine the advantages of both to suit how you need to connect with your target audiences For example, use online social networks to engage with people regularly attend real world networking events. Many of these meet ups have a presence on social media platforms such as LinkedIn, Facebook and Twitter, which you can use to engage conversation before the events—and identify beforehand who you would be good to speak with.

You can further split both online and real-world networking groups/events into the following:

➤ **Generalist networking:** These types of networking events, groups, and Internet forums invite businesses of any type to join, meet, and discuss. Their non-specific nature often means that they don't have a specialist theme or agenda, but are very good for meeting other people in business to open opportunities for collaborations, sales, and learning of non-specific business information such as how to deal with running aspects of your business and happenings in the local area that could be of interest to you.

➤ **Specialist networking**: This is the opposite to generalist networking in the sense that these events, groups, and Internet forums invite specific types of businesses and individuals to join. Unlike generalist networking, this is great for being able to target businesses and people with specific interests. Although this type of networking can be used as a sales channel in many circumstances, it is often a better source for finding contacts of interest and learning about industry specific news. As an example, a software developer isn't likely to find much work in a room full of other people who offer the same services, but they may find useful people to work with on future projects; thus opening opportunities to find key partners for bidding on bigger projects that require more resources than the individual developer can provide.

➤ **Professional / trade organizations**: Unlike the previous types, networking through professional and trade organizations is strictly about the skills of the trade that you operate in. This type of networking is very good for finding industry-specific information such as new technologies and laws that will affect how you work, as well as opportunities to establish your own credibility within professional trade circles. Generation of sales through this channel is the exception rather than the norm.

➤ **Formal business networking groups**: Formal business networking groups such as the many business breakfast clubs aren't suitable for everyone, but they seem to work for some people. These types of networking groups are businesses who make money from arranging regular business networking events for their group members, with their meetings having only one agenda—producing referrals for their members. To succeed at networking within these organizations, you need to know how to work their groups by establishing trust and having a simple description of what you do that their members will understand. Some services and products are much easier to get people to understand; for example, everyone knows what a website is, and the demand for new websites are fairly common, but software development services are a much harder sell because software needs and benefits are much more specific—surprisingly, many people don't know that apps are software! Joining this type of network isn't cheap - costing as much as £500+ per year, plus extra weekly fees for each meeting you attend. With today's social networking platforms such as LinkedIn, Twitter, and Facebook, the same results can often be generated without the cost and risk of losing your investment. It must not be forgotten that this type of networking organization exists only to make money from your business marketing and offers no promise of a return on your investment. Succeeding with this type of networking requires the following:

> ➤ **The right group**: Your business is generated entirely through referrals generated by the group's members. These people need to understand your services or product to understand what makes a good quality referral for you. It is a benefit to have other group members who work in compatible industries, as these are more likely to have access to the types of people wanting to buy your services in addition to already having a better knowledge of how to promote you.

> ➤ **Strong referral generation**: Many referrals from this type of group can be of poor quality, meaning anything from work that loses you money, through to leads who have never heard of you—i.e. leads will class you as a cold caller. This factor is heavily dependent on the group members; people who don't know how to create good quality leads and groups that pressure members to meet referral targets will result in members handing out any old lead to you. This is also a misleading trap to fall for, as this type of group can appear to be generating a lot of business for its members—while a bit of investigating may find that a minimal amount of the leads are converting to real business, with people losing money and time from poor quality work from those leads that do convert to business.

> ➤ **A strong networking personality**: With a networking personality, you can get people in the group to understand what you do in business, gain their trust you and open opportunities for collaborations the help other members—who may in return advocate you to people in their other network circles.

> ➤ **The right group mentality**: Avoid groups where there is too much of a focus on generating new referrals. Quality if always more important than quantity when it comes to sales leads; hence quantity often at an expense to quality. A group focusing primarily on quantity of referrals can be an indication of no quality control, with false impressions being given on the groups successes. Also avoid groups where many members only have an interest in what they can sell to the group. Your success in these types of groups depends group members taking a genuine interest in helping you with your business, which isn't going to happen if they are only there to make a few of their own sales.

Writing press releases

Gaining the attention of the press for your work activities is a great way to generate awareness of your services and products, as well as improving the perception of your brand. Hiring public relations agency is one way to get your business into the spotlight, can be expensive; with the right know how, you can write your own press releases for submission to selected media outlets and avoid the need to hire costly public relations agencies to do the work for you.

Know your audience

The most important rule of creating a press release is to make sure that it is written from an angle that would make an interesting news story; after all, you are trying to convince the media that people want to hear about your story. The news story needs to appeal to each media channel's audience; hence you might consider how the same story may need to be reworded for different publication and broadcasting channel. Let's look at the following example:

A new website application is created for a photography studio that allows their clients to view and provide feedback with alterations as well as to select options for the purchase of their photos online.

There are a number of angles from which the completion and launch of this project can be made into a newsworthy story. The following angle would be best suited for a publication targeting the local community of the photography studio whose specialism is in providing news stories from the local community:

Local photography studio ABC Photography and software developer James Jones have teamed up to create a system that helps to benefit the environment and provide convenience for clients through an innovative Internet-based photograph selection system, allowing clients to select their chosen photography from the comfort of their home. With no need to revisit the photography studio, clients of ABC Photography are already playing their part in reducing pollution of the environment, while also benefiting from savings made on time and fuel expenses.

To a publication targeted at a more technical audience, that is interested specifically in innovation relating to websites and Internet technologies, the news story would be written along the following lines:

> *Software developer James Jones has developed a new type of Internet system for photography studio ABC Photography who have a keen focus on innovating the photoshoot experience that provides a more convenient and enjoyable service to their clients. With the system's user interface developed completely with HTML 5, it provides a level of interactivity that has previously only been associated with Flash and as a result is completely compatible with iPad and iPhone devices. The Internet software allows clients to select their photography and make enhancements in real time before print.*

Take note of how the main subject of the news story is now the software developer, with the news story focusing on how the Internet software uses HTML 5 deliver the innovation sought by ABC Photography. This news story can indeed be taken further with a view to inviting the publication to interview James Jones in their magazine, or simply to use the content in the press release as the foundation for a news item. There would be little to no mention of the environmental benefits because this angle isn't relevant to the publication's specialist subject focus.

Finally, the story can also be written from an angle that appeals to other photographers:

> *Software developer James Jones has created a new type of Internet system that allows photographers to improve the convenience and personalization of photography provided to their clients. The system can be made available through a photographer's website and allows the client to make photographic alterations, in addition to adding adjustment requests and personalized messages for integration with the final prints. Current user ABC Photography are first to praise the benefits provided by software. "We have seen a 100% increase on the number of prints ordered by our clients who use the system via our website." says Jane Johnson—client account manager at ABC Photography.*

James Jones remains as the main subject of the story in this item, but the news is now about how his system helps photographers provide better convenience and personalization capabilities for their clients. Take note of how ABC Photography have been reduced to merely a user of the system rather than a partner in the development; this coverage has no value to ABC Photography as it is specifically targeting their competitors. This scenario assumes that the terms of the business agreement made between James Jones and ABC Photography allows for the system to be resold to other photographers.

Be specific

Your press release has two main obstacles to compete with:

➤ Available time of the journalists working for the publication you are trying to gain coverage from

➤ Other news items submitted that are competing for attention and space

As a result, the more popular the publication is, the better your press release needs to be to gain their attention. We've already gone through how to make a story newsworthy; the next step should be to present the press release in a format that's short and to the point. Let's look at our original example again:

Local photography studio ABC Photography and software developer James Jones have teamed up to create a system that helps to benefit the environment and provide convenience for clients through an innovative Internet-based photograph selection system, allowing clients to select their chosen photography from the comfort of their home. With no need to revisit the photography studio, clients of ABC Photography are already playing their part in reducing pollution of the environment, while also benefiting from savings made on time and fuel expenses.

There are a few key elements to how this news story has been worded to efficiently get the message across:

➤ The wording starts with *"Local photography studio..."*, indicating straight away that the news story is both local and about a photography studio. This eliminates the risk of the reader discarding the press release on the basis of uncertainty about it being a local news story

➤ The sentence continues with *"a system that helps benefit the environment and provide convenience to clients..."* which allows the entire news story to be summarized within the first sentence. This is a critical element of the press release structure, as we can guarantee that the reader can understand the gist of the news story with the minimal effort. A decision can then be immediately made as to whether the story is relevant to the publication

➤ The example finishes with a summary of the story stating, what has actually happened—that is, *"... clients of ABC Photography are already playing their part in reducing pollution of the environment, whist also benefiting from savings made on time and fuel expenses."*

Integrating your agenda

Gaining media coverage is all very good, but it's a waste of time and money if it doesn't provide produce any results that relate to your business strategy. When creating your public relations strategy and its associated media communications, you should identify:

➤ What outcomes you want from the wider and long term strategy

➤ Short term results you intend to achieve from the individual press release

➤ How you will measure your success; both the overall strategy and individual press releases

From this, you should be able to gain an insight to:

➤ Angles to use for news stories fit your agenda

➤ Responses you intend to generate for each mention in the press

> Methods and criteria you will use to monitor how successful your media strategy is performing to contribute to the success of your business

It's important to remember that not all agendas are quantitively measurable; that is you can't always measure success by something like the number of enquiries you receive. Let's examine success factors for an agenda of gaining credibility:

> Number of publications providing exposure of your name and brand

> Quality of publications providing your exposure

> Purpose of your exposure

Although it's easy to quantify the number of publications featuring your name and brand, none of the preceding points give us a specific number to represent how much more credible such exposure has made our brand appear. However, some important assumptions can be made:

> Not all media brands have the same weight - i.e. being featured on Sky News will get you more attention than the equivalent exposure on Random FM radio station

> Different types of exposure provide different levels of perception to your professionalism—for example, your e-mail being read on a radio show will have next to no professional value, whereas being invited onto the show as an expert s will gain you much more trust and credibility

> The perception amongst other professionals can be improved by being featured in high profile specialist publications than in generalist press media—in other words, being featured in PC Pro magazine as an IT consultant will gain more credibility amongst IT professionals than being a guest speaker for the same subject on Random FM radio station

> You will only be perceived as a professional on the subjects you are featured for—in other words being featured in the press for being an IT person will not help people to perceive you as a specialist software creator unless you are featured specifically for the subject of creating software

From these identifications, it becomes clear that success for the agenda can be measured on the basis of the weight and relevance of media coverage generated from the press release strategy. More general high profile media coverage such as Sky News is much more important for increasing the professional perception amongst people who don't have industry expertise, whereas coverage by industry specific publications will boost your credibility with people inside the industry—but not with those outside.

Make it easy to read

As previously defined, making your press release as attention grabbing as possible is a critical factor in succeeding to gain media coverage. Not only is it important to have your news worded in a way that grabs attention, but it also needs to be structured in a way that's easy for journalists to understand the news story, recognize your brand identity and to know who to contact should they wish to follow up the story.

Your press release should be constructed in the following order:

➤ **Company logo**: Provides the advantage of gaining easy recognition. If you already have a good reputation, your wording will be taken with more credibility. If you don't already have a good reputation, this is the first step in making yourself more recognizable for future press releases

➤ **Contact details:** For journalists interested in your news story, it's important to have you contact details in a place that's easy for them to see at first glance. Placing this at top means that minimal effort is required to find your contact details

➤ **Headline:** Your headline should be worded in a way that intrigues the journalist and generates a desire to read further. It should vaguely summarize the story using creative wording. Our photography studio example could be worded along the lines of *"Local Firm Shoots Greener Clients"*, with the headline being kept short and punchy. The headline should also be presented in uppercase to make it stand out from the main content

➤ **Subtitle:** Accompanies the main headline, giving a more clear insight to the subject of the news story. It should be a short sentence that outlines the story, such as *"Photography studio provides more convenient way to select photos—for both client and environment"*

➤ **Main press release content:**

   ➢ **Introduction:** A more detailed, yet still short overview of the story. This should be kept to two or three sentences that allow the reader to gain a better understanding of what the news story is about

   ➢ **Further Information:** Several paragraphs outlining the story in much closer detail. This section should feature information on benefits, results, statistics, future expectations and quotes that can be used when reporting the news story. In short, this section should provide all of the information required to make sure the journalist needs to invest minimal effort to feature you in the publication

   ➢ **Summary:** An outline of everything that has been mentioned in the news story, emphasizing the important parts that you want mentioned

   ➢ **Contact Instructions:** Just to make it clear who is to be contacted for further information. This makes it easier for the journalist to see after reading the story as well as minimizing the risk of them contacting the wrong person. In some situations, you could have aspects of your PR being managed by other person such as a PR specialist or someone with a specific expertise on the subject of the press release

Using a standard format such as described here for your press release provides a major advantage for getting your news story published; it makes it much easier for journalists to quickly scan your press release without investing much effort. The following is an example of how this type of press release would look:

ABC Photography

Contact: Jane Johnson   [For immediate release]
Tel: 0123 333 3333
Mobile: 07777 777 777
Email: jane@example.com

LOCAL FIRM SHOOTS GREENER CLIENTS
Photography Studio Provides Convenient Way to Select Photos – for Client and Environment.

Local photography studio ABC Photography and software developer James Jones have teamed up to create a system that helps benefit the environment and provide convenience to clients through an innovative Internet based photograph selection system that allows clients to select their chosen photography from the comfort of their home. With no need need to revisit the photography studio, clients of ABC Photography are already playing their part in reducing pollution of the environment, whist also benefiting from savings made on time and fuel expenses.

With the recession still hitting families hard, increases in fuel expenses and new congestion charges expected to be introduced within the coming months, the new photography selection system is welcome news for families investing in portrait photography. "It would have taken us over two hours to of travel revisit the photography studio, plus the added inconvenience of being restricted to an appointed time to see our photos. With the new selection system, we saved on the time needed to travel and were able to take our time to review the photos with friends and family who would otherwise have not been able to give suggestions in our selection for printing. The flexibility to choose a time of our convenience to review the photos has been an additional benefit to us due to taking time out of work being self-employed usually means losing out on opportunities to earn money.", says Karen Bishop – a client of ABC Photography.

The system was developed as part of ABC Photography's drive to help their clients beat the recession and improve the convenience of the service offered. "We identified that one of the most common concerns amongst our clients was the time and inconvenience to make a second trip to our studio for the review and selection of our photos, with our clients having to travel an average of 1.8 hours. As a company that strives to evolve in order to make our services both accessible and convenient, our new system is one of many steps that we have taken to improve our client experience. It's not often that you are offered with a solution to an issue that makes your life more convenience, saves you money and allows you to play your part in saving the environment.", says Jane Johnson – ABC Photography's client experience manager.

Recorded statistics show that the photography selection system has so far eliminated the need for 70 journeys this month alone, saving clients and the environment on a total of 126 hours of travel expenses and pollution, with a further 1,386 hours expected to be saved this year.

###

For further information on this story or to arrange an interview, please contact Edward Stuart on 0123 777 7777 or by e-mail at ed@examplep.com.

Figure 5.1: A press release that is easy to read, has an eye catching headline, emphasizes an interesting story, and makes it clear who to contact.

Tips for writing news stories

It's important to get the most into your news stories so that they can produce the type of response you want. The following are factors you should take into account when writing your press release content:

> ➤ Journalists are human, so keep them entertained with your writing. Make it fresh, informative, and interesting.

> ➤ Publications are there to provide content that interests their readers, so write your press release to be in the interest of the publication's readers and nobody else.

> ➤ Journalists are busy people who are under pressure to deliver to their editors, so make it as easy as possible for them to extract the information they require from your press release. This should include:

>> ➢ Creating a ready to print headline for them that sounds good and is attention grabbing.

>> ➢ Outlining the summary of the story within the first paragraph.

>> ➢ Integrating ready to use quotes within your main news story content.

>> ➢ Keeping the content of the press release as short as possible; usually within two pages, but ideally just one.

>> ➢ Placing the most important information of the news story near the top to ensure less effort is needed to reach it.

>> ➢ Make your contact details very clear so that they know who to contact should they have to.

> ➤ Never write a press release to make sales; you will only annoy the publications and risk damaging your credibility for future PR. Instead, make the story newsworthy—even if it's only announcing a new service, you can put an emphasis on something newsworthy, such as who it will benefit, what it has achieved, and/or new features you have invented that help with factors such as reducing costs or improving quality.

> ➤ Keep an eye on what is trending in the news, especially for anything relating to the publications you intend to get featured in. There will be a higher chance of you being featured if you are able to create a newsworthy story that matches trending news. Twitter is a valuable platform for this—news often breaks there before it gets into the mainstream media.

Enhancing the reach of your media coverage

Gaining exposure in the media isn't only good for gaining awareness of yourself among new people, it can also be a great way to improve your perceived professionalism and authority among people who already know of you and who you may interact with in the future. For any mentions you get in publications, you should spread the word to your existing contacts via newsletters, e-mail, Twitter, Facebook, LinkedIn, and any other medium you use to communicate—of course, without overdoing it!

Open project sources

The easier way of finding work is to use sources where prospective clients make their work requirements publicly known for people like yourself to bid for. On one hand, this provides a big advantage of being much easier and cheaper for you to find the work. On the other hand, the nature of the project being open for any number of people to bid for means that you will be up against a lot of competition. The key to succeeding with open projects is a mixture of applying for them in quantity, being selective in the projects you apply for and sending tailored proposals that meet the needs of the project owner.

Project sources

There are many sources to find details of projects requiring your skills. The following are descriptions of the main types you are likely to come across:

> **Project bidding websites:** These are websites that allow any type of business to publish their work requirements and anyone to bid for them. Unfortunately, you will often find yourself competing against less skilled/experienced people offering to work for minimal rates and for project owners who don't understand the benefits of hiring based on suitable experience over the cheapest price.

  Example: www.peopleperhour.com

> **Job boards**: These are similar to the project bidding websites, but have much better vetting and usually work with recruitment agencies who submit much more lucrative work opportunities. This avoids the issue of competing for low quality work and expectations often found with projects posted on project bidding websites.

  Example: www.cwjobs.co.uk

> **Tendering websites**: These are usually run by or for bigger organizations with the objective of finding suppliers who are able to provide the best convenience, quality, and price. You can be assured that opportunities posted for tender have more serious budgets, but also require much more effort to create a very detailed tender submission as well as the preference to be a bigger business than a one man/woman freelancer. It is often much better to form a team of freelancers when bidding for this type of work; expect to lose out on many bids before you win any.

  Example: www.thechest.nwce.gov.uk

> **Forums**: People often post details of their project needs on forums with a view to getting suggestions from other forum members. Some requests ask upfront for people to recommend a service provider, whereas others will ask for advice, which later turns out to be a request to buy services. Not all requests turn out to be opportunities to make a sale, and participating in forums shouldn't be about selling. When used in the right way, forums are great for getting people to know and trust you, who in turn will later recommend you to others—including those on the forum who request recommendations for suppliers.

  Example: www.ukbusinessforums.co.uk

➤ **Social networks:** Social networks operate in the same way as forums in the sense that that some people will openly ask for recommendations and advice that can lead to winning new work. Like with forums, the best strategy is to build a good reputation with community members and allow them to actively recommend you.

Example: `www.linkedin.com`

Being selective

Producing project proposals that are worth submitting for open projects costs time and time will in most cases be the only resource you make money from. It's important to identify that:

➤ Many open projects don't have realistic budgets.

➤ Owners of open projects often don't have realistic expectations.

The quality of open projects are often related to the sources they are listed under, with certain project bidding websites having a reputation for project owners having unrealistic budget expectations and bidders racing to offer the lowest price; there's only so much margin that you can compete on price with before a project becomes a waste of your time!

Fortunately, not all project owners use the same criteria to select their service providers, with some using price and others perceived quality as the deciding factor. The important issue for you bidding for these projects is to know how to identify which projects are worth bidding for that you can be profitable with. The following are some examples of the type of project you may see on these websites:

Example 1

```
Project Source: Project bidding website
Job Title: On going website PHP MYSQL
Job Description:
My website have stay with my current web developer for more than 6 months and I want
to see it go faster. So I need more people to carry on my PHP MYSQL and JOOMLA
Shopping Basket which now have the problem in Langauage Menu.

I would like to invite to bid for finish my Language menu .

For more datails please ask

Job Type: Programming
Budget Range : £80-£120
Budget Type : Fixed Fee
```

Figure 5.2: An example of a job specification showing clear indications that the buyer may be difficult to work with.

"If words of command are not clear and distinct, if orders are not thoroughly understood, the general is to blame..."

—Sun Tzu, The Art of War

The above example shows the following causes for concern:

➤ Although not a definite indication, poor grammar and spelling mistakes (see underlined text) can be an indication that there hasn't been a lot of effort or thought put into the job description, potentially meaning that the requirements haven't been properly planned.

➤ Another warning that poor grammar and spelling mistakes could indicate is a language barrier. Whether they are still learning the language you speak or it that they just don't have good communication skills, mistakes they make in their communications can become a problem for you gaining an understanding of what they want. For example, a few problems can occur if your client writes something along the lines of "I enjoy eating my grandma and her pets" when they should have written "I enjoy eating, my grandma and her pets".

➤ A vague description of the specific requirements gives further evidence that the project details haven't been fully thought out.

➤ The job description indicates that the project owner has already hired a previous developer that hasn't been able to satisfy their delivery expectations. This could genuinely be that the previous developer hasn't worked fast, or more alarmingly that the project owner doesn't have realistic expectations on the time requirements to deliver their project. This should be considered as a warning sign that the project owner can be difficult to deal with.

➤ People with enough experience in software development will know that adding more developers to a project can make progress slower by increasing the need for more communications and testing to ensure that contributions made by different developers don't conflict with the work of others on the team. This observation conflicts with the stated primary factor of importance being to develop the project faster and so hence is another indication that the client will be difficult to work with due to a lack of understanding of the technical issues relating to the project and unrealistic time scale expectations.

➤ A project owner who is wise and has a trusting relationship with their current developer would work them to expand their team. Not only is the developer in a better position to vet the quality of candidates, but they would be in a position to identify what type of developer(s) they can work with and are also likely to have contacts that they have successfully worked with on other projects. The project owner not taking advantage of this suggests that they may not be good at delegating tasks to the most suitable people and that they may not have a smooth/trusting relationship. These are all indications that point to the client being an obstacle to progressing the project.

➤ The project has a fixed price budget, meaning that you take on time versus budget risk. With the above indications pointing to the project owner being unknowledgeable about the technicalities of the project and having unrealistic expectations, you should expect them to make their work requirements sound more simple than they are, which is a cause for concern if you are expected to become committed to working at a fixed price regardless of what you discover after the agreement.

> ➤ The project budget is very low, meaning that there's a good chance you will be working for less than your target hourly.

> ➤ The requirements are defined very loosely, which makes it very difficult to identify what they are expecting to be delivered for the price; with buyers wanting to get their money's worth, this shows scope for unrealistic expectations that will result in you working much harder without your efforts being appreciated; with the possibility of the wording being a deliberate attempt by the client to keep the definition open for them to include extra work under the same pricing agreement. In the worst case scenario, you would end up working for almost free and have a dissatisfied client who doesn't appreciate the lengths you've gone to help them or the massive discount they've received on your time.

All indications point to the project owner needing extra care to ensure that their lack of technical knowledge and elements of unrealistic expectations don't become disruptive to the project. This in itself drives up a requirement for you to invest extra time in communications and so hence increasing your costs to support them. It may be worth your time to take on the work if the project owner is willing to pay for your extra time to cover extra support, but if they are only willing to pay a fixed price to cover time spent specifically on developing their code, then the price per hour you are paid can be significantly reduced through the unnecessary extra work generated by the client's difficulty.

In summary, this isn't the type of work opportunity that you want to be taking too seriously because all initial indications point to a poorly managed project that already has problems before you've got started and one that may not have good pay. At most, it could be worth sending a short enquiry to get more information on the project requirements and ask a few questions to make a better informed judgment, but try to limit your initial enquiry to a short e-mail to avoid investing too much time into something that isn't likely to be worth your effort.

Example 2

Project Source: Online discussion forum
Topic Title: Website Upgrade
Post:
I'm not in the market for this right now however it is something that has just crossed my mind and I wondered if its something that web designers can do or do.

I am learning HTML, CSS through coding and Dreamweaver and I am creating a basic site. However, its not as professional looking as it could be due to my lack of skills.

Figure 5.3: A project description with indications showing that the buyer has an understanding of their requirements along with good communication skills.

The following observations can be made from the above example:

> ➤ The forum poster states that this isn't an immediate opportunity to provide your services. Now is a great time to start stage one of the sales process for establishing the relationship (see later in this chapter: *The sales process*) to ensure that you are a prime candidate to approach for a quote when the prospect is interested in making the move to buy the services.

> ➤ The forum poster is looking primarily for someone to improve their current website, but has also indicated scope to expand their interest to provision of training services and other products you may offer such as a content management system. None of these should be suggested upfront, but can be identified and proposed in later stages of the sales process.

> ➤ The project owner has shown a likeliness to understand at least some of the technical issues of the service to be provided and so hence has a much lower chance of being a problematic client.

> ➤ The project owner shows evidence of being proactive with them already having started on their website and stating that they will be able to provide you with their logo. This shows that they have already thought about how the working relationship would work to some degree and suggests that they have forward planning skills that will be of benefit to you when working with them.

> ➤ Being proactive shows how the buyer has already thought about the requirements of the working relationship, hence reducing the risk of a situation where delays from the client introduce inefficiencies in your workflow.

In summary, this looks like the type of lead that's worth putting some effort into following up. Starting with the first stage of the sales process to establish a relationship with the prospect, a simple e-mail enquiry can be made to build a conversation that captures more details about their website and its requirements. Providing some tips and suggestions on what can be done with the website is a good way to build trust that opens the prospect to provide the information you need for understanding how your products and services are relevant to them, along with other factors such as timescales and budget influences. It is also worth taking a look at the website they have created so far to suggest other factors for consideration that they may not be aware of such as improving the website's loading speed and SEO; this would be fairly quick to check and would show that you've taken some time to take an interest in what they are hiring you for, which in turn may gain you trust that allows you to move away from competing on price.

The sales process

Often misunderstood as something that happens when a sale is made, the sales process is something that has several phases and doesn't end when the sale is complete. From the first instance of being introduced to a prospective client, through to closing the sale and maintaining the relationship, the sales process isn't just about making a sale, but more about maximizing the sales potential and building an ongoing relationship.

Stage 1: Establish the relationship

There are a number of channels that can be used to establish relationships with prospective clients; the key being to ensure that your name is mentioned or placed in the right location at the right time. Channels that are effective for establishing leads that in turn are used to establish new relationships include:

> **Word of mouth recommendation**: What can be considered as the most effective form of advertising, personal recommendations produce genuine interest in your services by people who are actively looking for what you offer. Through actively marketing your personal brand to generate trust that leads to word of mouth recommendations, you can extend your market reach by persuading people to recommend you to others - in effect allowing you to build a virtual sales force that listen for opportunities to recommend you wherever they go.

> **Advertising**: Good advertising is all about getting your message and details to the right people, at the right time and at the right place. This isn't as good as a personal recommendation because you don't benefit from gaining any trust from advertising and it can be costly if you make mistakes. If done properly, it's a good way to establish leads that you know have an interest in your services. Advertising works best when it is highly targeted because it allows you to refine your message to appeal more specifically to the people exposed to your advertising.

> Remember that this is the first stage of the sales process, so your advertising strategy shouldn't be focusing on closing the sale just yet. No matter what medium you are using to advertise, your objective at this stage should be to get people to make an enquiry that provides you with details of who they are, their interests/requirements and ideally information on their time scale and budget. This information would then be used in the next stages of the process to increase your chances of successfully closing the sale.

> **Online social media and networking**: Never to be confused as advertising platforms, social media websites like Facebook, Twitter and LinkedIn are a great way to get your name noticed by a targeted audience and to build a following who can recommend you to others. Although social media can be used to sell directly to your followers, there is a risk of you appearing to be a *spam wizard* if you advertise your services too much - resulting in people not listening to your message and/or unsubscribing from your social media channel(s). Social media is best used to provide useful information and commentary on current situations that engage the types of people you want to target in your marketing, whilst keeping the ratio to 80/20; that's 20% advertising and 80% informative content. Use social media to engage people in a way that gets you noticed and gets people to advocate you.

> **Real world networking**: Before this age of online social networking, the best way to meet people of interest was to go to organized business networking events. Business cards would be exchanged and arrange follow up meetings would be arranged; their purpose being learning more about each other's businesses, identify any scope for collaborations and introductions to people of interest. Real world networking is still as important as online networking because people will always want to properly know the people they do business with. Real world networking shouldn't be considered as a separate activity, but something that is integrated as part of a broader networking strategy that includes both real world and online networking to that take the full advantages that both have to offer.

> **Search engines**: A high quality source of targeted traffic, search engines like Google allow you to get your website to people who are actively searching for what you offer. The fast way to get your website listed on relevant searches is to pay for a sponsored listing in which you are charged per click; Google's Ad Words is an example of this, where they provide you with the tools you need to review and manage the search phrases you want to sponsor. The other way is to create well targeted content in the hope that the search engines will list you under relevant searches, but with no guarantees of search placement and it taking much longer to achieve success. Both methods have their pros and cons, with each needing tailored content pages to maximize your conversion of visitors to enquirers.

Whichever methods you base your sales strategy around, always remember that the first phase of sales is all about generating leads. At this stage, you are only looking to find information that can be used later when following up. As a minimum, you will want the following information from enquiries:

> Name

> Telephone number

> E-mail address

With this basic information, you are then in a position to follow up the enquiry and provide further information. In an ideal situation, you should also be able to collect the following information as part of the initial lead generation:

> Available budget

> Time scales for delivery

> Special or specific requirements

Stage 2: Recognizing the need

Having all of the suggested information from stage one will allow you to tailor your approach to become specific to the interests of the prospect. Leads should ideally be followed up first by telephone so that you become more human and also to gain insights from their reactions in your conversation, allowing you to adjust the flow of the communication in-line with what they show an interest in.

After the telephone conversation ends, the lead should be followed up with an e-mail summarizing the telephone conversation that ensures they have something to refer back to and the ability to respond should they have lost your details.

The process of recognizing the need may take several communications and meetings to fully understand what the client requires. Some leads may be hot in the sense that the prospect knows exactly what they want, whereas others maybe warm and require a lot more probing to identify their requirements. Either way, recognizing the need is all about allowing you to understand how you can be of help, which of your services can be provided to meet the requirements and possible identification of additional products and services they want to buy.

Stage 3: Proposing the Solution

At this point, you should have all the information you require to make a decision on the types of solution you can provide that are relevant to the buyer. Although being able to identify a solution to the problem is a good thing, it's not always enough to keep the buyer engaged with you; hence the need to consider how you will propose the solution. The following are suggestions that help to make your proposal stand out:

> **Provide options**:

>> Gives the prospect choice to make them feel in control.

>> Allows you to provide a range of prices that cover all levels of complexity and to avoid scaring the client away with prices outside of their budget.

> **Focus on benefits:** Try to avoid technical jargon and describe more of the benefits that the solution will provide. In most cases, the client isn't interested in *how* it's done, but more about *what* it will do.

> **Be unique:** Finding an original angle to describe and provide features that will benefit the prospect will give you a unique selling point that anyone else they may be speaking to isn't likely to be offering. This allows you to capture the attention of people who are already looking at other suppliers you are competing against. Being unique makes you stand out from the crowd and become more memorable, which itself could be the one factor that makes the difference between closing and losing a sale.

> **Be reactive**: Don't speak at the prospect when suggesting your proposal, but speak with them. Ask open questions that allow them to describe their ideas and control the direction of the conversation in ways that reveal information you never thought to ask about. By inviting the prospect to give input on your proposal, you will be able to identify if they have any concerns and avoid them going away with unanswered questions that could lead them buying their solution from elsewhere.

Stage 4: Closing the sale

If you have pitched the proposal properly, the prospect will show enough interest in what you offer for you to be able to make your move to close the sale. Closing the sale as soon as possible with a deal that is favorable to both parties should be your highest priority in the sales process, as any time spent where the client hasn't committed to buying from you is time where someone else can approach them with an offer that may seem to be better than what you are suggesting and jeopardize your time investment. Always aim to lock out the competition as soon as possible by getting the prospect to commit to a deal that involves an upfront deposit payment. Once a payment has been made, the prospect is then in a position where they will be wanting to get the best value for what they've invested and an extra incentive not to cancel talks on the project should a competitor attempt to poach them from you.

Never do work upfront without payment - this only opens scope for you to be taken advantage of and leaves you with no protection if the client decides to buy their services from elsewhere or cancel the project without payment, regardless of what they may promise beforehand. Two options considered to be standard for accepting payments are:

> ➤ 50% upfront and 50% upon completion.

> ➤ 1/3 payment upfront, 1/3 payment upon an agreed milestone and 1/3 upon completion, limiting your risk of non-payment only to the final 1/3 of the project.

You may often find it difficult to close the deal—especially if the client is a tough negotiator. The following tactics can be used to give you the upper hand in persuading the buyer to commit to hiring you:

> ➤ Use time limited incentives to make sure that the client has a good reason to commit sooner than later. Examples include providing a bonus feature at no extra cost or a discount if they can commit to buying within a specified number of days.

> ➤ Use time to your advantage by being able to guarantee your availability on specific dates to work on their project, but on a first come first serve basis. This is most effective when the client needs the project completed as soon as possible; if they are confident in your capability and are happy that your proposal is fair, they won't want to risk you becoming unavailable and not being able to meet their deadlines.

Stage 5: Delivery and evaluation

The sales process doesn't end once the sale is made. Most businesses make the mistake of focusing on generating new sales from new customers; how many times have you been unimpressed to find that the best phone contract deals are only available to new customers? The flaws in this sales strategy include:

➤ **New clients are expensive to generate**: The cost of conversion includes advertising and time required to make the effort to convert leads to sales. Never forget that time is money, even if you aren't physically paying someone else - your own time invested in marketing is time you can't spend on work you are getting paid for.

➤ **New clients are less likely to spend as much:** Providing bespoke services is never cheap and unless you are trading with large organizations, clients who have never dealt with you aren't likely to commit to large value without an existing working relationship to reflect upon. This means that sales from new clients are likely to be small projects where your sales conversion costs need to be directly deducted from their profit margin.

➤ **You can't trust new clients:** It sounds harsh, but you can't guarantee that new clients are good to work with if you have no previous working relationship with them. Big risk factors for all new clients include potential difficulty to work with and more importantly their ability to pay on time. Of course, clients are able to earn your trust once you begin to work with them and get paid.

By providing the client with an impressive experience of working with you and an end solution that they are amazed with, you will be able to produce an advocate who actively recommends your services to others as well opening scope for repeat business. Throughout the delivery of your services, there will be ongoing opportunities for you to assess the needs of the client, allowing you to identify opportunities to propose additional software/features at the end of the project. As the person with both the technical and business knowledge, you are in a better position to provide the client with ideas that they haven't thought about or even knew was possible; this is how the consultancy side of being a freelancer becomes part of the sales process.

A final review of the project upon completion is an ideal time to present both an overview of the benefits that the project provides to them as well as outlining optional steps to introduce additional benefits; all based on your observations and conversations engaged during the project. It may be that the client has immediate requirements to engage you in further work or that there are no immediate requirements. Either way, the process should repeat again from step one to ensure that the relationship is maintained for any future opportunities to work with the client.

Summary

Success in both careers and business is all about who you know, so pay attention to how you network to find the people who can open opportunities for your business strategy. Networking and marketing shouldn't only focus on sales, but also to find people who can benefit your business by providing news and other types of information insights that allow you to make better decisions. Networking is also a great way to build key partnerships with suppliers and people with specialist skills, while also helping to build a following of people who advocate your business—helping to generate awareness of your brand, products and services.

Where sales are concerned, it is important to follow a sales cycle to close sales. Avoid the common mistake made by many people in businesses who try to immediately close the sale. This can easily lead to losing sales through making the wrong pitch, or even worse is winning a sale that turns out to lose you money. Your sales cycle should make sure to have a process that qualifies sales enquiries to ensure their suitability for your business in terms of profitability and the type of client/customer you want to work and sell to. Other processes in the sales cycle should focus on building an understanding of the buyer's needs and interests so that you can later produce a pitch that perfectly matches all the criteria the buyer wants in order to give them the confidence to choose you for their project.

The next chapter introduces client types, describing what you need to know about the different characteristics you are likely to come across when working for people who hire you.

6

An Introduction to Client Types

Once you start to get freelance projects, it will quickly become clear that every client is different; some will be easy to work with, while others will be a bit of a handful. Being successful as a freelancer ultimately comes down to:

➤ Making clients happy
➤ Being profitable

The types of client you work with will have a direct influence on both of the above factors. If only every client was easy to work with, freelancers around the world would live lives with less stress and better cash flow; the unfortunate reality is that almost all clients will cause issues that affect your ability to satisfy them and/or be profitable with your projects. This chapter focuses on identifying the different client characteristics you are likely to encounter so that you can better prepare a strategy to make your clients happy, stay profitable and avoid conflict. Keep in mind that most clients you will provide services to will show a mixture of characteristics, with no two clients being exactly the same.

> *"If those who are sent to draw water begin by drinking themselves, the army is suffering from thirst."*

> *—Sun Tzu, The Art of War*

Before starting a project, we can learn a lot about a clients characteristics by simply observing how they act. The information gained from these observations can become a useful tool for making decisions on how to perform business with the client, minimize risk and avoid negative situations. As the saying goes, actions speak louder than words.

The ethical client

The type of client that is good to work with; the type who we would all like our clients to be. If a client can't be classed as ethical, then there has to be serious consideration as to whether it's worth providing services to them.

Characteristics

Ethical client tend to be:

> ➤ **Keen to identify a deal that is fair to both parties**: Ethical people understand that a fair deal leads to a win for everyone, meaning that they get the solution and quality of service required because you have the funds to make it happen. They also look at the scope for establishing a working relationship for future projects, understanding that a good relationship with people they can trust leads to receiving solutions faster with minimal problems.

> ➤ **Generous in what they offer**: Ethical clients often know what the market rate for your services is and will offer this as a minimum, while potentially suggesting bonuses as an extra motivation when their work is required at short notice or requires you to work extra time at weekends or evenings.

> ➤ **Keen to keep people happy**: Ethical clients make a priority of keeping the people they work with happy, whether it's rewarding good work or working with you to identify mutually achievable solutions to problems that may occur on a project. Ethical clients will try to avoid putting you in situations that cause unnecessary stress and understand that showing their appreciation for your contribution can make a big difference in your opinion of the working relationship.

Progression options

The most important factor to building a good working relationship with the ethical client is communication; without this, ethical clients will not be able to make judgments that truly reflect the situation. Information relating to the complexity, implications and time estimation for completion should always be communicated on a regular basis to ensure that the client can see the real picture of what is happening. Especially with projects of a technical nature, it is easy for ethical clients to see a different picture from what is happening in reality, hence giving scope for unrealistic expectations to emerge that lead to their disappointment when you aren't able to meet their demands. To avoid this, you should:

> ➤ Have a transparent process that is clear and direct with the client on all factors relating to the project.

> ➤ Provide regular reports on your progress so they can see what has been achieved; time tracking software can be used to monitor the time spent on individual tasks to produce detailed documentation for the client's review—a good way for you to emphasize where time is being spent.

> ➤ Pay special attention in your progress reporting to anything that isn't easy to see, such as research and construction of behind the scenes functionality, that are taken for granted.

>> ➤ Use the most relevant methods for the client to provide your progress reports—every client is different and will respond differently to different methods of communication. See *Chapter 12, Project Management*, for more information.

The difficult client

This type of client comes in many guises, but ultimately will cause you problems in one way or another. It's often better to not take on work from the more extreme of this type of client, but in most cases you will not have the luxury of knowing how difficult a client can be until you have started working with them.

Characteristics

Difficult clients will show at least one of a number of characteristics that you can learn to identify before you agree to engage in any work for them. These characteristics include:

> **Lacks a basic understanding of technicalities of the service you provide**: This isn't a definitive indication of a client who can be a handful to manage, but its's certainly a red flag that should raise your suspicion—especially when combined with one of the other warning signs. A client who doesn't understand the basics of the technicalities of the service you offer is much more likely to demand solutions that are not realistically achievable either on a technical level, in the time available, or within the budget they have. With the more extreme type of difficult client, this can lead to a distrust of advice that you give them and later a dissatisfaction and under-appreciation of the work and effort you have provided, due to their unrealistic expectations.

> **Pushy and wants everything yesterday**: Insistence that a new project needs completion at short notice is often an indication that they lack organizational skills—otherwise there would not be a situation where they need you to complete the work ASAP. If the indication exists, this characteristic is likely to reoccur with the client altering the requirements of their project without adequate notice and still expecting you to complete the project without delay. A client with this characteristic will want you to put their work as a priority above anything else you are working on. If not handled correctly, they will cause you problems with your work for other clients. In today's age of social media, these clients can also cause damage to your reputation by openly publishing negative feedback on review websites, including on your profile on social media platforms such as Facebook and LinkedIn, as well as any freelance websites you use for finding work. The problem with this is that there is no delicate way to provide a response that describes how the complaining client is in the wrong without scaring away potential buyers of your services; as far as they will see, it looks like a case of "no smoke without fire". A combination of this type of client personality with the previously mentioned lack of basic technical knowledge is a clear indication that the client will be a handful to manage. If you can identify this before work on the project begins, you should take serious consideration of whether it's worth taking on the work at all.

> **Doesn't understand the effort required to do the job**: This can be as a result of a lack of basic understanding of the technicalities of the service you provide, or more alarmingly, part of a dismissive personality. Either way, this characteristic is likely to cause problems when trying to negotiate and explain the required budget and time as well as what is possible.

> ➤ **A tough negotiator**: Negotiation is an important skill in business, with a good result being one that is a win for everyone involved. Difficult clients who are tough negotiators usually only seek what is a win for them, which can put you in a very difficult position as a service provider and can cause you to lose out on the project financially.

>> ➢ Tough negotiators may also use a tactic to make the project sound more simple than it is in order for you to agree to lower prices and shorter delivery time before signing an agreement. New freelancers without exposure to this type of negotiation are easy prey, who then become held accountable once the agreement has been signed.

>> ➢ The more extreme type of tough negotiator will ensure that all elements stated in a written agreement are fully followed through, regardless of how realistic their expectations are. It is therefore important that you define a watertight written agreement that has no scope for extras to be added through any loose wording used in the agreement; this should include the definition of what is considered to be reasonable support and turnaround times. This subject is covered further in *Chapter 12, Project Management*.

> ➤ **Lack of etiquette**: This is usually leads to communications from the client that sound much more rude and aggressive than they are intended to sound. Examples include swearing and writing e-mails in capital letters; which for some reason the client considers acceptable to use in a professional relationship. Lack of etiquette leads to an impression of no respect or value for your contribution to the project and can lead to you and any other collaborators you work with becoming demoralized. The question to consider with clients who lack etiquette is whether you want to be involved in working for them; their lack of professionalism can spread from just being poor communication to physical contact and other conduct that could pose a risk to your health and safety. The foundation of all good working relationships is a mutual respect between the client and the service provider—if this fails on either part, it opens too much scope for bigger problems to occur later in the project; can you or do you want to handle this type of client if you can simply find someone else to hire you?

> ➤ **Blames others for failing to deliver**: This should especially raise your suspicion of a client who could be difficult to handle if you are noticing them complain about a string of people who have apparently not been able to deliver the standard that they expect and/or if they are complaining about a previous service provider hired to do the job that they want you to do. It could be that the client has been unlucky in choosing the people they work with, but more often than not this is an indication that they are difficult to work with by either not providing the information required to complete the job or having unrealistic expectations of what can be achieved.

Progression options

Most clients will pose you with some level of difficulty to successfully satisfy their demands and remain profitable. The issue for progression is not whether a client has difficult characteristics, but more about whether their difficult characteristics will affect your ability to successfully and profitably complete the project without sacrificing your other commitments and business relationships.

In short, there are two options you have to conclude your involvement with a client who proves too difficult to deal with:

> ➤ **Identify a level of completion with new terms for the future of the working relationship**: Most clients will have some level of difficulty to work with, and there will often be cases where you have initially misjudged the difficulty of a client. In this scenario, you will have hopefully agreed upon a water tight specification (see *Chapter 12, Project Management*) that allows you to define the level of completion for the current work. Upon completion, a new agreement can be made that takes into account your new knowledge of working with the client to ensure a better working relationship that has less risk to you and offers better scope for profitability.

> ➤ **Identify an exit strategy**: A last option resort for scenarios where the client relationship proves to be unprofitable, unworkable and/or too high risk. A good exit strategy will allow you to end the client relationship without any hard feelings or leaving the client in the lurch. An exit strategy can include a level of completion for the current work with a handover to a new service provider or simply an immediate handover. Polite ways of ending a client relationship can include quoting prices that you know the client will not pay and making an introduction to a competing service provider.

The trusting client

Like the ethical client, the trusting client is one of the ideal types of client for a freelancer to work with because they leave you to get on with your work with minimal interruptions. However, the trusting nature of this type of client needs to be handled with care to ensure that the project progresses in the right direction and to maintain a good working relationship with the client.

Characteristics

Characteristics of a trusting client include:

> **Doesn't raise many questions:** Often as a result of not fully understanding the technicalities of your service, a lack of questioning indicates that the client is relying on you to get the work right, without too much input from themselves. This method of client engagement:
>
> > Allows for faster progress in projects that are simple and straightforward which don't need too much guidance from the client.
> >
> > Leaves too much scope for mistakes to be made from incorrect assumptions that result in the delivered solution not meeting the client's true requirements.
> >
> > To ensure that the project runs smoothly and results in success, this type of client requires special care to extract all of the required information.

> **Openly asks for your suggestions on what should be delivered**: This is a good indication that the client is open to suggestions and likely to be happy to progress the project entirely on your advice. You need to make sure that any advice you provide is accurate, which includes information and decisions based on your knowledge of individual factors related to the client.
>
> > Be careful about providing advice that you are not qualified and/or knowledgeable enough to provide—as this can backfire and be used as a reason to sue you if the client acts on your advice and suffers negative consequences as a result.

> **Has a vague idea of what they want, but not in too much detail**: A characteristic that can prove to be problematic if not handled properly, being vague in their requirements will require some initial effort to create a clear requirements list—not only to guide the client in the right direction, but also to protect yourself from feature creep later in the project.

> **Doesn't ask to review your work in high detail**: Like being vague in their requirements, this is another characteristic that can become problematic later in the project if not handled with care. A lack of effort from the client to review work you provide means that there is a much higher scope for them to blame you if anything goes wrong resulting from your work not fully matching their expectation or requirements.

Progression suggestions

The trusting client is usually a pleasure to work with, but as identified, their trusting nature can introduce issues that affect the progression of the project and the quality of the end solution. As a result, some special measures need to be taken to steer the project and the client in the right direction for success.

> ➤ **Work with the client to produce a full requirements specification**: Whether it's through a series of meetings or delivered as a formal training course style consultancy session, taking the time at the beginning of the project to thoroughly build a picture of the client's requirements and have this recorded in a written document to ensure that you are able to fully understand what is required. The written document also acts as a point of reference for describing what is required in the end solution; an asset that protects you against disputes about the agreed delivery and feature creep.

> ➤ **Research the client as thoroughly as possible**: By knowing as much as possible about the client, you move yourself into a position that ensures you can provide the best advice and decisions tailored to the client's needs as an individual business. This not only results in a better solution and service for the client, but also better protects you against repercussions based on uninformed advice you may provide.

> ➤ **Have everything signed off**: Having a formal procedure for the client to sign off every stage of the project makes them psychologically aware of your progress as well as prompting them to check that the work you have provided meets their expectations. Not only does this act to improve the client's feedback for the success of the project, but it also protects you against future change requests, feature creep and disputes on quality that the client may otherwise expect you to resolve at a cost to yourself.

> ➤ **Build a plan that covers the client's current and future requirements**: The trusting client who hasn't fully defined their requirements specification is also less likely to have a clear plan for both the short and long term progression of their project. This type of client shows a need for proactive management, which it is in your interest to help them identify the direction they need to take. As identified previously, make sure to only provide advice that you are qualified and/or knowledgeable enough to provide in order to minimize your exposure to being sued should anything not go to plan. You might also want to consider the use of a disclaimer in your service agreement that relieves you of responsibility of consequences from suggestions provided—in other words it's the client's responsibility to speak to specialist professional on the subject.

The nasty client

This type of client will often show most of the characteristics of a difficult client, plus some surprises of their own. For most people, nasty clients are best avoided at all costs; they're not worth the effort, stress, or humiliation that they can cause.

Characteristics

Characteristics of a nasty client include the following:

➤ **Aggressive behavior to others**: Aggressive behavior can come in many forms, whether it is speech, threats, body language, or physical aggression such as frequently throwing objects and slamming doors. This type of behavior indicates that the client either gives no consideration to how other people view them or that they have no self-control. Either way, this causes much scope for problems to occur if they disagree with your future actions; do you really want to risk bearing the brunt of their aggression?

➤ **Malicious gossip:** Aside from the acceptable level of banter present in most work environments, gossip that is sincerely malicious shows a clear disregard for confidentiality and respect for others. It is true that there could be genuine reasons for a client to have a cause for concern and unhappiness with people they work with and know of, but professionals tend to value all of their professional relationships and discuss their concerns directly with the people in question—or at least in private with those it is of concern to. Client behavior of this nature suggests that they can cause you problems through failing to communicate their concerns directly to you, hence causing unnecessary damage to your reputation when they decide to spread malicious gossip about you

➤ **Name calling**: Clearly an unprofessional characteristic, name calling by the client in any way that's not within the realm of reasonable banter isn't positive to anyone in the professional environment. It shows a lack of respect for the people they work with, which is the foundation that all good working relationships are built upon. If your client can't truly respect you and/or others as a professional, then the seeds are already sown for a difficult working relationship that poses you with a high risk of being undervalued, unappreciated and taken advantage of

➤ **Extreme sarcasm:** Although not always an indication of a nasty client, uncalled for sarcasm can be an indication of a dismissive personality trait. This can cause problems if the client's expectations can't be met on the basis of technical, budget, resource, or available time

➤ **Boasting of unethical deals**: It's one thing to benefit at the expense of others such as gaining free labor from people needing to gain work experience, but it's an entirely different issue to boast about how the situation has been taken advantage of. A person who boasts in this way shows a lack of appreciation and confidentiality as well as indicating that they take pleasure in gaining at the expense of other people. In general, this type of person should never be trusted because they are likely to take advantage of your working relationship and leave you losing out financially or otherwise for their own gain

> ➤ **Publicly dismissing the skills and efforts of others**: Like sarcasm, this isn't necessarily a clear indication that the client will cause problems in a working relationship, but should raise awareness of potential issues ahead. This type of trait indicates that the client doesn't appreciate the finer details of the skills and time required to deliver a service, which if true, will make it much more difficult to communicate and negotiate terms that are critical to the success of the project such as the required time, resources, and budget

Progression suggestions

Nasty clients are difficult to work with and provide minimal margin for actions to keep the working relationship running smoothly. These clients are high risk because their attitude can lead to situations that damage your credibility and profitability—possibly to a point where the client doesn't pay anything.

> ➤ **Cancellation**: The earlier you can identify the characteristics of a nasty client, the better positioned you will be to make an exit from your involvement with them. Ideally, this would be before the commencement of any work or signing of contracts so that you have no legal obligations or financial commitment. Where work has already started, it is still worth considering options to make an exit; ideally with getting paid for your time commitments, but even without payment, the cost of continuing could be significantly higher than writing off the amount you're already owed for the project, especially where there is a risk of the client not paying their bill

> ➤ **Payment upfront**: Never trust the nasty client because they tend to lack the traits required to ethically engage in business. Request payment upfront so that they can't withhold payment as a tactic to hold you to ransom for getting you to do unpaid work or bargain you down on price in return for a faster payment; even worse is when they have no intention to pay after getting their free extras. Payment upfront combined with other elements mentioned in this list provides you with additional negotiation strength when the client starts to use underhand tactics to take advantage of your time and skills

> ➤ **Clear documentation**: There is a higher requirement to document everything in fine detail because the nasty client can't be trusted to keep to their word or distort agreements. Project documentation should pay specific attention to exactly what you have agreed to deliver, when it should be delivered and at what price. This agreement should use watertight wording that makes it impossible for the client to claim an alternative interpretation that allows them to insert additional work or escape payment

> ➤ **Micro-milestones**: Keeping each project milestone short allows you to charge the client in advance of work commencement and can avoid situations where the client manages to swindle you into providing more work than you agreed to. When combined with clear documentation and upfront payments, this becomes a highly effective negotiation tool that protects you against unethical business practices used by nasty clients looking to take advantage with a view to gaining free labor

> ➤ **Written communications**: The nasty client's favorite forms of communication are the types that can't be used as evidence, especially when it may come to you extracting payments from them through the legal system. Spoken agreements are difficult to prove and even recorded telephone/video conversations may not be admissible as evidence if no permission was given by the client to make the recordings in the first place. It is because of the unreliability of spoken agreements as evidence that all significant communications should only be accepted in written formats, which includes e-mail as well as signed paper letters. For situations relating to teleconference, face to face or phone communications that detail important project requests/decisions, simply request for the client to provide an overview in an e-mail or letter, allowing you to keep this as part of your project documentation

> ➤ **Employees and collaborators**: Extra effort should be made to protect the people you work with against nasty clients through the use of formal policies and procedures. This is not so much to protect them from lesser issues such as verbal abuse you can expect from this type of client, but more to do with them becoming victim of unethical business practices that the client may engage to take advantage of their naivety to gain free labor, escape payment or even to gain commitments for unachievable goals. At best, this leads to a situation where people you work with are used as tools to get you obligated to delivering unfavorable business deals. The more serious situation is where the nasty client intends to use the commitments they gain as evidence to sue you for more than the project is worth; which may be the entire purpose of the client's project. It is for these reasons that you should ensure to make clear in any contracts that it is only yourself who has authorization to accept additions, alterations and commitments to the project plan. Policies and procedures should also be used to ensure that the people you work with are aware of how to handle communications and situations when dealing with the client; helping to avoid accidentally giving the client the ability to gain commitments and/or liability admissions through loose wording. Ideally, this risk can be reduced by eliminating communication channels that allows your employees and collaborators to speak directly with the client

The price-conscious client

The price conscious client will come in many forms; some are motivated by getting the best deal, some are restricted by their available budget, and others are motivated by a lack of knowledge, meaning that the only factor that they can evaluate value is with price.

Characteristics

The price conscious client will have at least one of the following characteristics:

> ➤ **Uses price as the main factor in their purchasing decision:** This is a characteristic that can cause problems with the project, as to win the work, you may have to push your prices so low that the scope you have to make profit doesn't cover anywhere near what your time is worth. Being self employed, you aren't covered by any minimum wage laws, hence you have to be careful not to quote so low that you end up working for less than you would earn flipping burgers at one of those fast food chains we all know of! You also need to factor in the overhead you spend on the client in terms of time; a client who requires more time to communicate with will mean more time spent on the project, even though it is not more time spent on the actual technical production you are being hired to deliver

> ➤ **Uses tough negotiation tactics to drive down costs**: People who have this quality indicate a good level of business acumen and as a result should know what realistic costs for their requirements are. Their tough negotiation tactics could be motivated by a lack of technical knowledge or simply to get the best deal. Either way, this can lead to difficulties in the project if you allow them to negotiate you beyond a point that is realistic. Not only will likely have to cut corners to remain profitable, but the client's tough negotiation tactics will likely force you to complete any specification agreement to the word, making it likely that you will work for far below what your time is worth and possibly make a loss

> ➤ **Expects the same quality output as more expensive solutions**: A clear indication that the client will be difficult to work with because they either don't have a realistic expectation of what can be achieved, or that they have no intention of working in a relationship that is mutually beneficial. This becomes part of a toxic combination when the client also uses pricing as the main factor for their purchasing decisions. There are a number of factors that lead to this expectation, such as a lack of technical understanding and the client having already compared their requirements to other more expensive options in the market

> ➤ **May compromise on quality to lower costs**: This is certainly an indication that the client is at least realistic.. The compromise on the quality accepted may come after some tough negotiation or it could be offered upfront, the latter certainly being an indication of a client who has realistic expectations of what is achievable and who could be good to work with. To protect yourself against future disputes with clients who turn difficult, it's important that you have any agreement on compromising the quality of the end solution documented in writing

Progression suggestions

Price conscious clients should be considered very carefully, as the budget expectations for the project can lead to problems that affect how you can achieve a successful completion, keep the client happy and earn a decent living. The key to success in the project lies in the following:

> ➤ **Information**: Make sure that the client understands the full details of what you are offering with your service to meet their requirements. They must understand that solutions provided by cheaper service providers may not offer all of the features, quality and experience you offer, so providing them with the information they need to make a fair comparison will help to avoid you being undercut by someone looking to cut corners.

> ➤ **Negotiation**: If the client is pushing you to lower your prices, you can offer to drop non-critical elements of your service in return for a lower price. This is a useful tactic to use because it allows the client to win in their price negotiation without compromising your profitability; therefore allowing you to maintain a standard of quality that will ultimately satisfy the client. Good negotiations result in solutions that satisfy all parties involved.

> ➤ **Education**: Making sure that the client understands the basics of the technicalities that your service offers is important, as it will save you from dealing with unnecessary phone calls and e-mails that damage your productivity. Educating your clients also helps them to understand the real value of what you are offering.

> ➤ **Tools**: Development and/or purchase of resources to help you become more efficient in providing your service and delivery of customer support and project management can lead to you providing a better service at a lower price without compromising your profitability. This type of resource is ideal for winning and successfully completing work for the price conscious client.

> ➤ **Productization**: As an extension of the previous mentioned tools, you can look into developing products based around the services you offer. This is especially good for selling to clients who are price or time-restricted, as it allows you to provide ready-made solutions at a fixed price without the need for unpredictable time investment. Your hourly rates can then be added to any standard product price for further modifications and enhancements required by the client. Good examples of productizing a service are website templates for website design and template contracts for legal support services.

Summary

There are different types of client that require different methods to work with. Clients are likely to show characteristics that fall into several of the categories mentioned in this chapter, which is what makes every client unique. The success of your projects will often depend on your ability to choose the right approach to working with the client, so there is an urgency to make sure you are able to identify what categories each client falls under before you start to develop the project with them.

Whereas clients will talk about multiple success factors, it is important to remember that there are only two factors that you should seek to address—being profitable and keeping the client happy will result in a conclusion to the project that satisfies both parties. Although this may sound obvious and straightforward, the difficulty in achieving this is affected by the characteristics of the client, with some characteristics being problematic to manage and posing undesired risks to your profitability and reputation.

In addition to having methods for dealing with the different client characteristics you encounter, generating savings to cover your expenses for several months will allow you to avoid situations where you are forced to accept work from clients you observe showing undesired characteristics. Being in this position allows you to be selective of the projects you take on so that you can avoid situations where bad clients lead to unjustified loss of money and damage to your reputation. Your time can instead be spent working with good clients who are easy to work with, appreciate your contribution to their project, willing to pay what you're worth and more likely to return for more of your services based on the trust they have developed for you.

With an understanding of how to identify characteristics of the clients who hire you, the next logical step is to understand how to manage them—the subject of the next chapter.

>7 Managing Clients

Knowing how to manage clients can make the difference between a project running smoothly, successfully and profitably. This chapter looks at methods to be used when working with clients in order to avoid problems that can derail the progress of the project and risk its success and your ability to make a profit.

Points of contact

Success in projects largely lies in good quality communication with the client and like managing the technical requirements of the client, it is much easier and efficient to get the message across when the lines of communication are simplified. It's for this reason that there should ideally only be one point of contact to communicate with in the client's organization so that:

- ➤ Agreements for work requests can't be disputed on the basis of authorization given by the wrong person—i.e. ensure that your point of contact has the final say and authorization.

- ➤ Work requirements provided are consistent—i.e. no conflicting requests due to the point of contact being able to have the final say.

- ➤ Repetition of communication is kept to a minimum by providing the designated point of contact the responsibility to relay information to the correct people, hence avoiding your time being consumed by multiple people calling or e-mailing you with the same questions.

- ➤ Support is easier to manage and co-ordinate—not only through the above mentioned reduction of communication repetition, but also by benefiting from the point of contact becoming more knowledgeable in the processes and issues relating to your service so that over time they can resolve more support issues without contacting you.

- ➤ Disputes are easier to manage and more likely to be genuine—it becomes very difficult to communicate dispute issues with multiple people who have different views of the situation, especially when complaints stem from information not reaching the right people in the first place.

Unfortunately not all client setups are ideal enough to allow for only one point of contact. In this type of scenario, several points of contact need to be identified at the start of the project that may include:

> **Project sponsor**: The person who has the final say on what is paid for any services to be provided. This person should always give a final authorization before any work proceeds to ensure there is no scope to dispute amounts to be paid once the work has been completed.

> **Co-coordinator**: The person who is responsible for co-coordinating the client's side of the project management and will be responsible for drawing up the project requirements as well as ensuring everyone has access to the right information— including those relating to support for end users.

> **Technical contacts**: The people who will provide the information and resources required to progress with the project. For more advanced projects, these are likely to be specialists in their field, such as a representatives of the IT and marketing departments who you need to collaborate with.

> **End user representatives**: A selection of real users of the solution you are to provide. Whether your are to provide an IT system, brochure or photography, feedback from a sample of people who will be using your solution is important to ensure that whatever you have created will be useful and/or appreciated by the people who will be using it. These people may also give feedback that leads to improving the solution by adding new features that add value and taking out or modifying those that aren't useful.

Not all of these contact types will be required by every project, whereas some projects will be flexible to have one person acting as two types mentioned above—such as the project co-coordinator being given authority act as the project sponsor with the ability to authorize payment agreements. Whether a full list of contact types is required or only a few, the important issues are to ensure:

> The least number of points of contact used to reduce your effort for managing the flow of communications is kept to a minimum.

> The right types of points of contact—a team who has the ability to provide the information and resources you require to progress as well as the authority to make decisions and commitments.

Performing risk assessment of the project

Regardless of whether you have a good working relationship with a client or not, all projects require an amount of risk assessment before and during their engagement. Although we all like to believe that our clients can be trusted and pose no risk to our business interests, it is basic business sense to have procedures in place that highlight potential risks of engaging any work provided by a client so that we identify potential problems early before they become a major issue.

The following are examples of considerations that should be taken into account when reviewing the amount of risk associated to a project:

➤ **Client personalities and politics**: These can cause issues that disrupt your ability to successfully complete the project. Are there any indications from your observations that the client could be difficult to work with? Are there any indications that politics within the client's organization may affect your work?

➤ **Business formation**: Limited companies and limited liability partnerships can be liquidated, posing a risk that their liquidation can leave you exposed to not being paid for your work. In addition to this, it is entirely legal for a business owner to transfer assets from a company they are about to liquidate to a new company in order to avoid paying their creditors—aka a phoenix company. The important factor to recognize with these type of business formations is that they are a separate legal entity to their owners, meaning that that you are dealing with the business entity and not the person. Never make the mistake of assuming that assets can be seized as a form of payment in the worst case scenario; even where the owner doesn't set up a phoenix company, assets they personally own are separate to the business.Sole traders can go bankrupt, making it very difficult for you to get paid for services you have provided if this happens. When someone is granted bankruptcy protection, they are released from any financial obligations they have, meaning that there is little you can do to regain any amounts you are owed; this can be a serious issue if you have incurred significant debts of your own to provide your services to anyone who declares bankruptcy. Complexities of a project's requirements can be massively over simplified if the client's description due to their lack of technical knowledge to describe all associated factors in detail.Pay extra caution when clients mention words like *only*, *easy* and *simple*. These types of words suggest that they perceive the work to be basic and therefore should require little effort and skill, commonly resulting expectations for a faster delivery at a lower cost than what it is realistic.

➤ **Practicalities of client requirements**: Clients will often have ideas of what they want that you know from your experience wont work. Clients will often listen to your feedback, but there are some who wont listen to your suggestions and will be adamant in proceeding with their own ideas—the dilemma being whether to work with them at the risk of souring the relationship when it goes wrong or to suggest that they hire someone else on the moral principle of only providing solutions that's within the client's interests. In addition to this, projects that you believe will fail could also have a financial element that affect the client's ability to pay your fee—in this case, it may be better to completely avoid the bigger risk of not getting paid by not taking on the project.

> ➤ **Implications of the client's requirements**: What are the consequences if the solution you deliver fails in any way? An air traffic control system poses much higher risk for consequences than an entertainment software system, even though both may require the same degree of skill, time and effort to develop.

>> ➢ What is it that you will be working to develop? And what are the dependencies that already exists? If you're being asked to make an update to the code for the above mentioned air traffic control system, you'd better make sure that you fully understand the design of the system and how each component integrates with each other, as introducing the changes you are asked to make can easily break other parts of the system without your knowledge. This principle isn't specific to software engineering, but also applies to many other professions such as accountancy, journalism and graphic design for brochures and books.

>> ➢ Is it safer to not make the changes?

Measuring complexity

A factor that can turn to become a problem is the complexity of the project. The very nature of spoken language is that the same sentence can be interpreted to have different meanings to different people. It should never be assumed that any project is easy—there's nothing more damaging to your industry and negotiation ability to have certain inexperienced service providers suggesting that a job is easy. This leads to the client:

> ➤ Assuming the job can be completed quickly.

> ➤ Expecting a lower price for your quote.

Unless you are working with a client who is clued up on the technicalities of the service you provide, details about the complexity of the work to be delivered should almost never be provided to the client other than to say it's more complicated to achieve than it sounds. Good reasons for this include:

> ➤ High risk of increasing expectations—especially for elements of the project that turn out to be more complicated to implement than expected.

> ➤ Gives the client scope to come up with unreasonable conclusions by measuring against previous tasks. This isn't good for elements of a project that sound similar to previous tasks, but require a lot more 'under the hood' work that isn't noticeable to the client.

> ➤ As it is often difficult to explain the complexities to the client in these circumstances, the client will often assume that you are elaborating on the additional effort required, leading to a potential compromise in your ability to negotiate on factors relating to payment and time scales for delivery.

> ➤ Unknown factors can make simple jobs more complicated.

> ➤ The client themselves can be an obstacle that turns a simple job into something much bigger.

With the above in mind:

> ➤ Never say anything is easy—it usually isn't and it compromises your ability to negotiate.

> ➤ Expect to find undisclosed information that will affect the work you do.

> ➤ Never commit to concrete delivery dates until you are happy that you have all of the information you require.

> ➤ If delivery dates are set to complete the project, ensure that you can identify components that can be dropped if complexity leads to you falling behind schedule. The components identified should be those that aren't critical to the functionality of the end solution and that can collectively save enough time to put you back on track.

Key performance indicators

Knowing in advance what the client is judging your performance on can provide you with the ability to focus your efforts on the areas that will capture their attention earlier in the project—allowing you to gain their confidence quickly. All clients are different, so you should avoid making assumptions about what aspects of your work will get the most attention.

Gaining an understanding of the client's key performance indicators comes from good communication—specifically in being able to ask the right questions in a way that the client understands. First impressions are also a major factor that will influence the how the client judges your performance; something as simple as explaining to the client what your work has involved and the benefits it delivers to them can make the difference between them being dissatisfied with your pace of work and being highly impressed with what you

> ➤ Ask questions at the start of the project about what they are expecting to see—if you are working on site, ask them at the start of each day about what they are expecting to see that day; this gives you a guideline on where your efforts should be focused, as well as early identification of any unrealistic expectations that need to be addressed.

> ➤ Identify the types of work the client values most—are they all about the visuals or are they more interested in working functionality?

> ➤ Never assume that delivering work to a good standard is enough to impress the client—make sure they know what you've done and why it's to a good standard.

> ➤ Discuss alternative options for anything you've identified as being a higher risk to develop—never be optimistic about delivery timescales and complexity.

> ➤ Define performance objectives as SMART:

> > ➢ **Specific** : In the sense that there is no scope for misinterpreting what is expected from you.

> ➤ **Measurable** : In that definitions for your goals are not vague and instead can be compared against metrics that can't be disputed at different stages of the project; i.e. instead of *to improve the loading time*, ensure that the wording is to become more specific such as *to reduce loading time to within 3 seconds*.

> ➤ **Achievable** : All objectives must be possible in order for you to meet them, whether it's technically, politically or with the available resources, skills and budget; we can aim to produce the best graphics, but we will never achieve this if we don't have the graphic skills.

> ➤ **Relevant** : Eliminate objectives that are outside the scope of what you deliver as part of your core skills; e.g. a client may confuse developing web software with delivering online marketing, in which you would need to eliminate any marketing objectives that are not directly related to software development.

> ➤ **Time-related** : Make sure that the client specifies the timeframe they expect the objective to be met within; avoid situations where they give you non specific suggestions such as *as soon as possible* or *whenever you're ready*—both of these have too much scope for the client to change their mind at any point, and especially where contracts are involved. Instead, time related objectives such as *to deliver xyz in 2 weeks* is specific to a point where you can evaluate upfront whether the objective is realistic.

Defining client expectations

Defining client expectations is important for the perceived progress of the project. Unlike managing their expectation, which is what happens once the project has begun, defining a client's expectations is about how you set their hopes before they have committed to buy from you. It is very easy to accidentally give the wrong impression about the complexity, financial and time requirements of their project, so being very aware about what you say in front of any prospective client is crucial to ensure that they avoid making assumptions that you are then later held meeting. Examples of delicate issues to discuss include:

> ➤ **Timescales for completion**: You should avoid mentioning anything about the completion time until you have the project specification fully finalized, good insight to the characteristics of the client and an understanding of all factors relating to the project. Many problems can be caused when you say something along the lines of *It could take x number of weeks/months, providing that we get all of the resources on time and we experience no problems, but don't take that as any guarantee!*, which often results in the client hearing *No problem, we can have it done and dusted within x weeks and we don't expect any problems—take that as our guarantee!*, when in fact the client turns out to be slow to deliver resources you require and causes problems both in terms of slowing your progress and having the assumption that you will deliver quickly regardless of issues encountered. If no time scales are mentioned, this type of problem can be avoided completely.

- **Complexity:** A classic mistake made by people who are new to freelancing is to assume or make work sound simpler than it really is. This causes the following major problems:

    - The client undervalues the skills required to do the job.

    - Increased risk of unknown factors relating to the work opening new complexities that increase the scope of the work requirements.

    - Opens scope for the client to assume quick progress on work that sounds simple, but in reality is difficult to produce.

    - Opens scope for the client to assume and/or demand a cheaper price based on their wrong assumptions for time requirements and undervaluing your skills.

    - Suggests to the client that anyone can do the job—resulting in you being perceived as easily disposable.

    - These are all the ingredients that can lead to a toxic problem in your project where the client begins to ask for more and more complicated features and additions that require much more time and costs than they expect. This type of problem can lead to a lack of confidence in your capabilities, resulting in the client ditching you for another service provider who they believe will be able to work faster and cheaper—which isn't good for anyone, especially if the client owes you money. Avoid this by never making assumptions on the complexity of the work and never mentioning words like easy, simple or basic in relation to anything you are to provide.

- **Price:** Clients who make assumptions on complexity will also make assumptions based on price. Like with these other factors, any mention of price should be restricted to only what your hourly rate is during initial briefings—never be pressured into suggesting any price on the spot, as many clients tend to mishear this as a final quote for the work and puts you in a difficult negotiating position should you find additional factors that will increase your time and cost requirements. Playing safe to avoid false expectations is always a policy that is best in the long run, but isn't necessarily good in the short-term if your competitors are making unrealistic or unsafe promises on time scales, complexity and price to make their proposal appear more attractive than yours. Should you feel this is the case, some of the following actions can be taken to gain trust and ensure that prospective clients are able to make an informed decision when deciding who to hire:

    - Provide documentation detailing the project development process as part of your sales literature—complete with information about key factors that they should be looking for in a service provider and how you meet the required standards.

> ➢ During your meeting with the prospective client, guide them through your project development documentation, informing them of the processes involved in creating their work and highlighting potential problems that can be occurred as well as consequences that can result from poor workmanship.
>
> Not only does this emphasize that you know what you are doing to gain trust from the prospect, it will also put the prospective client in a position where they can interrogate your competitors to identify those who are making false and unsafe promises.

Analyzing implications

Before starting to work on any project for a client, it's important to analyze all scope for implications that arise from your involvement. The most common implication of working on new projects is working with other service providers—who may be working with you as team members of the same project or on separate projects that require co-operation. To be successful, it's important for all parties to act within the best interest of the project and to avoid politics based on personal agendas.

It's important to identify the right strategy to use in progressing the project to completion and to satisfy quality, budget, and time scale delivery requirements. The following are implications that should be taken into consideration when evaluating these delivery requirements:

> ➤ **Work already started on the project:** In the best case scenario, existing work on the project will be developed to a high standard that will allow you to progress more efficiently and avoid implications on any changes you need to make. There will be a likely requirement to invest some time into learning how to make use of any existing work produced in order to allow you to maintain the quality and to take advantage of any resources developed to avoid time wastage and duplication of work.In less than ideal scenarios, existing work will be produced to a lesser standard that will result in you having to invest excessive time to check accuracy and ability to make changes efficiently. In the worst case scenario, it may be identified that restarting any existing work from scratch will produce a solution that is delivered in less time, is more accurate and will have advantages for future productivity and maintainability; Such decisions should never be taken lightly, as this will result in massively extending the work requirements of the project—the question being whether any extended effort requirements will help deliver the project within the required budgets and time scales in both the short and longer term. When opting to create a replacement, another issue worth considering is whether there are any components that can be reused in the new implementation; this will certainly be the case when the system already has production data in use.

> ➤ **Politics of the client's organization**: It's important to know who to approach with which information to avoid implicating yourself in scenarios where people become unhappy or discover information they shouldn't have access to Client politics can result in certain people withholding information that is required for you to make accurate decisions and progress with your work. This can be as a result of people perceiving the project to be a threat to their position or simply due to a personal dislike of other employees of the client who are involved with your work.

> ➤ **The client's business processes**: A client who runs their business or department with highly efficient and structured processes is more likely to apply the same type of methodology to working with you, resulting in them developing a structured process for working with you on the project. A client who is disorganized in managing their business or department is also likely to be disorganized when working with you, resulting in potential problems to get information and feedback from them. The solution that you are to provide needs to fit within the client's business processes. The same solution for a business with a set of business processes won't necessarily work for another business of the same type that has different business processes. The key issue to identify is that all businesses are different— even if they offer the same products and services targeting the same market.

> ➤ **Individuals working on the project** : whether they are employed by the client or are other service providers.

> ➤ **Skills and expertise**: Always know what work to delegate to the right people and which opinions should be taken with higher authority.

> ➤ **Communication abilities**: Knowing which is the most effective way to communicate with individual team members will avoid many problems. It's very damaging to a project's progression when other members fail to listen or misinterpret instructions that result in lost time through duplication of work.

> ➤ **Team management**: It's important that the team is properly coordinated to avoid members producing work that doesn't fit with other components produced by the team.

> ➤ **Politics**: Some people may act for what's in their own best interest over that what's best for the project. This can be especially true for people who want to appear to be making a more important contribution and who want deflect blame on themselves for anything that goes wrong.

Defining an exit strategy

Although it should always be the intention to successfully complete the project in question to a level that the client has requested and is satisfied with, any number of situations can occur that will limit your ability to complete and deliver the project. For this reason, there should always be a strategy to exit the project without leaving the client in the lurch. Exit strategies should include:

> ➤ A definition of notice period to be given to the client to ensure that they have enough time to make any preparations—if any.

> ➤ Potential suppliers that you can introduce to the project to replace you.

> ➤ Training procedures for any replacement supplier(s) to be engaged as part of the handover phase, ensuring that the new service provider is able to use the work you have provided to a sufficient standard and without wastage of time.

Analyzing the client

You can't assess the risk that a client can pose to your success and profitability on a project unless you have information beforehand about how they operate. Although there is no substitute for being able to measure a client from previous experiences of working with them, there are a number of ways that you can obtain an amount of information that will help you in estimating what risks a client will pose to any possible project and working relationship.

Commitment

A client's commitment to a project will often be a defining factor in a successful implementation—no matter how good your project management and technical skills are, your output will always rely on what the client inputs. There's an IT acronym known as **GIGO (Garbage In Garbage Out)** that accurately describes the issue in that if the client doesn't put the required effort into the project, then they wont get what they want out of the project.

Although it's difficult to see how important a client sees their project, a number of factors can be taken into account when evaluating and testing their commitment:

> ➤ **Planning assistance**: This could be in the form of traveling to you for meetings and/or providing a detailed list of all of their requirements. If they are able to fully commit to helping you in the first stages, then the chances are much higher that they will be committed enough to provide the on-going assistance you will require once the project has started—whether it be feedback, testing or defining additional requirements.Keep in mind that clients have different levels of technical abilities; hence not all clients will be able to help you with everything you suggest. However, even clients who are technically restricted should show a minimum commitment to take time out to see you face to face—ideally traveling to you at least once, which shows more commitment to achieve their requirements.

➤ **Response times**: Slow response times to information requested relating to the project is an indication that the client is too busy with other aspects of their business; similar but worse to slow response time are unpredictable response times, which introduce difficulties for you to plan your workflow. This isn't good for projects because it leads to either the end solution not matching the client's expectations due to lack of input, and/or inefficiencies caused by delays and duplication of work caused by delays in the client feedback..Clients who have a slow response characteristic often complement this by having an expectance for you to respond to their requests ASAP and have a quick turnaround time. This becomes problematic when you aren't able to plan your schedule because you don't know when you will be able to progress to the next stage—plus you will also have other projects to manage that will make it difficult to quickly react to feedback that isn't scheduled.

➤ **Quality of information provided** :A detailed specification showing what is required is a good indication that the client is committed to the project through their prior time investment and are therefore likely to assist in providing further information and feedback that you require to successfully implement and complete the project to a standard that everyone is happy with.Some clients may have an idea of what they want, but may not have the abilities to define their requirements in a detailed document. In this scenario, you can test their commitment by offering to help them build their requirements specification. If this is the scenario you face, the client's commitment should be tested through ensuring that they have full input—if they have you define all of the requirements for them, then this could be an indication of a problematic working relationship and leaves you vulnerable to features of delivery that the client assumes should be part of the standard delivery, but aren't defined in their specification.

➤ **Feedback and execution**: To give a detailed and bespoke service, you will provide a lot of advice and will often write reports as part of your consultancy. A client who is committed will take this information on board and will provide feedback—even if they don't agree with your suggestions. A client who keeps asking the same questions and or gives no feedback that is positive or negative indicates a potential lack of commitment to listen and/or read your advice. This can be problematic for project planning that requires the client to provide feedback and actions to be implemented for the project to proceed and succeed. This factor can be tested transparently through your initial consultation process. Using a few open questions that allows the client to provide their opinion of what you have said in a meeting and on any written materials you have provided them with is a great way to see if they have taken the time to at least made a small effort to listen and/or review the information that you have prepared for them.

Ethics and difficulty

The most effective way to evaluate whether a client is difficult to work with or not is to spend a number of days working with them at their office. From this, you will be able to gather information on their office culture, how the client deals with other suppliers, their work ethics and staff opinions of the key decision makers that you will be working with. From this, it becomes easy to see first-hand how they deal with that may occur when you are working with them and to identify any warning signs—such as the client withholding payment from suppliers, boasting of unethical business deals, complaining of other service suppliers and lack of trust of employees to their employer.

The main downside to this method of observation is the amount of time required to dedicate the number of days to work on site with the client as well as giving the impression that you are already committed to taking on the project. As a result, this type of observation activity is best reserved for higher value contracts for which you can negotiate to have a trial starting period to deliver your services.

Secondary research is another option that can be engaged either in addition or as an alternative. In this this type of observation, you would gather information from other people involved with the client, whether this be staff, suppliers or anyone else who has been involved in working with their business. From using a mixture of direct and indirect questions depending on who you are speaking to, it will be possible to build a picture of what the client is like to work with.

Financial

A critical part of making any potential project worthwhile your involvement is to be paid—not just at some point, but on time and for the right amount of what your time investment is worth. Failure of clients to pay what they owe on the dates that they should and the right amounts can lead to your business, lifestyle and family suffering as a result, so knowing beforehand if the client can be trusted to be ethical on payments allows you to put procedures in place to protect yourself from being financially taken advantage of.

Researching the level of financial risk that a client poses can be fairly straightforward if you know where to look. Reports on submitted accounts for limited companies are available to purchase online at Companies House (www.companieshouse.gov.uk) via their WebCheck service. In a similar way, financial information can be obtained about individuals through performing a credit check via one of the many online agencies who provide credit scores for individuals.

Researching publicly available information is only one part of the puzzle, as company accounts and credit checks will not reveal information relating to bad business ethics and late payments to regular suppliers that will cause you problems. To gain an understanding of this, it is worth researching the client's existing suppliers and other people they have dealt with to get feedback on questions about their business relationships with the client. Social networking websites like Twitter (www.twitter.com) and LinkedIn (www.linkedin.com) are useful for this type of research, not to mention the old fashioned business networking methods.

Learning and execution

All clients have a different level of technical capability, which will usually be one of the factors that defines your working relationship with them. Some clients will be knowledgeable in everything that you do and will want to hire you as an extra pair of hands, whilst others will have little to no knowledge of the technicalities and will fully rely on your advice. Between these, you will get many more clients who have some amount of technical knowledge, but not enough to do everything themselves.

The learning and execution element of a working relationship should be central to any plan that is defined for working with a client. Some clients will be proactive in working with you so that both you and they can learn about what is required by the project to succeed, whereas others will leave the finer details to you and simply demand that the bigger picture be achieved—in which case, it's up to you to be proactive and identify how everything is to be achieved. Both of these clients pose their own types of risk to the success, a profitability of the project and therefore need to be approached differently.

Clients who are proactive in the working relationship will often have set ideas, which is usually good, but can be a problem if you know from experience that their specific requests will cause technical problems or make bad business sense. In this scenario, it is best to analyze the end goal for what the client wishes to achieve and present options to proceed that are as close as possible to how they want it implemented without compromising on the technical or business maintainability that you know will later become problematic. Using and developing political skills comes in very handy for this type of scenario, as the same meaning can be written and said in multiple ways, each of which will be interpreted differently to the client—the aim being to guide the client in the right direction without making them feel that it's you who is making the major decisions.

On the other hand, the type of client who isn't proactive in engaging the project's development will not cause any of the above mentioned issues, but will provide the risk of not giving enough information. If not managed properly, this can lead to a lot of wasted time on parts of the project that aren't important or in the worst case scenario the end solution not being what the client wants. The key to managing this type of client is to give them regular incremental updates on your progress, showing them the benefits of what each update makes to the bigger picture and getting them to confirm that they are happy—or to provide feedback on what they would like to be altered.

The type of learning and execution style of a client can be observed through initial engagements with the client—whether through an initial consultation, general conversation or starting to work on the project. Clients who are more proactive in the project development will talk a lot more about the specifics of how it is meant to be implemented. If they are proactively providing you with materials and suggesting how things should work, this is a good indication that you are best to let them be in the driving seat of the project and then diplomatically intervene when you can see they are heading in the wrong direction.

The less proactive type of client can usually be observed as speaking more about the end goal and not as much as about how it will be achieved. As they see the bigger picture, they are likely to openly ask questions on your opinion on what should be done next. This is where you should define the tone of communications as the leader in the project, but ensuring that you keep the client updated at every step.

Consistency

Many clients will start their working relationship with you without fully knowing what they want. All clients vary in their clarity of vision for what they want, and as their consultant it's your responsibility to extract all of the information needed to proceed with the work and avoid problems that may occur later.

Clients who show a high degree of inconsistency need extra attention to avoid causing headaches for both parties. As standard practice, a project should:

> **Start with a formal written specification**: Not only does this help to avoid misunderstanding the depth of the project requirements, it also protects you against disputes relating to what is to be delivered for the agreed price.

> **Have all requirements clearly defined in the specification**: Wording within a specification that is vague leaves too much scope for the client to expect more than what you perceive to be agreeing to. Especially with clients who are inconsistent, this will usually lead to additional requests being defined as part of an original requirement and leaves you exposed to being taken advantage of if you are being paid a fixed fee.

> **Have everything signed off**: Having the client sign to confirm that they are happy with any agreements or work that you provide protects you against any future accusations that the work was unsatisfactory resulting in requests for free alterations or refunds. Although we like to believe that all clients that we work with are ethical, there will be a minority who will pull any tricks they can to get free labor.

> **Be broken down into milestones**: This is a good way to show the client how much work is involved and to ensure that there are specific sign-off points to protect you from being asked to make further alterations without additional payment.

> > Through using a formal and documented approach to managing clients, you produce a paper trail that helps to avoid any confusion as well as to make the client more aware of their ambition with the project.

Negotiation

An art form of it's own and deserving of it's own dedicated chapter (see *Chapter 8, Negotiation*), the ability to negotiate well is an important part of the mix that makes a successful freelancer. Without good negotiation abilities, your projects will have a higher risk of failure and you are more likely to be earning less than it's worth to take on the work you win.

Good negotiation strategies aren't about being able to win one over on the client, but are more about finding a solution that is mutually beneficial. Every project will have a different priority on time, budget and scope of the delivery—by knowing the order of importance, you can tailor your negotiation strategy to become more appealing to the client without compromising on your profitability.

Cash flow issues

Whether intentional or not, it is very easy for clients to waste your time—especially when you are charging a fixed fee and where you aren't being paid until completion of the project. If not managed properly, this type of issue can cause you many cash flow problems, as not only will such client behavior reduce your profitability on their work, it can:

> ➤ Reduce your availability to make money from other projects—especially if the client is demanding all of your time exclusively.

> ➤ Reduce your productivity, such as through excessive support requirements, hence reducing your ability to complete other work timely and profitably.

> ➤ Extend the date that you can invoice for their work though additional requirements generated.

> ➤ Extend the date that you can invoice other clients through your decreased productivity.

A typical example of this type of scenario is a design client who is constantly changing their branding requirements for a project. Even if they are offering to pay extra for each change, they are still causing a cash flow problem for the service provider who has agreed to accept payment upon completion of the project by causing more work that extends the invoicing date—for which it is standard for the client to have 30 days beyond this to pay the amount owed.

Such nightmare cash flow problems are not often caused intentionally by clients, but more through communication issues, set procedures and/or a lack of business acumen by either the freelancer or the client.

Avoiding cash flow problems

The solution to avoiding cash flow problems will always lie at the start of the project when negotiations and definitions of terms take place. After this phase, it becomes much more difficult for the service provider to then negotiate outside what is written in any signed agreement, whether it is an increase in the available budget, the specifics of what is to be delivered or the date(s) of payment for the services provided. A good agreement that avoids cash flow issues will:

> ➤ Define in detail what is to be delivered and leave no scope for misinterpretation that can lead to extras being defined as part of loosely worded text.

> ➤ Ensure that project phases are paid for in advance to avoid the possibility of the client not paying for services provided through bankruptcy or liquidation; clients who are not willing to make a deposit and commit to a payment schedule may be an indication of them having payment problems in general—giving you an opportunity to reject the project before it becomes a problem.

> ➤ Define a procedure for changes to the work agreement, ensuring that change requests only come through designated representatives of the client who have the authority to authorize an increase to the available budget. The procedure should insist that all such requests be documented in writing to avoid a scenario where costs for work that deviate from the original agreement are disputed on the basis of no authorized permission given.

Summary

Client behavior has a big impact on your ability to work on a project, so having formal policies and procedures in place will help to avoid problematic situations occurring that can derail the project. Time spent on researching the client and their project requirements before you commit to anything will pay off in the long run by allowing you to make better decisions, especially in situations where you discover that the client has a poor credit history, hence making you aware of an increased risk of them failing to pay for your work.

No matter how good your technical and project management skills are, the success of the project will always be dependent on the client's commitment to the project. This includes the client's willingness to provide you with the information and resources you need to get the job done and to the standard that they seek. Have policies in place that make it clear to the client what is expected of the, making sure that you don't try to fill in the missing pieces—not only does this increase your costs, but in all likeliness will result in some unknown mistake being made that the client can hold you to account in an attempt not to pay their bill or even sue you.

The bottom line of all projects you spend your time on should always be about getting paid for your work, so make sure to have policies and processes in place that don't leave you vulnerable to cash flow issues when clients delay paying you for several months and who may use the amounts owed as a way to force you to do extra unpaid work.

With an understanding of how to manage your clients, the next step is being able to negotiate—whether it is the details of the project specification and price you are being paid, or for situations that may occur in a project that needs an outcome that suits everyone's interest. The next chapter looks at how negotiation skills can be used to assist in taking projects to a successful conclusion that favors all parties.

>**8**

Negotiation

A critical ability to have in your toolset of business skills is the ability to negotiate. This isn't a skill only applied to business environments, but pretty much every area of life. Being a good negotiator allows you to turn unfavorable situations to your advantage, whether it be the house chores you are expected to do or how much you are being paid by a client for your work.

"Thus, what is of supreme importance in war is to attack the enemy's strategy."
- Sun Tzu

The Winning Formula

There are three main areas that a freelancer needs to negotiate a good deal to ensure the best chances of satisfying the client and to be profitable:

Timeframe

Often, and especially those who don't understand the technicalities of the service you offer, clients have unrealistic expectations for how long it should take to deliver the solution they are hiring you to provide. Having a specific focus on the timeframe element will allow you to persuade the client to offer a delivery schedule that is more realistic to achieve. This is because it doesn't put you under pressure in a way that risks late delivery. It also avoids the project interfering with the time you have committed for other work you may be involved with.

Budget

The factor that is closely related to the timeframe and depth of the project, the project budget needs to reflect both what is delivered and when. A bad result in negotiating the project budget will not only restrict your profitability for the project, but will also affect your ability to deliver on quality and within deadlines; you can much of the work yourself, but if you have to start hiring other people to help meet deadlines or deliver parts of the project that are outside of your expertise, you will run into problems if you don't have enough cash to pay them.

Aside from how the budget affects your ability to deliver, a poorly negotiated budget can also lead to you losing money on the project either directly through spending more on resources than you are being paid or indirectly through losing out on time that could have been invested on more profitable work.

Depth

The depth factor is all about how detailed the requirements of the project are. Clients will often ask for much more than they need, over complicating the project and massively increasing the amount of time required in the process. The depth issue is often also made worse when clients who don't understand the technicalities of their requirements, leading to assumptions being made about time and budget requirements. that many aspects of their requirements are simple and should only take minutes or hours to produce, when in reality what sounds simple is a complicated task that takes days or even weeks to deliver.

In situations where a clients assume a week's worth of effort can be produced in just a few hours, negotiating on the budget and timeframe becomes very difficult if the client is adamant that their request is simple and refuses to listen to your advice. This type of situation can be avoided by reducing the depth of the project, allowing you to minimize any complexities involved that may damage your ability to meet the client's expectations and remain profitable. This is state of the specification's simplification is called the MVP – the minimum viable product.

An example of depth reduction would be where a client has high expectations that you know to be unachievable in terms of time, budget or what can technically be delivered. Starting the project with a direct focus on negotiating a reduction of the specification's complexity to become the bare minimum required for the project to benefit the client's ambitions will help to identify where development efforts must be focused and identifies unnecessary features that may cause problems in completing the project. Being able to successfully negotiate the client's expectations to the minimum requirements means less risk for the project and more options to upgrade later as and when time, budget and technology becomes available.

Strategic Negotiation Phases

Negotiating a deal for a project is very rarely something that starts and finishes in just one session. Instead, negotiation is something that remains ongoing throughout a project – especially when a client is asking for more without suggesting additional payment or alteration to the delivery date. The process of negotiating agreements for in freelance and contract projects can be split into 5 stages:

Stage 1: Evaluate Priorities & Characteristics

Before you can start serious negotiations on delivering the project, you need to know what the client places a higher priority on and whether they are realistic on all parts of the winning formula. Clients and their requirements come in all shapes and sizes, often with the client's situation dictating what elements they place a higher priority on. Although you may have already worked for the client, you must never assume that their priorities will be the same for the current project. For example, price could have been a priority for previous projects, but a new situation dictating the need for the new project could make price irrelevant and delivery time becoming the top priority. Identifying this provides you with a strategic advantage, allowing you to suggest an express delivery charge that would allow you to bring in extra resources to complete the project faster or simply to better compensate you for working out of hours.

"Knowing the enemy enables you to take the offensive..." — Sun Tzu, The Art of War

Some clients are much more generous than others, meaning it's important to identify the difficulty level of all buyers to offer a fair price for your time. Serious negotiation and drafting proposals take a lot of time that you don't want to be investing in people who aren't realistic about the time or budget required to build their requirements. If not managed properly, you could end up spending more time on negotiating than what the client is willing to pay for the entire project, making it more attractive to cut your losses and not take on the project after all.

Some methods you can use to filter serious buyers who meet "your" requirements to make the profit margins you want include:

➤ Asking them directly about their budget.

➤ This could be via e-mail, telephone or as part of a questionnaire.

➤ Asking them about what they've spent on other aspects of their business.

➤ Through asking them about what they've invested in other areas of their business, you can get a clearer picture of the price bracket that they want to spend based on industry standard prices.

➤ Reviewing the size of client's business and the prices of the services or products that they offer.

➤ A small business selling services and products at bargain basement prices is more likely to only be able to offer such low prices by cutting corners on their own costs.

➤ Asking detailed questions about the client's requirements.

➤ Clients will often make their requirements sound more complicated than they need to be, hence identifying alternatives to anything complicated can be used to satisfy their needs whilst saving on time and costs at the same time.

➤ Asking detailed questions about why and when the client needs the final solution.

> ➤ The typical view of many clients is that they need everything yesterday. Although this may be the case with a small number of your projects, the majority will not be as urgent. Questioning a prospective client about their motivations for the project and the reasons for their urgency will allow you to gain a clear picture of the situation so that you can tailor your negotiating accordingly.

Prospective clients who indicate unrealistic expectations in terms of budget or delivery timeframe are not always an instant case for rejection. In some cases you will be able to propose an entirely different solution to what they are asking for, which allows you to win the work, satisfy the client and be profitable with the project. If this is an option, it's important to identify what the alternative solution is as early as possible to avoid wasting effort on what can't be agreed for the original proposal.

Stage 2: Depth Reduction

The ideal project for anyone who is self-employed is a project that is easy to deliver and highly profitable. Projects that require extensive expertise and skills to deliver are much more likely to increase risk, time and cost requirements.

> *"The greatest victory is that which requires no battle."* — Sun Tzu, The Art of War

Although it may seem more advantageous to you as the service provider to avoid depth reduction, it is actually a benefit to both parties:

> ➤ **Reduction of risk** means that there is less scope for anything to go wrong within the project – whether that is the project taking longer to complete than originally anticipated or faults in the final delivery. Both of these examples are likely to affect your cash flow and profitability, hence eliminating factors that pose a risk will avoid situations that affect your ability to satisfy the client, maximize your profitability and ensure that the project doesn't affect your cash flow.

> ➤ **Minimizing the cost** to deliver the project will mean that you can either maximize your profit or pass on the savings directly to the client in ways that allows you to become more competitive on price. This is advantageous when you have identified price as being a major influence for the client's project and their decision making.

> ➤ **Minimizing the time** for completion means that you have options to add in margins for anything unexpected and plan the project around your other commitments. The client will also benefit from being more likely to have the project delivered by the date they have stated they need it as well as to see the benefits of the project sooner – which could mean more savings or more money generated.

> ➤ Depth reduction is especially useful to freelancers who are working on fixed price projects and/or where payment is only received upon completion of project milestones. Although depth reduction can reduce the overall payment received for the project, it is better to be paid more for each hour you've worked than it is to work more hours for a lower hourly rate. Options remain for selling additional features to the client, as well as providing you with availability to take on projects from other clients.

Stage 3: Define Time scales

Timescales for delivery of a project will have an impact on your ability to manage your workload, as well as the quality of the end result. Freelancers and contractors are often posed with the problem of the client asking for too much to be delivered in too little time – meaning that the only way they can achieve this is at the expense of time available to other clients and/or working out of hours. It needn't be this way, as with a bit of negotiation based on information obtained from the previous stage to 'evaluate the priorities and characteristics' of the client, a timetable of delivery can often be presented that both satisfies the client's requirements and provides you with enough margin to manage anything that is unexpected.

> *"When we are near, we must make the enemy believe we are far away..."* — *Sun Tzu, The Art of War*

After reviewing the priorities of the client and learning more about their situation, your conclusion will often be along the lines of the client needing some type of prototype version in the short term that will be refined over time to become the real working system. Examples of this include:

➤ A minimum viable version of software that has the most urgent features available in the first version and later releases incorporating features that aren't as urgent..

➤ A draft article for a magazine that shows the structure of what is to be written, but isn't full edited, featured with quotes or fully fact checked – these will be added for the final version.

➤ A book or website design showing the general theme to be used and flow of content, but without any of the bespoke illustrations or text content to be used in the final release.

➤ A website that has several sections available for the launch date and new sections added later.

It's not uncommon to find the urgency suggested by prospective clients to be somewhat exaggerated. Never be tempted to promise to meet a client's deadline to win the work when you know that their expectations aren't realistic or where there is only a small time flexibility margin for you to meet the deadline – something unexpected is almost guaranteed to happen, such as the client not providing the full resources you require in time or them being difficult to manage. Instead of focusing your pitch to win the work by promising to deliver on the date they expect, you should negotiate on how and when the solution is to be delivered – opening scope for you to satisfy the prospective client's more urgent needs whilst remaining realistic on what can be achieved.

Stage 4: Terms of Delivery and Engagement

In most situations you will have a standard set of terms and conditions for which you will provide your services, covering standard issues relating to terms of payment and delivery of your service. In some situations, a prospective client will have unique requirements such as a non-disclosure agreement for you to agree to before the project can proceed. It's important to identify the major difference between defining your own set of terms for commencement of a project and signing anything provided by anyone other than yourself; the difference being that any terms provided by anyone else is likely to be written in favour to assist with their interests and agendas.

> *"If we wish to wrest an advantage from the enemy, we must not fix our minds on that alone, but allow for the possibility of the enemy also doing some harm to us, and let this enter as a factor into our calculations."* — Sun Tzu, The Art of War

In short, you should:

- ➤ Have a standard set of terms and conditions for your normal methods of engaging and delivering a project.

- ➤ Treat any documents needing your signature from the prospective client with suspicion – ask many questions to get an overview of what the document's agenda is and read the document in detail; this is especially true for NDAs (non disclosure agreements), which may restrict you from mentioning the project on your CV or portfolio – even worse would be anything that restricts you from working on any similar types of project, hence reducing your work opportunities..

- ➤ Never sign any agreement upfront – always ensure that you can take the agreement away to thoroughly read through in your own time. This will provide you with the advantage of being able to read through all aspects of their terms at your own pace without feeling pressured by the prospective client who is watching and waiting for you to read the terms, which in itself may affect your ability to properly interpret the agreements agenda.

- ➤ Read any agreements objectively – leave no scope for vague wording to have multiple meanings and highlight any parts that raises cause for concern. Anything identified with the wording that isn't rectified before you sign on the dotted line can cause you major problems if anything went to court, as vague wording can open scope for the client to dispute what has been agreed and cleverly worded clauses can result in you agreeing to things you aren't aware of. In the worst case scenarios, these wordings can lead to you being unpaid, being committed to spending more on the project than the client pays you and providing ownership intellectual property that isn't included in the intended agreement.

- ➤ Show the agreement to a solicitor or someone with relevant knowledge if you are in any doubt to the implications of any parts of the prospective client's agreement or aren't able to fully read and understand the document.

- ➤ Negotiate changes to the wording of anything you've highlighted as a cause for concern.

> ➤ The majority of clients will not have a devious agenda and will only be looking to protect their business interests on an ethical level, with many providing agreements for you to agree to based on standard templates – hence wording that causes you cause for concern often comes from the client using a template that they haven't fully adapted. However, as a principle in business, no prospective client should be trusted to a point where you sign any agreements without thorough scrutiny of all clauses and wording. This isn't about mistrusting the prospective client, but more about being aware that:

> ➤ Prospective clients may have a different view of the working relationship than you, hence opening much scope for future disagreements that can sour the relationship.

> ➤ The expectations of both parties for what is to be delivered and the associated terms of use and ownership of intellectual property may be different, hence allowing for future disputes if unchecked.

> ➤ Prospective clients may have unethical agendas that will harm your business.

Apart from the last point raised, it's clear from the above that thorough scrutiny of terms provided by the client is more about preserving a good working relationship. It's also true that prospective client's may have a hidden agenda that will harm your business interests in ways that are both related to the project and otherwise. Although this is more likely to happen with people you have never dealt with before, it is entirely possible to occur with client's you've built a better relationship with who have previously proven to be reliable and trustworthy. More often than not in these cases, the sudden deviousness will be as a result of a change of personnel, whether it be new management or an introduction of new people who influence relevant decision makers. Good negotiation isn't about winning one over on the client, but more about coming to a compromise that has mutual benefits to both parties. In realizing this, it's possible that the client may object to having some of their terms altered or omitted from the agreement. The key to resolve this type of scenario will be to present alternative options that offer to protect their interests whilst avoiding any conflict in the interests of yourself and future scope for the working relationship. An example of this could be where a client is requesting a feature that is complicated and time consuming to develop and test. With some investigation into the motivations behind their request, you may find that what the client wants to achieve can be delivered with little to no additional code being created by suggesting a simple alteration to an existing feature. Once again, the information obtained from step one of the negotiation phase 'evaluating priorities and characteristics' in addition to further questioning about their concerns and agenda will allow you to become creative in offering alternatives that are attractive to the client. Common areas of concern that a prospective client may want to be assured of are:

> ➤ Provision of confidential information to their competitors.

> ➤ Provision of the same solutions to their competitors.

> ➤ A guarantee of future support and accountability for anything that goes wrong.

> ➤ Whatever options you decide to provide as an alternative, the following are major issues that you will need to consider to protect your own business interests:

➤ Provision of any type of exclusivity will limit your ability to do future business. This could be in the form of stopping you from working with companies who operate in the same market as the client, or using resources you have developed outside of the client's project.

➤ A guarantee to provide future support may tie you to working for a demanding client that you discover that you don't want to work with due to them being difficult and/or unprofitable. Avoid this by making sure there is an exit clause that is fair to both you and the client.

➤ A level of accountability should always be defined on your terms – especially if you are providing services and solutions of a technical nature. Being held responsible for consequences resulting from faults resulting from defects in your code is one issue, whereas being held responsible for consequences resulting from misuse of the solution by the client is another. Always ensure that any agreement that holds you accountable for anything defines 'exactly' what you are responsible for and that it leaves no scope for misinterpretation.

➤ Clauses for provision of support and acceptance of accountability leave a lot of scope to be abused by less ethical clients to gain free labor.

➤ Always define exactly how much support is given and to what extent.

➤ Always ensure that your accountability for faults of the system is fair. Never allow this to be taken advantage of by allowing the client to request additional work to be provided that is beyond rectifying the original problem. For freelancers and contractors who have a refund policy or contract clause concerning competency and workmanship, ensure that the terms are written so that a refund or repeat of work is only given upon a fair review of options to rectify any faults – if they indeed exist and going as far as to include an independent third party to provide an assessment if required to protect yourself against less ethical clients who try to gain a refund or free labor by tampering with the system or reporting faults that either don't exist or that aren't part of the agreement.

It may become clear after a lot of negotiation that the client will not make any concession on some or all of the clauses you have identified. In this scenario, you need to consider whether it's within your interest to proceed with the project and at what price if you do. If you decide to proceed, it's important to make acceptance of unfavorable conditions to be worth your time by compensating you for any lost business and future work opportunities, as well as any increase of risk. Your considerations should include:

Financial and strategic consequences of providing exclusivity on time or resources you have developed.

Make a note

Time example: A project for a law firm having a clause in its contract stating that you are not able to work for any other law firm for 2 years after the completion or termination of the project.

➤ How will this limit your ability to take on new contracts?

➤ Have you specialized in bulding a reputation exclusively in this sector?

➤ Can you adapt your skills and experience to become relevant to other sectors?

➤ Do other sectors pay as well as this sector?

Make a note

Resource example: A clause in the contract states that all code delivered to the client becomes their exclusive property. This has implications if you are to make use of code already created to accelerate development of previous and future projects. Additionally, you have no authority to accept such terms for open source components you make use of.

➤ What is the cost to future projects of not being able to use the quick start code?

➤ Will it increase their cost to a point where you lose your ability to be competitive in the market?

➤ Can the client take advantage of this clause by claiming ownership of other code you've written in a similar style?

➤ Can the client cause interruption to your previous clients by issuing them with a cease and desist on usage of the code you sell to them?

➤ Is there a risk if other clients suing you for any disruption that the client could cause to their business through gaining exclusive ownership of the code you plan to sell?

➤ These examples illustrate the worst that can happen when contract clauses aren't negotiated properly. If agreeing to these terms, you have an obligation to protect previous clients who are using the resources you are selling the rights to (the code in our example) and to ensure that the resource is sold at an additional premium price to the main project. There is no point in selling exclusivity on resources you have developed separately to the project if the client isn't paying a premium for it, and this is especially the case when you are being paid by the hour – otherwise you are literally giving away your intellectual property. The separate price for any resources you agree to give exclusivity should cover any lost work opportunities you expect. In most situations, this will increase the price of the budget by many times over and will give the client a reason to reconsider your proposals.

Unrealistic delivery dates:

➤ Timescales for delivery that aren't realistic can open you to be held accountable for any losses that the client incurs as a result of late delivery. This in turn gives them scope to sue you for compensation or ask for a full refund if the working relationship turns sour.

➤ Time scales for delivery that aren't realistic are also likely to result in rushed work that results in faults and other quality related issues. Again, this provides the client with scope to sue you for compensation or demand a full refund on the basis of the losses theyincur.

Stage 5: Price Identification

When providing a fixed price quote or estimate, it's only when the depth of the complexity and the time scale for delivery have been fully identified and negotiated that you will be in a position where you can identify the expected costs of the project – otherwise known as your break-even point. The break-even point is the lowest price that you can afford to provide without losing money on the project; either by working for less than your time is worth or spending more money than what you are paid. This happens when hiring additional help or investing in equipment and other resources such as hosting facilities required by the project. It's not usually advisable to aim to break-even on projects, as this would give you no margin for error in your project planning; you should instead intend to make an additional profit that you can use to invest in your business expenses and also to compensate against any previous or future projects that cause problems to your profitability and cash flow.

There is nothing wrong in starting your negotiation with a higher price, especially if you are negotiating with a difficult client who likes to haggle. The one big advantage of starting with a higher price is that you can always make a reduction if the client doesn't give a positive reaction – something you can't do without losing money if you start at your lowest price.

The strategy to start negotiating with the highest price should never be considered as simply starting with the highest price you can offer, but more about the highest suitable price. This is especially true when you are negotiating a deal where the price factor is a high priority, which is usually the case when dealing with people at the budget segment of your market, where buyers primarily seek to buy at the lowest price. Depending on how you have decided to position yourself in the market, you may not want to deal with audiences who place too much emphasis on getting the lowest price. After all, there is only so much that you can compete on price without losing the ability to compete on quality!

Summary

Although there is no single method that works for every circumstance, it is clear that negotiation is about using the right type of strategy for the right type of situation. The main component of all situations you will apply negotiation towards is the person you are negotiating with. Knowing their characteristics and what influences them will allow you to identify which approach to negotiation is likely to be the most effective.

The majority of negotiation you engage should be looked at achieving a win/win outcome. This means that you need to look at the situation from both your own perspective as well as the perspective of the other person. In the case of clients looking to hire you, negotiation often revolves around price. Different clients have different motivations that affect how they negotiate the price they pay – what you must identify is whether they are looking to negotiate the price they "want" to pay or the price they "can" pay. Knowing the difference between "want" and "can" allows you to engage negotiation methods that produce a better response; someone trying to negotiate a lower price because they can't afford the full price is more likely to be open to consider eliminating part of their requirements in exchange for a lower price.

On the other hand, someone wanting to get a lower price just for the sake of a perceived better deal will want everything without compromise – a completely different situation.

Success in negotiation comes from the use of give and take, where being flexible to give in one factor results in taking away of another factor. In the case of negotiating the budget of project, this could be to provide a lower price by eliminating the less important features – something that is likely to appeal to someone who can't afford the full price, whilst still emphasizing to someone who just wants a lower price that they also have to sacrifice if they want to negotiate.

The final part of negotiation is to make sure that the agreement is clearly understood by both parties and fully documented. This avoids problems from misinterpretation or even deviousness of one party whose intention is to covertly force the other to give more at a later date; this type of strategy is never good to consider because it leads to long term distrust that can damage the ability to cooperate for the success of the project and missed opportunities to generate new business.

9

Software Development Resources, Patterns and Strategies

Methods of developing software have increased in sophistication and technical complexity over recent decades. The emergence of sophisticated software patterns are neither coincidence nor random; the evolution of software development as a discipline has been molded by the business environments that software projects exist to serve. This means that the code patterns and tools used to define software have been continually refined to address the types of problem that are common to all software projects. Not only does an understanding of software patterns provide you with the ability to get your projects to the fastest and best start, but an understanding of them also allows you to become more employable for working with other programmers who use the same standardized patterns for their projects. Similarly, many of the programming frameworks used in contract projects are based on these standardized patterns, meaning that your understanding of code patterns will significantly reduce the amount of time required to learn these frameworks.

Sophisticated code patterns are not just to be considered an element of the software system being produced, but also as an enabler and reflection of the business model (see *Chapter 3, Defining your Business Model*).

Software problems: A recap

One theme that's consistent throughout this book is that the human factor can be problematic. This is not an observation meant to be pessimistic about the prospects of working with people, but of the exposure to problems that people introduce to software projects. These probelms include:

> Programmers — make mistakes, resulting in poor quality code that introduces security vulnerabilities and restrictions to react to future situations.

> Project managers — underestimate the complexities of requirements and ability of their programmers.

> Designers — over complicate designs, resulting in unnecessary complexity and project risks when integrating their designs into code.

> ➤ Clients — fail to define their software requirements in a literal way that software people can make sense of and change their requirements over time.

> ➤ Everyone — gets ill, needs holidays and change jobs.

Knowing in advance that the involvement of people in software projects are a risk can be used to your advantage by understanding how to manage your code to decrease the risks that people introduce. Considerations for this include:

> ➤ Keeping the number of people involved in the project's activities to a minimum.

> ➤ Specifying code patterns and standards for programmers to use.

> ➤ Providing designers with the ability to integrate their designs themselves.

> ➤ Allowing the software to be adaptable for unknown future alteration requests.

> ➤ Developing the software to be compatible with unknown future platforms.

It is for these reasons that software programming methods and patterns such as object oriented programming and n-tier development such as with **MVC (Model-View-Controller)** have emerged. Although these methods require a steeper learning curve to get started in software development, any learning effort is more than repaid when it comes to avoiding "technical debt" that can occur through problems that people introduce.Platform compatibility

There will never be a 100% certainty of which operating systems and hardware will be in popular use in the future, which is a big issue if a requirement of your software is to be compatible with mainstream consumer platforms. Additionally, software projects that have long development cycles also risk being developed for platforms that become obsolete by the time development of the software has been completed. Examples of this include game consoles that typically have a lifecycle of 5 years, and embedded systems that may become redundant. However, why develop code for a fixed system specification when there are ways to develop code that can be ported to different platforms with minimal or no changes?

Portable code components

It makes sense to develop your code in ways that can be reused across multiple platforms wherever possible. For projects that target devices capable of showing web pages, it is worth considering which features of the software requirements can be developed using HTML, Javascript and CSS – commonly referred to as HTML5. Although this is a very different approach to traditional methods of developing software, there are indications that this will be a more common method in the future; several operating systems including Google's Chrome OS and Mozilla's Firefox OS for smart phones, laptops and smart TVs designed specifically for their apps to be developed with HTML, Javascript and CSS. Even Windows 8 and 10 offer the ability for apps to be developed with Javascript and HTML, showing that this method of software development has become a serious option.

Developing portable code with HTML5 can be performed using one of two strategies:

Pure HTML5 applications

Software applications that are meant to be run online can be accessed through a web browser in the same way as any website. This is also an option for software that requires offline functionality, with modern web browsers allowing websites and web apps to be accessed without an Internet connection — subject to browser constraints. With platforms such as iOS and Android allowing these pages to be bookmarked and accessed from the user's app list or home screen, web apps can be made to appear and function in the same way as their native counterparts, but without the hassle of needing to have your app approved via the platform's associated app store.

The alternative option for developing your software application in pure HTML5 is to make use of a wrapper such as PhoneGap — a freely available middleware application that allows you to package your HTML5 code for distribution and access in the same way as a native application. This is an obvious advantage if you want your software application to be marketed and found in app stores such as those for Android and Apple devices. Another reason for using this option is to access features not available to the browser, such as the ability to exceed the app's data storage beyond the restrictions set by the browser—typically 5MB at the time of writing.

Not all platforms require the extra effort and complexities associated with middleware such as PhoneGap. Platforms such as Chrome OS and Firefox OS are designed to run all of their apps using the HTML5 standard, whereas Windows 8 and the Chrome desktop web browser allow for apps to be developed using the HTML5 standard for use as an offline application that can access features such as local file storage and unrestricted application sizes that are not available through the web browser.

Hybrid applications

The other approach to developing software applications with HTML5 is to combine the software components that have been developed with native code. This is achieved through the use of web views—a window presented in the user interface that shows the results produced from a web page, which in this case would be a locally stored version of the HTML5 component you've developed. The previously mentioned PhoneGap also includes a framework that makes this approach possible.

Native code has a number of advantages over HTML5, primarily relating to the ability to be executed faster — something that will be a high priority for graphically intensive applications such as games that need to run on minimal hardware specifications. However, improvements in HTML5 rendering engines used for web browsers and operating systems are continually closing the gap between the performance of native code and Javascript through HTML5. Similarly, hardware specifications are constantly improving to a point where performance issues at the start of the project will eventually become irrelevant.

Where the development of features written entirely in HTML5 are not enough to meet the performance requirements, it makes sense to identify a selection of the software features that would be suitable to be developed using HTML5 standards and to have them integrated into the native portion of the software through web views—meaning that additional development time on these components can be saved for any situation where the software is required to be ported to a different platform.

The option of using HTML5 as a software development standard solves a large portion of the problems previously identified in software development relating to the risk of the specification changing in later stages of the project to include making the software available on platforms that were not specified at the start of the project. However, HTML5 does come with a set of its own issues in that it is an evolving standard; new capabilities that may be introduced later in your project's lifecycle will take time to become available in different browsers, with some browsers taking significantly longer than others others to embrace new standards - Internet Explorer, ahem! It is worth checking out the website www.caniuse.com , which is very useful for finding how much support there are for features of HTML, CSS and Javascript from the different browsers.

HTML5's features for responsive design through CSS provide advantages for creating user interfaces that can adjust their layout to best suit the screen size and/or device type — e.g. detecting if the display is on a projector, TV, desktop computer, touch screen, big screen or small screen. With these detection features not always being easily available using native methods of developing software, HTML5 provides an out of the box solution that is guaranteed to offer future proof presentation for visual elements of the software project. Additionally, the ease of how visual elements can be formatted with HTML and CSS without the need to edit any of the main Javascript code means that there is the opportunity for you to provide the responsibility of any formatting change to designers on the project in a way that will not allow them to break your main functionality code.

Code translation

Whereas the HTML5 strategy relies on the target platform having access to the ability to make use of the HTML5 standard in order to present the application, the opposite way of producing portable code is to use software development tools that are capable of translating code to your target platforms. Two examples of this are Appcelerator's Titanium and Monkey-X from Blitz Research.

In the case of Monkey-X, code is written in a language that is a hybrid between Visual Basic and Java. This code is then translated to your desired platform language for compilation. For example, compiling your app for Android would result in the Monkey-X code being translated to Java and compiled to an apk file. Additionally, Monkey-X allows you to create new commands for target platforms in addition to extending the language to support new target platforms; users have already created compilation targets for Amiga and others.

With Monkey-X translating its code to native code for target platforms, the real advantage of this programming tool is the ability to producenative code that is highly efficient — a feature required for intensive multimedia software such as games that rely on real-time interactions and processing. Target platforms available at the time of writing include Windows, Mac OS, Linux, Android, iOS for iPhone/iPad, Windows Phone and Playstation Vita.

Rescued by object oriented programming

With the exception of languages like Java, **object oriented programming** (OOP) isn't mandatory, but is a skill worth developing if you need the flexibility to adapt your code to changing requirements; an important ability if you are to follow agile development principles. Academics and hardcore coders will often talk about the four concepts of object oriented design using jargon you may find difficult to remember; often without any relation to the business benefits of object oriented programming. Similarly, there are a lot of people who talk about OOP without knowing how to use it properly to get the intended benefits! Neither of these approaches are effective for understanding how to use object orientied programming to support your business model; whether it's for flexibility, efficiency or the need to respond to changing requirements and politics. We will break away from this ineffective traditional approach by avoiding the unnecessary jargon and looking primarily at the business motivations for using this programming style to develop software systems — after all, the primary purpose of your freelancing, contracting or product development is to be successful as a business in being able to write software profitably within the budget you have available.Self-contained code for better maintainability

The technical term for this is encapsulation, which is just a fancy way of saying that object oriented code allows for software to be made from mini programs whose code are independent from the main program they are being used to create. This means that the same definitions can be used for elements such as names for variables and functionality (methods) without them affecting the other mini programs (objects) that are also being used by the main software system being developed. This is in contrast to traditional procedural programming, where using an existing variable name in one part of the code could break the functionality of another part of the code that relies on the same variable name.

The business advantages for this feature of object oriented programming include:

> ➤ Easier to coordinate multiple programmers in software development by allowing each programmer to work on their own independent modules. This reduces time, costs and risks associated with programmers needing to co-ordinate their code with dependencies of code created by other programmers.Example: Having a large team working on a software system where programmers are continuously making changes and adding new code has a high risk of people accidentally introducing new flaws. These flaws include accidental use of variable and function names already in use, as well as use of variables in way that are not intended. Object oriented programming solves these issues by allowing programmers to create functionality as independent mini programs that are not affected by separate code being created by other programmers on the project.

> ➤ Ability to base new projects on pre-existing code without restrictions being imposed.Example: With code created as mini-programs, it is possible for the project team to create a library of functionality that can be reused in new projects that share similar functionality. This means that the team can save time in having to rewrite functionality and also from repeated testing. Programmers are not restricted by functionality they don't require because they can pick and choose which functionality they want to make use of.

> ➤ Reduced requirements for testing due to elimination of shared references., resulting in faster project completion at a lower cost.

>> ➤ Example: With code being wrritten as independent mini-programs operating independently to each other, there is no need for programmers to be fully aware of how code is created outside of their module. This allows for local variables to be named as needed without any risk of affecting code in other areas of the system.

> ➤ Ability to better engage test driven software development practices by developing each part of the software system as individual components. This allows components to be individually tested for expected output before their integration into the main software system — ideal for test driven development approaches that use raw data comparisons to identify functional accuracy.

>> ➤ Example: The software team is able to assign specialist testers who are not involved in the development of the main software code. This is only possible because the software has been designed in a modular way using object oriented programming. These testers can write code based tests to call objects created for the software and check to see whether they are returning expected values. Feedback can be given to the module object's programmer on any tests; with these tests being automated, the programmer can adapt their code until it passes the automated test without the need of the testing team needing to write further test code.

Maximising reusability, minimising duplication

The ability to allow code to be highly reusable whilst limiting duplication is achieved through what is referred to as inheritance; a feature of object oriented programming that allows new code to automatically gain features from previously programmed components. In contrast, traditional procedural programming has each new functionality defined separately, possibly with duplicated code for features that share similar functionality.

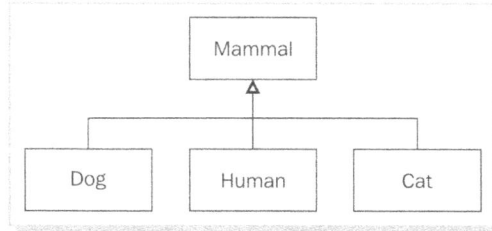

Figure 9.1: Inheritance is presented as the definition of creatures. Dogs, humans and cats are extended from mammals – meaning they share all functionality defined as being a mammal, but also have their own unique properties and functionality defined within them that makes them what they are.

The business advantages for this feature of object oriented programming include:

➤ Ability to develop a code library that can be used as a starting point for multiple projects. This allows for the ability to reduce time and costs by allowing new code to "inherit" functionality that already exists from previously written code. Example: A project requires extensive functionality for a customer relationship management system. Programmers have already developed functionality for many of the required features such as for storing and presenting details of people. The project can reuse existing code by making the new people management code "inherit" the same functionality from the original project.

➤ Faster response time to the need to update code common to multiple projects, especially where time is a critical factor such as updating security vulnerabilities. Example: The team identifies that the original code used for people management has a security flaw. Fortunately, the code can be quickly fixed in one line of code and automatically updates any components that "inherit" the original functionality. This is much better than copying and pasting code, such as would have been with procedural programming, especially where the need to repeat fixes may miss one of the repetitions. Additionally, the programmers can reduce testing requirements because the fix only needs to be tested in one place; as opposed to testing every copied location if the code had been physically duplicated.

Functional adaptability

Another way that object oriented programming provides advantages for maintainability and adaptability is through a feature that allows programmers to create multiple versions of the same functionality (polymorphism). This allows for functionality references to act differently for specific types of situation. The ability to define adaptable functionality in this way has several business advantages:

> ➤ New functionality can be added to legacy code in a way that doesn't break existing functionality.Example: The software team can take objects they have already coded to use as a blueprint of a new project. The new project requires some of the existing code to act differently in some situations. New versions of object functions (methods) can be created in a way that allows both the new and original versions to be called whenever they are required. This allows functionality to be modified for specific requirements of the new project without any risk of breaking legacy functionality that should stay the same.Risk, cost and time requirements can be reduced by keeping code components simple to write and easy to read.Example: The software team hire a new junior programmer. The new programmer has less experience than everyone else on the team and so doesn't understand some of the more advanced code patterns that have been used. The new programmer is not aware of how the software system works, so there there is careful consideration on how to train them on using the code. Fortunately, the software is designed in a modular way that allows the team to set new tasks for the programmer without the need to understand anything outside of the mini-program (object) they are coding. The junior programmer can also overwrite existing object functionality (methods) without the risk of breaking other parts of the system that they are unaware of. This means that the junior programmer can become productive almost straight away with minimal learning requirements and at no risk to functionality outside of their working space.

> ➤ New functionality and modifications can be quarantined to reduce risk and its associated costs.Example: The new programmer doesn't have the level of experience or training to be aware of how software systems can be exploited through user input. The software team are aware of this and are able to use polymorphism to keep the junior programmer's code components separate from their counterparts in the live system until they have been thoroughly tested by the testing department. The team can keep the junior programmer's modifications in quarantine until they can provide feedback from testing, while still allowing the programmer to continue writing code that doesn't affect the live system.

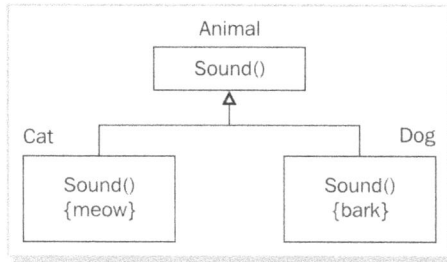

Figure 9.2: The concept of polymorphism showing how an animal object can have a sound method, which has a different version of functionality called depending on whether the object is of type Cat or Dog

Clarity of solution implementation

The central feature of object oriented programming is the ability to define functionality and architecture similarly to real world entities – i.e. objects, types, properties and methods. The ability to define code in a way that closely resembles the language used to describe the problem and solution has multiple business advantages:

> Programmers and analysts are able to better understand each other due to the same terminology being used in both a business and programming context.Example: The business analyst on a project talks about business entities such as people and their tasks; they have no knowledge of any technical programming jargon. Programmers who speaking to the business analyst know exactly what people and tasks are in relation to the code because the system has objects of type people and tasks with all of the actions (methods) named in using the same terminology spoken by the analyst. Similarly, programmers are able to speak to the analyst about the technical architecture of their code without confusion because everyone uses terminology and concepts that both programmers and analysts understand.Terminology and concepts are more likely to be understood by clients, therefore making it easier for programmers to speak directly to clients without confusing them.Example: Like dealing with the analyst, programmers become conditioned to talking about the code using terminology that the client will understand. When the client speaks about new features and relationships that don't exist in the software architecture, the programmer immediately understands which parts of the code need to be adapted from the objects, methods, attributes and relationships mentioned in the client's description.Reduces risks of miscommunication that lead to faults, time wastage and increased development costs because everyone is able to refer to the same terminology and apply their existing knowledge to how this is managed in the system implementation and operation.

> Example: Programmers on the project can be more confident when producing code based on descriptions provided by analysts and the client because the same terminology is shared by the code and its requirements description.

➤ Blueprints (classes) can be made to describe the general object instances that will reflect each part of the problem being modeled. Each of these individual object instances can later be customized with unique reference names, properties and abilities (methods) that make them best suited to reflecting the part of the problem they were created to reflect and provide a solution to; all using the same language definitions provided to the programmers from the analysts and client that are involved with the project.

> Example: When the business analyst investigates the client's business structure, they identify that there are different types of people and different types of task. Some people are managers and other people are workers; they all share common features, but also have some features that are unique to their role, such as managers being able to sign an authorization. Programmers immediately understand that managers and workers can be made as new object types extended from the people object, allowing them to have all of the features of people combined with their own unique abilities such as managers signing authorizations.

➤ The use of objects to define system functionality allows the system architecture and code to be created in a way that directly reflects the real word using abstract concepts such as inheritance that also allow for the description of relationships that increase efficiency through elimination of code repetition.

➤ Example: The programmers receive a new feature request to be added to the project. The feature requires the definition of a new object type, which is described as requiring part of its functionality from the "Activity" object blueprint (class), and the rest of its functionality from the "Processes" object blueprint. Programmers can create this new object blueprint very quickly with hardly any code – firstly by creating the new object to extend (inherit) the functionality of the "Activity" object blueprint, then also to extend the functionality of the "Processes" object blueprint. This approach also provides the advantage of the new object blueprint inheriting any maintenance upgrades and fixes made to the original.

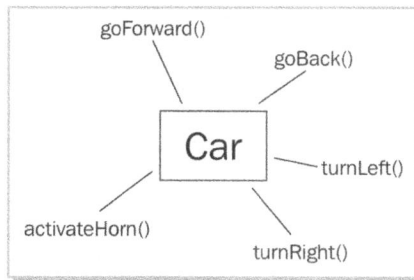

Figure 9.3: Object oriented programming using objects with names and methods that correspond to the client's language terminology help to avoid confusion when programmers are speaking to people with less technical knowledge and vice versa.

Strategic efficiency with MVC

Regardless of which software development language and tools you use to create your software, the top priority should be to develop your code inline with a strategy and method that produces both short and long term efficiency. With the exception of prototyping, ,it should also be kept in mind that short term efficiency shouldn't come at an expense to long term efficiency; using such approach usually results in unnecessary problems occurring at the end of the project that become harmful to the project's success.

One solution to developing software with strategic efficiency is a code pattern called MVC, which is an abbreviation for "models, views and controllers". MVC is a variation of n-tier architecture design, where n is the number of tiers (layers) that the software is modeled through. In the case of pure MVC, the software is constructed through three tiers that combine to form the following agendas:

> ➤ Separation of functionality, presentation and content.
>
> The ability to keep the software functionality for data processing completely separate from any parts of the code responsible for managing the visual presentation and content. This provides a massive advantage for containing risks related to refining how the application's user interface and content is presented, such as:Limiting your involvement in design changes:
>
> Ability to provide designers with the ability to construct their own user interface markup without the risk of them breaking functionality means that you can avoid unnecessary work and getting involved with design politics. This is useful when your project is running on a fixed price budget, or where it becomes highly problematic to get the design defined and accepted.
>
> Example: A designer on the team you are working with is always changing parts of their design. This becomes a problem when you have a list of other development tasks that you also need to complete. Keeping the visual formatting separate from the main functionality opens the opportunity to provide the designer with the responsibility to take control of the visual formatting and avoids your task list from growing out of control.
>
> > ➢ Avoiding visual design and content creation delaying feature development.
> >
> > Example: The project specification is finalized, but the programmer is waiting for content and design to components to be provided by the content team. The programmer is still able to progress with their work by developing their functionality around a skeleton that allows for the design and content to be integrated at a later date.
> >
> > ➢ Ability to produce automated testing of individual functionality components—referred to as unit testing.

> ➤ Example: The team needs to make sure that new changes to the code haven't broken previously working functionality. Manually performing the long list of tests each time code is modified is both time consuming and costly. Fortunately, the MVC architecture allows for individual code units to be tested against expected outputs; these tests only need to be written once and can then be run to produce immediate warnings for any tests that fail. This means that tests can be repeated regularly without increasing time and costs – hence opening opportunities to reduce the risk of unnoticed faults getting through to the live release.

> ➤ Increasing data security by reducing code and improving efficiency. Producing reusable components.

Components that can be reused throughout the project and in other projects result in reduced time for development, testing and future maintenance. Reduced time means more margin to correct mistakes made in other areas of the project and/ or to reduce the cost of the project — especially if it is outside the budget of the client.

➤ Delivering consistency and maintainability.

Functionality and visual presentation updated in one area will automatically be updated everywhere else that the same component has been used. This provides a guarantee for consistent output throughout the entire application; regardless of how many times the presentation or functionality is used in different parts of the software design.

Example: The client requests an alteration to the people details screen; they want the telephone number to have specific formatting and validation. They request a guarantee for telephone numbers to be 11 characters in length with valid dialing codes. The programmer develops this feature exactly as requested by the client, but the client later complains that the feature is not working when they are testing it on other screens in the application where telephone numbers are present. This is a problem if the programmer hasn't used an MVC style architecture because it requires manual identification of every location in the application that uses a telephone input field; this is a significant drain on time and budget if there are dozens, hundreds or en thousands of this repetition. In this case, not only does the code need to be developed and manually copied to each location, each repetition needs to be manually tested – leaving no guarantee for every occurrence to be fully and correctly updated. MVC solves this problem by allowing the feature to be developed once and automatically become available everywhere in the application without the need for the programmer to be aware of where the individual telephone input fields are used.

With an understanding of the purpose for MVC, we are now in a position to identify the different components that MVC based archietecture make use of.

MVC: Models

The processing functionality of MVC architecture are stored in components referred to as "models". Combining this this with the previously mentioned object oriented programming (OOP), models can be created as objects that contain methods for each individual activity that the software needs to perform. These methods can then be called at any point in the software application without any further effort to define the functionality.

Adaptability strategy

An important consideration for the design of models is how their functionality will need to serve the different areas of the software application. Model size is a concern that needs to be balanced; so called fat models have an increased complexity that lead them to become bloated and difficult to maintain, whereas skinny models don't have enough adaptability to be efficiently used across the full software application. Another consideration of this is the relationship between models and the controllers that use them; logic placed in controllers are not reusable across the application, but placing too much logic into models makes them fat, hence the phrase fat model / skinny controller.

A set of principles to be aware of that can assist your decision of where to place the code weight in your application is the Law of Demeter, which states that:

> ➤ Each unit should have limited knowledge about other units — i.e. units should only be aware of units they require to execute their own functionality.

> ➤ Units should never talk to strangers — i.e. those that don't have any relevance to their functionality and purpose.

> ➤ Code should only talk to immediate friends — i.e. avoid mixing functionalities of different types that have no relevance to each other.

The outcome of adopting these principles tends to be code that is more maintainable and adaptable due to the minimization of inter-unit dependency. This provides an advantage for adapting and maintaining the internal structure of components such as objects and their containers, allowing them to be changed and/or replaced without affecting long list of dependents. The downside to this approach is that there may be a need to write more wrapper methods to execute this strategy, requiring additional work investment and a possible noticeable difference in execution speed. This execution performance may become noticeable if the application is server based software under heavy usage.

Some areas of the software may require model functionality to act slightly differently than standard, especially where the model methods have been updated with new functionality and still need to retain compatibility with older code elsewhere in the system. The dilemma of this situation is how there is a need to define the functionality to behave differently depending on how it is called; hence allowing the same functionality calls to adapt itself to different situations.

Languages such as Monkey-X and Java that support the use of polymorphism features such as object functionality overloading (see figure 9.4) can provide the ability to support different versions of model functionality to reflect the situation they are being called. This is achieved through each version of the functionality being defined with a different set of parameters or type of returned output.

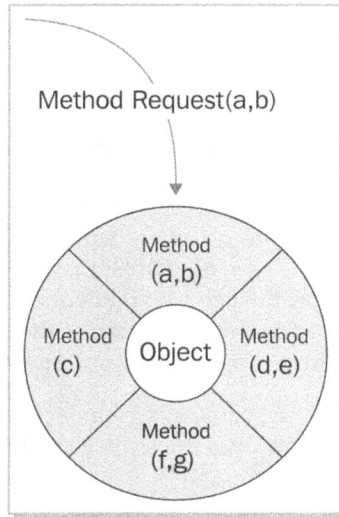

Figure 9.4: Overloading (polymorphism) is where objects can have several versions of the same method. The method chosen will be the version that matches the request's parameters.

For languages that don't support polymorphism features such as functional overloading, or where this seems inappropriate, functionality can be designed to check for indications of the situation they are being called to address. These indications allow the method functionality to identify the most appropriate behavior for the required output response. A way to use this for legacy compatibility would be to detect parameters being provided; with any code calling legacy versions of method not providing parameters that were added for newer functionality. Similarly, checks can also be performed on how data is being performed; such as whether a data item is a string on integer; or if a string is just plain text or using JSON formatting.

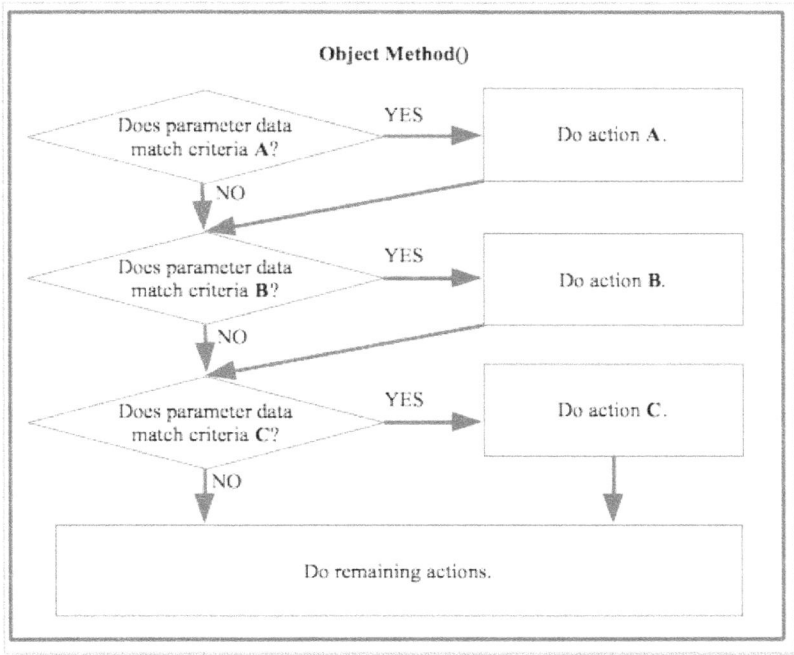

Figure 9.5: Logic can be stored inside object methods to allow them to react differently based on how they are called. This allows the same method to be used in different ways or as a solution to keeping compatibility with legacy code.

Some languages that don't support polymorphism are also strict about how references to object methods must use all of the parameters in the order they are defined. Even when this isn't the case, parameters still need to be provided up to the point where the required parameter is located. This poses a problem because ugly functionality parameters increase the difficulty of calling and upgrading methods with new functionality – especially whilst retaining compatibility with legacy code. In the worst case scenario, this leads to code becoming overly complicated, with functionality calls looking as confusing as the following:

```
Something.doAction("","",Null,Null,5,Null,"","","","",true);
```

This has major problems for productivity, maintainability and security:

Long lists of parameters make functionality calls unreadable, making it difficult to read code and train new programmers on using them.

Increases dependency of programmers on documentation – reducing their productivity each time they need to check for orders of parameters, etc.

Increases the risk of mistakes being made due to easy placement of parameter in the wrong location.

Introduces security vulnerabilities that may be difficult to notice – e.g. placement of parameter in wrong location results in provision of data and functionality to the wrong type of user.

Increased difficulty leads to more time spent on writing code, along with increased testing requirements; more tests required and more time spent per test.

The way around this is to design your methods to accept a single parameter of type object—the object provided as a parameter can then be used to contain any information you wish to pass to the method and will not be inspected by the language compiler when you are changing the types and amounts of parameters you are providing in the object.

A solution to the problem is to design functionality methods with just a single parameter; a data structure containing the different parameters that are relevant to the functionality. Javascript allows for this through the use of JSON to define objects as a parameter:

```
Something.doAction({
    "amount":5,
    "visible":true
});
```

Similarly, PHP allows for associative arrays to be provided directly as parameters to functions and methods:

```
Something->doAction(array(
    "amount"=>5,
    "visible"=>true
));
```

Where your language of choice doesn't allow for data structures to be provided inline as a parameter, there is always the option of providing parameters as a JSON string, which is converted to a data structure inside the function/method. Take note how the following example uses single quotes to define the parameter as text so that the JSON text can easily have double quotes – otherwise use an escape character to allow for double quotes to be placed inside your string:

```
doAction('{"amount":5,"visible":true}');

function doAction(parameters){
    settings = JSON_parse(parameters);
    result = do_something(settings.amount);
    if(settings.visible == true){
            show_something(result);
    }
return result;
}
```

This approach addresses the problems associated with using multiple parameters. Advantages include:

> Makes code clearly identify which parameters are being used.

> Avoids the risk of data being placed in the wrong parameters by making programmers explicitly state their associated parameter name.

> Allows for parameters to be placed in any order or eliminated – reducing the need for reliance on documentation.

> Adding new parameters has no effect on legacy code due to their order in funcationality calls no longer being an issue.

> Easier for new programmers to gain a general understanding of what is happening in the code without extensive reliance on documentation.

Advantages

Several advantages to using models in your software development include:

> **Write once and use many times** - Meaning that software can be expanded very quickly when new features can be constructed from existing functionality in models.

> **Rapid maintenance** - With no repetition of code and each functionality derived from a singular location, modifications to functionality are made in one location. This single modification automatically updates every location in the application where the functionality is present.

> **Improved testability** - With functionality defined modularly inside model containers, the majority of testing requirements can be automated by code written specifically to test code. Any code tests that fail can provide detailed reports of what failed and their reasons – saving many hours from finding the root cause of faults found in manual testing. With functionality being defined from a central location, there is also a guarantee that tests will produce consistent results throughout the application where the same conditions are met.Automated testing provides two advantages. The first and primary advantage is the quality of testing, where tests can be repeated with confidence for accuracy and thoroughness once they have been successfully created the first time. These tests can then be used to identify new bugs that may have been introduced through recent maintenance of system; this is in contrast to human based testing that relies on knowledge of where to test in order to identify new flaws, allowing a lot of scope for testing requirements to be "forgotten". Additionally, manual testing may not provide detailed information on tests that fail due to lack of knowledge of the code and its dependencies – or simply that the tester doesn't have as much skill in writing. Automated testing can be created to guarantee a consistent level of reporting that – with original programmers of the code being able to create the tests and their reporting.

The second advantage of the automated testing abilities of models is the reduction of time and costs required by manual testing. With automation code being able to run each test in as little as a fraction of a second compared to minutes or even hours for a human, tests can be performed in a way that avoids delaying progress in other areas of the project and without using human time that would otherwise increase costs. The avoidance of time and cost implications also allow for tests to be performed earlier and more frequently in order to identify and correct faults the earliest opportunity - helping to avoid problematic situations at the end of the project.

Other considerations for improving testability with unit testing include the use of metrics to estimate how much of your codebase has supporting tests and the level of detail and quality that the tests evaluate against; not all testing is equal and there should be careful consideration to what is being tested and their purpose. Automation of testing only becomes useful if the tests created are themselves correct, hence tests should also be tested — a method to perform this is called mutation testing, where source code is change in an attempt to make their associated tests fail; hence identifying any tests that are incorrectly reporting passes when they shouldn't.

> **Consistency** - The use of models to define functionality that is provided to different parts of the software application means that all functionality is managed from the same source, guaranteeing consistency throughout the software application. This is in contrast to having functionality distributed and replicated through different parts of the software application where consistency cannot be guaranteed, especially when new maintenance requests are received to update functionality in a specific area of the software application without reference to other parts of the system that the same features are replicated.

> **Integration potential** - With the ability to access functionality with consistency, it becomes possible to allow the software system to be integrated into other platforms and device applications through the construction of an API layer that calls the services of models. This approach to software development addresses the issue of future proofing modern software projects against currently unknown demands. Especially relevant to this are Internet based systems that could include future requests to allow devices such as smartphones and tablets to access data from the main system; or where third party systems are required to access data. Models make it very easy to create an API layer that makes data available to third party systems using controllers (see later) that decide how models are tho be used for providing and accepting data.

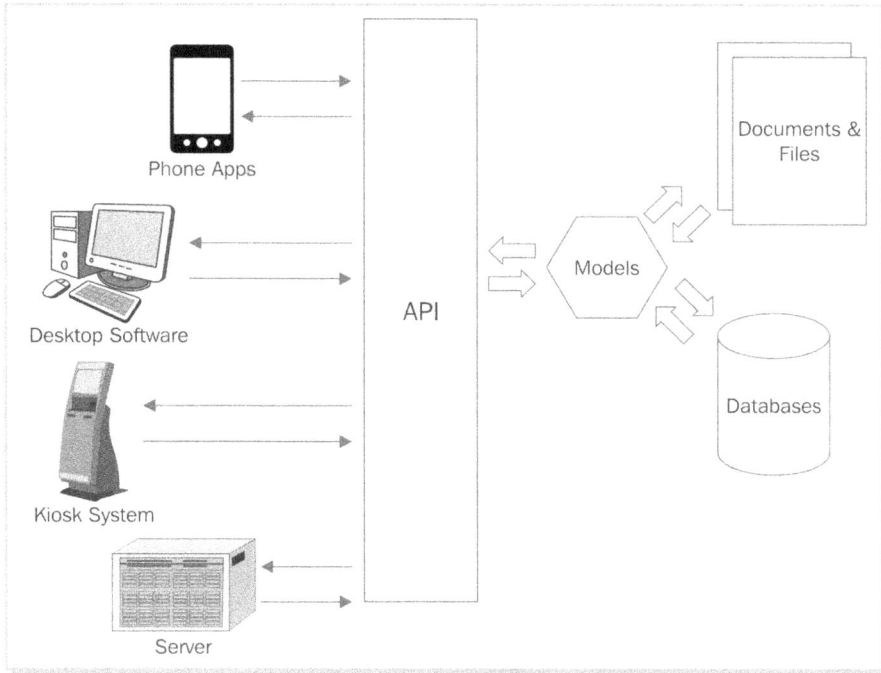

Figure 9.6: Models can be used as an integral resource of API layers of data provision services. This allows a guarantee for consistency of data provided through the API and direct system access, as well as other advantages for compatibility, flexibility and faster development cycles.

MVC: Views

Views are components of the MVC architecture that are similar in concept to models, but specific to managing visual presentation. Each view is typically stored as an individual text file with visual markup defined through a variant of of XML, which in web applications would be standard HTML—itself being a standard based on XML.

Views in action

The views used in MVC software applications exist as one of three variants:

➤ **Screen templates** - Visual presentation markup that describe how a screen, web page or e-mail should look. Screen templates may contain fixed content presented each time the screen template is shown, as well as placeholders for additional content to be inserted when then screen content is called.

➤ **Input controls** - Not to be confused with MVC controllers (see later), input controls are components designed to be used throughout the software application for capturing user input. Their design may include markup to enable the component to appear or function in a specific way as well as having the ability for any data provided to be presented within the input control.

➤ **Content snippets** - This type of view exists to standardize how specific types of content are presented as part of the software application's screens. An example of this type of view could be a notification template, where the view is called with the text to display as part of the notification; this would be highly useful in supporting multiple languages. Another example could be a menu that is made available to display in different parts of the software application; providing a guarantee for consistency of available options.

Advantages

The use of views in your code has many advantages for maintainability and consistency that give you more ability to react to evolving project specifications.

➤ **Consistency** - Provides a guarantee for each repeated version of content or visual component to be consistent regardless of how many changes have been made. This is contrast to the copy and paste approach, where different versions may become inconsistent when changes made to one version are forgotten to be made to other versions that have been copied and pasted.

➤ **Efficiency** - It becomes increasingly time consuming to update visual components and content that has been duplicated throughout the system. This becomes a serious issue where an element such as a menu, notification layout or screen design is repeated tens or hundreds of times throughout the application, especially if they are being updated on a frequent basis. Views solve this problem by having components defined only once, meaning that any update is made in a single location to automatically update all appearances throughout the application — regardless of whether it is repeated ten, one hundred or one thousand times.

➤ **Adaptability** - The efficiency for changing views also influences the application's adaptability — whether it be for consistency of upgrades, or providing presentation tailored to specific platforms; such as providing a different user interface for smartphone and desktop usage. Updates to the visual presentation that would be considered too high risk or impossible to achieve within the time or budget available can become achievable through minimal time requirements and risk associated made possible through the efficiency that views offer. The speed at which this can be achieved also opens the opportunity to provide clients with samples of how visual changes look in the live software application without investing major effort.

➤ **Testability** - The elimination of duplication reduces the need for testing because anything that works with the same settings in one part of the software application will work with the same settings elsewhere in the software application. The result of this is that short term testing of visual elements can be initially tested on a small sample of functionality, with heavy testing only being required prior to the release of the software.

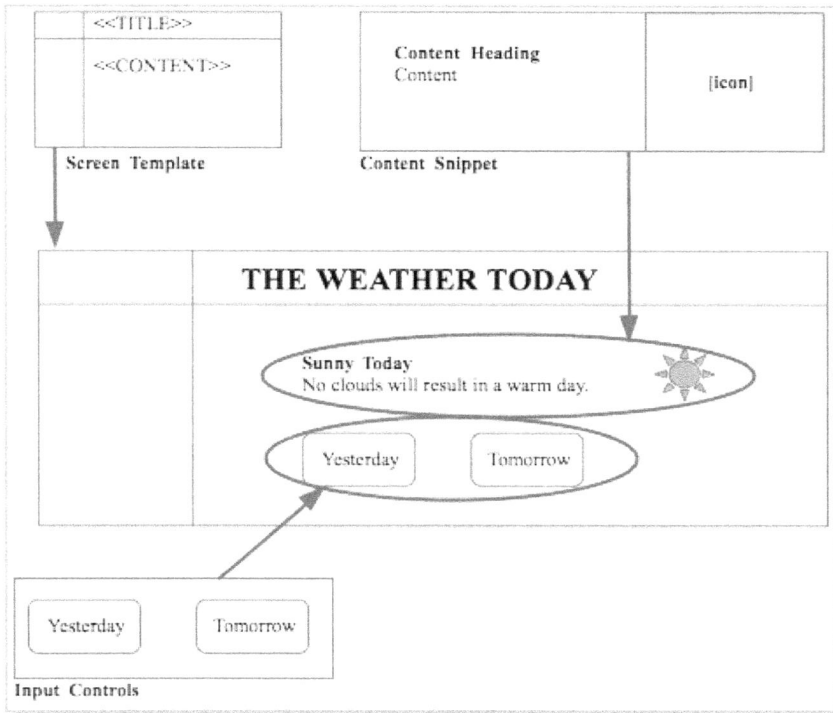

Figure 9.7: Example of a page created from multiple views. In this case, the screen template has a content snippet and input controls inserted into it.

MVC: Controllers

If your software was a movie, controllers would be the director. The role of each controller is to manage how models and views are being used in response to how the user interacts with the application. Controllers direct what happens — but not how, which is the responsibility for models (functionality) and views (presentation) that they call.

Controllers in action

With each controller being responsible for managing the flow of operations for their specific part of the application, a typical controller's structure will look similar to the following:

➤ Call the model's functionality that matches the requirements of the controller.

➤ Identify a default output by calling a default view and model functionality if required.

➤ Listen for some type of user input.

> ➤ Identify whether user input matches criteria for reaction; if so do one of the following:

>> ➤ Call the associated model functionality and use its results in content created from views to be presented to the user.

>> ➤ Redirect the user to another controller if required.

>> ➤ Output any content generated from views and models.

>> ➤ Decide whether to return to listening for new user input or to exit.

The only processing performed by controllers are in passing details from model functionality to views and vice versa activated by user input.

Advantages

Controllers have several purposes that provide advantages to software development:

> ➤ **Customization of model functionality** - The results returned from model functionality can be manipulated to suit the specific purpose they are being called for without the need to add unnecessary complexity directly to the model. This avoids any risk of breaking compatibility with other areas of the code that use the model, hence avoiding additional testing requirements from being introduced. An example of this could be converting data returned from a model's functionality into JSON that can be used with Javascript in a web application view.

> ➤ **Control of views** - Controllers can decide what the most appropriate view is to match the situation. In many cases, controllers will just have one default view to choose from, but other situations could have the chosen view being decided by conditions such as input received from the user or the response given from models. For example, a model returning a response indicating that the user has provided correct/incorrect information could be used to choose the most appropriate views for content response and presentaiton layout. Similarly, controllers can call upon models to identify the privileges assigned to a user; upon which the required views are called inline the response received. The controller can decide to call different views for notifications and access to additional software functionality as required.

> ➤ **Connecting results of multiple model functionality** - Some data processing functions may consist of several processes. Instead of placing duplicated code in model functionality, the system can use controllers to call individual model methods in the order they are required. This allows the controller to take responsibility for passing results between models in any order that's required. This approach of using controllers to allow models to speak to each other allows for more advanced functionality from a simplified set of code due to the ability to keep models and their functionality simplified.

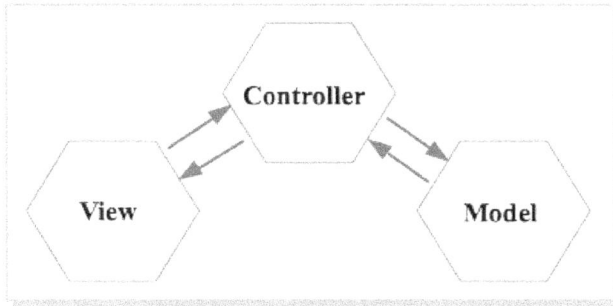

Figure 9.8: The controller acts as the middle person, deciding how views can pass information to models and vice versa. It can also be used to decide how models are connected to other models, as well as combining views with other views, allowing for advanced functionality and presentation from simplified code

Strategic data management

The ultimate purpose of all serious software applications is to produce knowledge that has a positive impact on the real world. A major factor that influences the success or failure of information systems is the quality of the data they manage and produce. The dependence of software systems on data quality leads to serious causes for concern:

> ➤ Modern software projects need to be highly agile to accommodate the changing requirements of clients; especially those who don't fully understand what they need. The fixed specification approach advocated by the waterfall model is no longer adequate for most projects; the waterfall model being a formal set of project phases that start with the requirements definition and progress through to design, implementation testing and review in a fixed order.

> ➤ It is rare for clients to communicate their specification changes in relation to the entire software system, meaning that they will ask for changes to a specific part of the system without any mention to other areas that also need to be updated for consistency throughout the system.—this often resulting from their assumptions that what is obvious from their perspective should be obvious to people developing the system.

The consequence of software projects being agile combined with the assumption that clients often make about how their requests should be understood leads to higher risk for inconsistencies occurring over time. At the very least, this leads to a higher requirement for testing to ensure that all modifications are made consistently throughout the system. This is a problem because rigorous testing can only ensure accuracy to the point where the software development team are share the same understanding as the client, and where the both the time and budget are available to invest for the the level of testing required.

User interface consistency with data binding

Data binding is a feature that can be integrated into your code that ensures consistency of data wherever it is presented or changed through your software application's user interface. The ability to connect data directly to user interface components provides multiple advantages to counteract the risk of data presentation and management becoming inconsistent through agile development:

> ➤ Easy management of user interface components such as text input boxes, radio buttons, lists and text presentation.

>> ➤ Defining the relationship between data and a user interface components offers to guarantee consistency for data presentation and capture throughout the system. When data presented through a user interface component is modified, the system will identify all other places that the data is presented in the system – and update these presentations with the new version of the data. The only concern of developers is to make sure that each data item is connected to the right user interface components using the right functionality.Simplification of code for data processing.

>> ➤ There is no longer a concern to develop any type of code that updates user interface components after data processing has been performed; data binding will automatically identify user interface elements needing to be updated when a data item has been altered.

> ➤ Reduced testing and analysis.

>> ➤ With data binding taking care of the relationships between data items and their associated user interface components, developers don't need to be concerned about the wider impact of change requests because the code is able to manage consistency throughout the application. In addition to reducing this responsibility of programmers, it is also an advantage for new developers joining the project who may not be initially aware of how the different parts of the software share the same data sources; hence reducing risk for new faults being introduced.

Data binding is a common practice in software development, so the chances are that you will be able to implement this feature in your code with minimal effort by using a third party library/framework or directly through the programming language you are using. For example, web applications using Javascript can make use of one of many libraries and frameworks such as AngularJS that readily support data binding; or for browsers that support it, the native Object.proxy() method can be used to bind data without the need to integrate any third party components. Tools such as Modernizr (www.modernizr.com) and Kangax (kangax.github.io) can be used to detect whether Javascript features are available from the browser, hence allowing you to write fallback code when code when features aren't available; there are many so called polyfills available online for newer HTML5 and Javascript features.

For projects that need to implement a custom version of data binding, the following diagram describes a model that can be used:

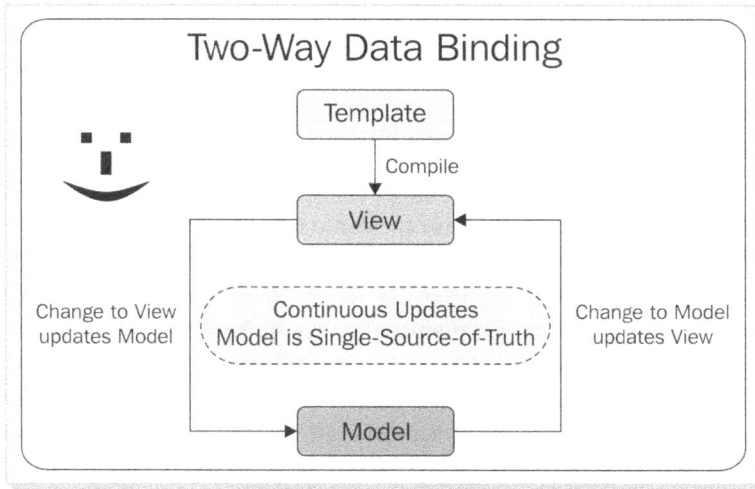

Figure 9.9: Two way data binding ensures that both visual presentation and their associated data are always up to date regardless of how they may change.

Example: The client requests the addition of some existing information fields to a screen in their application. No mention is given to how adding these fields are also present elsewhere in the application, hence the fields are added without further consideration. After presenting the client with the update, a complaint is made that the information entered on the screen isn't appearing in the "same" field presented on other screens. Without data binding, this is a problem because there is no guarantee that the programmer will know where every associated user interface component has been placed in the application; especially if code has been created by programmers who are no longer on the project. Using data binding from the beginning solves this problem by ensuring that every user interface element updates its attached data when modified, as well as updating what it presents when its attached data is altered. This means that user interface elements will automatically manage their consistency without the need for the programmer's involvement.

Database consistency

Where your software makes use of a database management system (DBMS) such as MySQL or Microsoft SQL Server, it makes sense to use these components to their full potential. Making full use of database features provides the following major advantages in keeping your code agile and consistent for data management:

> ➤ Consistency of data and its processing can be guaranteed for software applications that exist in multiple forms such as separate apps for web, mobile and desktop. This is due to all versions of the software sharing the same data source and will receive the same results regardless of how the data processing rules may change over time.

> ➤ Data management is kept centralized and confined within one system, meaning that any changes to data processing rules can be kept consistent throughout all instances where data is called — especially where your software application exists in multiple forms such as separate apps for web, mobile and desktop.

> ➤ Reduces the risk of change requests that are specific to data management leading to new faults being introduced to other areas of your code.Keeping your data processing logic confined to the database means that data processing rules can be updated without needing to alter your main application code.

> ➤ Improves response time to data management change requests by eliminating unnecessary requirements to duplicate data functionality in different versions of the application.

> ➤ Improves efficiency, including reduced testing requirements, leading to lower development costs and more time to invest in other areas of the software project. Efficiency can be further improved by the ability to deploy a database specialist for the management of the database.

Relational database tools

There are several features commonly available in mainstream database management systems that can be used to manage the majority, if not all, of your application's data processing:

> ➤ **Views**: Allow you to define how data is selected from multiple tables using any rules you wish to apply for restricting the search results.

>> ➢ Highly useful for situations where data required by your application is distributed across multiple tables, allowing you to keep your main application logic simple by calling the view in the same way that it would call any database table directly—keeping the data management confined to the view defined inside the database.

> ➢ Keeps your database architecture maintainable by avoiding the need to duplicate the view's logic throughout the database. By having view logic contained in a central location, updates can be made to the view with a guarantee that all dependencies will automatically be updated.

> ➢ Offers the opportunity to control access to data called by different users or parts of the application where you may want to define different rules for access, logic or formatting.

> ➢ Provides flexibility to adapt the database without affecting the main software application — useful for situations where the application has already gone into production use and distributed to real users, but where the client still needs to modify how data is managed.

➤ **Stored Procedures**: These are subroutine functions that can be called with parameters to make use of in their processing. The parameters, if provided, can be used as part of the subroutine's logic such as for conditions of data being called from tables and views. The results of these data calls can also be processed by the subroutine before they are returned – or simply used as part of additional data calls.

> ➢ Allows you to simplify the main application codebase by confining logic specific to data management within the database.

> ➢ Simplified application code reduces risk of faults and increases development productivity.

> ➢ Centralized data management directly from the database eliminates duplication of data processing functionality that would otherwise exist in multiple versions of the software applications. This results in reduced time and costs for development and maintenance and testing.

➤ **Triggers**: These are another type of functionality that can be embedded within the database, but are specific to reacting to events that occur — unlike stored procedures, which must be manually called.

> ➢ Ideal for ensuring consistency of data:
>
> Apply validation rules on data being inserted and updated within the database.
>
> Preparing additional data records when new data is inserted—e.g. creating new job roles for each employee record created.

> ➢ Allows data to be formatted before being inserted into the database.
>
> Ideal for securing user input that could prove harmful when output— e.g. stripping out Javascript that could be harmful for web applications.
>
> Ensuring that specific types of data input are realistic — e.g. numbers that must be within a specific range.

➤ **Relationships**: Defining the management of relational data within the structure of your database allows for the database and software application to be simplified.

> ➤ Avoid orphans (redundant data records left after their parents have been deleted) by using the *foreign key* constraint combined with *references* and *on delete cascade* to make the database aware of how data records are related — and in turn how to automatically delete child data when parents are deleted. This allows you to:

> ➤ Ensure integrity of your data by guaranteeing to avoid data orphans.

> ➤ Simplify your database structure by reducing the need for complicated triggers and stored procedures.

> ➤ Simplify your software application code by reducing the need to call multiple stored procedures and/or perform manual checks on the database.

The SQL for a relational database using these constraints would look something similar to the following example which defines a middle table describing relationships between categories and items — using *foreign keys*, *references* and *on delete* to state that the current record will be deleted if their associated foreign records in either the categories or items table are deleted:

```
CREATE TABLE categories_items (
  categoryID int unsigned not null,
  itemID int unsigned not null,
  PRIMARY KEY (categoryID, itemID),
  FOREIGN KEY (categoryID)
    REFERENCES categories (id)
    ON DELETE CASCADE,
  FOREIGN KEY (itemID)
    REFERENCES items (id)
    ON DELETE CASCADE
);
```

NoSQL: Alternatives to relational databases

Database development has traditionally been synonymous with fixed structure relational design and the use of SQL, a language for defining and querying relational databases. This approach has advantages for easy access to data and old school waterfall approaches to software development where project specifications are fixed before any software development is started, but can introduce problems and inefficiencies on agile projects where iterations and changes to the specification are frequent.

More recently, new approaches to defining databases have been developed that are more suited to agile approaches to software development, which ultimately provide more flexibility when defining and accessing data. These new types of database are referred to as NoSQL, or Not Only SQL, where rather than being a category of a single method for developing databases like relational databases do through SQL, the NoSQL approach covers four approaches to database development:

➤ **Key/Value stores**: The simplest type of data storage, consisting of of a data structure where each element has a unique reference key used to access the data item. The data values stored in this type of database can be strings, integers or floating point numbers — languages such as PHP and Javascript allow more advanced data to be stored by converting object data to JSON or XML string representations for storage and converting these strings back to objects when their key values are required. This is an easy to manage solution for managing small data objects, but becomes increasingly inefficient as the complexity of data objects grow.

➤ **Document databases**: Modern data formats such as XML and JSON make it possible to describe complex data in a format that is searchable, meaning that information documents created in these formats can be combined to form databases of information. This is the next step up from key/value databases, adding the ability for nested values to be associated to each key and offering better features for searching data. Something of interest to anyone in using these formats to describe data is that popular open source databases systems including MySQL and Postgres have started to support the parsing of JSON data strings; meaning that you can create a relational database that stores JSON document/ object data that can be queried as part of SQL requests — read more on this later.

➤ **Graph databases**: This approach to databases relies on creating a data model that consists of individual nodes containing data and connections to other related data nodes. These nodes can exist on the same system or on another server, hence allowing the database to be distributed across multiple systems for easy scalability.

➤ **Column Oriented Databases**: These databases are designed to store large amounts of data that can be distributed over multiple machines in a way that is more efficient than row column based relational databases. Their approach to storing data makes use of objects defined through formats such as JSON, with individual reference keys being made of a combination of a unique *keyspace* (equivalent to a table name in relational databases) and item reference key (equivalent to a primary key in relational databases) that combine to provide a reference to an individual data object. These data objects then have data stored as field items (called columns) and groups of data fields (called column families)— these are structured in the same way as you would consider creating normal JSON or XML documents, such as those used in document databases.

By default, relational databases are typically more difficult to scale up, which isn't good when your system expands from dealing with small amounts of data to massive amounts in the way that Facebook did. There are ways around this if you have the skills, time and/or inclination to learn about the configuration of database clusters; this being where you spread your database system across multiple database servers and synchronize them to work together, hence avoiding the default limitations by spreading the workload. Tools such as Amazon RDS also help to reduce the work required to manage this approach to the scalability of relational databases.

NoSQL databases have a natural advantage in this area because their non-relational design allows their data to be distributed across multiple machines/servers without the need to add complexity to your software code. Although this is achievable with relational database systems, this comes with the added need for you to develop complexity into your codebase or server management for managing the ability to link and synchronize data stored in different databases on different servers. Remember, added complexity is never good because it increases risk for faults, development costs and time requirements.

With NoSQL data being based around how objects are modeled through JSON and XML, an additional advantage of this approach is the ability to pass object data generated within code to be stored in the database without any need for modification; unlike relational databases, where an object's data will at least be stored in separate fields, and possibly in separate tables. The NoSQL approach not only simplifies the storage of data from your application, which in turn can be retrieved without the need for modification, but it also allows you to make changes to your object data without needing to be concerned about updating the database — objects that have missing fields will not lead to the database returning errors, hence this being ideal for agile projects where new data features are added as the project progresses.

SQL and NoSQL: The best of both

Although NoSQL databases have advantages over traditional relational databases for scalability and keeping projects agile, this is not to say that NoSQL approaches are a perfect solution to your software's data management requirements, nor that relational databases be disregarded as an option. For all the advantages that NoSQL approaches can provide to database development, there are still major drawbacks that are otherwise taken for granted with relational database:

> **Data consistency**: The NoSQL approach to database design relies on collections of data being dumped into the database without any need to guarantee consistency in how data is structured and defined. This lack of enforcement for consistency can lead to data duplication and search results that are inconsistent due to a lack of relational database functionality such as joins.

> **Analysis difficulties**: Inconsistency and lack of enforced formal structure to data can make it difficult to analyze data — especially when NoSQL databases typically lack methods to analyze data though a query language that's as easy and efficient to use as SQL.

Furthermore, not all projects require the full advantages that NoSQL approaches offer for data management; especially for small scale projects that are known to stay small scale and where their data requirements are mostly fixed to a standard specification that will always remain the same. An exmaple of this is the type of functionality required by small scale e-commerce websites, which tend to be based on standard open source systems and have little or no modification requirements beyond their initial setup. It therefore should come as no surprise that the application of NoSQL approaches to some types of project would be overkill that leads to unnecessary complexity through the loss of data management and analysis features available by default in relational database systems such as MySQL.

RDMS with NoSQL

There is no rule to say that software systems need to rely on a single data management strategy, which is precisely the case when it comes to using relational database systems and NoSQL approaches to data management. Several popular relational database systems now provide features to query NoSQL data stored as JSON or XML in text or blob fields. This provides an ability for your software to make use of both relational data management and NoSQL techniques from the same database system.

Offline databases vs online databases

Internet connected software applications have the option of storing their data online or on their host device. Which option is best depends on the purpose of the software application and how it is being used. Considerations include:

➤ Availability of server resources:

    ➢ **Problem:** Not all projects have access to the hardware resources required to provide full access to an online database. This is especially true for projects that provide features that can lead to users producing high volumes of data. In turn, these features increase server costs through increased requirements for data storage and processing.

    ➢ **Solution:** Offline databases can be used in part or whole to reduce or eliminate the need for data storage and processing to be performed on the server; hence transferring this responsibility to the user's device, which eliminates the project owner's operation costs for data storage and processing.

➤ Dependency on the ability to access data.

    ➢ **Problem**: Data stored online will not be accessible without an Internet connection. This isn't a major issue for systems based on fixed location wired or wifi Internet access where there will always be a high certainty of Internet access, but this can't be guaranteed applications based on mobile devices that are being used on the move, hence any dependence of online data access could limit or cripple the software application's ability to function correctly.

> ➤ **Solution**: Providing features to temporarily store data offline when there is no Internet connection can allow the software application to continue functioning until an Internet connection is established again. In this case, any data produced would be submitted online to be processed and synchronized.

➤ Number of people who will contribute or alter data.

> ➤ **Problem**: There is a need to ensure that different users are able to view the latest version of data, especially when data can be modified by multiple users.

> ➤ **Solution**: Offline databases are primarily suitable where multiple users make their updates from the same device without the need for the data to be submitted elsewhere. Any other situation that involves more than one person to access, contribute or alter data is more suited to being managed by online databases that can access requests and provide data to multiple users using any type of device.

➤ Requirements for customized versions of the data for individual users.

> ➤ **Problem**: Systems that provide the ability for individual users to have customized data storage will increase the complexity of their design, leading to increased time, costs and risks associated with the database maintenance and management.

> ➤ **Solution**: Customized data features can be implemented in a separate database; especially where the main database is online, the use of an offline database can be used to store data specific to the individual user until, if at all, it is ready to be published to the main database where it can become part of the standard data made available to multiple users who have permission to access the data.

➤ Volume of data being accessed.

> ➤ **Problem**: Large amounts of data being accessed from an online database will introduce waiting times for the user. This can become frustrating if large amounts of data are frequently being accessed, resulting in the software application appearing to be slow and unresponsive.

> ➤ **Solution**: Access to locally stored data will always be faster than access to online data, which has to travel hundreds or thousands of miles through the Internet. Using an offline database to cache frequently accessed data from the online database will produce what appears to be instant access to data, hence reducing loading times to a point that may not be noticeable to the user.

The consistent pattern that can be identified by the above problems and solutions is that both online and offline databases can be used to support each other for the best outcome. Modern web browsers allow this to happen for web based applications through in browser database storage available through local storage and IndexedDB APIs.

API-oriented system architecture

The most obvious way to write a software application is to develop the entire logic embedded into the application. This approach has advantages in terms of rapid development of the software project with minimal dependency on external systems in order to reduce complexity, but limits future efficiency of the project's development when software features need to be shared across multiple platforms. This limitation could come in the form of there being different versions of the application for desktop, mobile and web, or in the form of integration into third party systems such as websites and software developed by other software developers. These issues are easily resolved when your software is designed around an API (Application Programming Interface) based architecture.

Why create an API?

The role of an API is to provide data services to external applications, of which your software application would be one of them. Data services are both the provision of data as well as processing of data for storage, meaning that functionality developed into your API needn't be replicated across multiple versions of your application. This approach provides several advantages:

> ➤ Reduced long term development time and costs.

> > ➢ Once a feature is developed into the API, it is available for integration into any external system without the need for further feature development; the only additional time required is for integration of the API into external application. Components of this integration could be made as reusable code for use across multiple projects that share a compatible architecture and/or programming language.

> ➤ Reduced testing requirements.

> > ➢ The elimination of the need to recreate functionality across multiple platforms/systems means that the need to repeat the testing of separately developed version can also be avoided. The only testing required is to ensure that the API integration has been performed correctly.

> ➤ Guarantee of consistency across all systems.

> > ➢ Data services provided through the API will be consistent, regardless of what type of system is submitting and/or calling data. This means that there is a guarantee of all systems being treated equally with regards the results they receive. What these systems do with the data is a separate issue—i.e. if they perform additional data processing separate from what is provided from the API.

> ➤ Control of data functionality.

> > ➤ With the data processing functionality kept separate from the main software applications, there is more control to change rules that dictate what data is made available. This is useful for situations such as where changes in an organization's policies or law affect what data is to be made accessible; a centralized approach to data provision through the API allows these policy changes to be executed efficiently and consistently across all versions of the application and for all users. Costs for development and testing are therefore significantly reduced.Although using an API based approach to developing your software may have an additional time cost in the short term, the benefits are more than repaid in the long term for any software project that needs to distribute data functionality across multiple systems. This also includes the opportunities to guarantee consistence and control of data distribution for users who have inidivual installations of the same software application.

Delivering data

Although there's more than one way to deliver and accept data from your API, the easiest method to implement as well as to integrate into external software applications will be through HTTP. This method of developing an API relies on producing plain text output served to software applications using the API. This approach is easy to set up and also benefits from the availability of standard HTTP codes that indicate errors such as 404 when nothing is available from a specified URL.

The following is an example of a plain text response that could be sent from a HTTP based API:

REPSONSE:OK | ID=123 | ROWS UPDATED=3

The client application would read this response and identify each part by using the the "|" – possibly by exploding the string into an array. The problem with this approach is that there's no context described within the format of the text string. This poses the following disadvantages:

Future alterations may break compatibility with systems already using the API.

Future requirements for data may change, meaning that existing data types for parameters may change. This requirement could cause a problem in which programmers face the option of breaking compatibility with systems using the API or making the API more difficult to use by adding unnecessary parameters.

Can become difficult for programmers to use.

At the very least, a long string without whitespace formatting will make it difficult for programmers to parse data. If the response must have values in a fixed location, this means that programmers need to be more dependent on referring to documentation, resulting in lost productivity and increased risk of introducing fautls. Additionally, a non-standard text format means that time needs to be spent for parsing the string format to capture the data; which itself could have faults.

Difficult to describe complex information.

Simple informaiton such as an individual number or piece of text are easy to describe, but some information requires a combination of multiple data types, including numbers and text. This non-standard plain text approach has limited support for this, meaning that the API would need to restrict how it describes data or add unnecessary complexity for its integration to external systems.

Fortunately, several standard formats have already been designed to describe data structures, context and data through plain text—ideal for delivering data through HTTP based APIs. The most common of these formats are XML and JSON, as demonstrated in the following examples:

```
<RESPONSE>
  <STATUS>OK</STATUS>
  <ID>123</ID>
  <UPDATED>3</UPDATED>
</RESPONSE>
```

XML allows formatting to be added to text based communications that can be processed easily by the receiver. It is also flexible to allow the order of information to be changed as well as for new additions.

```
{
  "type":"response",
  "status":"ok",
  "id":123,
  "updated":3
}
```

JSON is another format that allows text based communication over HTTP that is easy to process and flexible for future alterations.

Although both formats deliver the same results, JSON has several major advantages over XML:

➤ Better efficiency.

➢ Requires less text characters to describe data structures, meaning that large amounts of data can be transferred using less space.

➢ Smaller data transfer sizes result in faster data downloads with less bandwidth usage. This results in a reduction of associated hosting costs and improved speed of software functionality that relies on data from the API.

➤ Easy to integrate into Javascript.

> Web and hybrid application components that are developed using Javascript can, if considered suitable, embed data provided as JSON directly into any code without the software application/server needing to parse the data beforehand, hence meaning less processing required.

It is for these reasons that many newer web service APIs such as those offered via Facebook and Twitter are based on JSON and not XML.

Developing a HTTP based API

With the purpose of an API being to provide an interface between the server based data features you have developed and any external software applications, an efficient method of developing your API is as an extension of the MVC approach to building software systems.

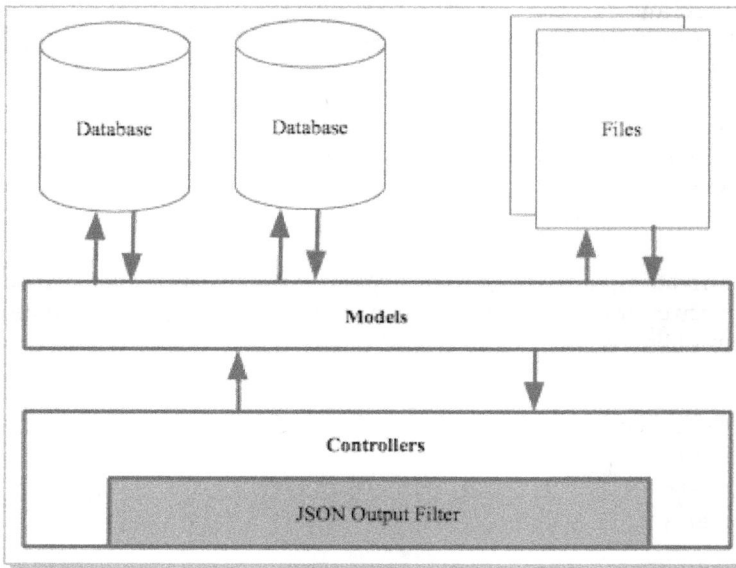

Figure 9.10: A structure of how a HTTP based API could be created with the same controllers that use the same models and resources as your main system. These controllers would have an output filter to publish data in a chosen format—e.g. JSON.

The diagram shows how an API can be constructed using the previously described MVC pattern by making individual controllers accessible from specific URLs, which in turn call models to retrieve data. Controllers simply convert any data returned by models to the required output format — typically XML or JSON.

Many server side programming languages support this type of translation through a single command; for example, PHP can output any data object through HTTP as JSON text using the following code:

```
echo json_encode( $data );
```

API design

Like developing any other software component, it is important to consider the best structure for the development of the API before any programming commences. Like with MVC and n-tier architecture for the structure of you main application code, REST is a formal pattern for API design that is worth considering in your projects for maintainability and adaptability. With the aim of your API being to efficiently provide data access to multiple software applications, there are a few design considerations to make for the design of API for long term maintainability and productivity:

> **Versioning** - There may be a requirement to release a new version of the API that breaks compatibility with the previous at some point. This introduces the problem of breaking any software already making use of the API. The risk of this occurring can be avoided by designing a version namespace as part of the API call parameters. This allows for future versions to be added in a way that doesn't break breaking software that depend on old versions of the API. A URL used to access a HTTP based API may like like the following: `http://api.example.com/version2/some/feature.json`

> **Functionality grouping** - Two important requirements are to allow productive programming of software using the API and the ability to extend the functionality of the API as required. Programmers shouldn't need to repeatedly refer to documentation in order to figure out how to use your API's data services — a logical and consistent structure for calling API features will make it easier for programmers to remember and/or guess how to access functionality. Additionally, a well planned design will also provide better opportunities to be extend the API with new features in a way that doesn't cause conflict with existing functionality.

> Designing functionality grouping into your API allows you to create a design that is logical, easier to use and extensible with minimal effort. The key part in identifying such a design is to identify how to group functionality in a way that keeps the structure of the API minimal and simple. One good way for this is to reserve top level namespaces (within your version namespace) to reference the version being accessed. The following example shows how a HTTP based API may use a URL based on this design to provide a product list with parameters provided through GET: `http://api.example.com/version2/product/list.json?categoryID=1234`

> ➤ **Informative** - There is no guarantee that software making use of your API will call data that they have permission to access, exists or even call the service in the correct way. An API that allows software developers to be productive will respond to these situations by providing clear details of the error(s) occurring in their API request. The more clear the information is provided about the error, the less time software developers will need to spend on figuring out why their code doesn't work — something that will save you many hours over time if you are writing software to make use of your API.

Another feature that will be required for handling feedback from your API will be the ability to inform software about the outcome of data service requests. This is similar to how information would be provided to the software developer, but needs to be in a more direct and simplified way that can be processed by code. The specific purpose of this response feature is to allow software to react to the specified outcome of their requests, such as deciding what should be presented to the user if their request fails. The best way to allow for this will be to provide a field specifying a code number relating to one of the known outcomes of the API request — e.g. success, missing parameters, access denied, etc.

The following example shows how a HTTP based API could provide a response formatted as JSON to provide an error that can be used by both programmers and their software in responding to the issue:

```
{
  "result":{
    "type": "error",
    "code": 3,
    "message": "Access denied to requested data."
  }
}
```

Where there is a successful request to the API, the response should still provide details of the result in addition to containing the data being requested. This needs to be delivered in a way that any additional details separate to result data and result description can be added without breaking compatibility. The following example shows how a successful request to the API would result in data being returned in its own segment of the response — allowing for result details and any other information to be included in their own spearate segments:

```
{
  "data":[
    {"id":1,"name":"product 1"},
    {"id":2,"name":"product 2"},
    {"id":3,"name":"product 3"}
  ],
  "result":{
    "type": "success",
    "code": 0,
    "message": "Data has been listed."
  }
}
```

API security

It's important that the data made available through the API is only accessible to systems and apps that have permission to access their data. Components can be used as part of your technical implementation to secure your data include:

> **Fixed keys** - The simplest method of restricting access to data not meant to be publicly available is to implement the requirement for all data requests and submissions to require the provision of a key code/password known only to the API and the client application. This security is adequate enough providing that the security key is never exposed, guessed or discovered by malicious Internet users who desire to attack the system. However, the weakness of this approach is that it is difficult to change the key once external application installations are making use of the API key.

> **ID based keys** - The next step up addresses the issue of fixed keys being exposed or leaked. ID based keys are provided as a unique key code to each system using the API. This approach means that any disruption or vulnerabilities resulting from the exposure of an API key can be limited to the system that the key has been assigned to. Apps that make use of multiple installations can optionally make use of unique keys assigned to individual user accounts where this is manageable — or simply make use of one key for all app installations and enforce users to upgrade their app should the key be exposed, guessed or discovered.

> **Session tokens** - This extends the concept of providing unique authentication keys to individual clients of the API by making the keys provided valid for a limited time. This authentication requires the client to provide some form of ID for the initial handshake validation, upon which a session token is generated by the server and provided to the client with details of its life duration. The client is then responsible for taking this information and using it as part of data requests.

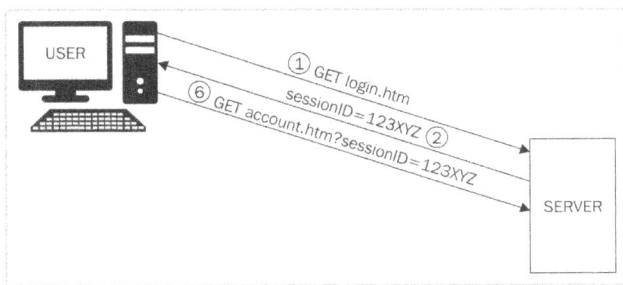

Figure 9.11: Users provide authentication details over HTTP for the server to inspect. The server creates a session for the user if the details are correct and returns a token for the user to reference with data requests.

➤ **IP addresses** - Limiting access to the API's functionality through IP address is a good way to limit scope for abusing the API to users operating from a specific location or server; this certainly rules out random attackers with no knowledge of the API's workings. ID based keys and session tokens can also take advantage of this by attaching valid IP addresses to client profiles stored on the server. The downside to this approach is that it isn't suitable for home users, who tend not to have a fixed IP address.

Testing strategy

With the exception of the most basic programs, no software exists without faults in some form or another. It's important that your software is tested thoroughly enough to ensure that there are no faults that affect performance to a point where the software is considered to be a liability or unreliable. A large part of reliability comes from the strategy for testing the software, with good strategies making the difference between discovering serious faults and them going unnoticed.

Some considerations for how software is tested during and upon completion of the project should include:

➤ **Testing effort consideration** - The effort required for testing will grow in proportion to the size of the project. As more features are added to the software system, more testing will be required to test each of them for every version update. Even where features haven't been altered in the new release, a thorough testing strategy should ensure that all features are tested prior to a new release to avoid the possibility of less obvious dependencies introducing unexpected faults. Additionally, the more complexity that is introduced to the system, the more effort that is required to plan testing in order to identify and protect against the growing number of different faults that can emerge.

➤ **Test driven development** - This is a method of developing software in which the project specification is defined as a series of tests that the software must be tested against. Code is developed as a series of units, each performing a specific functionality matching their associated test requirement; these units are typically very small and highly specialized in what they do. The project is developed in a way where each unit is created to be tested against a set of expected outputs based on known inputs. Once these units are known to pass all of their tests, they are integrated into the main system.

A unit test is a piece of code written to test another piece of code against expected output. If the code function `check_crossTheRoad()` were controlling a robot to cross the road, one of the unit tests could be designed to test decision making when crossing at traffic lights; in this case, the robot's functionality can detect:

➤ The *red man* - meaning don't cross the road

➤ The *green man* - meaning that the robot can cross the road

Two unit tests can be created to ensure that this functionality is working correctly — the first would be to test with something like `check_crossTheRoad("traffic-light", "red-man")`, which should return `false` because the rule for "traffic-light" and "red-man" is to not cross the road; the test only reports a pass if the result of `check_crossTheRoad()` is `false`. Another test could be `check_crossTheRoad("traffic-light", "green-man")`, which is designed to report a pass if `true` is returned. This process of testing is referred to as red/green/refactor (nothing to do with the red/green man example), in which the programmer is regularly on the look out for tests that turn up as red (fail) and will refactor code until all tests return green (pass). It's important to note that although a unit may fail a test, the fault may lie within one of the components that the unit is dependent upon; hence the focus also being on investigating how code can be refactored if necessary when tests fail.

Making use of this method to develop software helps with the type of project that has a high level of complexity, such as projects relying on many calculations. This allows software to be developed without programmers needing to fully understand the full complexities of the entire system requirements; e.g. no need for programmers to be maths experts to develop functionality producing calculations based on the provided formulas. This approach allows for full focus to be placed on one part at a time so that programmers can work faster on developing features in a way that they can verify accuracy against expected outputs.

> **Defining testing roles** - A common mistake in software projects is to assume that programmers should perform all testing because they created the code. Although programmers may test as they develop their code, programmers are the least effective people for tracking unexpected faults because their equipment and mindset are set to test the software against optimal situations. For example, a programmer's computer may have preset configurations such as cookies set during the programming activities that are not present on a real user's computers, hence leading to tests being passed in the programming envionrment that would otherwise fail in real world use. Ensuring that the system is thoroughly tested by people unconnected to writing the code will address the issue of these types of faults going undetected, while making use of people who have no knowledge of the system will also help to expose unexpected user input that could become problematic. This is the job of QA (quality assurance), yet it is surprising how many organizations are not aware of this.

> **Unit testing** - Some types of tests are required to be repeated on a regular basis to guarantee that their features haven't been broken by the latest code updates. The problem with this is that repetition is costly and increases the chances of human error being introduced to the testing process, resulting in tests not being performed correctly or missed out completely. Where software is developed as individual units through styles such as object oriented programming, much of this repeated testing can be automated; either through specialized software such as PHP Unit (`www.phpunit.de`) for PHP and N Unit (www.nunit.org) for C#, or by writing a script/mini-program to test code components against known inputs and their expected outputs. This approach means that testers can have a program in which they click a button to start the tests and receive a list of all components that are failing so that action can be taken to make corrections.

This method of testing is best suited to programmers writing the software because it is all about testing the code, as opposed to testing how the software functions in real usage. With programmers having an understanding of how the code is developed, they are able to write new tests as required – in addition to reacting to new faults identified in the test reports.

Security considerations

The problem with securing software systems is that clients often dismiss the importance of security efforts until something bad happens. With security faults almost never being obvious to identify from regular testing, there is a need to invest specialized effort to identify security vulnerabilities. The combination of client's negligence and the need for specialist knowledge to perform the required testing create a toxic combination that can lead your software systems being misused in ways that can resulting in anything from data being stolen through to your system being deleted and malicious software being installed to your server. Although security is something that can never be 100% guaranteed, you can build a processes and philosophies into your software development strategy that will help to minimize the amount of security vulnerabilities your software is exposed to:

➤ **All systems can be hacked** - There will always be a way for people to abuse software in ways that the application's developers were not aware of during production. Knowing this beforehand gives you the advantage of being able to put procedures in place to minimize potential damage should this happen to your software.

➤ **Assume your system will be hacked** - Making the assumption that your software will be hacked will put you in the position of being able to put a strategy in place that keeps any disruption to a minimum. Your strategy should include both technical and policy elements that are activated as soon as any attempt to hack your system is detected — whether it be successful or not.

➤ **Build security into your code — don't add it later** - The structure of your code should be created in a way that has an emphasis on making sure that known security risks are tackled at every opportunity rather than leaving these considerations as an issue to be added at the end of the project.

➤ **Whitelisting** - Define what you will accept over what you won't accept - It is impossible to identify all of the different types of input that may harm your system, hence instead of blacklisting everything you know not to be accepted as input (blacklisting). Instead, be specific on what you will accept (whitelisting) by restricting the acceptance of data to what you know to be safe, hence providing a guarantee that keeps you in full control of what your code accepts and rejects. This approach avoids scope for dangerous input to be forgotten – or where future changes make some types of input dangerous. An example of this would be where your web application is written in PHP; you obviously don't want to accept PHP files as part of your upload features because this can lead to attackers hijacking your server by executing code they upload. Additionally, you may be unaware of other executable languages that run on your server, or where future server changes activate additional scripting languages such as Perl and Python.

The whitelisting approach guarantees to secure the system against the unknown and future changes.

➤ **Make use of multiple layers to secure data and functionality** - Knowing that that your code will have some type of security vulnerability somewhere, regardless of how much effort you invest into making sure this doesn't happen, means that you shouldn't rely on any individual security feature to guarantee security against the type of attack they are meant to protect against. Just like in safety critical systems such as planes, your code should be designed with secondary backup features and processes that secure known vulnerabilities should the primary version fail. This is highly useful for situations where system maintenance activities accidentally introduce faults that result in primary layers of security failing.

➤ **Focus attention on areas accepting any type of input** - Input provided by third party systems or users should be classed as high risk because these are where attacks on your system will be launched from. This means that special consideration should be given to how these areas are designed and tested to minimize risk of exploitation, while maximizing opportunities to identify vulnerabilities before the system goes live.

➤ **Never trust any input provided from the client side** - No information provided from client side applications should be considered as safe — not even data that is meant to be generated from client side code. Especially with regards to web based applications where system generated input can be embedded into the client side user interface using hidden input fields, client side tools such as those available within web browsers can be used to change HTML and other content used to submit hidden information to your web server.

➤ **Understand the code components you use** - Many software applications are exposed to vulnerabilities through the use of third party components that contain faults or are purposely designed for malicious purposes. Always research any third party software components that you plan to use by researching online reviews and checking the code yourself if possible. Avoid going trigger-happy on the use of third party components, especially plug-ins for open source software systems such as WordPress — each additional component you use increases the chance of you using code that introduces vulnerabilities to your system.

➤ **Keep it simple** - Complexity in your code introduces higher scope for faults and vulnerabilities that escape your detection during testing. Eliminating any unnecessary complexity means that you reduce the risk of this by increasing the manageability of your code, while also reducing its testing requirements.

➤ **Design robust and agile code** - Code patterns such as the previously mentioned MVC and n-tier development that are designed from the beginning to allow future adaption will provide a significant advantage in your ability to manage security issues. Although these patterns alone don't guarantee the elimination of security vulnerabilities, they allow rapid response to any issues exposed and ways to offer multiple layers of protection with minimal effort. This can make difference between the system being vulnerable for minutes, hours or days.

➤ **Never trust the user** - Most users will not have malicious intentions, but it only takes one malicious user to abuse your system for the damage to be done. Innocent users can pose just as much of a threat to your system's security such as through the use of weak passwords, storing information such as credit card details that your system isn't designed to secure against and giving their login details to other people. Not trusting the user means that you are more likely to integrate features that will minimize the types of problem that both malicious and innocent users can create.

Version control

Version control tools are useful for addressing changing requirements the risk of functionality between updates. These are software applications that help you to keep a recorded history of your code, images and any other files associated with your software project. Major advantages of using version control include:

➤ **Easier co-ordination between programmers** - The need to manage access and distribution of code increases rapidly when working on a project with other programmers. When this isn't managed properly, programmers risk overwriting the work of other programmers by not having the most up to date version of code, or where they are writing to the same code files at the same time. Version control tools avoid these risks by allowing programmers to request the latest versions of code and to lock access to them when they are adding new updates.

➤ **Taking a step back** - There are times when rolling code and other files back to a previous state can be of benefit to a project; typically to save time. An example of this would be when a difficult to track bug has been introduced, where rolling back to a previous version of the code requires less effort than tracking and solving the bug. Another example would be where the client has requested some change that they later decide to cancel and request to revert back to the original; version control avoids the need to invest time in undoing code alterations by simply reverting back to the version before the changes were made.

➤ **Acceptance management** - Another situation where version control can be used to support the management of programming teams is where there is a need for the lead programmer to verify the acceptance of code submitted by other programmers on the team. This could be to ensure that junior developers and new team members have developed code to an acceptable quality or where code has been fully tested against security issues and other factors of concern. Developers can submit the updates through the version control system for storage and access, but only people with authority such as the lead programmer can accept submissions to become part of the real version of the software project.

➤ **Learning what happened** - Everything submitted can be accompanied by a description about the submission. These descriptions can be used to describe the changes made, hence allowing you to track what has changed in the history of a document; useful for identifying where bugs may have been introduced.

Concept glossary

Popular version control tools that are oriented towards software development, such as Git (`www.git-scm.com`), tend to be provided as command line tools, meaning that you will need to learn their commands. There are also user interface tools that you can download separately to use with these tools. Concepts that are worth your investigation when considering the use of version control in your projects include:

> **Repository** - A repository is a directory used by the version control software to store the versions of files and their details that relate to your project. The version control software manages this directory on your behalf, so there is no need for you to know anything about how they work; just where they are so that you can direct the version control software when working on them.
>
> Repositories come in two types — local and remote. All projects will have a local repository, which is the location you submit all of your changes to as you work on your project; your local repository is what belongs to you.
>
> Remote repositories are stored somewhere outside of your computer, either on a local network or on the Internet. This type of repository is highly useful for any project that uses more than one programmer or content developer — and even as a backup solution for solo projects; hence is always worth considering. Network repositories are where team members submit final versions of files they are working from for availability to other team members and inclusion in the final version of the software project — see about commit.

> **Clone** - A clone is simply a copy of a repository directory. When starting an existing project, or where you are introducing new team members, you will make a clone of the original project for yourself/them to work on. When working on team projects, you will typically clone a project from an Internet or local network URL.

> **Commit** - Changes you make need to be submitted to the version control repository being used to store your changes; submitting your file updates is called committing. Individual changes you make are committed in your local repository, in which you keep doing this until you are ready to make a final commitment, in which your updates are sent to the remote repository to be made available to everyone on the team.
>
> Version control tools usually provide you with the ability to attach a description with each commit you make. This is a useful feature that allows you to look back in the future for understanding how the project was developed — and to identify where bugs may have been introduced. It is for this reason that it is recommended to make each commit based on one theme — i.e. fixes for feature A and not fixes for feature A, B and D.

➤ **Staging Area** - More specific to Git, the staging area is a place that can be used for temporary storage before they are committed. This is useful for allowing you to decide which alterations you want to include as part of a commit — hence no need to worry about the order of your changes affecting what you commit; i.e. you can work on fixes for feature A, then feature B and then feature A, and make two separate commits — one for fixes of feature A and the other commit for feature B.

➤ **Branch** - Being able to branch parts of a project provides you with the ability to keep alternate versions of code and content separate, while still existing parallel to each other. This could be used for keeping the untested development versions of a software system separate from an older version tried and tested version that doesn't have the new features.

➤ **Merge** - Where branching is the ability to create an alternate version of part of the software project, merging is the ability to combine these alternate versions together. This would be used in situations such as when a new feature has passed testing, where merging the code and content developed in the development branch would make the new updates available in the main branch.

When used properly, the use of version control is a solution to avoid many problems associated with growing project teams and provides individuals with the flexibility to adapt code without the fear of breaking something that affects the entire project. In worst case scenarios, version control will always offer the ability to roll back to a version where the code was fully working — providing you remembered to commit regularly!

Summary

Success in software development is heavily influenced by strategy for the construction of each component. Good code strategy directly influences your ability to react to changing client requests, whether this be through the client not clearly describing the project brief, or needing adaptability for changes in their operating environment. When it comes to making assumptions about software projects, the only safe assumption to make is that specification changes are likely.

Changes to software specifications are always bad news, but code that has been developed to accommodate this can make the difference between changes being slow/painful and fast/efficient to implement. Understanding code principles for object oriented programming, patterns such as MVC and system architectures for APIs will allow you to design code in a way that provides higher degrees of flexibility and scalability across multiple platforms so that your software projects can be upgraded quickly, efficiently and without restriction from legacy code. Designing your code in a way that is modular also allows for easier upgrades, testing and confinement of faults, including security vulnerabilities.

Although it is tempting to rely on a plug and play approach to software development, especially when using open source software, it is important to ensure that the code you are using is reliable and secure. When using open source components, the use of metrics can be used to evaluate their suitability, such as the project's maturity, response time to bugs and project activity. Third party components can provide additional functionality with minimal time investment, but components that are poorly coded and/or are integrated in a way that is poorly planned can undo the benefits you have worked to achieve in the design of your main system. It is for this reason that special care should be taken when considering and integrating third party components — especially in relation to security.

10

Software Development Methodology

The creation of all creations is a method, with software development being no exception. Although there are many methods that can be used to develop software systems, it is important to identify the type of method that best suited to the software you are developing and the situation you operate within. The methods used to develop large scale software systems involving many people may not translate to the type of small scale projects you are likely to be involved with as a freelancer — not due to how the technology works, but due to the social implications of working with people. This is what the study of software methodology is about — the identification of software development methods to efficiently accomplish the production of software to an acceptable standard.

This chapter looks at the features of established methodologies that are relevant to freelance projects so that you can identify the processes relevant for developing your own style of freelancing.

Social factors of software development

For those who have never experienced writing software for a real client, it can be tempting to jump straight into writing the code to get the job done. The lesson learnt very quickly is that developing software for clients is very different to developing the same software as a personal project or a coursework item for a school, college or university course. Both code and hardware system requirements could be exactly the same, but the big difference is the people factor — in the real world, software developers have to contend with social factors that are never part of personal projects or coursework:

> **Unknown requirements**: Unlike coursework where there is a clear specification of what you are expected to create, clients often only have a vague idea of what they want — typically in the form of *what* it should do and not *how* it should do it, but there are also times when clients don't know "what" the software should do. A good example of this is how people may want an e-commerce website to sell their products (what), but don't know how they want it to function (how).

> ➤ **Changing requirements**: The issue of changing requirements emerge from one or a mixture of clients not initially knowing how they want their system to function, clients not fully understanding how their system design will affect their business processes, or changes in the client's business environment (laws, competitors, technology, etc.).

> ➤ **Collaboration**: Bigger projects will require collaboration with other programmers, content creators, designers and people with other types of skills. The effort of collaboration needs to make sure that people are working on productively on the right tasks to an acceptable standard. Collaborators are likely to have different skill levels, especially in programming — meaning the need to make sure that collaborating programmers with lower skills are assigned to the right tasks, in addition to being taught about required code patterns and strategies needed for the project.

> ➤ **Politics**: The more people there are involved with the project, the more scope there is for social factors such disagreements to become a barrier to progressing the project. Politics can lead to software developers being provided with misleading information as well as being drawn into irrelevant disputes that hamper their productivity.

Formal software development methodologies go a long way to address these issues, whether it be through formalizing communications, assigning responsibility or avoiding/engaging legalities. The use of tried and tested methodologies in your freelance and contract projects will help you to avoid undesired scenarios that are time consuming and potentially costly. leading to unjustified dissatisfaction of your clients. As a business, it also makes sense for you to have a successful process that you can replicate across all of your projects to ensure their profitability.

Features for preventing problems

Above all, it should be mentioned that there's no single method of software development that is suitable for all software projects. The qualities of a good software development methodology are the features that provide solutions to the problems facing a project, hence software development methodologies that focus on providing solutions to non-existent problems will have less relevance than methodologies that are designed to address the problems that do exist within the project. The first question to be answered shouldn't be about which methodology to choose, but what are the problems faced or likely to be faced by the software project?

Formality

Although it may not sound like a feature, having an element of formality will help to keep the project on track by providing a process that people are aware of. With formality come rules and requirements, which in turn produce discipline — required by the development team and the client.

It is the outcome of formality (requirements and discipline) that benefits projects; not only does it make sure that the development team knows what it should and shouldn't be doing, it also points out to the client what they need to be doing — especially when the development team needs their input to progress.

As a freelancer or contractor, you may work alone directly for the client or as part of a team. Both of these working methods should have some element of formality, even if only to cover your own back. Considerations could include:

> **Appointment of decision maker(s)** : It is agreed by everyone involved in the project that only this person or people have the authority to make decisions relating to the direction of the project.

> **Feature requests written in a specification document**: Making sure that each feature is clearly worded without any scope for ambiguity.

> **All change requests to be made in writing and dated with the signature of an appointed decision maker for approval:** This would occur after the decision maker has been made aware of the implications of the change request — e.g. delay in the project delivery, risk of additional testing requirements, etc. Any implications should be written into the description that the change request authorization document. This formality provides accountability that avoids scenarios involving you being asked to make changes that haven't been requested by the client; this is a significant issue when people involved in the project have their own agenda that's not compatible with those of the assigned decision maker(s).

> **Time sheets:** Having a written record detailing activities relating to the project will provide the client with a better understanding of effort and time being invested. This helps to control the client's understanding of how the software development process works and avoids situations where the client makes assumptions about timeframes and costs for features that sound easy and quick to develop, but in reality are time consuming and difficult.

> **Meeting documentation:** Making sure there is a formal agenda for meetings and that notes are created to document all issues covere will help to make sure that everyone involved can attend the meeting fully prepared and that time isn't wasted on covering irrelevant topics and repeating anything already covered. Keeping a record of all meeting documentation also allows you to backtrack later in the project to identify what was agreed in meetings if required.

> **Specifying availability**: This factor works both ways, where you need to be available to do the work and the client needs to be available to provide resources such as information and content you need to get the job done correctly and on time. Having an element of formality to identify the availability of both parties will avoid situations that affect the progression of the project such as your other project commitments becoming a barrier or where the client may take a holiday that results in a delay to your work due to a requirement of information not being met. Similarly, having a formal agreement relating to your availability helps to avoid the client making assumptions about you not spending enough time on their project — especially where the client doesn't understand the complexities involved in developing the software features they have requested.

Flexibility

The need to adapt for unexpected or changing situations shouldn't be underestimated; not even for projects that appear to have concrete specifications that are unlikely to change. Although formality provides advantages for structure and discipline in the project's development, too much formality can prevent the type of flexibility required to successfully react to unexpected circumstances. An example of this would be where there has only been one decision maker appointed for the project who isn't contactable when an important decision is required; having the flexibility for someone else to make decisions when the primary decision maker is unavailable would help to avoid this situation becoming a problem.

There are many ways in which your software development methodology can incorporate flexibility:

Working hours

For the most part, software development is about writing code. Code is only a valued contribution if it does the job — and a major bonus if it is developed to be maintainable. Unfortunately, writing code, and especially good quality code, requires programmers to be "in the zone"; a reference commonly used to describe the state of mind where the programming problem's solution can be clearly identified, hence resulting in the programmer being highly productive. Not everyone is a morning person, meaning that a lot of people are more productive towards the end of the day. With software development relying on the quality of the programmer's output, the traditional formality of set 9 to 5 working hours enforced by most office based businesses becomes counterproductive to getting the most output from the programmers on a project. It is for this reason that flexibility of working hours can have a positive impact on projects in terms of the delivery and cost by producing more output with less time requirements by only investing time that is highly productive.

Code patterns

It is technically true that there is no wrong way to develop code as long as it works and the outcome meets the requirements specified for the desired software. With this in mind, there are still bad and good methods to develop code in relation to business strategy— the better code having advantages in adaptability, testing, security and other issues. So although any method of programming will eventually get the job done, better methods of programming will reduce problems, costs, risks and time requirements to make you more profitable and able to meet criteria for quality and completion time. Programmers have already identified so called code patterns that are a good fit to meet the demands of software projects, hence you can learn about these patterns and adapt them to fit your (or your team's) programming style and project requirements. Think of code patterns as being similar to writing, in which there is a pattern that you use for splitting your content between paragraphs, chapters, diagrams, etc. - all useful tools for specific parts of your writing.

Code patterns shouldn't be flexible in the sense of consistency for programming style, but they should be developed to be flexible to withstand changing requirements. This means investing more time to write code that is reusable and adaptable for the long term. Although this requires more effort initially, the benefits become apparent later in the project when alterations and additions can be implemented in a few lines of code with minimal time and skills. The skills element of this benefit also means that what would otherwise be considered to require advanced programming skills can be given to junior programmers to reduce the project's costs and release more experienced programmers on the project for other tasks.

Specification management

Project specifications change for many reasons, therefore your project's methodology should reflect this by providing a process to facilitate changing specifications. This could be in the form of breaking the project into release milestones where formal goals are identified for each release with the ability to refine the specification for future releases, or where an approach is taken to developing the software that refines it until the client is happy. The important consideration is to make sure that whatever process you use to reflect changing specifications also makes it clear what changes there are to the costs involved.

Skills deployment

Where you need to hire people who have skills or time you don't have, it is worth considering whether sub-contracting or employing is the best option. When budget is a concern, sub-contracting could be the safest option; providing the flexibility to only pay for the hours required — as opposed to employing people where time waiting for the next phase of the project to commence will still cost you in wages/salaries. Contractor fees are more expensive on a per hour basis, but they don't have any of the wastage and hidden costs such as employee insurance, training and equipment. Although you should make sure that your sub-contractors are legally considered to be contractors to the project and not under your employment — in the UK this is called IR35 and is worth reading up on.

Link: http://www.contractoruk.com/ir35/what_is_ir35_rules_explained. html

Prototyping

Working on a prototype before developing the real product will give you a lot of flexibility to make changes without needing to worry about the implications of how change requests from the client introduce the risk of new bugs appearing in the code, or where inflexible code will cause problems to add the new requests. Prototypes can be created without the need to use specialist software; using PowerPoint or Keynote to create an interactive presentation will allow you to get the quality of feedback that clients would otherwise only provide once the software development has started, by which point it can become difficult to undo code you have created. An added bonus of prototyping with PowerPoint or Keynote is that these are general purpose software that the client is likely to have enough IT skills to add some of the changes they want, meaning less difficulties in you needing to interpret ideas the client struggles to communicate.

Planning and analysis

The art of planning for freelance projects is a fine balance between the extremes of absolutely no planning and too much planning. Heavyweight methodologies such as PRINCE2 and SSADM—two methodologies that are overkill for most freelance projects, make significant use of analysis and report writing activities to correctly define everything required before the software development begins. These are good in theory, but not so good in practice when it comes to executing the typical freelance project you're likely to get involved with. The reasons for this include:

Time requirements

The typical freelance client wants to see results fairly quickly. The level of planning detail demanded by heavyweight methodologies add a significant amount of time to projects that freelance clients aren't likely to be patient enough to wait for.

Knowledge requirements

Although the purpose of analysis activities in heavyweight methodologies is to identify the problem and the most suitable solution, many freelance clients don't understand enough about their requiements in order to give good quality information to fully identify the problem and solution.

An example of this is almost every small business wanting a website — these businesses are primarily motivated to purchase a website because they want a presence on the Internet to be like everyone else. The sad reality is that most of these businesses fail to make use of their websites and consequently lose money on their investment because in many cases, a website is least suitable option for the problem they have poorly defined.

While these businesses say they want a web presence and make the assumption of needing a website, what they really need is a way to make sales and enquiries via the Internet; of which options such as Amazon, eBay and specialist directories such as Tutor Hunt are a much better option because they provide both the platform and the audience without the associated software development and marketing costs. For many businesses who target consumers (as opposed to other businesses), having a Facebook page will have more marketing success than a dedicated website. Even where the creation of a website is justified to provide confidence to the client's customers, this type of business will often request a large website with unnecessary features, when what they really need is something very simple to present basic information needed by their customers. This is a clear example of how a lack of knowledge and ability to describe the main problem leads to an inadequate analysis that proposes an unsuitable solution.

Budget

Most small startup businesses, which are likely to be the main source of your freelance work to begin with, don't have huge budgets. The sophistication of heavyweight methodologies adds significant time overheads to kick starting projects — so much that the amount of time required to do a fully detailed analysis such as with SSADM could eat up the entirety of the client's budget before you get to write your first line of code. This factor alone would rule out the use of detailed methodologies for most freelance projects, regardless of how suitable they are on a technical level for solving the problem.

Changing requirements

With the majority of clients not truly knowing what they want or fully understanding the problem they are trying to solve, combined with changing factors in their business environment, you will often discover that the scope of your projects change and expand throughout their lifecycle. It is not uncommon to find what was initially intended to be a week's worth of work turning into a project that spans months or even years. With this type of project, a lot of planning that occurs at the start of the project becomes redundant midway through the development, meaning that time and money has been wasted on analysis activities that have no impact on the project delivery. Furthermore, each change results in the requirement for the existing plan to be updated to reflect changes in the requirements, hence further increasing the time and budget required.

With all of these factors weighing against the use of planning in your freelance methodology, it would be easy to assume that planning is a bad thing for freelance software development. The truth couldn't be further from this assumption — although it's safe to say that the detailed planning championed by the heavyweight methodologies are overkill and ultimately unsuitable for the majority of freelance projects, there is still a need to have a form of planning that is lightweight for activities to be executed efficiently and profitably on a smaller budget, but adequate enough to define expectations and keep the project on track to meet key milestones and completion.

The level of planning and analysis required for freelance projects is dependent on the project in question, with the primary factors dictating the required effort being budget, time and complexity. The main planning and analysis considerations for all projects should include:

Problem definition

Clearly identifying the problem to be addressed without influence of how the client is describing the requirements in relation to a preferred solution.

Culture analysis

Understanding the people that the project relates to will form a large part of identifying the best solution to the problem, as well as understanding how to manage the client and their employees. The culture analysis shouldn't be restricted to the people directly involved with the design and development of the project, but also to people outside of the project development such as the end users of the software such as the client's customers and suppliers. This activity helps to identify social barriers posed to both the software development process and the end product, both of which will highlight which of the potential solutions would be the easiest and least risk to implement.

In terms of the previous website example, a culture analysis would reveal that the target audience of all businesses can be found on pre-existing web platforms, whether it be eBay, Amazon, eLance or Tutor Hunt. This analysis would also identify how these potential customers are already familiar with the pre-existing platforms and having enough trust to make payments through them; all of which pose a significant barrier to building a custom built website to do the same job. Furthermore, this analysis would also identify that regardless of how good the software provided for content and e-commerce management, not all businesses have the capabilities to execute the required ongoing content strategy to make their website a success — in some cases giving the ability to change and add content on the website can lead to some clients adding poorly written content that destroys brand credibility.

Technology evaluation

The technology relating to the software shouldn't be underestimated. Care should be taken to ensure that the vision for the solution is in line with the technology that is both available and in use. Projects should avoid over ambition by being designed to require technologies that are not in use by the target audience — one example of this would be developing a mobile app that requires higher than average phone hardware and OS specifications, therefore limiting the number of users who can use the app. With this said, which is especially relevant to mobile apps, thought should also be given in relation to the expected state of the market by the end of the project completion. Where mobile apps are concerned, hardware specs rapidly improve every year, with the average phone user upgrading every two years. This has a significant impact on projects that have a long duration; with the average technology specification in use at the end of the project being significantly different to those in use at the start.Environment evaluation

Factors that are outside the control of the client lead to situations that affect the project requirements. Understanding the environment that the client's business operates in will lead to a better understanding of how the definition of the problem may change throughout the duration of the project. By understanding how the environment will affect the project, new considerations can be identified for the requirements of the software's programming implementation for flexibility that will allow accommodation of new feature requests that result from changes occurring in the client's business environment.

Risk analysis

The element of risk should never be underestimated; whether it's factors that have a direct impact on the code or whether it's the risk of the client not paying their bill. Understanding the risk allows for procedures to be put in place to eliminate or minimise their impact should they occur.

Viability analysis

Identification of options to solve the problem without bias to any individual solution, regardless of what has been suggested by the client is important. Viability should be considered as the achievability within the timeframe and budget given by the client, as well for the end result being realistically capable of producing the short and long term outcomes desired by the client.

Milestone identification

Breaking the project into smaller objectives makes it easier to show the client how far away you are from completion, as well as to identify if you are on schedule — and for action to be taken early if not.

Timescales

Having an estimate for the delivery of milestones and their breakdown tasks is good for your own time estimates as well as for allowing the client to see regular updates on how the project is progressing.

Factors requiring planning and analysis need to relate to the type of client the project is for, the people you will be working with in the client's organisation and even the team you are hiring or working with. This side to planning and analysis methodologies is completely focused on people oriented issues; referred to as a soft methodology, this is different to the previously mentioned methodologies and activities whcih focus purely on the technology implementation. People issues should never be underestimated because they always have an impact on the progression of the project. The same project for two different clients could have a significant difference in cost and time purely based the people factors relating to the client's employees and their company culture. Important soft elements of your methodology should include considerations for:

Understanding characteristics and learning styles of the client and their employees

Every business is different, so it's important not to assume that what works with one client will work with another. People are creatures of habit, and understanding this will provide you with an advantage for learning patterns of behaviors and characteristics in your clients that will allow you to predict their actions and reactions to situations that emerge in the project. This foresight is important for allowing you to be proactive in avoiding problems — instead of being reactive to problems after they've occurred.

"If those who are sent to draw water begin by drinking themselves, the army is suffering from thirst." - Sun Tzu, The Art of War

Soft methodologies such as Peter Checkland's **Soft Systems Methodology** (**SSM**) address this issue by having a specific process to model the different roles people play in situations. The model refers to situation role players as actors, owners and customers, describing each in relation to their environment, experiences and perspectives that influence how they become involved with the project. By understanding the model, you are able to develop an understanding of their motivations and limitations so that you can identify the best way to approach the project with minimal friction, disappointment and confusion simply by communicating the right message to the right people. After all, adequate decisions can only be made by appropriate people who have the current insight and authority; you are simply wasting your time, if not also opening the door for bad decisions or expectations, by speaking to the wrong people about project issues they shouldn't be involved with. This process also forms a solid foundation for setting expectations that the project performance will be measured against.

Setting expectations and performance metrics

When it comes to setting expectations and performance metrics by which the project performance will be judged by, the first thing that should come to mind is to keep objectives **SMART** — specific, measurable, achievable, realistic and timely. SMART objectives should be the foundation of your plan for setting the right expectations so that your performance metrics can be met. People with experience in any type of engineering or management field will have learnt quickly that it is much easier to promise than to deliver, with software development being no exception. The saying of "loose lips sink ships" is a good phrase to have embedded as part of your team's mantra so that situations can be avoided where people accidentally say things in front of clients that needlessly increase expectations.

The risk to avoid in all software development projects is providing any type of suggestions that fall outside of the SMART agenda. This happens a lot easier than it may sound; especially if you have junior software developers working with you who interact with the client at meetings or through e-mail. This is more common in digital creative projects that involve software development, where it is easy for people to get over enthusiastic and under estimate the complexity and time requirements of their ambitions. In these scenarios, what is expected to take hours to create can turn out to take days or weeks, resulting in projects being delayed, budgets exceeded and most critically the project team failing to meet performance metrics, potentially leading to the client discontinuing the project. A form of soft methodologies such as SSM is required to control this type of situation to avoid emerging difficulties leading to conflict and blame. In turn, software developers are able to avoid distraction by team/client politics, resulting in more of their time being spent productively to progress the project.

Resolving conflict

It would be naïve to think that your projects will be executed and completed without conflict of some form. Not all conflicts are severe, but all are conflicts nonetheless. All conflicts originate from agendas or communication breakdown, with the majority resulting from the latter. Avoiding conflict in most cases comes down to having a clear communication strategy — especially when you are dealing with projects that involve multiple people. Make sure that the right people receive the right communications, complete with the ability to remind them and record agreements in writing. Time is a factor of all projects that distorts perceptions of agreements; the more time involved means the more scope there is for people to forget or be selective in remembering the finer details. When agreements are documented clearly in writing, problems of selective and distorted memory of agreement details magically disappear.

The other cause for conflict are the agendas of people, which are always something to look out for. These conflicts are difficult to avoid due to the person or people with the agenda actively steering the project in the direction for conflict. Understanding what these agendas are will allow you to plan in advance an adequate response to the situation. Sometimes the solution lies in identifying how to appease the people with the agenda without derailing the project, whereas other times it may be best to isolate the people who are causing problems so that their impact on the project's progression can be minimized. It should be noted that there is a fine balance between appeasing people so that embroilment in politics can be avoided, and making harsh decisions that may offend people. Always understand who you are answerable to so that your efforts can be focused on appeasing them; when it comes to conflict caused by agendas, many problems are caused by people bending the truth or telling outright lies.

Avoiding involvement in client politics

Politics between you/your team and the client are enough for you to be concerned about without also being involved with the client's internal politics. Make sure not to willfully or accidentally engage in client politics, which includes making comments on individuals, decisions or situations that don't directly involve your work. It is very easy to accidentally step into a client's internal politics by commenting on their activities or individual employees. Even if only jokingly, this can lead to perceptions of you taking sides in their affairs that result in mistrust creeping into your relationship with employees of the client who have a direct impact on your ability to work on the project. Your embroilment in client politics adds unnecessary barriers to meeting the project's performance metrics; in the most extreme cases can cause a complete failure of the project.

Documenting agreements

Something that should be involved in all soft issues is the documentation of agreements. These agreements don't magically provide solutions to the technical elements such as resolving broken code, but they are a framework for keeping the project on track to an agreed specification. This benefits everyone, helping to remind develoers what needs to be done, while making sure that the client has a reference to what they've requested. Having a policy for documenting agreements also helps to avoid conflicts caused through agendas by clearly identifying who is requesting alterations to the project specifications. This allows for any devious actions to be traced in a way that allows the client to take action and avoids you being held accountable.

Communicating ideas, agreements and opinions

The foundations to all soft problems are in perception, and an important part of how perceptions are created is through communication. Good communications can mean the difference of good ideas being correctly interpreted as they are intended, or incorrectly interpreted as bad ideas - resulting in the software being produced without features that can make the difference between its success and failure.

As a minimum, the use of document templates for Microsoft Office or Libre Office should be considered for many communications; especially those that need to be documented. The use of templates for communication allows for consistency as well as to remind people who are writing communications of what they should be asking or providing information about. Examples of templates that can benefit communications include change request documents, progress report updates and requirements analysis communications; all of these communications can benefit from improved quality by prompting writers to detail who, what, when, where and why. Consistency in template formatting also makes it easier for people looking to find specific information if the template format is designed to have a specific section that is easily identifiable when speed reading.

Having a plan to execute and resolve all of these issues will allow you to manage your projects in a way that avoids, or at least minimises, the risk of people issues becoming barriers to progressing the project.

Methodologies of interest

Although some have been briefly mentioned earlier in this chapter, this section looks at several methodologies that are either suitable or specifically designed for software development. The descriptions of these methodologies are meant as an introduction to their suitability rather than as a detailed instruction manual for their execution — of which there are dedicated.

Waterfall model

The waterfall model is a structured process for developing software that for the most part emphasises on progressing from one stage to the next in a logical order, and reverting back to a previous stage when the current stage cannot be completed to a satisfactory standard. Its focus is on creating the design specification upfront before coding implementation begins — a process that works in ideal environments that never change and where clients are able to perfectly communicate their requirements upfront. The relationship between each stage of the development cycle is represented in the following diagram:

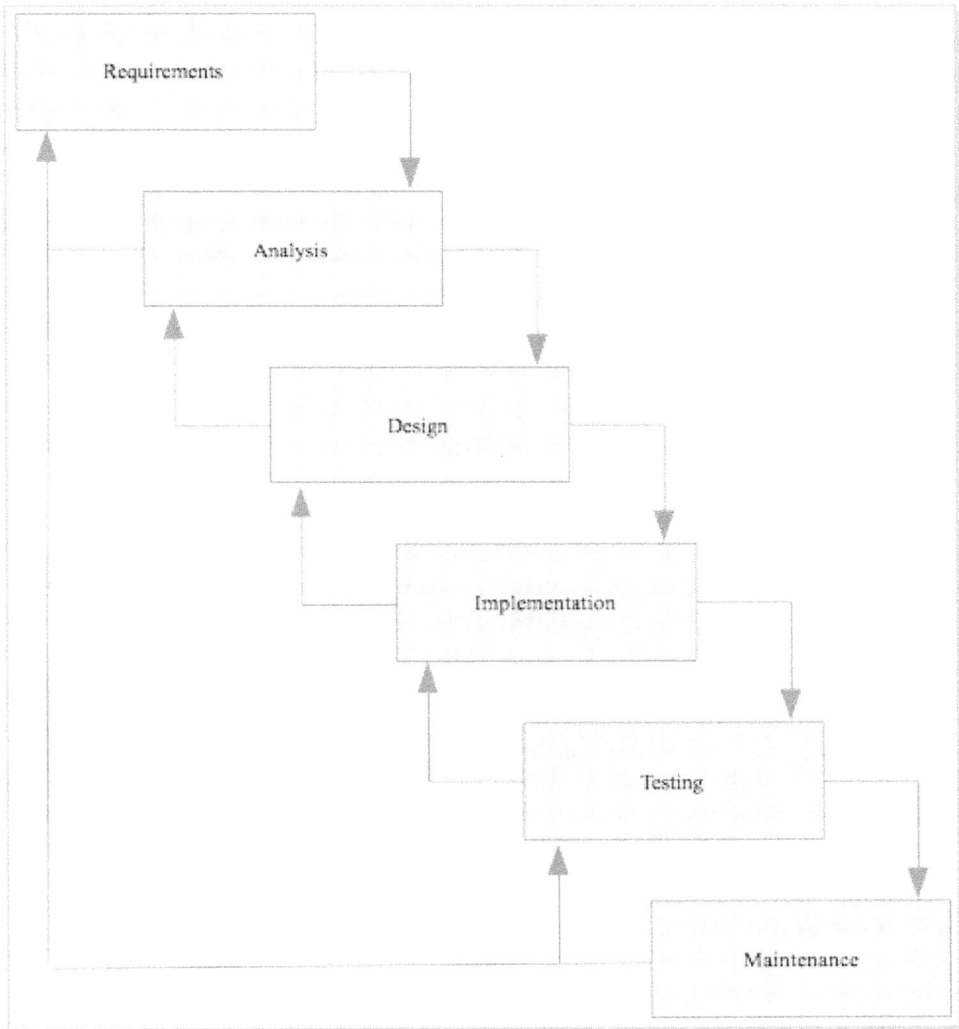

As demonstrated in the diagram, the waterfall model splits the software development project into six specific stages that focus on a specific type of activity. These are:

> **Requirements**: Defines the desired outcomes of the project; this activity looks at describing the problem to be solved in relation to individual characteristics that the chosen solution must have.

> **Analysis**: Looks at the problem in more detail to identify potential problems, assumptions made, client characteristics, available budget and delivery timescale options in relation to available solutions that meet the identified requirements. This analysis allows for the identification of the most appropriate solution that fits the current situation — which may not be the most technological advanced solution, or even software based. In essence, the analysis phase is also a feasibility study for the project.

> **Design**: The process of defining how the chosen solution will be implemented. This process is a mixture of defining the logical processes and component structure of sub-systems such as databases and communication modules, as well as visual components of the user interface. The ideal design documentation should be created to a standard that describes exactly how the chosen solution should be developed.

> **Implementation**: The creation of the identified design. An ideal situation would consist of the design documentation being handed to creators (software developers, designers and/or whoever else is required) who can create and integrate each of the documented design components without any need to communicate with the client or understand their business processes.

> **Testing**: Once the design has been implemented into a working solution, the process of testing how it works in relation to producing expected results against raw data and real use by end users begins. This phase aims to produce a list of any faults within the implementation — which may in turn be based on the provided design. Each fault found results in an alteration request being passed to the the software testers (and designers where relevant) who in turn develop a fix for the fault.

> **Maintenance**: When the system passes all tests to a satisfactory standard, it is published as a live release. Further faults may still be found in the live release version, as well as new adaption requests being made by real users of the system. The maintenance stage looks to engage these requirements to solve faults and restarting the development process for integrating new feature requests.

Like anything, there are situations where the waterfall model is ideal, and other situations where it is less suitable. The following are a list of its pros and cons:

Some of the pros include:

> **Discipline**: The set structure of the waterfall model forces developers and their teams to work in a structured way that accommodates the project's progression from one stage to another.

➤ **Focus**: The main emphasis of the model is its progression from one stage to another, meaning that team members and the client are always aware of the project's current stage. This avoids situations such as creatives adding new design features when the implementation stage is in progress, as well as making it clear to the client when the window for modifying their requirements closes.

➤ **Controlled**: The emphasis on fully defining the problem and design of the system before any code is written makes sure to avoid time wastage caused by change requests and new feature additions being added during the development of the code.

➤ **Perfection**: The structured process of defining the problem and design before any code is written allows for a more accurate and better quality design of the system to be created. This higher quality design gives better direction to the software developers, leading to the software to more accurately fit the problem without appearing to be disjointed through the addition of important features as an afterthought that haven't been properly thought through.

➤ **Knowledge**: A factor that relates to the quality of the design for the implementation is the ability of knowledge to be transferred between all parties involved in the project. Combined with a formal process for documenting accurate, relevant and high quality communications, the waterfall model allows for knowledge generated at each stage to be passed to the people involved with the next stage. This means that there should be no scope for latter stages of the design and implementation to deviate from the identified requirements of the project. This is especially important for business focused projects that require the services of creatives to create visual design components; while designers may make excellent creative decisions, they are not disciplined in business theory and most likely not exposed to the full details of the business motivations of the software project. The structured process of the waterfall model produces a chain of command in which knowledge only flows in the directions for either dictating how the next stage is to progress or where feedback is provided for reconsideration of anything unfeasible or impossible to implement. This chain of command also makes it very easy to trace deliberate efforts to deviate from instructions provided — e.g. unauthorized changes in the design can be traced to the designer if the developed software matches the provided design.

Some of the cons include:

➤ **Understanding**: The buyer of the software development services often doesn't fully understand the problem they are trying to solve. This also means that they don't understand how they intend to solve it with software until they see a working version that they can evaluate to provide feedback. The structure of the waterfall model for progressing linearly from one stage to the next makes it unsuitable for clients who require this type of flexibility. For these clients, the main risk of the waterfall model is how it can put them in a position of having to accept an end result they don't want or having to make a significant investment to implement the requirements they identify in later stages.

> **Estimation**: Complicated projects where the client is not fully aware of their requirements pose a problem because estimates for time and costs can only be provided once the work is well underway. The risk with this is that by the time the full requirements are identified, the client may realize that they don't have the time or budget required to develop the project. In the worst case scenario, initial stages of the waterfall model may eat up too much of the available time and budget before estimates can identify production costs. This can potentially lead to a dispute over what the client has paid for, especially if the client gets no software because their budget didn't last to the production stage.

> **Assumptions**: The nature of the waterfall's structured progression means that knowledge transfer is heavily weighted in one direction from one stage to the next. This means that there is a lot of scope for decisions to be made based on assumptions in the earlier stages that lead to problems in later stages - especially for the implementation. Without the ability for experts, such as programmers who are responsible for executing latter stages, to have input in earlier stages, there is a lot of scope for incorrect assumptions to be made that cause problems. An example of this would be assumptions about available technology, time and cost implications that lead to unexpected problems in developing the software. The most likely candidate of these problems would span from stages such as the design and functionality requirements, where unnecessary requirements are specified and features designed in ways that are more complicated to develop than they initially appear. Such features can cause major problems for keeping the project to estimations made earlier in the project, as well as design concepts setting the client with unrealistic expectations that turn out to be unachievable in terms of the budget, timescale or technology.

> **Testability**: Although the waterfall model has the ability to revert back and forth between individual stages, the emphasis of the project progressing one stage at a time makes it difficult to test the accuracy of stages preceeding the implementation due to not allowing for multiple stages to occur at the same time. An example of this would be where testing of the implemented design reveals how the solution doesn't provide the desired output; the lack of testing in parallel with design and analysis activities provides a vulnerability where assumptions are made about problems being within the developed code, where in actuality the fault may lie within the design, analysis or even the requirements definition. This vulnerability exposes the project to significant time wastage in investigating the wrong problems, resulting in the risk of deadlines being missed and budgets being exceeded.

> **Flexibility**: The structure of the waterfall model allows for only one stage to be engaged at any one time. This opens scope for projects that exist to respond to changing environments where events require rapid response. The rigid process of the waterfall model may mean that any adaptations made in this method are already out of date by the time they are completed.

Conclusion

The waterfall model has many advantages for making sure that the project progresses in a disciplined and linear fashion that makes it easier for all parties involved to identify where the project is at in its lifecycle and what is to come next. The waterfall model's linear progression structure also provides the ability for a chain of command that has minimal scope for stages to accidentally deviate from the project plan —deviations originating from personal agendas being easily traceable to the person responsible.

The main problem with the waterfall model that makes it unsuitable for many projects, including the majority of small scale freelance projects, is its requirement to fully understand the customer's problem. This makes the waterfall model unsuitable for small scale projects where an estimate for time and cost are required before starting the project. However, the process of fully defining the problem and resulting requirements as part of the waterfall model ultimately results in much time being saved overall — providing that critical assumptions can be avoided that affect latter stages of the software development.

Incremental model

The incremental model is based on the waterfall model, but looks to address the issues caused through long development cycles by splitting the project into smaller projects presented as individual releases. If the project was to create a house, we may look at building individual components such as the following:

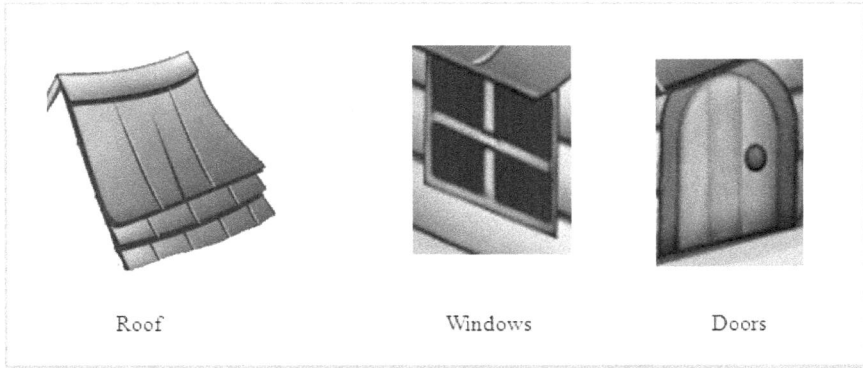

| Roof | Windows | Doors |

Upon completing and integrating everything on the creation list, the final product would take shape:

The execution of this project using the incremental model would look something similar to the following diagram:

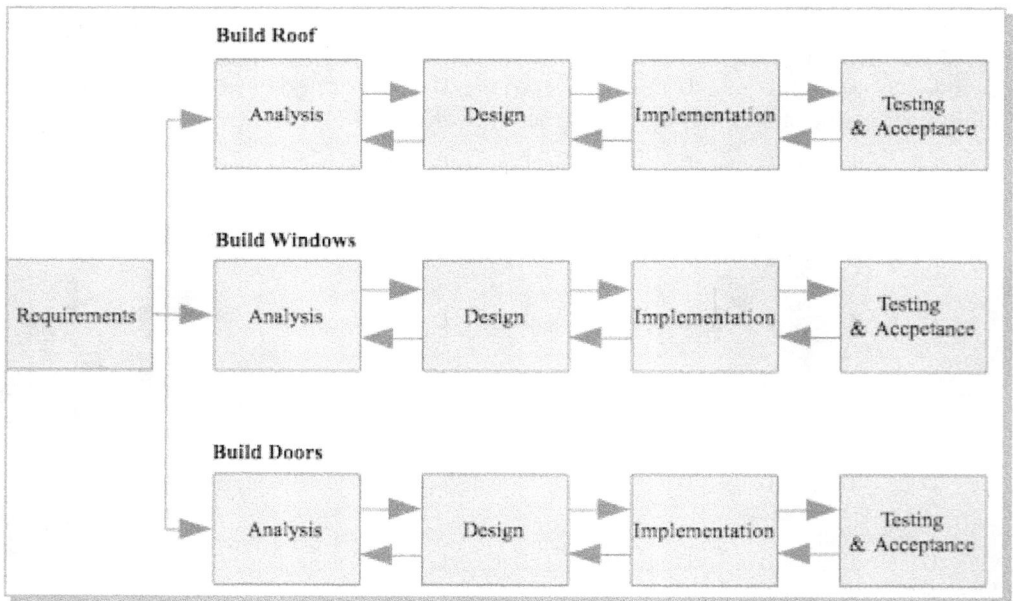

The incremental model addresses some waterfall model's major issues, but also has issues of its own.Some of the pros include:

> **Flexibility**: The breakdown of the project into individual components means that there is more flexibility for the development of new feature requests introduced later in the project life cycle.

➤ **Delivery**: Allows the client to see working components much more quickly than the waterfall model, hence avoiding many issues such as clients perceiving progress to be too slow.

➤ **Discipline**: The incremental model still uses a structured approach to developing software, meaning that it still has the advantage of keeping everyone on track and avoiding issues of people engaging in activities they shouldn't.

➤ **Control**: The development of individual units means that problems can be controlled by restricting their influence to the specific component in question. This is handy to ensure that disruption to the development of other components in the system can be minimized or eliminated, as well as reducing the impact of these problems on any project completion estimates.

➤ **Adjustability**: There is better control for reconsideration of decisions already made; such as for components that turn out to be too costly, timely or impossible to develop. This factor is strengthened where initial requirements are not defined too strictly. The ability to create each component as a project of its own means that their design can, to an extent, be adjusted to suit what is possible for implementation without affecting other components in the wider project.

➤ **Parallel development**: With components being developed independently, there is the option of developing them in parallel with other components. This makes sense where the project has multiple programmers/teams who can take on the responsibility of individual components, or where code can be reused across the software system.

➤ **Testability**: Testing becomes a lot easier with the project split into smaller components, meaning smaller components can tested more thoroughly with less delay. Scenarios where faults in components escalate to other components being developed incorrectly can be avoided due to these initial faults being identified before they are integrated into the main system.

➤ **Feedback**: The ability to release the system incrementally means that end users can use the system earlier in order to provide feedback that allows for better informed decision making for further development. This feedback helps to avoid poor decisions that prove to be costly and problematic, as well as the generation of new ideas that make the system more useful.

➤ **Costs**: Initial costs for getting a working version containing core features will be much lower than the waterfall model because there is no reliance on completing the project to the full specification before the initial release. This also has an additional advantage of saving the project from unnecessary time investment on features that later prove to be unnecessary after; hence providing an opportunity to reduce overall costs occurring in wasted effort on features that don't provide envisaged benefits.

Some of the cons are:

> **Understanding**: There is still a requirement for the client to fully understand what they want to achieve with the project. This is not good for clients who only have a vague idea of what they want to achieve, who refine their requirements as they learn about how the most appropriate solution fits with their business setup.

> **Estimation**: Although it becomes easier to provide an estimate on initial components identified for the project, there is still the problem that most clients will not be able to specify their requirements in enough detail that would lead to a full list of components to be developed in the project. This leaves a lot of questions unanswered, hence resulting in a need to add more requirements later. The addition of new components throughout the life cycle of the project means that initial estimations for time and budget requirements will be unreliable — although estimates for individual components are more likely to be accurate providing that no changes to their original requirements specification are introduced.

> **Dependency risk**: There is a risk of developing system components that are dependent on other components that are not yet fully defined or have a risk of changing in a way that affects the component. In terms of the house example, this would be where the outer walls are built based on the inside rooms of the house, but where changes are later made to these inside rooms requiring them to be double their size — hence also requiring adjustments to both the outer walls and roof of the building to accommodate these requirement changes. These changes may also impact less obvious components, such as the measurements and numbers of windows and doors.

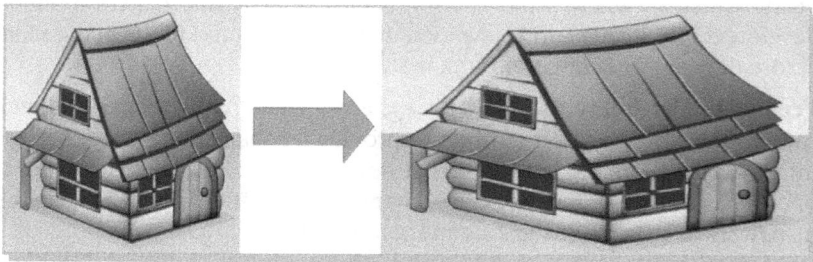

Example of how changes to inner components have an effect on external components.

> **Assumptions**: The development of components are still vulnerable to problems arising from assumptions, although to a much lesser extent than the waterfall model. This is due to how analysis is spread across individual stages instead of being performed entirely at the beginning. While assumptions can still be made, the delay and focus of analysis on stages that become relevant allows for assumptions to be made at a time when more information is available. The outcome of this opens the ability to limit the impact of wrongful in a way that confines them to the component they originate from.

> ➤ **Time**: Modular development is likely to introduce some additional time overhead when compared to developing the project linearly from start to finish. This additional time overhead comes in the form of additional communications and startup repetition such as detailed analysis of every component that would otherwise have only been required once in the waterfall model.

> ➤ **Costs**: Increased time means increased costs.

Conclusion

The incremental model offers a structured method to develop software that is more flexible than the highly structured but rigid waterfall model. It also provides the ability to present working versions of the software to the client earlier and at regular stages, as well as opening opportunities to use a more flexible release strategy.

Cost and time benefits are debatable with the incremental model. On one hand, the incremental model lowers the risk of wasting development time and budget by offering the ability to get working versions of the system to customers much earlier than the waterfall model. This allows for feedback that can avoid time being invested in developing features that turn out to be unused and/or of no benefit. On the other hand, the waterfall model is a lot more efficient in terms of avoiding unnecessary communications and duplication of activities, with overall costs being lower if all features defined in the initial requirements and analysis stages are accurate.

Although the incremental model addresses many of the concerns identified with the waterfall model relating to the client needing to fully understand what they want, it still suffers from a reliance on this to a lesser extent for the identification of accurate estimates for time and budget. Smaller estimates can be provided for each component, which are likely to be more accurate, but estimating time and cost of the entire project is likely to be difficult due to how clients can new requirements over time.

Spiral model

The spiral model is similar to the incremental model, which in turn is based on the waterfall model. The main focus of the spiral model is the management of risk, and therefore is ideal for projects where a large element of risk needs to be managed. The spiral model differs from the waterfall model in the same way that the incremental model differs; it has a structured approach to software development, but it doesn't have a fixed linear approach to completion.

Like the incremental model, this introduces elements for flexibility, but at a cost of introducing time and budget overhead.

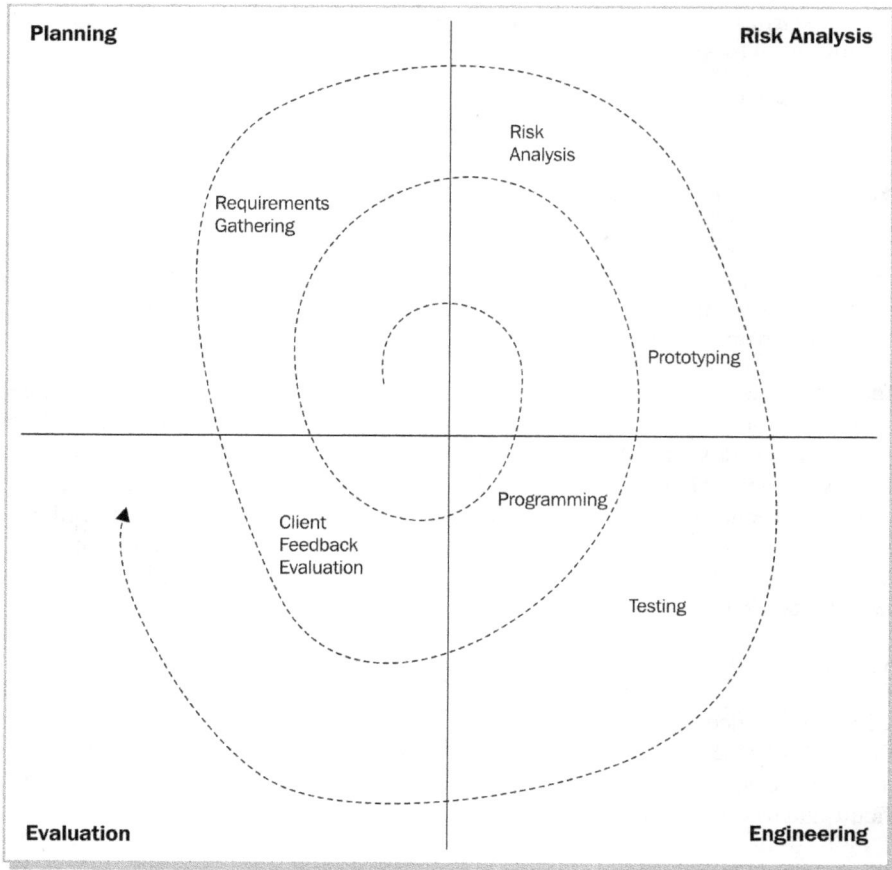

Planning   **Risk Analysis**

Risk
Analysis

Requirements
Gathering

Prototyping

Programming

Client
Feedback
Evaluation

Testing

Evaluation   **Engineering**

Projects using the spiral model repeatedly iterate through four phases, with each iteration referred to as a spiral. These spirals consist of:

> **Planning**: Every spiral starts in a planning phase that identifies the requirements for the spiral to be considered successful. These requirements come in two forms — business requirements and system requirements. The primary focus looks at the business requirements, as these ultimately dictate what the software implementation should be, which in turn has a direct influence on the system requirements. A common example of this influential relationship between business and system requirements is in the implementation of web based software applications that rely on the user's browser to provide the visual interface. Although modern browsers offer beneficial features that are faster to implement, the business requirements dictate that the solution be compatible with the widest number of customers, meaning that compatibility with older browsers becomes a high priority in the technical requirements.

A significant factor of defining the requirements is the ability to conduct high quality communications that can be clearly understood with minimal scope for misinterpretation. The formality of having an emphasis on communications in this stage allows the software development team to be updated on any situations or alterations to the known objectives that will affect any existing software development plans. This allows for action to be taken in the planning and risk analysis phases of the current spiral before any new software development commences.

Once the software team are aware of the requirements for the new spiral, work can commence on identifying how the next batch of features are to be developed into the system. This planning of risk factors directly impacts how software features and system design are developed. , as well as influencing project management related activities such as the assignment of tasks, timescale estimation and budget management for the new spiral.

➤ **Risk analysis**: The aim of this stage is to identify risks associated with the current spiral and alternative solutions. The risk analysis phase will often result in the production of a prototype of the next phase's implementation, allowing for some insight on what is to be expected in the production process and likely feedback from the client — i.e. what sounds good on paper may not produce the expected outcome when implemented in terms of quality, cost or timescales. The prototype allows for the identification of potential problems in these areas, and for alternatives to be proposed if identified problems can't be solved or avoided.

➤ **Engineering**: With the plan in place and risks ironed out, the spiral can proceed to developing the software component. This phase includes developing the software code as well as the testing.

➤ **Evaluation**: Upon completion of the new software component, it is presented to the client and end users for feedback. This allows the project team to gain feedback on opinions relating to progress made and satisfaction. Where the project isn't progressing as quickly as planned, both the client and the project team are able to review actions for future spirals to correct the problem — or even whether the client is to adjust the available budget and timescales available to the project.

Like with the previously mentioned software development models, the spiral model has its own set of pros and cons.Some of the pros include:

➤ **Risk management**: The main focus of the spiral model is on the management of risk, so it should be no surprise that risk control is the main benefit. With the project being split into smaller spirals, the model allows for review and analysis of risks that emerge before and after each development phase. This major emphasis on reviewing the progression of the project allows for situations that can grow into bigger problems to be identified early and for appropriate action to be taken to avoid them or minimize their impact.

> **Approval and documentation control**: Where projects have multiple people making new feature requests, it is important to have a process for authorizing and documenting requests so that confusion can be avoided later in the project. The importance of this increases for projects that run long enough for people to forget what they've been asking for or where people change job roles; something that becomes more common when working with large organizations. The ability to integrate processes for documenting plans of each spiral at their beginning means that conflict based on perceptions can be avoided, while also providing the client with the ability to control of the direction of the project.

> **Software previewing**: With software being developed as smaller components, the client is able to see the project take shape one part at time. If the client doesn't like what they see, they are able to provide their feedback at the end of the spiral so that adjustments can be made in the next iteration to put the project back on track to their satisfaction.

> **Flexibility**: The monitoring of the project combined with the modular development of software components allows for change to be introduced during any cycle. This is in contrast to more rigid models such as the waterfall model that would only allow for change to be introduced after the complete system has been developed.

Some of the cons include:

> **Costly**: The overheads introduced by the increased effort for planning, risk analysis and evaluation means that there is a significant increase in time and cost requirements. The question is whether this additional effort will save the project from mistakes that prove to be more costly than the cost of the increased effort? The answer to this will be different for every project.

> **Expertise requirements**: The execution of advanced planning, analysis and evaluation requires specialist expertise in these areas — especially when the results depend on acquiring high quality accurate information.

> **Risk analysis dependency**: The additional expertise requirements are further impacted by the model's reliance on risk analysis to steer the project in the right direction. This means that not only are spirals likely to go wrong if mistakes are made in their risk analysis phase, but also that the entire project could be in jeopardy from the start if people with inadequate skills are given responsibilities for risk analysis and its supporting information activities for planning and evaluation.

> **Unsuitable for small projects**: The overhead for planning, risk analysis and evaluation would more than likely eat up the entire time and budget available for small projects before any code is written. Additionally, small scale projects are likely to have significantly less risk than bigger projects, meaning that the benefits offered for risk control would be minimal.

Conclusion

The spiral model is most ideal for bigger projects where the emphasis is getting the software right first time and delivered within the agreed timescales. The spiral model can also be a benefit for fixed price projects where there is enough budget due to its ability to identify and manage risks at the earliest opportunity.

The downside of the spiral model is that the amount of effort dedicated to managing risk adds a significant time and cost overhead to the project; which could cost more than the mistakes the model aims to avoid. This is more likely to be the case for smaller projects where there is less risk of things going wrong in the software development. The additional cost and time requirements also rule out the spiral model as being an option for small projects that don't have the timescale or budget to accommodate the thoroughness in planning, risk analysis and evaluation.

A major factor that the spiral model can be used to address is where projects have large element of uncertainty. The flexibility to evolve the project at each spiral means that the project can withstand anything that isn't clear at the beginning of the project. Using the spiral model allows for iterations to occur in a way that delays production of software components until their associated uncertainties have been eliminated. At the same time, software components can be developed to be partially complete, with later iterations adding remaining functionality once their requierd clarity has been introduced.

Agile development

The concept of Agile development is a style of software development adopted by many practices and methodologies; these are collectively referred to as agile methods and practices. Agile methods and practices for software development all share a common focus on developing the **Minimum Viable Product** (**MVP**) to meet the project requirements; the emphasis being to reduce activity effort by eliminating planning and development of features that could be developed into a future release. The focus on minimizing effort for planning by reducing releases to very short development cycles eliminates the wastage introduced by the more structured methods such as the waterfall model; short cycles get more immediate feedback from the client, avoiding time spent on planning and developing unwanted features.

In contrast to more formal project management methodologies such as PRINCE2, Agile development is more of a framework to fit compatible project activity methods that can be hand-picked for implementation. This flexible way of implementing Agile development means that software teams can tailor it to fit how they already work, as opposed to being forced to make their setup fit the methodology. The flexibility of Agile development means that there are many ways that it can be executed; meaning that you are likely to need to learn new methods to do the same job each time you move to a new development team.

The following are Agile based methods and practices you are likely to come across should you decide to embrace Agile development in your projects:

> **Continuous deployment** : The process of deploying software on a regular basis, with new features and fixes being introduced. Adoption of this type of deployment is more common with web based systems, especially on the server side where user installation is not an issue. More recently, this approach has also been adopted by client side software such as web browsers that upgrade automatically to the latest version supporting new web standards, and computer games that access patches and downloadable content. These are contrasting examples of the different ways that continuous deployment is used; one being to reduce upfront testing and the other to extend functionality.

> **Agile modeling** : A method of modelling software systems that is ideal for small development teams working on projects in fast changing environments. Like with most things in Agile development, the main emphasis is on creating a model that is good enough and able to be adapted whenever required — with no intention to create a perfect model; which in turn would likely become out of date as new requirement changes are introduced. Producing a model that is good enough, but not perfect, also means that less time is required to produce the model, allowing feedback from the client and end users earlier so that new changes can be introduced in line with discoveries about changing requirements.

> **Extreme programming** : A method of programming that has a main focus on customer satisfaction and their changing requirements. This is achieved by developing software in a way that allows for continuous feedback from the client and end users so that the team can identify how they are progressing in line with the latest requirements and expectations. The process of constant communication with the client in turn affects the execution of programming the software by keeping programming of functionality short, modular and simple so that clients can be regularly presented with ongoing communications and presentations. This results in rapid programming cycles that are highly focused on delivering features that have the client's current attention.

> **Pair programming** : A practice is used in Agile development to share knowledge between programmers, especially new programmers being introduced to a project. Pair programming makes use of one programmer to write the code and the other programmer to instruct and guide; an interactive method of learning as well as a form of code review.

> **Test driven development** : Related to test-first programming concepts found in extreme programming, this method of software development is based on developing each code component to pass a specific test. This is in contrast to having testing as a separate phase at the end of the development cycle. Several variations of test driven development exist to focus of specific development themes, such as client acceptance and suitability of functionality in real use cases.

➤ **Planning poker** : Mainly used to estimate the amount of time and resources required to develop software components, planning poker is a meeting where members of the team use numbered cards to provide their estimated size of individual tasks. The combined estimates for each task are then discussed in detail to identify the reasons behind each member's estimate in order to arrive at a group consensus for the task — this is a way of performing "wisdom of the crowds", where the combined estimates of the entire team is more reliable than an estimate of an individual member.

➤ **Velocity tracking** : An activity closely related to planning activities such as planning poker, measuring the velocity of the team and its members is about identifying productivity. Many factors can affect productivity, which in turn has an impact on the team's ability to meet the estimates they have produced. The project manager can keep an eye on this by using a maths formula that identifies how the team is performing — as well as individual members if required. The purpose of velocity tracking isn't so much to do with holding the team and its members to account when slippages occur, but as way for corrections to be made to estimates when slippages occur.

➤ **Scrum meetings** : A way of regularly performing short meetings that are highly focused and to the point. These meetings are meant to keep everyone in the team updated on what other members are working on in, allowing for planning review and retrospective insight to learn from mistakes and activities that lead to success. Team members typically make their contribution to the meeting in less than a minute, usually standing up to "encourage" a brief description of their latest activities.

➤ **Story driven modeling** : Another method of modelling the software system, but with a focus on using concrete example scenarios to produce object diagrams that define what the software system should be. Additional focus is also given to how the presentation of object diagrams may evolve throughout the execution of the scenario.

Some of the pros include:

➤ Allows clients and end users to see a working version of software sooner.

➤ Opens opportunity for iterative feedback that eliminates ambiguity of communications from the client — helping developers to create more of the right features.

➤ Accommodates the risk of changes to the specification from the ground up, meaning disruption to software development is kept to a minimum.

➤ Emphasis on only doing just enough means that time and budget is invested more efficiently and avoids the risk of wastage of investment in planning that becomes redundant when changes to the requirements are introduced.

Some of the cons include:

> ➤ Risk of project management being too relaxed, resulting in the project going off track through lack of client coordination — i.e. not defining what the software should be developed to do.

> ➤ Risk of project management being too relaxed, resulting in the project going off track through lack of team coordination — i.e. not developing the software to match the client's specification.

> ➤ Lack of emphasis on formal documentation and design can lead to the development team making wrong interpretations of what is being requested by the client, resulting in software features being developed in the wrong way. This leads to increased costs and time to undo and correct.

> ➤ Lack of formal procedures mean that people making decisions need to be capable of making good decisions justified by adequate technical and business knowledge. This makes Agile development unsuitable for teams who have limited technical and business experience.

> ➤ Lack of formal procedures exposes the team to higher requirements for justifying actions when things go wrong — i.e. standard procedure can't be used as an excuse.

SSM: Soft Systems Methodology

Described as a systemic approach to solving real world problematic situations, Soft Systems Methodology is unlike the previous methodologies mentioned in that it focus is on resolving people oriented situations. The methodology is designed to address so called "soft" problems, whose results can be seen in projects, but are difficult to identify their root cause; whether it be getting the best co-operation from the client or maximising productivity of the development team. This is in complete contrast to other methodologies that primarily focus on the production of the final output — which for software projects would be code, data and content that form the software system. As a result, Soft Systems Methodology can be used to compliment other methodologies such as Agile development that focus on the technical production side of software development.

The following are brief descriptions of primary activities promoted by Soft Systems Methodology:

> ➤ **Data collection** : Data is collected for review using a range of standard collection methods such as surveys, measurements, observations and interviews. Effective data collection requires careful consideration in the design of questions used to capture data. With this data capture leading to discoveries of unknown factors relating to the situation, there is a need to capture data using the right questions using the right format — i.e. knowing when to use quantitative and qualitative questioning.

➤ **Situation definition** : Initial modelling is performed as written observations and simplistic diagrams that describe the wider situation of the problem. This practice helps to identify the situation without a bias towards what the problem is perceived to be and allows all factors to be taken into account in later stages, meaning that potential causes that are underestimated can be identified for further investigation. Boundaries of the situation can also be defined as part of initial modeling, which can be expanded or reduced depending on what is discovered. A specific focus is placed on identifying factors such as structures, processes, climate, people and issues — especially those that lead to conflict.

➤ **Problem modeling** : Later modeling activities focus on building models that are specific to describing the problem. Soft Systems Methodology starts this process by identifying the significant contributors to the situation — these being:

  ➢ **Beneficiaries** : People or other entity types that benefit from the resulting output

  ➢ **Actors** : People or other entity types who contribute to producing the output.

  ➢ **Transformations** : The changes required by the situation's systems and processes.

  ➢ **Perspectives** : The different views of the situation.

  ➢ **Owner** : The person responsible for the situation being investigated.

  ➢ **Environment** : The external factors that affect the project.

➤ It's important not to assume that all situation beneficiaries will be external to the development team, as soft problems can just as easily occur between members of the development team. An example of this would be how content producers such as designers and instruction writers conflict with programmers due to lacking the ability to directly control of how their content and designs appear in the software product — and with programmers not being able to take immediate action on their change requests. This scenario has the potential to become a situation for Soft Systems Methodology where content creators become beneficiaries of a solution that provides them with the control they seek for integrating their content into the software system.

➤ The activities that beneficiaries engage will play a significant role in both the problem and the solution in one form or another. Our example situation where content creators rely on programmers to integrate their content changes produces the conflict where content creators are dissatisfied with the time taken by programmers to make their changes and often to make changes exactly how they want them. The transformation in this situation is the new solution that allows content creators to integrate their content without the need to rely on programmers. This results in scope for complaints to be eliminated making more time available to programmers for working on other activities. The transformation is also likely to have a direct impact on the project's methodology — affecitng everything from how the design process is executed through to identifying who is involved in different communications for requests and how releases of the software are test; with content creators now being responsible for content corrections such as spelling mistakes, instead of this being the responsibility of programmers to update.

> ➤ The different views of actors and beneficiaries are an important factor to consider for identifying a solution that satisfies everyone's needs without causing additional problems. An investigation of this in our example scenario may reveal that although content creators are enthusiastic about the idea of gaining control for integrating their content and alterations, the programmers have a different perspective with concerns about how the development of tools to allow this will potentially increase their workload for its initial development and ongoing support, plus an additional concern that providing too much control to content creators could result in parts of the software being accidentally broken with unstructured content updates. In this case, content creators would be unaware of the faults they create, resulting in extra work for programmers to track the faults – and opening scope for a "blame culture" to emerge. This investigation of the different perspectives discovers a full range of pros and cons to be aware of when selecting a solution to the problem that will help to avoid shifting the situation from one type of problem to another type of problem that is equally or more detrimental to the progression of the project.

> ➤ The owner of the situation is most likely to be some type of manager who has specified the need for a solution to a problem they are aware of, but in some situations could be someone who is directly working on the project, or even the client. In our example situation, the owner(s) of the project could be the content developers who are granted their demands on the ability to control their content, or it could be the programmers who raise the issue and become the owners as a result of an unmanageable workload. Depending on how the situation plays out, the owner(s) will have a unique a set of factors relating to:
>
>> ➤ Whether they can help or stop a solution from being developed.
>>
>> ➤ Motivations that persuade them to help developing a solution.
>>
>> ➤ Causes for owners to become an obstacle to developing a solution to the problem.

It is important to select the right owner of the project who can control and prioritize these factors. Projects often have a hierarchy of decision makers, with people at the top level having the ability to overrule all decisions and sub-level decision makers being appointed for their specialist knowledge. Getting the best out of decision makers is dependent on your ability to select the most suitable decision maker for the decisions to be made.

The environment that the situation exists within has a direct influence on what solutions are available. The environment may include factors that are completely external to the project such as law, market resources, competition in the industry and personal lives of team members, of which you have little to no control over. For many situations, environment factors will also provide some element of control. In our example scenario, an investigation of the environment could reveal the available budget for a solution to the problem—which would then dictate which solution implementations are valid. The available budget as an environment factor is something that could be negotiated — and result in a bigger budget if successful.

Additionally, an investigation into the external environment may reveal off the shelf tools that can be purchased for integration into the software development process that would allow content creators to make their changes. This would at least solve some of the issues raised from the perspective of the programmers relating to concerns of the cost and time to develop and support internally developed content creation tools. Even where these development tools are priced outside the available budget, knowledge of the costs, time and risks to develop an in-house equivalent can be used to produce a more persuasive case for increasing the budget to buy the tools — especially when it will produce almost immediate benefits to productivity compared to needing to wait several weeks or even months for internally developed tools to be created.

Some of the pros include:

> Ideal for building a better understanding of non-technical factors causing the problem — specifically people related issues.

> Will identify social bias and communication issues that become a barrier to productivity and progression of the project.

> Can identify problems that can't be detected by methodologies specific to software development.

> Easy to implement without any specialist equipment or software — just pen and paper.

Some of the cons include:

> Doesn't provide any solution to identified problems — just a detailed description of the cause.

> Heavily focused on people for analysis, therefore its accuracy is dependent on being able to access people and their willingness to be truthful — can be difficult to implement in highly political situations where information is purposely withheld.Not specific to software development, hence doesn't solve problems specific to software development.

Conclusion

Soft Systems Methodology is not specific to software development and therefore can't be used as a standalone methodology for software projects. The methodology excels at solving the type of problems that software specific methodologies typically fail with — the people oriented "soft" issues that become barriers to software development.

In the case of the given example where content creators demand more control over the integration of their content into the software product, a software development specific methodology would likely suggest the need to develop new software tools to allow designers and copywriters to add their content without the need to submit their content to the team's programmers. Although this solution could be implemented, the solution would definitely have a financial and time cost, plus there would be the risk of allowing content creators to introduce new issues based on assumptions such as the definition of a small file size. All of these can lead to additional problems that need to be resolved at additional financial and time cost.

In contrast, the use of Soft Systems Methodology would likely identify a twofold solution to the problem;the first stage being the provision of a visual template for use in PowerPoint or Keynote that allows copywriters to see how their content would appear in the real software product, while the second stage would be to provide the graphic designers with training they require to understand important principles of software development. This training would cover concepts such as DRY (Don't Repeat Yourself) and management of file sizes, while also providing access to a separate draft installation of the software that they can use to change placeholder image files that have been added by the programmers without the risk of affecting the real version of the software product. Each change can then be reviewed by the team's programmers before they are imported to the real version. This approach uses Soft Systems Methodology to identify the people issues that are the root cause of the problem to identify solutions that satisfy the humanistic requirements of training and visualization before making use of any costly and time consuming technical solutions that themselves could introduce more soft problems.

The solution to the example scenario shows how looking at the people based soft issues occurring in software development can provide project management with a big advantage in maintaining efficiency for time and budget investment by avoiding personal conflict based on the demands of individual professional disciplines. Firstly, by having action seen to be taken to solve perceived problems helps to avoid members of the team becoming disgruntled through perceiving to be ignored — which can escalate into bigger conflicts. Secondly, using the Soft Systems Methodology tools to model the situation identifies an efficient low risk and low cost solution that may not be obvious from the initial problem description given by the intended beneficiaries; especially if they have a bias towards an intended solution.

Designing your methodology

Now that you are aware of the issues surrounding software projects and clients, you are now in a position to use this insight to design a methodology that can be applied to your freelance projects to counteract the types of problem likely to be encountered. Your methodology should take the best parts of tried and tested methodologies such as those identified in this chapter.

Formal structure

It is useful for both yourself and your clients to have a process that is formal and structured. Highlighting this to the client at the beginning of the project can play a big part in setting the right expectations and avoids situations where they become unrealistic in what can be achieved in relation to time, budget and available technology.

Consider making use of the following identifications made in this chapter in one form or another:

➤ **Waterfall model** : A process based on the waterfall model in which the status of the project can be clearly defined will help to avoid situations where the client tries to skip to later parts of the process or undo previous parts that have already been completed. This reduces the risk of time wastage from testing too early or managing design additions during the programming phase.

➤ **Policy** : A formally written policy describing how situations are to be handled throughout the project will help to give the client a better understanding of what to expect as well as to give you legal backing should the project go very wrong.

➤ Policies should be included to support your implementation of a waterfall model style stage structure to ensure that:

  ➢ Clients sign a completion document for each stage of the project that has been completed.

  ➢ Clients are aware that changes to signed completion can't be altered without changes to the suggested completion date and cost of the project.

  ➢ Changes requested by the client are also formally documented.

  ➢ Authorisation for changes and completion signage can only be made by the people identified as the project's decision makers.

➤ **Agreements** : Ideal for setting in stone expectations and implementation of policies.

➤ **Documentation** : Documenting meetings and major actions in the project such as the acceptance of software features and change requests will help to provide a paper trail for requests and agreements when people forget what was previously agreed. This helps you to avoid situations where requests are made and forgotten about, such as when a client asks you to take out features of the software and then later ask you why the said feature isn't available.

➤ Make use of templates for documentation to ensure theirconsistency along with their completition including all required information — e.g. date, details, people involved, authorised by, etc.

Team communications policy

Although the intention should be to work with the client and other parties involved in the project, it should also be remembered that these people have much less technical knowledge than you about the implications of software development.

Much care should be taken on how all wordings are presented to the client and other collaborators of the project because:

> **A little knowledge is a dangerous thing** : This saying is highly accurate with regards to software projects where the client and other collaborators have some understanding of the technical issues involved with your work, but not enough to have a full understanding of all implications. The problem with the client and project collaborators having incomplete knowledge is that it often leads to a belief of their requests being a lot simpler to achieve than it really is. This leads to the problem of increased expectations regarding time for delivery and number of features.

> **Loose lips sink ships** : In terms of software development, the ship would be the project. Whether it is yourself, members of your team or suppliers contributing to the project, saying the wrong things in the company of the wrong people can lead to people developing unrealistic expectations. As much care should be taken of what is said when in the company of external collaborators as should be taken when speaking in the company of the client because these people can just as easily communicate their misconceptions to the client when you aren't there to correct them. A focus to control what is said and how they are worded will go a long way to avoid the evolution of "titanic expectations" that doomed to run into problems from the start; just like the ship!

These issues can be corrected by having a formal team communications policy that allows everyone to be aware of how issues can be discussed when in the company of not in the immediate team. Examples could include:

> **Discussion of features that are extensions to the specification** : Discussion of potential future features risks collaborators and the client making the assumption that discussed features are to be implemented into the current version, causing increased expectations that can't be satisfied with the currently available time, budget or technology resources.

> **How the software is to be developed** : This has a risk of providing an incomplete picture of how the software is being developed, potentially leading to an over simplified view with the impression that that the impossible should be possible. This may also lead to collaborators forcing bad decisions to be made that affect how the software is developed, causeing problems for future maintainability and implementation of features. The fallout of these bad decisions then become your responsibility to clean up.

> **Progression of the software development** : This can lead to assumptions about rapid progression of smaller and easier tasks being representative of larger and more complicated tasks. This risks the team unwittingly setting higher expectations for faster delivery by allowing the client and collaborators to perceive the project to be ahead of schedule.

> ➤ **Estimates** : Speaking of estimates in many cases leads to perceptions of mentioned completion dates and/or budget as being set in stone. Estimates should only be mentioned when they have been fully researched and in a way that emphasizes how the estimate is not set in stone, hence subject to change. Team members, especially software developers with less commercial experience, are often too optimistic on what can be achieved and too enthusiastic to get started on new work without researching the full facts. This is a perfect combination for providing wildly inaccurate estimates that provide the impression of being a promise; affecting your ability to profitably and successfully complete the project.

Planning

It has been identified throughout this book that that the majority of freelance work are small scale projects, most of which don't have enough budget to do any heavyweight planning. However, this is not to say that planning has no place, as even the most basic planning can make the difference between a project being delivered successfully and ending in disaster.

The key to planning in freelance projects is to have the flexibility to decide how much planning is suitable for the scale of the project. More complicated project should be assigned more time for planning, with their budget being adjusted to accommodate for additional planning effort if required. Complicated projects with a tight budget that can't accommodate for planning are likely to be more hassle than they are worth, hence abandonment should be considered before you become committed to the client by starting on its development.

The following are useful activities to consider in project management for all types of projects:

> ➤ **SMART objectives review** : A feasibility review of each objective set by the client to ensure that the project can be delivered to their expectations should be the first priority of any planning strategy. In the worst case scenario, it will lead to an identification that the project would not be worth progressing, saving you a lot of headaches. SMART stands for:
>
>> ➤ **Specific** : Does the client know what they want to solve with the project? Most will not necessarily know how they want the software to solve their problem, but they must at least know the specific attributes that define the problem.
>>
>> ➤ **Measurable** : The objectives of the client must be measurable — objectives that can't be measured have no way for you to measure how progress is being made and will leave you exposed to the client continuously demanding more.
>>
>> ➤ **Achievable** : All objectives must be achievable within the project's budget, timescale and with the available technology and skill resources. Objectives that can't be considered achievable with all of these factors pose a high risk of disrupting the entire project.

> ➤ **Realistic** : Are the people defining and reviewing the objective being realistic? Anyone can say it is achievable, but research must be performed to find facts confirming these judgements to be realistic.

> ➤ **Timely** : Can the objective be achieved within the available time? Factors such as holidays and risk of team members needing to take unscheduled time out of work should be taken into account for this review.

➤ **Gantt charting** - A Gantt chart is a visual chart that illustrates the start and end dates of project tasks in relation to each other. This is very useful for both the development team and the client to quickly see the size of individual tasks in relation to others, as well to see where the project is up to.**Critical path management** : Every project has a critical path, which is the longest combination of activities to the project's completion. Although this sequence of activities has the longest duration through the project, it is identified as critical because any slippage with these activities will guarantee the late delivery of the project. Placing an emphasis on ensuring the timely completion of all activities that fall within this path will result in the project being completed for the target date. Developing

The development phase will make use of your chosen style of implementing the code to form the software - chapter 10 discusses this issue in full detail. Code architecture and style is as much a business issue as it is a technical issue in the business of developing software, emphasizing the importance for your code strategy to accommodate for the following:

➤ **Speed** : Development needs to be fast enough to be completed by the target completion date — whether this is dictated by the client or the available budget.

➤ **Maintenance** : Code needs to be adaptable for when the client requests changes during the current project execution or as a future maintenance upgrade. The need for maintainable code will conflict with the need for speedy development because more time will be required, but this will pay off through the project and/or in future maintenance from time saved, hence there needing to be a good balance.

➤ **Reusability** : Developing new components is expensive in terms of time, but code that is developed to be reusable across many projects will open opportunities to spread the cost across future projects in a way that speeds up development time.

➤ **Risk** : Software development is always a risk, especially when software faults can lead to real world impact such as the client losing money or becoming vulnerable to legal action. Code should be developed in a way that reflects the level of risk that the corresponding functionality represents. As a minimum consideration, features considered to be higher risk should have code that clearly highlights what could go wrong so that whoever works on future maintenance can be made fully aware; hence avoiding code being broken and the introduction of new faults. Features that are high risk should also include backup features and failure reporting. Such backup features ensure that the system can continue to operate without causing harm to people who rely on the system, while reporting allows whoever is responsible for maintaining the system to be made aware of the fault and the situation data that caused it. This combination allows for the impact of risks to be minimized and for faster reaction to correct faults identified.

Testing

The success of the project's end product will be heavily dependent on its testing, so this stage of your methodology shouldn't be neglected. With there being different types of testing, this shouldn't be an activity that is considered to be performed at just one stage of the project or by an individual person. The following are considerations to take seriously in your testing strategy:

> **Acceptance testing** - Without doubt, there is a need to have the client confirm that they accept the state of each feature developed upon completion so that ongoing tweaking can be minimized. Although clients who are pressed for time or afraid of using technology may be more than happy to sign their acceptance of features without properly checking may initially seem good for progressing the project faster, this will only result in the client coming back to you to with change requests later — causing conflict that is harmful to the project's progression if they have already signed their acceptance.
>
> With software being an interactive format, you can embed features within the systems you develop that allow you to ensure that acceptance testing is performed to the required standard. The following are ideas to consider in your acceptance testing implementation:
>
> > Web based applications presented through HTML pages can use unique links that can be tracked by your web server code when they are accessed. Unique links for testing can be sent to the client so that you can identify which pages have been accessed — and follow them up if they haven't.
> >
> > Web based applications can also make use of client side cookies and local data storage, allowing you to track other information such as what has been tested on the web page and how long was spent. This is useful for being able verify that features were tested as required — and to provide feedback to the client if they've missed something out.
> >
> > Client side applications, including phone apps and desktop based applications, can be developed to track actions performed by the client and send the tracking data generated to a server based application developed with PHP or another scripting language — which in turn would store the details in a database for later review. A simplified version of this would be to e-mail the tracking data to your e-mail account, meaning that there would be no need to set up the server side scripting and database component.
>
> **Technical testing** - This type of testing should occur throughout the full development phase in one way or another. At the software development level, testing of code should be tested by software developers as they develop their code. This type of testing shouldn't be confused with any type of final testing, as the aim is only to identify that their software components are working in theory so that the development of the next task can be started.

➤ **Final technical testing** - A type of technical testing should be considered a separate task to developing the software, and ideally performed by people not involved with developing the code. This ensures that test results aren't contaminated by ideal settings made available on developer machines such as cookies or configuration files that have been set as part of the development process, but not made available by default. Final technical testing also looks at testing software components with much heavier and complete data that represent a wider range of scenarios — something that would slow software development too much if this were to be performed alongside software developmentd.

➤ **End user testing** - You can guarantee that end users will use the software in ways that were never thought of or intended by the software development team or the client. Having someone test the system who isn't biased from exposure to technical knowledge or experience of how the system works will allow you to identify two significant categories of information:

The mistakes people make when interacting with the system that prevent them from using functionality — e.g. not reading instruction prompts that lead to them not being able to submit forms because of missing mandatory input.

Faults in the software exposed through unexpected user usage that developers and the client didn't think of.

➤ **Automated testing** - Allowing some of the testing to be automated has the following significant advantages:

> ➤ Guarantees that thorough testing is performed considtently to a high standard providing that the tests are properly defined.

> ➤ Guarantees that testing is performed correctly providing that the correct data is provided.Rapid identification of faults introduced to new builds of the software.

> ➤ No cost of human testing time allows for repeated testing to be performed without a cost to the project.

> ➤ Causes of faults can be pinpointed without the need to guess.

➤ **Security testing** - This is a specialism of technical testing, but could be considered as a testing activity to be performed as an activity of its own if the development team doesn't have anyone with enough experience of ethical hacking.I In this case, activity should be out outsourced to a freelancer, contractor or company who can provide this as a service; possibly a specialist.

In short, security testing focuses on making sure that no input features of the system can be abused, and typically focuses around the prevention of common attacks. For web based systems, this would ensure the prevention of SQL injection, cross-site scripting, manipulation of APIs and the like.

Distribution of testing - As suggested by the previous considerations, testing should never be considered as a job just for one person. Testing should be distributed across multiple people who each have their own specialisms that can be contributed, whether it be technical knowledge for technical testing, or lack of knowledge to ensure that the system produces no unexpected results when users perform unexpected actions.

Summary

A methodology is a formal set of methods for engaging an activity. In the case of software development, the focus is not only the creation of software, but also managing the many other related activities including communications, requirements definitions and team collaboration.

The use of formalized methodologies in software development helps to avoid the occurrence of common obstacles. An awareness of methodologies developed for use in software development will help you to avoid problematic situations already experienced by other software projects, hence helping you to increase your productivity and profitability. At the same time, a formalized process will help you to keep the threat of politics from derailing the project in question, while also helping to ensure quality by setting standards for activities such as testing and requirements definition that result in the right features being created to serve the project's ambitiont.

11

Creating Quotes and Estimates

The cost of a project isn't a major issue for you when the client is paying on per hour worked basis, but is a difficult issue when working to a fixed price. Accuracy of identifying a total price is still important for projects paid by the hour because clients will not be happy to receive a bill that is multiple times higher than you originally suggested. Knowing effective methods for producing accurate estimates for both fixed price and time based projects will save you a lot of headaches when it comes to getting the client to pay.

A good consideration for all estimation is Hofstadter's Law, which emphasizes the difficulty of accurate estimation for tasks of substantial complexity—despite all best efforts and actually knowing that the task's complexity. The law simply says that what you are estimating will always take longer than you expect, even when you take into account Hofstader's Law. It is often referenced by programmers in discussions relating to project management and productivity such as the mythical "man month" and extreme programming.

Maths to the rescue: The basics

There is no fixed way to produce an estimate for work to be produced, but using knowledge with math's can be a powerful combination that allows you to minimize the risk of under pricing your projects as well as to make better decisions.

All project costs are a combination of your time and the use of required resources. Your ability to develop code and content quickly and efficiently is directly dependent on the quality of input you receive from the client, who in turn is dependent on their suppliers and partners. The situation is presented in the following diagram:

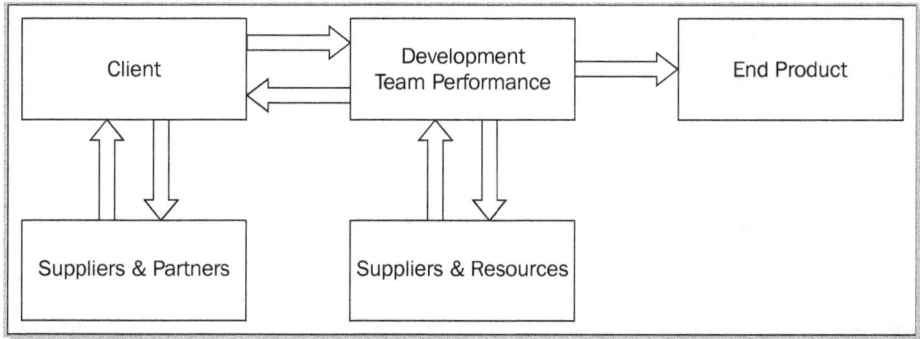

Your pricing method needs to reflect these factors that affect your ability to produce the end product. To recap, the following are the factors that your pricing calculation needs to incorporate:

➤ How the client's input affects your software development performance.

➤ How the client's input affects the costs incurred through using suppliers your suppliers and resources.

Performance rating

Monitoring work performance is the first step to identifying how pricing and estimates of any type should be calculated for individual clients. Two factors are immediately affected by performance:

➤ Time

    ➤ Better performance will result in higher productivity that reduces the amount of time required.

    ➤ Used to estimate how long individual tasks or full projects will take in relation to the expected amount of time it should take.

    ➤ Significant scope to be impacted by the client's input or project factors such as inheriting pre-existing code that is undocumented and/or difficult to adapt.

➤ Price

    ➤ Time and resources required for a project result in a cost for time invested, hence the quality of performance that results in the usage of time and resources will impact the price of the project's activities.

> ➢ Input from the client can lead to additional costs being incurred from suppliers, partners and use of resources.

Although time and price are closely related, knowing how your work can be affected by factors such as the client's involvement that affect your performance can prove useful in project management for estimating completion dates and organizing workflow. It should also be noted that inheriting projects that have already been started by other people also has a cost to your productivity—at least in the short term and possibly also in the long term. Examples of this include:

➤ **Difficult to manage code**: It can never be guaranteed that code developed by other software developers has been developed to a high standard to allow maintainability, especially where the client has their initial software development team based on the lowest price—which although is not always the case, such prices are offered through cutting corners or lack of experience, both of which result in reduced quality of code that will cause you problems.

➤ **Lack of documentation** : Similar to the previous issue, documentation is often neglected by developers who have develop their code to a tight budget or timeframe. Although previous developers will fully understand their code and be able to pick up where they finished, you don't have the luxury of this knowledge when you take on projects that you haven't been involved with from their beginning. No documentation means the need for you to invest a significant amount of time testing each part of the code to learn how it works, plus a high risk of introducing bugs that will cost additional time to resolve. The impact on your product resulting from any lack of documentation, including commented code, should never be underestimated.

➤ **Lack of technical tools** : Limited or no access to software development tools such as version control, revision history and test suite will affect your ability to efficiently pick up development of code you inherit on the project. Certainly where the code you inherit has a large amount of complexity, there will be a need to invest a significant amount of effort to investigate the code in order to understand how the code architecture works and also to develop unit tests that ensure your changes don't break functionality in areas of the system you are unaware of; in some cases, it can take less time to rewrite the entire project than to engage these activities.

➤ **Unmanaged client expectations and perceptions** : Clients may believe that their software is more complete than it is, or that more is technically achievable than is possible due to communications with their previous software developers that haven't revealed the full facts. Any unmanaged expectations and perceptions need to be addressed at the earliest opportunity to avoid unnecessary time being invested on activities that don't benefit the project's progression.

Understanding your performance when working with individual clients can therefore be an asset that allows you to produce more accurate estimates and quotes. The basic formula for calculating performance of an individual task or project is:

Performance = Time Invested ÷ Expected Time

This formula provides a figure that indicates how close your actual time investment was to how much time you had expected it to take for completion. The target will always be to get a performance of 1 or less, which indicates that the expected time was either equal to or less than the actual time invested.

Let's take the example of a project that we've quoted based on a standard 8 hours of work, which in actuality turned out to take 12 hours to complete:

Performance = 12 hours ÷ 8 hours = 1.5

This scenario has the performance formula return 1.5, showing that the work took one (1) and a half (.5) times longer than had been expected—or to put it simply, it took 1.5 times longer. With the result being above the target of 1, it is clear that something has gone wrong in the delivery of the project. The calculation at least identifies that there is a need for further investigation to identify the reasons, as well as adding the identified performance rating to the client rating.

Client rating

Creating a rating for individual clients is ideal for fairly adjusting standard prices based on your previous experiences with the client and works both ways for increasing and decreasing the amount you decide to charge. Good clients who are efficient to work with benefit from receiving a better rate, whereas clients who cause problems receive a poorer rate. The best part of this method is that rates given to clients can't be disputed as being biased on a personal level because they are calculated based on the facts of the client's previous performance—this alone can be used as an incentive to make clients more cooperative.

Client ratings are not produced for mates rates (a phrase used for providing a special discounted price for friends), but are a straight calculation using only facts of their average previous performance. The basic formula for this would be:

$$\text{Client Rating} = \frac{\text{sum of previous ratings}}{\text{number of previous ratings}}$$

This calculation uses all of the previous performance ratings by adding them together and dividing them by the number of performance ratings recorded to produce an average of all performance ratings related to the client.

Example

In an example scenario, we have a client that has worked with us on 4 previous projects. Details of their performance are:

➤ Project 1 = 2.5
➤ Project 2 = 2

➤ Project 3 = 1.75

➤ Project 4 = 1.5

The numbers show that the client was initially very time consuming, leading to a performance cost of two and a half (2.5) times of what it should have taken. This could have been due to many factors such as needing to repeat meetings, telephone calls and many e-mails—each of these adding unnecessary time to the project. Although they have improved with each project, the numbers show that working with the client still takes more time than expected. Using an average is ideal because:

➤ Although the numbers show that it is unlikely that the next task's performance rating will be as much as 2.5, it is still possible that it will be higher than project 4's performance value of 1.5.

➤ Performance will almost certainly be higher than the target value of 1.

Using these numbers in the formula provides:

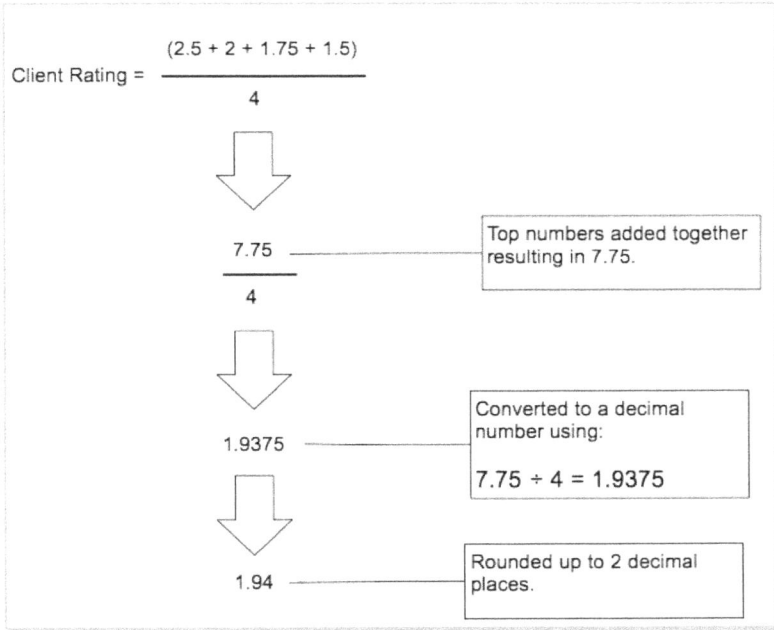

$$\text{Client Rating} = \frac{(2.5 + 2 + 1.75 + 1.5)}{4}$$

$$\frac{7.75}{4}$$

Top numbers added together resulting in 7.75.

$$1.9375$$

Converted to a decimal number using:

$$7.75 \div 4 = 1.9375$$

$$1.94$$

Rounded up to 2 decimal places.

The result shows that the client rating is still higher than the previous two projects, even though the client has shown improvement. The client rating can be updated after completion of each new project, allowing them to get a better (lower) rating if they are able to contribute to a better performance rating.

Estimation

From what has been learnt about the client, we can apply the client rating to calculate an estimate for time and price of new work requests. This method is much more likely to be accurate than a guess because it is based on data collected from previous performance that may indicate an ongoing pattern.

The time estimation for a project is simply multiplied by the previously produced client rating , hence the formula becomes:

Time Estimate = Ideal Time x Client Rating

There are three strategies for identifying an estimate for pricing depending on what type of project you are selling to the client:

> Time

 > Charging the amount you want o be paid for each hour your work.

> Value

 > A fixed price method that doesn't reflect the amount of time provided to produce the software.

 > Use this for anything that you are selling that is pre-made, customizable and offers to benefit the client by reducing development time.

Time based price estimates are straightforward; with the aim being to charge a fee for each hour you, work, you multiply the amount of expected time by the amount you want to charge per hour. The basic formula for this would therefore be:

Price Estimate = Time Estimate x Hourly Rate

Projects also incur additional costs relating to services and resources purchased for use on the project, hence you may also want to include these in the price. This would require the basic formula to be adjusted to become the following:

Price Estimate = (Time Estimate x Hourly Rate) + Fixed Costs

Price estimates don't need to be purely time or value based. For example, a project that requires a number of hours to customize could consist of a combination of time based and value based pricing. Although this type of project could be calculated using value based pricing, with the customization time offset against the total sale price, there would be a significant enough risk of some clients increasing the customization time to a point where it becomes unprofitable to include the customization.

Small scale projects with thin margins are especially vulnerable to this, when the calculated value based price makes the assumption that a small technical configuration taking a few hours in ideal situations, when the reality is that some clients for one reason or another will significantly increase the customization time through issues such as changing their minds, lack of clarity in their communication or adding new requirements. This can become a serious issue where the client introduces inefficiencies that increase the time to many times more than the original price accommodated for—in the worst case scenario, this cost of this misjudgment could be worth more than the value of the entire project.

A solution to the issue of using value based pricing for projects that have an element of bespoke work requirements such as customization is to provide these elements of the project as a separate estimate in addition to the fixed value based price. This provides two main advantages in managing the budget:

➤ Your risks are minimized to only fulfilling the elements of the project that have known costs associated with them.

➤ You have the ability to use the estimate status of the remaining components to negotiate with the client—whether it be to adjust the price to accommodate unexpected time increases or to persuade them to compromise so that the components can be completed within the original estimate.

These advantages minimize your risk to a point where you can be confident that the project will be profitable. Just make sure that anything priced under the value based pricing is accurate!

Example

Continuing the example that produced a client rating of 1.94, our example scenario has the client wanting to add a reservation system to their website. We have already developed a system that can be added to websites in order to allow them to accept and manage reservations, so the project will only be a case of installing and customizing the system.

This example has a mixture of a value based pricing, used for the product that we can sell to the client, and time based pricing, which would be the time to set up the product. Charging only for the time would mean that we aren't getting paid for developing the original system, hence the product system has a fixed price for each client it is sold to. The following are the factors associated to our pricing:

➤ Hourly Rate = £30

➤ Reservation System = £1,000

➤ Typical installation, configuration and testing = 4 hours

Together with the previously identified client rating of 1.94, we have everything we need to create our estimations for time and price. Firstly, our time estimate would be performed as follows:

➤ Time Estimate = 4 hours x 1.94 = 7.76 hours

Previous experiences with the client suggest that we should expect to invest more time than usual to perform the installation, hence the time estimate of 7.76 hours. Typical activities that will increase the amount of time required are those that are open to subjective criticism such as the design of the reservation pages and any type of activity that is heavily dependent on the client providing accurate information and resources— which would be the case for the testing in order to make sure that the reservation system has been correctly configured.

Now that we have the time estimate, a price can be estimated for the installation:

> ➤ Price Estimate = 7.76 hours x £30 = £232.80

Finally we add the price of the cost of the fixed costs to the price. With items using value based pricing being classed under fixed costs, we simply add the price of the reservation system purchase to the price estimate already calculated:

> ➤ Price Estimate = £232.80 + £1,000 = £1,232.80

Quotes

The only difference between providing an estimate and a quote is that a quote is a guarantee that the price stated is fixed for what's been agreed. Stating a delivery date is like a quote, but can never be absolutely guaranteed due to the risk of unforeseen circumstances that lead to slippages.

The problem with selling your services on a quote basis is that anything you get wrong in your estimation may lead to you to reducing your profitability, or worse—losing money on the project. It is because of this that it is a good idea to only consider selling your services on a quote basis once you have enough experience of running freelance projects.

When a client wants you to quote them a cost that you become obliged to deliver a project at, they are in effect passing their risks associated with the cost of the project to you, including the time costs resulting from any of their inefficiencies such as inaccurate communication and being too fussy in accepting components of the project that are subjective to opinion. With the wrong type of client, quote based pricing can open a can of worms that the client's cost concerns would have otherwise kept under control.

When faced with a client who insists on you providing a quote and not an estimate, consider the following:

> ➤ Whether you believe they pose too much risk to provide a quote.
> ➤ Whether the complexity of the project poses too much risk to profitably complete.
> ➤ Clearly attaching conditions to the quote that limit the scope of how it could be abused—such as the amount of time the quote is valid for acceptance and the number of revisions that can be made in project components that are open to subjective interpretation.

> ➤ Adding a significant percentage to your estimate to cover to cover the risk element being passed to you.

> ➤ Increasing your estimate to a point that would make the client reconsider accepting the original estimate.

With regards to the last point regarding the addition of a margin to incentivize the client accept an estimate instead, there is a fine balance with this. You will want to remain competitive, but at the same time make the price difference large enough for the client to see it being worthwhile to accept an estimate. For this reason, you may want to present both estimate and quote side by side so that the potential cost savings can be emphasized.

This method of calculating the price of a quote is the same as calculating an estimate, but with an added percentage added to the estimate. This means that the first step in this process is to calculate the value of the percentage you are adding to the estimate:

> ➤ Percentage Amount = (Percent ÷ 100) x Estimate Price

We then add this amount to the estimated price for the final quote:

> ➤ Price Quote = Price Estimate + Percentage Amount

Example

Our price estimate for the addition of a reservation system to the client's website was calculated to cost £1,232.80. The client has insisted that they would like us to quote a final price and not an estimate. Although the price estimate has already been calculated to accommodate the client rating to include the expectance of inefficiencies based previous experience of working with them, providing a quote is high risk if we can't be fully sure that we have accommodated all factors.

To accommodate the added risk, we want to add a percentage to the estimate price that gives us a large enough margin to ensure that we still earn our target profit margin if anything unexpected happens—and to avoid making any loss on the project. It is decided that there is still the risk of unknown factors, including the unknown amount of support that the client will require, hence we will go with adding 40% to the price of the project:

> ➤ Percentage Amount = (40 ÷ 100) x £1,232.80 = £493.12

Now that we know the price that 40% amounts to, we add this to the previously calculated price estimate created for the project:

> ➤ Price Quote = £1,232.80 + £493.12 = £1725.92

Risk management

Especially in the production of quotes that you become obligated to fulfill, the management of risk is an activity that should be engaged throughout the process of the project, which starts at the point where the requirements are being investigated and prices are being calculated. In our example of providing the client with a website reservation system, we have already identified the following risk factors of concern:

> ➤ Small project means that there is less margin for error if the estimate is wrong.

> ➤ Small project means that we are less able to adjust the budget allocated to different parts of the project to compensate for mistakes that cost the project.

> ➤ There are unknown factors relating to both the client and their requirements.

Counteracting risk

The first activity to engage in the production of the quote would be written terms that specify the conditions that quote will be valid. These terms are as important as the price calculated for the quote because they make sure that the client is restricted from doing or requesting anything that would pose a risk to your profitability. An effort should be made to ensure that the specified terms counteract each of the identified risk factors, such as:

> ➤ A detailed specification of the work to be undertaken—chargeable separately to the client if they are unable to provide this themselves.

> ➤ Definitions of limitation of each feature identified in the specification—restricting the client from adding features that are implied by the wording, but not explicitly specified.

> ➤ Conditions for the client's participation that the validity of the quote is dependent upon—providing the client with accountability for their actions and adherence to their responsibilities.

> ➤ Definition of consequences—further emphasizing what is expected from the client for the quote to be valid, with specific examples of situations where the quote will become invalid, additional charges are introduced or where any specified delivery dates become unachievable

The application of terms and conditions shouldn't always be applied in such a draconian way, especially where the client is happy to proceed with an estimate. However, even where the client is aware that the prices you are providing are as an estimate, it is still worth providing documentation to specify factors such as the specification that the estimate price was produced from—if not only to keep the client aware that the price stated is an estimate and not a quote.

Calculating risk

With the consequences of identified risks having an effect on the time and cost of the project, it makes sense to have the ability to incorporate risks as part of any estimation calculations. Risk has two components:

> ➤ The probability of the risk becoming a reality.

> ➤ The consequences of the risk if they become a reality.

The dilemma of risk management in estimating the time or cost of a project is incorporating a realistic balance that covers the likelihood of the risks becoming a reality. In more extreme cases, risks with a high cost and low probability cause a dilemma for project estimation and planning because:

> ➤ They are unlikely to happen, hence incorporating their full cost would likely make the estimate inaccurate and may risk make our project estimate or quote uncompetitive.

> ➤ The cost of the consequence when it happens has a serious impact on how the project is able to keep to the original estimate for time and/or cost.

The way that risk is treated in project estimation can be similar to how we treat risk in our everyday lives. Take for example identifying how to travel from location A to location B, where we can use a taxi who gives us two different route options. The following diagram models the risk and costs associated with each route:

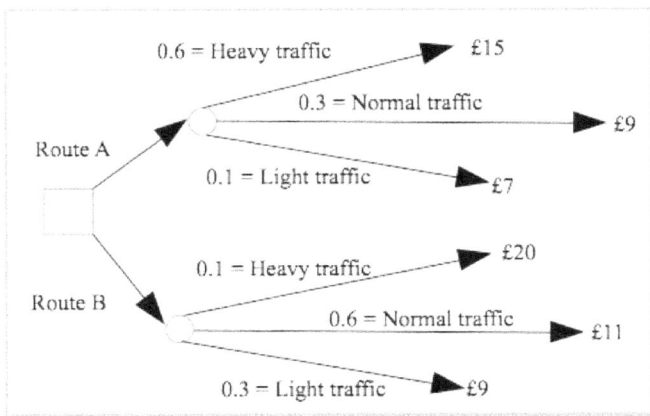

The simplest conclusion we can see from the diagram is that all outcomes in route B are more expensive than all outcomes in route A. This simplistic view of the situation can be misleading because we have not considered the probability of each outcome actually occurring. Probability is expressed as a decimal number between 0 and 1, with 0 representing impossible and 1 being 100% certain. We think of probability in everyday circumstances in percentages, which can easily be converted to their decimal equivalent by dividing the percentage by 100, which will result in our probability between 0 and 1.

Identifying the probability of outcomes such as those identified in our example model should be identified from informed information sources such as historical data, surveys or opinions of experts—see the section of this chapter titled Maintaining estimation accuracy.

After taking into account the probability of each of the outcomes of the routes, we can see that the most likely outcome for route A being heavy traffic due to a probability of 0.6, resulting in the taxi fare being £15. This is in contrast to the most likely outcome of route B having normal traffic, also due to a probability of 0.6, but resulting in the taxi fare being £11. We now have a completely different conclusion in that route B is likely to be cheaper than route A, despite all equivalent outcomes being more expensive.

Although our method of identifying the best route now provides a more informed insight about the likely outcomes and resulting cost associated with each route, we still have an element of uncertainty because there is still a 0.4 probability of each route having an alternative outcome that would result in a different expense. We can use the probabilities of all outcomes in each route to identify the most likely price by multiplying each price by their associated probability and adding all results under each route together. This would then result in:

> Route A = (£15×0.6) + (£9×0.3) + (£7×0.1)
> = £9 + £2.70 + £0.70
> = £12.40

> Route B = (£20×0.1) + (£11×0.6) + (£9×0.3)
> = £2 + £6.60 + £2.70
> = £11.30

The results of these calculations show that route B as being slightly more expensive, but still not as expensive as route A, whereas route A is can now be viewed as slightly less expensive as previously identified.

In the scenario of deciding a route to take for our taxi journey, neither method of analyzing the outcomes provide us with the complete information we need for making the decisions required for an individual journey. To make the best decisions, we'd use all three methods to identify the information we need:

➤ We would identify the maximum cost that each route could cost to ensure that we have enough money to pay the taxi fare.

   ➢ In a scenario where we only have £15 to spend, we know that route A can be guaranteed to meet our budget, regardless of traffic conditions.

   ➢ We would ensure to have at least £20 available to spend if we were willing to take a risk in order to save money, which would be the most likely outcome.

➤   The most likely outcome can be identified for an individual journey.

    ➢   With route A having a 0.6 chance of having heavy traffic, we know that the outcome for all journeys are likely to be the most expensive option. The probability of the second most expensive option can be combined with this to produce an almost certain probability of 0.9 that the journey will cost either £15 or £9.

    ➢   In contrast, route B has the probability of the most expensive option as only 0.1, meaning that the combined probability of normal and light traffic are almost certain at 0.9 probability that the journey will cost £11 or £9.

➤   The inclusion the likelihood of getting the most expensive outcome for journeys that are repeated on a regular basis.

    ➢   Although we know that heavy traffic is unlikely for route B, the probability is that it will occur once in every ten journeys, hence should be reflected in the likely price we pay for multiple journeys.

    ➢   Although our taxi journey example is based on the price of the taxi fair, we can also use the same method for estimating risk implications involving time and any other project factor that is measurable with numbers. It is also important to identify that although cost is often proportionate to time requirements of a project, other fixed costs can also be combined that take the total cost out of proportion with the time requirements. In the case of our taxi journey example, this could be where a route has costs incorporated such as a bridge toll, meaning that it isn't just the taxi meter that is charging for the time of the journey.

The risk associated pricing you use for your project pricing becomes dependant on the situation and the amount of risk you are able to take in relation to your profitability. Like with our taxi journey example, it may be worth risking the possibility of some reduced profitability on your project if there is a likelihood that you will make more money— however, you should only take this option if you can afford to absorb any unlikely costs should they happen.

Recovering unaccounted costs

As with anything related to risk, some things don't go to plan, resulting in situations where projects start to run over budget—a problem for you if you are working to a fixed price, meaning you lose money on the project in terms of time and/or costs incurred to complete the work. Although the client's rating would be adjusted to reflect the unexpected time and costs associated with their project, this is only useful for adjusting the price of future work to anticipate the same issues occurring again, and not to recover losses that have already occurred.

There are two options available for situations where a client's project has incurred unexpected costs that have lead to a loss in your profitability or outright loss on the project:

> ➤ Accept the loss and try not to repeat the mistake.

> ➤ Attempt to recover the loss.

It is important to remember that freelancers are ultimately in the game to make a profit, hence losing money is a serious issue. Your time also has a value, so make sure that you calculate any time above your estimate as part of losses.

One solution to recovering the costs of projects that have resulted in you losing money or the potential to earn money is to add the amount as part of the fixed costs element of future estimates and quotes you provide to the client. This method relies on you being able to:

> ➤ Provide the client with an incentive to hire you again—hence the importance of satisfying them with the original work.

> ➤ Remain price competitive whilst recovering your losses.

Small losses can be recovered quickly by adding their full amount onto the next project/phase that the client hires you to produce. Larger amounts, or those that are large in relation to the total amount of the project, need to be broken down into smaller amounts and therefore collected over several projects/phases.

Examples

Continuing our example where the client requested a website reservation system, we discover that the project has overrun by 15 hours. The first step is to calculate the value of the time lost:

Time Value = 15 hours x £30 = £450

We are aware that the upcoming work requests from the client are smaller jobs than the original system and therefore wouldn't be able to include this £450 in a price that would be competitive—hence risking the client looking for someone else who has the advantage of not needing to recover the £450. We know that the client is also likely to hire us for two other small projects in the future, providing us with a total of three opportunities to make recoveries:

Recovery Installment = £450 ÷ 3 = £150

The new recovery amount of £150 over three projects is a more likely to be accepted by the client and will keep your pricing competitive.

Maintaining estimation accuracy

It is easy to be misled when working with a small sample of data. This can be a serious issue when quoting a fixed fee for a big project if the quote is based on facts and figures that turn out to be inaccurate or irrelevant. Some factors that should be considered when calculating prices for quotes are:

> ➤ Experience of working on an individual project may not be a true reflection of how easy or difficult it is to work with a client.

> ➤ Different types of project have different levels of difficulty to implement.

> ➤ A client may have better skills in some areas than others.

> ➤ Client staff may move jobs and be replaced by new people throughout the project, resulting in whole new values generated for the client rating.

> ➤ The client's personality, commitment, competence and contribution skills may change over time—leading to an improvement or deterioration in efficiency of the working relationship and the decreased accuracy of the client rating data you have previously collected.

With the above in mind, it is possible to use more advanced methods to calculate the client rating and their resulting job quotes that better reflect evolving work relationships and the differing complexities of projects. These calculations, especially those for bigger projects, rely on the knowledge that:

> ➤ All projects are made of a series of smaller phases, hence each phase should have an associated cost to deliver.
>
> Where the client insists on a quote for a project considered to be large and/or complicated, your risk can be reduced by providing an estimate for the entire project and quotes for individual phases as they occur.

> ➤ Accurate estimations are dependent on accurate client ratings and realistic perceptions of the ideal time required to complete a job.
>
> Avoid the temptation to be overly optimistic, especially if you are trying to undercut the competition to offer a bid with the most attractive price, or where the client is pressuring you to commit to timescales that are unrealistic.

> ➤ The working relationship with the client is rarely either easy or difficult.
>
> Clients will be easier to work with for some types of tasks and more difficult to work with in others. Avoid making assumptions about the client based on previous experiences of working with them that are not similar to the current type of task you are estimating.

With the client rating being the critical element in adjusting estimates to account for known factors relating to the client, the key to maintaining accuracy of estimates is there largely to do with how client ratings are calculated.

Average client ratings

The most basic method of keeping quotes accurate is to base the client rating being used on the average of individual client ratings generated from each individual project engaged so far. Our original example used this method, in which each completed project was evaluated individual to identify its client rating, which in turn is added to the client ratings of previous projects in order to define a new average client rating that reflects the client's performance across all projects.

Using a client rating based on the average of all projects is good for situations where the project meets one or more of the following conditions:

> The project is reflective of the typical projects you have already delivered to the client.

> You are unaware of the bigger picture that the project exists within that will affect the client's performance on the project.

> There are not enough projects available to make use of the additional methods for generating the client rating.

Where the project doesn't meet any of the above conditions, there is an unnecessary uncertainty that poses a risk of the average client ratings being positively or negatively influenced by projects that are irrelevant to the current project being estimated.

An advantage using an average client rating in this type of scenario is that they tend to adjust themselves in the long run, providing that there are future projects/phases where they make enough improvements to cover any losses you experience from unexpected decreases in their efficiency.

Example

To demonstrate how using an average client rating can introduce inaccuracies in a scenario that doesn't represent the typical average project, we will perform an estimate on a project scenario where the client hasn't previously worked with us at such a technical level and therefore requires more support—this being the part that has scope to significantly increase the time investment required.

To recap on the client rating produced in the original example:

$$\text{Client Rating} = \frac{(2.5 + 2 + 1.75 + 1.5)}{4}$$

$$= 1.94$$

We see from this that the client is steadily becoming more efficient to work with, even though the average client rating still provides a rate that is near the half way point between their best and worst project performance. With the average client rating being above the target value of 1, it tells us that we should expect the client to take longer to work with on the typical project—in this case, it is telling us to expect to take nearly double the amount of time.

With our project scenario containing elements that are unfamiliar to the client, we can expect the possibility for any of the following to happen:

> ➤ More effort to manage the client through communication and planning - With the client being unfamiliar with the technicalities of this type of project that they have no experience of being involved with, there is a fair chance that they will need at least some additional element of support to check that they are understanding communications as expected and are able to be aware of what contributions they are required to make and when they should be delivered.

> ➤ Miscommunication with the client that lead to the repetition of work - This could be a lack of clarity in how the client words some requests or completely forgetting to provide information. This happens when the client is unaware of the importance of information—if they are at all aware of what the information is in the first place.

> ➤ Requirements to provide the client with additional training so they can contribute to the project - This could be in the form of teaching them how to use software they are unfamiliar with so that the can provide the data that your software components depend upon, or it could be in the form of providing knowledge about some technical activities.

Our scenario could have an element of miscommunication that leads to some of the work being repeated, which isn't good if have provided a fixed price quote. The average client rating may accommodate for this if the client has already shown inefficiencies on previous projects, which fortunately would be the case in our example scenario—providing enough margin for any such inefficiency to cause the project time to be almost double the ideal project time. This shows that the average client rating is at least reliable to a point in this scenario, providing that the ideal time for the project was realistic to begin with.

Where the average client rating could go wrong in this project scenario is if the repetition of code or other time investments required to train and manage the client are a serious enough issue to more than double the time. Maybe you would be happy to accept a small reduction in profitability on this project, which average client rating calculations would adjust itself to recover unaccounted time in future projects/phases—providing that the client becomes more efficient. However, when the problem comes when the client increases the project time to an amount such as three, four or five times the amount of time it should take.

Selective client ratings

Average client ratings can be made more reliable through being selective in the projects used in the calculation to ensure that the result reflects the expected efficiency of the client in the upcoming project/phase. Considerations that could be taken into account when selecting suitable projects to base the client rating on include:

> ➤ Whether the client has been progressively improving with each project - As their skills and ability to engage in a working relationship develops, the client will become more efficient in their collaboration and communications.

> ➤ Characteristics that previous projects with the current project/phase - Evaluating the client's performance on previous projects can be an illusion if the characteristics of these projects are not closely analyzed to identify their similarities to the current project. Where previous projects are not similar to the current project, it can appear that the client is able to perform better than they are capable of achieving with characteristics of the current project that prove to be different, more complicated or problematic to deal with. These characteristics may come in the form of some type of technical knowledge, skills, processes or communication ability that are required to be performed efficiently.

> ➤ Elements that are standard across all projects - There are likely to be some skills and processes taken for granted that are repeated across all projects. Clients who are initially unfamiliar with these before working with you will not need to repeat learning and mistakes to acquire the knowledge of these skills and processes.

The vulnerability of this method of generating client ratings is in the selection of projects. Being only human, the selection is vulnerable to mistakes in human decision making, whether it be through assumptions made about the suitability of projects being selected or being overly optimistic about the client's abilities.

Example

With our example scenario indicating that the client has little or no experience of participating in the current type of project, it would be more realistic to expect the efficiency of their engagement with the project to become similar to the first project. However, with the client already working with us on previous projects, it would be safe to assume that they will have gained skills and knowledge required to work with us that are transferrable to all projects, hence their performance in collaborating with us may not be as inefficient as the started with. For this reason, we will consider the following projects to reflect the characteristics of the upcoming project:

Project 1 - This project showed how efficient the client was to collaborate with when they first engage the type of project that they've not worked with before. Their lack of understanding of processes and skills required to collaborate at this point is similar to the current scenario.

Project 2 - This project showed how the client was able to make an initial improvement, which may have included elements that are repeated across all projects. With the previous projects being similar to each other, we are choosing to select the second project to accommodate the minimum amount of improvement we expect and to exclude later projects where the client has had more time to practice skills and understand processes that were specific to the previous type of projects.

With the projects with similarities identified for our selection, we are now ready to perform the calculation that identifies the client rating used for this project's estimation:

$$\text{Client Rating} = \frac{(2.5 + 2)}{2}$$

$$= 2.25$$

The result shows our selection indicating that we should expect the client's efficiency for this project to revert to a level that is only slightly better than when they started to work with us, which is what we would be expecting for a type of project that requires complexities that the client has never collaborated with us to produce.

The result also indicates that the client would be expected to become more inefficient than the average client rating would suggest—an increase of 0.31. Although this may sound like a small difference, it could be a large amount of money if the project is valued at thousands or tens of thousands of pounds instead of a few hundred pounds.

Proportionate client ratings

The third and final way that we look to enhance our client rating calculation is to estimate the client's efficiency for each individual phase of the project. This method requires more effort to evaluate the project, but stands to produce more accurate results if the project is evaluated correctly. It makes sense to identify that:

➤ The client's efficiency will vary throughout the project.

There will be some types of task that the client will be better at performing than others, especially if they already have relevant skills and/or knowledge that they use outside of the project.

➤ The client may learn and improve throughout the project.

Projects that have a longer duration will provide the client with the opportunity to improve their efficiency in the collaboration as they work on the project.

➤ Specific types of activity may involve barriers that other activities don't.

Barriers such as politics within the client's organization and their reliance on suppliers who are unreliable can affect the client's ability to be efficient in their contribution to the project. Without a full understanding of all of the factors relating to the client, it will not be possible to understand why they become inefficient, but analyzing the client's efficiency on each type of task or phase in a project will allow you to identify recurring patterns that lead to the client's efficiency decreasing when specific types of activities, people or suppliers are involved.

> There will be different levels of risk in estimating some types of activity, especially when we have to base opinions on third party sources.

Accurate estimation is dependent on being able to make calculations based on accurate information. We would ideally want all of this information be to be personally vetted by ourselves or someone we can trust to be knowledgeable on the subject so that the risk of anything being underestimated or overestimated can be minimized. However, mistakes can be made and it is difficult or impossible to fully verify all information, especially those that are outside the scope of our knowledge. We therefore need to reflect the scope for any unreliability of information used in our estimations as a risk.

With it being identified that the client's collaboration efficiency will differ throughout the project for different types of tasks, it makes sense that more accurate estimations can be generated by investing more effort into producing a breakdown of all of the project's activity types, which in turn can be used with existing knowledge of the client to produce a set of client ratings for each type of activity. These client ratings can then be used to produce estimates for the required time and budget required for each individual part of the project, as opposed to simply performing a single estimate to cover everything.

Any uncertainty about the reliability of the information we are using, whether it be about its accuracy, scope for unexpected results or increased complexities that could introduce unknown situations, can be applied by defining this uncertainty as a risk—see the previous section in this chapter on the subject. Applying risk to the client rating calculation allows for an adjustment to be made on any expected client contribution where we have an uncertainty about the reliability of judgments we are using about their abilities.

Example

Our scenario has a level of inaccuracy because there is an assumption that the new project will have a similar progression pattern as the previous projects, even though their characteristics are not completely the same. We also want to incorporate the ability to estimate the level of inaccuracy within our estimation resulting from the possibility of inaccurate information or the occurrence of unlikely scenarios that may occur.

To solve this issue, we can consider the reliability of the information we have used to to produce the client rating for estimating individual tasks as a risk. Our example has the client claiming to be fully proficient in managing data, which will be a big part of their involvement in the testing phase of the project.

The problem is that we already know from previous experience of working with them that they 3 out of 7 times they claim to have skills, they are not as proficient as they claim to be—typically taking double their expected time to complete the task. We can use this information to identify the probability of the client's claim being inaccurate:

> ➤ Accuracy Probability = 3 ÷ 7 = 0.43

> ➤ Inaccuracy Probability = 4 ÷ 7 = 0.57

Now that we know the probability of the client's claims being correct and therefore incorrect, we are now in a position to scale the client rating that is being given according to the risk of the client being incorrect. We know that the client rating for testing activities in previous projects averages 1.2 and that their client rating doubles for activities they incorrectly claim to be competent at, hence we will expect their client rating to become 2.4 if they are wrong for this phase of the project. We would calculate this as:

```
> Client Rating = (1.2 x 0.57) + (2.4 x 0.43)
              = 0.68 + 1.03
              = 1.71
```

We now have a client rating for the specific testing task that the client will be involved with that is proportionate their historical accuracy of their claims to be competent as well as reflecting the increase in their client rating for efficiency when they have been incorrect.

Summary

Although using math's is more complicated than simply guessing a price for quotes and estimates, the extra effort produces a result that is more informed and therefore more likely to be accurate. This more informed result in turn reduces the risk of your projects resulting in lost profitability or even an outright loss—this being where your costs to deliver the project is more than the client is paying you.

The less complicated type of project can in general be estimated as a standard package price—e.g. a 5 page website with bespoke design and conversion to web code to be X hundred pounds, and then Y pounds for each additional page added. This is a reasonable way to approach projects that are low risk in terms of complexity and where you are competing in a price competitive market. Using a client rating based on your knowledge of previous dealings with the client, or of other clients who show similar characteristics to the client in question, allows you to adjust any simple estimates you are considering for the project according to how efficiently you can expect to work with the client based on their characteristics.

More complicated projects can use more detail in estimation to a point that smaller projects may not have the budget to accommodate in such planning. Advanced estimation may still look at identifying a general cost for the entire project, or to invest a significant amount of effort to predict the cost of each phase—a safer approach, that would more than justify any additional time costs.

Self employment and business in general is all about risk management and you will always have to take some type of gamble when taking on new clients. The only difference between a fool who gambles recklessly and a wise decision maker is that the wise person will only take calculated risks based on reliable information. Although you may have little information to start with for calculating the price factors for an individual client, this can be developed fairly quickly to allow you to gradually become more accurate at pricing their projects.

12

Project Management

Whether you are developing your own product or taking on a new client project, the first issue that needs to be tackled is identifying how the end result will be created. For client work, this is more important because you will always be judged on how the client *perceives* you to be meeting their requirements and not on your *actual* performance. The right project management allows you to avoid this conflict of interest by prioritizing progression by focusing on:

> ➤ Priorities that are important to the success of the project.

> ➤ Aspects most noticeable to the client.

> ➤ Features that allow others to start making their contributions.

> ➤ Simplifying complexity of individual components.

> ➤ Versions to be produced for specific purposes.

With the right order of progression, you will be able to ensure that the client perceives to see progress whilst there is actual progress in the development of the project. It's a delicate balance to identify the right project plan, as listening too much to how the client wants the project to proceed can lead to problems in efficiency and other aspects of the project that affect both the delivery date and quality of the end result.

Client perceptions

Certainly in the short term, doing everything possible to make the client see progress will have many advantages for keeping their confidence in your ability; it is often tempting to take shortcuts to achieve this. In the longer term, this approach usually leads to many problems—especially when the project has a higher level of complexity. Examples of these problems include:

> ➤ **Research that hasn't been thoroughly verified** - Regardless of whether you are a journalist, business consultant or a software developer designing a data flow model to match the client's specifications, research that hasn't been verified for its accuracy will lead to the end outcome of the project being flawed.

> ➤ **Work that hasn't been structured to provide flexibility** - It doesn't matter whether you're a programmer writing software, a designer setting the layout for a brochure or someone creating a report document, it's almost always a guarantee that there will be a need to make some type of change(s) to the original requirements. If the work you've created isn't structured with efficiency and maintainability in mind, these change requests are likely to cause havoc that introduce scope for mistakes to be made and an increased amount of time required to make them.

Make a note

Imagine creating a website or software application that contains 100 pages/screens; each having their own headings, font styling and other visual presentation features. Everything has run smoothly on the project until the end, when the client asks for a last minute change to the fonts and color schemes used; this would be a 2 minute job if the work was done in a structured manner, but a serious task that could take a week or more to develop and test if the work had been developed in a rushed way without thought to structure and maintainability.

In the worst case scenario, the unstructured approach to developing this project would result in the requirement for manual alteration and testing of each individual screen, while the structured approach would only require minor modifications to a presentation settings file—such as a CSS stylesheet used in websites and web based applications.

> ➤ **Verification that hasn't been thorough** - No matter what type of software development you are involved with, it's important to constantly check the work produced so far to make sure that all components fit together. Skipping on this leads to more corrections that need to be made at the end of the project, meaning that the client can't rely on the work until it is fully complete; an issue that can be improved with a structured testing and development methodology . At least by investing time to perform verifications during the development of the work, the client can access previews that are more reliable for them to demonstrate or use to add their own data, information and suggestions

In most cases, the client will be eager to see progress on the development of their project. The relationship between the two types of progression philosophies and the client's confidence in your ability to deliver is demonstrated in the following diagram:

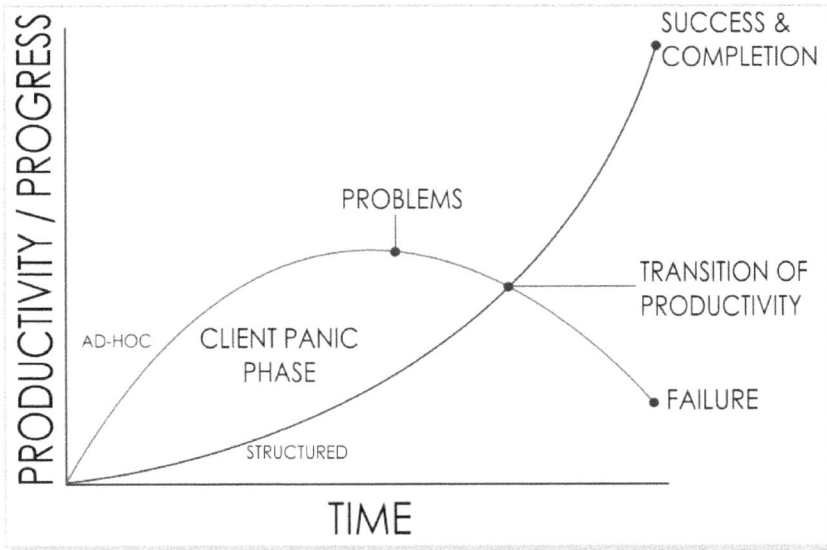

As can be seen from the above diagram:

> The structured way of working starts with a much slower progression than the unstructured ad-hoc approach.

> The progression rate of the unstructured approach decreases over time, whereas the structured approach starts to gather momentum.

> At some point, the pace of progression for the structured approach overtakes that of the ad-hoc approach.

> At some point, the ad-hoc approach leads to being unproductive—resulting from having to replace previous work due to change requests that take much more time due to the inflexibility of the work produced.

> The grey area between the progression of the two approaches represents the amount of panic by the client. The ad-hoc approach allows the client to be happy at the start of the project, but results in panic at the end, whereas the structured approach starts with a panic and ends with the client being happy and confident.

With the exception of prototype and throwaway projects, the structured method is clearly the way to go, as it allows for the best outcome in terms of time to deliver, quality and efficiency for future maintenance and expansions; the use of formal methodologies can be used to deliver a structured roadmap and identification of when tangible results are to be expected. The main problem with this approach is that it starts with a panic from the client and could be disastrous if not managed properly, possibly leading the client losing faith and abandoning the working relationship before the project reaches the point where they see the benefits. This is especially true for client personalities that show big elements of impatience (see *Chapter 6, An Introduction to Client Types*). There are two options to resolve this:

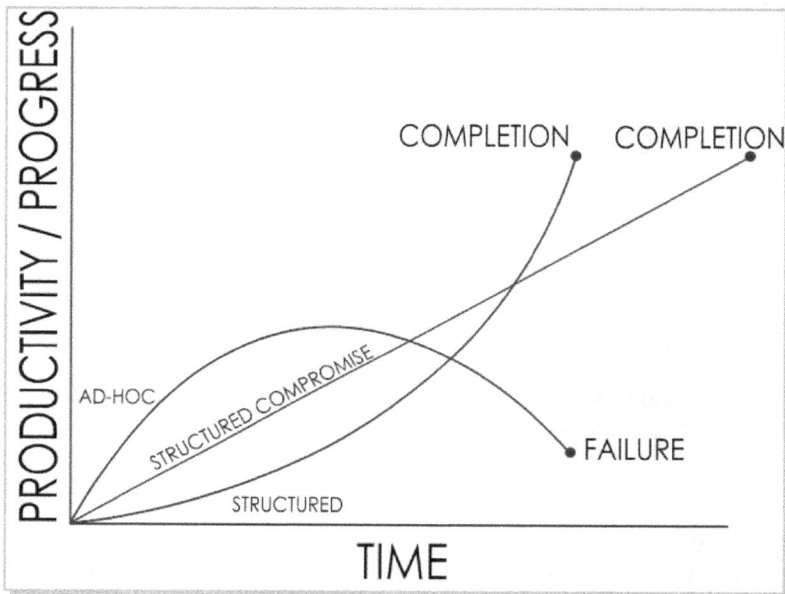

The first option for building the client's confidence is to carefully identify how to trade off the most structured methods of progression against the quick and unstructured. As can be seen in the above diagram, this isn't ideal, but it at least allows for a good level of efficiency and isn't a bad thing if the budget and deadline for the project allow for it. The key to succeeding with this strategy is in selecting the least critical elements of the structured approach to trade for the most noticeable and least flawed elements of the quick and unstructured approach, hence allowing you to satisfy the client without compromising your longer term progression and efficiency capabilities.

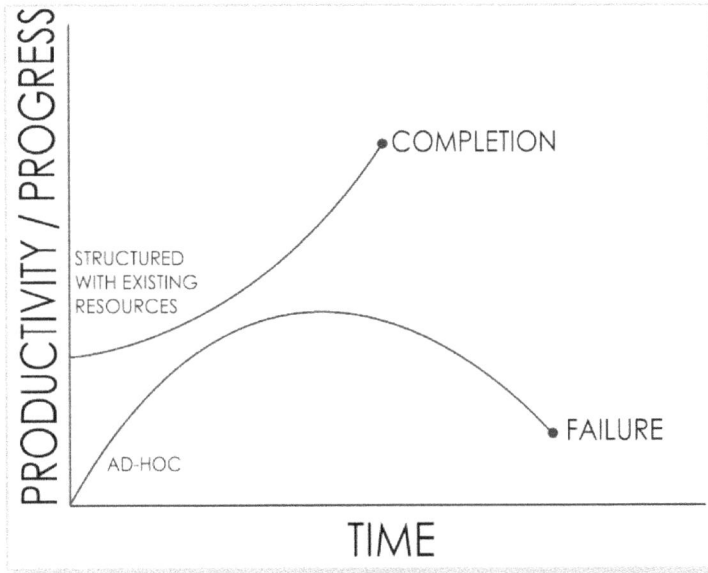

The second option, illustrated in the above diagram, starts with a set of resources that allow you to start several steps ahead in the project. These resources could be developed by yourself, accessed as open source tools or purchased depending on which options best suit your strategy. Examples of these resources include:

> Document templates for common types of report—e.g. business plans and sales reports.

> A code framework for software, making it possible to produce complex features more quickly.

> Template designs for websites.

> Ready made open source software—such as Wordpress for managing blog websites.

> UI framework for designing user interfaces—e.g. Bootstrap for websites and web apps.

> UI wireframe prototyping—i.e. creating visual mockups before the production of UI code.

> Royalty free stock photography for use in websites and brochures.

> A model library for animators, allowing scenes to be built quickly with common objects like tables and chairs being ready to drag and drop into scenes.

Whichever resources you select to enhance productivity, it is important to choose the right ones that are in general good quality, can be used with each other and that fit into your way of working. When researching the types of resources you will be buying or developing, you should pay special attention to finding answers to:

- ➤ How flexible is the resource for the range of projects you expect to deal with?

- ➤ What level of flexibility will the resource offer when clients change their requirements midway through projects? Does the resource make it easy to undo work such as by altering various settings?

- ➤ Does the resource impose any restrictions? If so, how could this affect your projects in worst case scenarios?

- ➤ What is the difficulty level to learn to use the resource? Will this introduce a problem if you need to bring other people onto the project?

When working with scenarios and/or clients who are difficult to predict, the best way to tackle the project will often be to identify in clear terms what can be provided for an initial version and then build on it from there; this being the minimum viable product (MVP), with new features being added with incremental releases. This will provide you with two main advantages:

- ➤ Faster route to market so that you can start trading sooner.
  - ➢ Recover your investment sooner.
  - ➢ Enable the system to begin funding its own future development.

- ➤ Allows you to test the market and develop future features in-line with identifications of market trends.
  - ➢ Avoids the risk of investing in features that unexpectedly fail to generate an interest and therefore fail to recover your development investment.
  - ➢ Allows you to make informed decisions about your product development inline with what your audience wants - and not what you think they want.

Methods of communication

An ability to communicate effectively will always be central to a successful project. Not only is it important to communicate the right information when needed, but also to use the best method for individual communications to avoid the project going off track. The following are an identification of the different types of communication methods that can be used in your project management, complete with details of their advantages and disadvantages.

Meetings

The most detailed and responsive method of communication, face to face meetings provide many advantages that can't be matched by other forms of communication— including the ability to more accurately interpret body language, exchange physical materials such as documents and also to have a more structured upfront conversation about issues relating to the project.

Although face to face meetings are very good for collecting details and observing non-verbal information from the client, their time consuming nature mean that they are best kept to a minimum on an 'as needed' basis. This isn't to suggest that face to face meetings should rarely happen, but more that they should be set weekly rather than a daily basis. Due to their time consuming nature, it's important that face to face meetings have a defined structure that meets all agendas and avoids wastage of time. A meeting agenda should:

> ➤ Define all issues that need to be discussed.

> ➤ Avoid repetition of issues discussed in previous meetings unless new information has come to light on the subject.

> ➤ Allocate a maximum amount of time to invest in discussing each issue to avoid spending too much time discussing minor issues and not enough time on the major topics.

> ➤ Identify a summary of points that are to be answered in the meeting.

Face to face meetings can also be disruptive if not managed properly:

> ➤ Always ensure that meetings are scheduled—whether it is face to face or online via systems such as Skype, never let clients believe they can pop in to meet you unscheduled as this will reduce your productivity on work you are engaged with.

> ➤ Unplanned meetings and those without a structured agenda usually lead to repetition of previously discussed issues with no new information or solution identified, hence resulting in a meeting that has no value to the project.

Telephone

Not as good for quality of communication as meeting face to face, but still a very effective method of communicating because a conversation can still happen in real time and although the client's body language can't be observed through a telephone call, it is still possible to obtain additional information through observing how they vocally react to information such as being shocked or confused.

Telephone conversations are a good medium between the ability to reactively collect information in real time and the ability to communicate efficiently, as telephone conversations rarely last hours and can be used to get fast responses for specific questions. The real-time and direct access elements to telephone conversations mean that using this method of communication is especially useful when information is required immediately—by calling the person, the question can be asked directly for an immediate answer without delay, unlike other methods of communication that rely on having to pre-arrange a meeting or non-real-time conversations that can easily go unnoticed or ignored. In addition to these advantages, the real time vocal communication elements can also be used to better verify interpretations of the message to minimize scope for misinterpretations that lead to wasted time and undesired results in the project.

Conference calls

Conference calls are an extension of the regular telephone conversation that provides an advantage of being able to involve a group of people, often without the need for them to travel. This advantage is useful for projects that have multiple decision makers and service providers who may be separated by a large geographical distance. Additionally, conference calls can also make use of video, making this option something that sits between a real face to face meeting and a telephone conversation.

Like face to face meetings, conference calls require much more planning and organization than a regular telephone call because of the need to arrange a time, agenda and availability of people needed for the conversation. This added complexity suggests that conference calls should be limited to only when they are required, such as for weekly progress updates and discussing new requirements.

E-mail

Unlike the previous communication methods mentioned, e-mail isn't real-time and so hence has a different set of advantages and disadvantages. The main advantages of using e-mail for communication are:

> Convenient to send information at a time that suits you, whilst also providing the recipient with the convenience to retrieve and read it at a time that is best for them. This is factor becomes more important for people working in different time zones or out of regular working hours.

> Efficient and easier to communicate information and instructions. There's no need for the receiver to worry about writing information and instructions because they are already written in the e-mail and can easily be stored for later reference.

> Reduced scope for misinterpretation because the communication is recorded in writing, hence no Chinese whispers effect.

> Information can be easily formatted to make better sense to the recipient to further help avoid misinterpretations.

> ➤ Documents, video, and imagery can be attached to e-mails, allowing for faster provision of resources that are required for the progression of the project.

> ➤ A paper trail of communication is produced, which not only can be used to find information and instructions relating to the project, but can also be used to resolve any disputes that may occur on what has been agreed for delivery.

> ➤ Avoids the scope for unnecessary distractions from your work, allowing you to remain productive regardless of who and how many people are sending you e-mails

Although there are major productivity advantages in using e-mail for communication, there are also some drawbacks:

> ➤ The non-real-time nature of e-mail means that you can't always guarantee that the recipient has received what you've sent. A number of issues can lead to this, including mistyping the e-mail address and the recipient not being immediately available. At least with real-time communications like telephone calls you are made immediately aware if you have dialed the wrong telephone number or if the recipient isn't available to immediately provide feedback on your communication.

> ➤ Another concern of the non-real-time nature of e-mails is that they are sometimes placed in the spam folder—meaning that the recipient may not see your e-mail at all.

> ➤ Written communications can be easily misinterpreted because there is no indication for tone of voice or ability to react to the recipient's response in real-time. As a result of this, a genuinely sincere message can be interpreted as being sarcastic and lead to an unnecessary conflict that is harmful to both productivity and the working relationship.

> ➤ Non-real-time communications like e-mail make it much more difficult to detect signals such as surprise or anticipation that would be useful to use in tailoring your response to communications.

> ➤ Older people and those less engaged with technology and/or writing will find using e-mail more difficult to use, resulting in poorer communications with this method. For these people, extra effort is required to use e-mail as little as possible.

As a result of such drawbacks, e-mail should always be used in addition to real-time communications like telephone and face to face meetings to ensure that you and client can engage communications that are efficient and most effective for the progression of the project. Combining e-mail with at least one form of real-time communication will help to avoid problems that can occur from the drawbacks of e-mail communications, whilst opening many new opportunities for better progress.

Social media

Social media is a new type of communications tool that has emerged over the past few years. It's not entirely new, as equivalents of many of the components have existed separately. The main advantages that these platforms provide are centered around the:

> ➤ Convenience of having access to all of the tools you need to effectively communicate from the one place.

> ➤ Reach to efficiently communicate directly with the people you need to.

> ➤ Easiness to share information with specific groups of people.

> ➤ Readily available analytics tools – useful for identifying trends project activity.

These advantages help to make social media specifically useful for tasks relating to project management, marketing and public relations. Although there are several advantages, some caution should also be taken with social media:

> ➤ It's very easy for shared information to offend or to be miscommunicated, resulting in political problems on a project.

> ➤ Public social networks like Facebook can reveal private information of individual employees that reflects badly on the business brand.

> ➤ Personal opinions of individuals can bring a business and it's projects into disrepute.

With a view to avoiding such scenarios, it's worth considering making use of a social media policy that people who you work with and therefore reflect have influence on your reputation should abide to.

Post

The slowest of all the mentioned communication methods, post is inadequate for much of today's fast evolving world where a response is required instantaneously. Although the time issue puts it at a big disadvantage, its one big selling point about using the post to communicate is the ability to send physical content, making it ideal for sending:

> ➤ Documents that require a physical signature.

> ➤ Physical items—such as a product, a prototype or components.

> ➤ Written communications to the technology shy and less financially fortunate.

Although it's often taken for granted these days that everyone is capable and comfortable with using computing devices to send e-mails, there are still many people who aren't able or don't like to use technology—such as older people and those who are less financially fortunate. If your business involves communicating with people who fall under any such categories, then postal communications becomes a much more important than the digital methods like e-mail and social media.

Even for the majority of people who take digital communications for granted, there are special circumstances where postal mail remains the best option:

➤ Marketing material is more likely to get noticed because it needs to be physically handled and can't be 'deleted' at a press of a button like an e-mail can.

➤ Important notices like final payment warnings are best sent by postal mail to ensure the message at least gets to the correct physical address to be physically noticed. There is no guarantee that an e-mail will reach the intended person— such as being blocked by spam filters or the person not checking their e-mail.

➤ Recorded delivery can be used to ensure that someone physically received the message—perfect for situations where proof is required that the communication was received, such as court proceedings.

➤ Provision and request of sensitive information. Although digital communications technologies are more than capable of securely transmitting sensitive information, organizations like HMRC (the tax man) and banks prefer to only request sensitive information by post due to the many ways that fraudsters easily confuse less tech savvy people with authentic looking fake e-mails designed to steal information and make payments.

Allocating the right people

When working with other people, whether they are employees of the client, your own employees or third party suppliers hired by either you or the client, it's important to know how to delegate project tasks. Questions that you should be thinking of include:

➤ Who is capable of achieving the task?

➤ Who is ideal for the task?

➤ Who is available?

➤ What are the limiting factors?

Although some of these questions seem to be asking the same thing, each highlights an individual set of answers that form the foundations of all good decisions.

Who is capable of performing the task?

The most obvious question is possibly the most important question that people often get wrong when they are delegating tasks beyond their knowledge. This is especially true with Internet projects where the realms of software programming merge with skills of graphic design and marketing; each having their own specialism. This type of diverse skill set that is often considered to be just one skill – that of website creation is typical of how a project's requirements for specialist skills are often by those not in the know. A closer look at this example shows how the general service of creating a website can require the full range of experts with skills and experience from different disciplines, which may include the use of collaboration methods such as DevOps; an agile framework for combining activities engaged by development and operations staff:

Design : All about creating the visuals for the project to enhance perceptions and usability.

Skill	Description	Works with
Graphic design	Creation of general design themes for the project. Involves selection of color schemes, creation and alteration of graphic components to create a concept that matches the desired visual brand.	■ Photographer ■ Client side developer ■ Illustrator ■ Advertising
Illustration	A specialism of graphic design that is about creating new images. This requires more skill and more time than using pre-existing illustrations as part of a design theme.	■ Graphic designer ■ Interface designer ■ User interface designer
Icon design	Similar to illustration and can be classed as part of user interface design. Icon design is specifically about the illustration of visual icons that will help improve the user's navigation through visual symbols and so hence requires skills and knowledge of both the illustration and user interface design disciplines.	■ Interface designer ■ Graphic designer
Photography	A completely different skill requiring a different set of equipment to the other mentioned design skills. Photography is all about capturing the most appropriate photographic resources for the graphic designer to use in communicate the message of the project and brand in their design concept.	■ Graphic designer
User experience design (UX)	Unlike graphic design, which mainly focuses on how content is presented to the user, user experience design has its focus on identifying how functionality and content can be presented in a way that allows the user to become more productive. This skill has less focus on creating graphic elements and more focus on identify design features such as to simplify the amount of options presented via a user interface.	■ Client side developer ■ Graphic designer ■ Icon designer

Programming : All about creating the functionality that makes content and design components work as intended.

Skill	Description	Works With
Server side programming	Server side programming is about the creation of code that works behind the scenes—you can think of it as the equivalent of theatre production staff who do all the work in a play to make sure that the actors can deliver a great performance. The server side code is what controls functionality of the website, including how data is sent to the database and what information is output to the website visitor.	■ Client side developer ■ Database developer ■ Server manager ■ Software analyst
Server management	A website needs to run on a server and the server needs to be configured properly to run the website. This includes making sure that the right software is available on the server to run the website, that the software settings are configured in the right way for the website code and to make sure that the server settings are secure enough against hackers.	■ Graphic designer ■ Interface designer ■ User interface designer ■ Software analyst
Client side development	The opposite to server side development, this is about creation of code that runs on the website visitor's computer. This is the code that shows the visuals of the website and allows for interactivity—both in terms of interactive animations and sending information back to the server.	■ Interface designer ■ Graphic designer ■ Server side developer
Database development and administration	The database development and management is all about creating the resource that is used to store information that the website needs to manage. This might be for storing orders for an e-commerce website or member accounts for a website that has user login accounts like Facebook. Any website that is more than a brochure website is like to use a database—even brochure websites that use a content management system will have their content coming from a database. The database needs to be designed to meet the demands of the website and later needs to be administered for tasks like future upgrades and cleaning of data.	■ Server side programmer ■ Server manager ■ Server side programmer ■ Software analyst

Skill	Description	Works With
Software analysis and design	Advanced websites are ultimately software systems—the only difference from traditional software being that they exist online and are operated through a web browser. As a consequence, advanced websites require a well thought out strategy for the construction of their code to ensure that the end result meets the purpose and can cope with future adaption requirements. Software analysts are the people who review the business processes and convert their findings into a system design for the different types of programmers to base their code on.	■ Client side developer ■ Server side developer ■ Database developer ■ Security analyst ■ Software tester
Security analysis	With websites existing online and accessible by anyone, the stakes are much higher for their functionality to be abused and information to be accessed by people who shouldn't have access. The role of the security analyst is to work with the system designer, developer(s) and tester to ensure that it can't be abused by users who have a mischievous or criminal agenda.	■ Server side programmer ■ Client side programmers ■ Server manager ■ Database developer ■ Software analyst ■ Software tester
Software testing	It's important to ensure that the website functions as it should—the more complex the system is, the more scope there is for something to not work right. The software tester is a separate person to the main programmer(s) and acts as a person with no programming influence on the system with a view to finding anything that doesn't work properly. Although the programmer(s) will have engaged some of their own testing during the development, some types of bugs are likely to be present in the system that either the programmer hasn't noticed or haven't appeared due to the programmer's equipment having different settings to real world users of the website.	■ Software tester ■ Software analyst ■ Client side developer ■ Server side developer ■ Server manager ■ Security analyst ■ Database developer

Marketing : All about generating attention and awareness to generate incoming traffic to the website.

Skill	Description	Works With
Content writing	Contrary to the belief of many beginners in website projects, the most important element of the project is always the creation of good content because without good content, design, programming and marketing have no purpose. The content writer is central to the creation and marketing of the website, creating content that appeals to the target audience, effectively communicates the message ins a persuasive manner and is recognizable to the search engines.	■ Social media marketer ■ SEO analyst ■ Advertising co-coordinator ■ Public relations
Search engine optimization (SEO)	A large amount of traffic can be referred to the website by simply being placed for search phrases on search engines like Google. The role of the SEO analyst is to identify which searches are relevant and worth being listed for, and then to identify and engage strategies that result in the website being listed in target search results—leading to the website gaining traffic from active searchers. The SEO analyst will often work with content writers and public relations to achieve their goals.	■ Content writer ■ Public relations
Advertising	The quickest and easiest way to get traffic to the website—by simply paying for it. The advertising coordinator will identify the best sources of advertising to generate targeted traffic and will work with content writers, graphic designers and social media marketing to ensure that their adverts are appealing to entice people to visit the website and then to follow through and perform anticipated actions such as making a purchase. The advertiser will use a number of advertising mediums including print and online advertising combined software that monitors the results of their advertising investment to identify which sources and advertising campaigns are producing the best results.	■ Content writer ■ Graphic designer ■ Social media marketer

Skill	Description	Works With
Social media marketing	Unlike other forms of marketing like SEO and advertising, this type of marketing is all about engaging with customers directly on a social level. This means that the strategy should initially be less about the selling and more about the social engagement—the benefits coming later from brand awareness, learning and increased ability to generate recommendations that lead to sales. The social media marketer works with public relations, graphic designers, programmers and content writers to produce content components that engage the target audience and achieve marketing goals—such as more website visitors and registrations.	■ Graphic designer ■ Content writer ■ Client side programmer ■ Advertising co-coordinator
Public relations	Positive attention from any type of media will often result in new visitors to the website—especially from other website that have a large readership. Public relations not only benefits the website by referring traffic from other websites, but also will positively influence search engine listings to place the website higher in their rankings, leading to more traffic being referred.	■ Content writer ■ SEO analyst ■ Social media marketing

From the above overview of all skills involved in making a website project successful, it's clear that it takes more than one person to achieve everything that is required. Even for small website projects that don't require advanced programming, a large element of marketing, design and content creation is required—it's unlikely that one person will be an expert in all three fields, yet failure to get them all right will result in the website not achieving it's purpose.

Who is ideal for the task?

Although elements of a project like programming a website may require just the one skill, it's important to know the full picture and as a result if the work requires specialist or generalist skills. With the website creation example, a server side programmer is likely to have skills in database development and depending on the complexity of the task you have, they may be able to do the job if:

> The work doesn't require very specialist database administration and development knowledge.

> The work is associated to their involvement with server side programming.

> The task isn't a high risk operation—e.g. can it result in the entire database being deleted if something goes wrong?

This is a classic example of how a generalist task can be delegated to anyone with skills in the same domain—as long as the specifics don't require knowledge that is too specialist or requires engagement in activities that are too high risk. On the other hand, providing this task to a web designer or web marketer would be entirely out of the question because their work is in a completely different domain, meaning that they won't have any generalist skills that they can use to complete the task.

The decision on who is best suited to the task shouldn't only be based on whether it requires specialist or generalist skills, but also:

> **The skill level of the individual** - A specialist will be better than a generalist in most cases, but there are always some exceptions. An example would be a highly experienced server side programmer who has worked with a lot of database projects being more experienced with database development than a junior developer who specializes in database development and administration.

> **The level of involvement with the project** - People who are highly involved with the project will have a lot more detailed knowledge about how everything works, including roles and responsibilities of other people involved. Certainly when it comes to complicated activities like programming, having more involvement and knowledge of how everything works makes a person better suited to make updates and changes than someone who may have more industry experience, but less understanding of the project's components.

> In addition, people who are new to a project will need time invested for learning and supervision – even if they are experts in their field. The big questions being - is the task something that can be used to ease a newcomer into the project or is it urgent to have it completed as soon as possible by someone who is already experienced with the project?

> **The risk of the task at hand** - All tasks have different levels of risk and knowledge such as industry experience, project experience and personality style should be taken into account. As an example, the specific task of penetration testing for security vulnerabilities in software and websites is best provided to a programmer who has specific knowledge of common methods used for hacking systems similar to what is being tested. On the other hand, the same programmer may not be suitable for a task that involves detailed knowledge of how the code works if they haven't had a lot of experience in working on the project.

> **Political motivations** - Although someone may technically speak be the best person to do the job, the reality may be very different—especially when politics are involved. At one extreme, it could be that this person has previously had disputes with exiting team members or simply that the client is not willing to pay the rate for a senior developer and so hence limiting your options to the junior developers who are available.

> **Available budget** - This is a factor that is very closely related to political motivations. It could be that the client is financially restricted to what budget they have for the project or simply because they refuse to pay above what they specify. Under any of these circumstances, a review of what is required and the potential implications is needed before a decision is made on who is suitable for the job.

In an ideal situation where the client is paying by the hour, a decision can be made on what the job requires to deliver a good result. A more junior person will be cheaper to hire, but in many cases will not be able to produce work at the same speed or quality as someone more experienced. Some clients will refuse to listen to the cost benefits of hiring people with higher levels of experience for the job, whereas jobs with basic skill requirements won't benefit from extensive experience—it's from these identifications that the cost factor should be combined with other decision factors to decide who is best for the job.

As can be seen from these considerations, the ideal person for the job isn't the same as the best person. Indeed, the person who is on paper the best person to do the job could in reality be the worst option given real world circumstances. Through taking the identified factors into consideration, a decision can be made that is more likely to result in a more successful outcome as a result of minimizing all risks for anything to go wrong.

Who is available?

It's logical to say that people can only work on a task if they are available, and their best productivity will be when all focus is given to one task. This isn't a problem when the required people are available, but there are situations when using the right people can cause implications for other parts of the project. Factors to consider include:

➤ Length of the task to be delegated.

➤ The importance of the task to be delegated.

➤ The importance of the work that the person is currently involved with.

➤ Productivity consequences of distracting a person from their current work.

➤ Expected and unexpected leave for the person—e.g. maternity leave, holidays and illness.

In situations where the ideal person for the job is already be engaged with other tasks, there are a number of options available:

➤ **Request that they drop their current commitments to resolve the new task** - This should only be used as a last resort for tasks of the highest priority; stopping people from working on their current work leads to lost time in productivity as well as an increased risk of faulty/unfinished work going unnoticed.

➤ **Wait for the ideal person to become available** - A perfect option for non-urgent tasks. This can sometimes be difficult to judge—especially for clients who have a habit of claiming that everything is urgent.

➤ **Select a less ideal person to engage the task** -Depending on the complexity, politics and budget available, this could be a good option. The less ideal person may not be someone who is less skilled for the task, but could be someone who is for example more senior and therefore more expensive—their time may cost more than the ideal person, but less than it would cost the project to delay the task, hence the added cost being considered as a premium for a fast turnaround.

Regardless of whether the ideal person is available for the task, a contingency plan should always be in place for whenever they become unavailable. The plan should identify the next most suitable people to take over the work as well as a plan to ensure that instructions, information and resources that are required to complete the task can be communicated. Often, this will involve the use of written documentation and some form of hand over training.

What are the limiting factors?

Everyone and everything has their limit; leading a project to success depends on realizing this. Limiting factors can come in many forms:

> **Time** : No matter how urgent the task is, people can only be made to work at a pace that is realistic. If the task needs to be completed sooner than is realistically possible, then extra people and/or resources need to be considered to achieve completion by the deadline—however, keep in mind that having more people working on a task doesn't always speed up progress. Other options include reducing the depth of the task and/or negotiating a more realistic delivery date with the client.

It's important to keep in mind that pressuring people to deliver work within unrealistic time scales leads to work that is rushed, resulting in a solution that may not work and requirements for more time investment for testing.

> **Skills** : A common mistake made by people hiring skills that they don't have an understanding of is assuming that everyone will produce the same output. Price is often a major factor in decision making, and people with higher skill levels and experience tend to charge significantly more for their time This becomes a problem for projects restricted by budget, where unknowledgeable decision makers view the lowest hourly rate as being the best value option. The downside to this style of hiring is that people with less experience and skills tend to work slower, require more training and are more likely to make mistakes that increase future development and maintenance costs. The lower hourly rate becomes a false economy when the overall costs become much higher than paying someone with the experience and skills required to deliver it faster without mistakes.

Knowing the skill limitations of the identified ideal person in advance will allow the ability to plan in advance for providing more advanced tasks to be provided to a more appropriate person as well as saving on time and avoiding mistakes that prove to be costly and time consuming to correct.

> **Pressure** : People will always work better and have better loyalty to a project when they feel valued and not over pressured. Applying too much pressure to people can lead to a higher turnover of staff as well as additional work absence caused by stress. A bit of pressure can be good to ensure people keep focused—knowing how much pressure an individual can take can mean the difference in them remaining happily productive with their work, and failing to contribute their full potential to the project.

> ➤ **Commitment** : People's ability to commit to the task in question will differ depending on their personal, work and technical capability circumstances. As an example, tasks that may require people to work outside regular working hours may cause a conflict with people who have children, whereas tasks that require full time working commitment may cause issues for people who may only be available to provide their services on a part-time basis. By knowing commitment capabilities of people in advance, it is possible to build a working strategy that allows whoever is chosen to engage the task in a way that is mutually convenient and avoids situations where work isn't delivered due to the project member being placed in awkward situations.

> ➤ **Politics** : Business is all about politics and freelancing is no exception. Whether it's an issue of negotiating the level of expertise to be made available to complete a task or issues relating to where, how and when the work will be engaged, the political factors will form the basis for which the limitations of all other factors should be based on.

Written agreements

Most worthwhile projects will require some form of agreement to be signed, and even where this isn't the case, it's worthwhile having a set of your own terms and conditions written. Although a contract is technically considered to be in place where there is a payment and verbal or written agreement involved, only a written agreement gives both parties reliable evidence of what has been agreed. Aside from the issue of protection against future disagreements, having a written agreement is also a useful tool for making sure that there are no incorrect assumptions made by both parties, which themselves can lead to conflict that derails the project. The following are considerations to make when looking to write up and agree to any formal written agreements:

> ➤ The ideal terms set for a project will be one that you have created yourself—this eliminates the possibility of you underestimating the definition of any clauses or requirements.

> ➤ Never immediately accept terms for delivery of work from a client who doesn't know about the technicalities of your service—instead, thoroughly read through their terms and make alterations to all items that can potentially lead to issues based on lack of knowledge from either the client or yourself.

> ➤ Ensure that delivery quality is defined in detail within the terms to protect yourself against clients who are unrealistic about what is achievable and/or wanting take advantage by claiming a refund based on quality of work that is otherwise delivered to a satisfactory standard.

> ➤ Ensure that there is a get out clause for both parties. Anything can happen in your personal life that will entirely change how you are able to commit to the project, as well factors relating to the client.

➤ Ensure that terms are defined for all change requests and communications. The wording should include reasonable hours to contact you and notice for work given. This protects you against unreasonable clients who believe it is ok to disturb you at night. and who expect their work to be put above the priority of your other clients – even going as far as to have you work through the night for them.

> ➤ With that said, it's not uncommon to charge extra for time spent over weekends.

➤ Make sure that the terms clearly state the conditions for delivery on any agreed deadlines. The wording must protect you against changes to the specification and revelation of previously undisclosed information; it is entirely unrealistic for the client to expect you to meet the deadline if they make alterations and additions to the specification that double the amount of work required.

➤ Clearly state exactly what the price charged to the client includes:

> ➤ Cover in detail issues such as support and alterations to the specification.
>
> ➤ Never leave scope for the client to make alterations that could increase the time required to develop the system and provide additional support without increasing what you are paid.
>
> ➤ Wording covering your support liability should limit this aspect of the service by time in some way—such as by hours or number of enquiries within the support period; this protects you from the type of client who would take advantage of using the support service as a way of gaining extra labor for free and makes it clear to all clients what is considered as reasonable for support.

➤ Make it clear in your wording which elements of the project are within your control and which elements you can't be held responsible for that could lead to missed deadlines or issues relating to quality.

> ➤ Examples of this include integration of third party software system suggested by the client and APIs from external systems used to provide data that your code depends upon.

➤ Ensure that there is a section to hold the client responsible for failure to provide the required feedback to progress and complete the project. It is unrealistic for the client to claim a refund for poor quality and/or missed deadlines if they themselves have failed to provide the information and resources such as content you need to complete the work.

Feature creep

The issue of feature creep, where additional feature requests are added over time, is common to the majority of software projects. For developers who don't have a huge amount of experience in managing software projects, it becomes very easy to let feature creep get out of control by not realizing what is happening and/or being too polite to the customer. Feature creep becomes a serious issue where:

> ➤ The client is paying a fixed price for the work, meaning that additional features are outside the scope of the project's price quote and therefore means you are giving free labor.

> ➤ A completion deadline is part of the agreement, especially where there is a bonus involved or where the client has grounds to take legal action for late delivery on the basis of damage to the client's business.

There are many reasons why feature creep occurs on software projects, and knowing their cause allows you to identify the most appropriate actions to resolve them as they occur. The following are common factors for feature creep that you are likely to experience in your freelance and contract projects:

> ➤ **Assumptions of the original agreement** - In most cases where this occurs, it is simply a misunderstanding between the software developer and the client regarding the scope for detail and complexity that a feature in the specification has meant to represent. Regardless of how innocent this may be, the issue can cause friction in the project that leads to the software developer losing out financially and lost trust from the client. The following are steps that can be taken to avoid this type of issue from occurring:
>
>> ➢ Word details in written agreements and specifications to explain the level of detail for functionality of every feature to a point where it can't be argued that undisclosed requirements are classed as being defined under ambiguous wording in the agreement.
>>
>> ➢ Rather than specifying what functionality isn't covered, look to word details to be specific on what is covered and restricting the specification and agreement to only cover the scope of what has been written.
>>
>> ➢ Make use of lean software development principles to reduce the scope of the project to the minimum viable product - only the functionality essential for the software to be useful for its purpose - Not only does this reduce the risk of extra functionality causing problems based on assumptions, it allows the client to have a working version faster at less expense.

➤ **Changing business environment** - Successful businesses are a product of how they react to the demands of their environment, whether it is sales driven by through changing demands of buyers, changing legislation or emerging threats from competitors. All of these factors affect the requirements for your software, and the longer the development cycle, the higher the chances are that something will happen in the business environment that results in changes/additions being requested. Although change often can't be avoided, the following actions can be taken throughout the project to anticipate and manage it:

   ➤ Use robust software development patterns that allow for changes and additions to be embraced efficiently—see *Chapter 10, Software Development Methodology*.

   ➤ Use a lightweight software development methodology that provides flexibility for change, as opposed to a heavyweight methodology that contains too much planning to allow fast reaction to changing needs halfway through the project—see *Chapter 9, Software Development Resources, Patterns and Strategies*.

   ➤ Consider using short release cycles and lean development principles to reduce the risk of business environment changes making software functionality redundant—this is covered in more detail later in this chapter.

➤ **Committee politics** - Where there are multiple stakeholders involved in a project, committee politics can become an issue where too many people ask for too many features, and where everyone is pressuring you to put their feature as top priority. This can be avoided by:

   ➤ Identifying the primary decision maker and having them provide you with development requests that have been fully vetted to their satisfaction—a single point of contact who relieves you of being directly involved in their organization's politics.

   ➤ A well defined project specification and written agreement created before the commencement of any programming, making the level of detail clear of what is to be developed and the procedures and time/price implications of change requests.

➤ **Hyping client expectations** - When communicating with clients about the software project, be careful not to unnecessarily increase their expectations. Extra care should be given to how features and possibilities are described, as well as any imagery shown. Avoid being optimistic about what is possible, whether in terms of timescale or technical achievability. Where there is scope for the client to assume more advanced features that have been agreed, extra effort should be made to define any limitations on the features to be developed in both the project specification and written agreements signed by both parties.

> ➤ **Assumptions of user needs** - People who have no background in software projects are often tempted to cram as much into their requirements in the belief that more is better and that it makes their software product/service more appealing to a wider audience. This type of approach leads to new additions being requested after the initial agreement, with these extras often being described as part of existing features. This problem comes from two factors; the client not being experienced in dealing with software projects, and also not fully understanding what they want from the start. When faced with this scenario, extra care needs to be taken to educate the client about the impact of trying to cram too much into their design—i.e. additional features increase the time to market and the risk of investing in features that don't get used. By educating the client about software release cycles (see later in this chapter), you can persuade the client to separate non-urgent features that can be revisited after completion of the main system.

Clients often don't fully understand the problem they are trying to solve with the software project they are hiring you to develop, meaning they will realize the need to add or refine features. Like with other reasons for changes and additions to the specification, this introduces an additional time requirement and therefore needs to be covered by the available budget. This issue can be avoided by:

> ➤ Use of prototyping before commencing development of real code. This provides the benefit of allowing the client to see how the final version would function and the ability to request changes and additions before commencement of code production. A significant cost advantage can be gained by avoiding the need to *undo* code, which can be timely to review, alter and test – hence it being expensive.

> ➤ Getting the client to focus on the releasing just one component at a time. This helps both you and the client to understand how the functionality should work in more detail, resulting in a better functioning result to address the problem the software is designed to solve.

Risk assessment

Many issues can occur before, during and after the completion of a project that can affect the client's perception of its success. Knowing the risks that lie within a project allows you to take measures to prevent them from becoming an issue, or at least contain them from becoming more serious than they need to be.

Project nature

Not all projects are equal, and this is certainly the case when it comes to software projects. If you are creating an entertainment app such as a smartphone game, making the app enjoyable to use will be a top priority, whereas creating an air traffic control software will not have any emphasis on enjoyability and will instead focus more on issues such as reliability, scalability and fallback safety features for scenarios where system components fail. These examples show how diversified software projects can be, and hence how their relevant risks should dictate the style of project management.

Team politics

Most projects where there is more than one person involved will have an element of politics to some degree. We've already covered how this can happen with clients for whatever reason, but it can also happen with people in the development team, whether it be with project managers, designers or programmers. Like with clients, the majority of project politics are caused by the different visions of the people who are progressing the project and assumptions made. The following are typical areas that should be managed by the team project manager:

> Decision by committee:

> > With your role as software developer being central to all other activities on the project, it is difficult to avoid getting involved in the politics between other members; this not only affects your productivity, but can also lead to the introduction of faults within your code and you being held responsible for actions of other people.

> > Decision by committee also reduces how fast the team can respond to the need for change. At its worst, team members can become undisciplined in order to achieve their agenda to a point that they are destructive to the project's progression; an example of this being features not designed to the project specification because members on the project are too emotionally attached and as a result are designing the system as their own product instead of as a product for the client.

> Solutions for decision by committee should include:

> > Identifying someone to become the dedicated decision maker. This person will liaise with the client to acquire information about their ongoing requirements, and will closely monitor progress of the creative/ development team to ensure that what is being developed matches the project specification. This person would also be responsible for monitoring all communications regarding the development of system features to ensure that scope for misinterpretation or manipulation can be minimized.

> > Ensuring that members of the project are not emotionally attached to the project, whether it be having an agenda to create the system primarily for their portfolio, or where they are paid royalties – which motivates people to become personally attached to design and development decisions.

> > Welcoming the input and suggestions of team members, as long as they are communicated through the team's decision maker for final decisions.

> **Blame culture** - When things aren't going well on a project, some types of people are more than willing to point the blame at the next person. With programming the software being central to the project, you should be aware of how this can put you in the firing line with such people. Look to have procedures in place that protect you from being the victim of these politics, which could include:

>> Minutes taken in all meetings to ensure everyone has a record of what's been agreed.

>> Having a document for confirming authorization to commence development of requested features, allowing you to show who made the requests if they are later disputed.

>> Having a sign off document to confirm satisfaction of each completed milestone, allowing you to show that confirmation was given of completion to a satisfactory standard.

> **Manipulation** - Some people on a project team can be problematic due to having their own agenda. This becomes a serious issue if they are also capable of being deliberately manipulative, which can lead to situations where you are led to believe incorrect information that suits their agenda. An example: A freelance team member has an agenda to use the project to enhance their portfolio and to increase the amount they are paid from the project. Their motivations lead to the team member suggesting features that not only increase the requirements for their services, but are also complicated to develop and unnecessary for the client's requirements. The team member pushes their agenda to be developed into the project by telling you that their features have been requested and authorized by the client, leading to you coming under fire when it is discovered that unauthorized features or alterations have been developed into the software. As a result, the project extends from 3 months of development work to spread over 3 years due to extensive coding, testing and design requirements. In the worst case scenario, manipulation can lead to a dispute in a dispute with the client; if nothing has been signed, it could mean that you are left with thousands of pounds/dollars worth of your time unpaid. You can minimize the risk of this by taking the same measures for managing the blame culture, in which you have processes to document and verify all requests you are asked to develop. Make sure to also have spoken confirmation by main the main decision maker(s) in a conversation to eliminate the risk of signed documents being tampered with and/or requests being worded in a way that is misunderstood by you and/or the decision maker(s).

Expectations

The most important element of managing any project is setting expectations for what will be delivered. Get this wrong and you set yourself to fail before you've started the project. The following are six areas to consider for evaluating the type of expectations you want to set for the client:

> ➤ Budget
>
>> ➤ An ideal project would have an unlimited budget to allow the deployment of the best quality time, expertise and labor to progress the project to a successful completion of the highest quality. Although an unlimited budget wouldn't always guarantee access to the best resources, it would certainly go a long way to make it possible if used wisely with knowledge.
>>
>> ➤ The problem with real world projects is that they are almost always affected by an available budget. Whether it is due to cash flow or profit margins, money is one of the two main factors that affect what is possible. Good project management allows for money to achieve more results through higher efficiency and productivity, but there will always be a limit to what a budget can achieve, so make sure you set expectations to be realistic on what a budget can achieve and don't let yourself be bargained down by clients who want to get the lowest price. Even if you lose a project bid to someone quoting an unrealistically low price, you can still be there to offer your services when it all goes wrong and without needing to worry about being out of pocket or vulnerable to legal action resulting from how the budget limits you from fulfilling your obligations.
>
> ➤ Time
>
>> ➤ The other major factor affecting capabilities to meet expectations is time, which itself is closely related to budget – time is money as they say! Time may be limited due to budget restrictions, or it may be limited due to the need to meet a completion deadline. Either way, clients need to be aware of what is realistically achievable within the available time. Software features can also be labeled in order of their importance so that less required features can be dropped or delayed for a future release should there be any slippage in the project plan – see more about this in *Chapter 10, Software Development Methodology*.

- ➤ Skills and knowledge
  - ➤ Whether it's your own skills or people you are working with, being realistic about your capabilities will allow you to avoid allowing the client to expect more than what you are capable of delivering. Although skills and knowledge can be gained through the lifespan of the project, there is a time requirement to develop such skills and knowledge to a standard where it can be usefully deployed within the project. This is where more experienced developers can justify their higher costs through an ability to deliver more productively, hence lowering the real overall costs for developing advanced code components that a more junior level developer would require more time to deliver.

  It is important to identify that the skills and knowledge required by the software project fall into three categories:

  Development—i.e. knowledge and skills for writing writing code.

  Industry—i.e. knowledge and skills about the client's industry, customers and competition that will allow you to make better judgments about the software requirements and implementation.

  Soft—i.e. the people skills for knowing how to manage the client and retain their confidence.

  - ➤ Skills and knowledge can also be used to develop resources that allow for better productivity. This may be in the form of content generation tools that allow data required by the software in development to be created through drag and drop GUI based input instead of manually entering code or data, or tools that capture client input to avoid inefficiencies such as duplication of work or features that are dropped from the requirements after they have been developed.

- ➤ Technologies
  - ➤ Enthusiastic clients often have big ambitions that match their enthusiasm, sometimes which can't be met with the technology available—whether it be availability within the budget or that the technology has yet to be developed. An example of the latter being how hardware for Internet of Things (IoT) are allowing new functionalities for software applications that wouldn't have been possible before 2010.

➤ Resources

    ➢ Resources are often related to technologies, especially when they are built on available technologies that the project uses, but they are separate to technologies in the sense that they are developed or customized to boost productivity ability of the project. This may include developing authoring tools to speed up data generation that the software in development relies upon; an example being a GUI point and click tool to capture image coordinates, avoiding the need to manually write code and test for ever co-ordinate for interactions. These resources appear within the project over time to make you and your team more productive, but are not immediately fully available unless you've already delivered projects to the same specification.

➤ Law and ethics

    ➢ Although something may be technically achievable, it may not be possible to legally or ethically deliver. Clients may ask for inappropriate features of their software such as an ability to hijack the host computer/ phone to deliver advertising and capture details, which could be considered as illegal under the Computer Misuse Act 1990. Other requests may be completely legal, but raise ethical concerns depending on the views held by the public or the software developer. A website designer was once exposed in a local newspaper for being hired to create and manage an adult-themed website, which although not illegal, could have lost him potential business with other clients who would worry about having an association with the story tarnishing their brand. Being clear with clients from the start of the project about what can be lawfully and ethically achieved will avoid assumptions being made that put you in a difficult position once the project has commenced.

There is a hierarchy in which expectation factors affect each other, which is demonstrated in the following diagram:

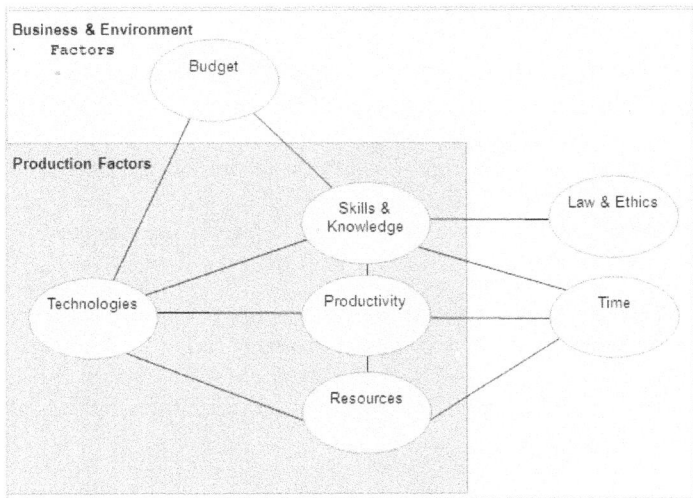

Legalities

It would be naïve not to expect something to go wrong in your projects, so understanding the implications of what can happen when delivery dates are missed and bugs within the code are left unnoticed will go a long way in allowing you to analyze the risks posed by being involved with the project. In the worst case scenarios, setbacks can leave you open to claims for:

> **Loss of earnings** : A client could claim that the delayed delivery of your software has led them to lose money from lost sales that they were expecting to make from the delivery date, and as a result could attempt to use the legal system to force you to compensate them for their calculated losses.

> **Loss of business opportunities** : Where faults in the software lead to data being lost, whether it be through data not being stored or data being deleted, the client could make a legal claim for compensation to the value of what they consider the lost data to be worth. Their compensation claim could be in relation to loss of opportunities to generate earnings, in which it they assume that each of the lost data items would have generated new business, or they could claim that the lost data is essential to their business operations, in which they would be claiming for compensation from lost productivity and business opportunities.

> **Financial losses** : Where faults in software lead to direct financial losses such as e-commerce websites dispatching orders without taking correct payments, or where the client is subjected to litigation resulting from software faults, the client could in turn take legal action against you to indemnify them against the claims they are subjected to.

Fortunately such claims are not so common and are only a higher risk where:

> The data being processed is highly sensitive or valuable—e.g. storing bank account details on the system database.

> The client deliberately causes problems with the software development process—potentially with a view to claim more money back from you than they are paying in the first place.

The solution to vulnerability to legalities is to have clauses in your terms and conditions that are specific to protect you against the types of situation that can occur. Care should be taken to ensure that your terms are worded accurately and in depth enough to cover the situations you are by default vulnerable to, as well as to reflect the law—your clauses are only valid if they are compliant with existing laws. Make sure to make your terms clearly understandable to eliminate any scope for the wording to be interpreted with a different meaning. A good set of terms and conditions should:

> **Have an introduction section to define meanings of important words:** This provides a clear definition of important words used in the agreement in a way that eliminates scope for the client to have the terms ruled invalid should it be taken to court based on a different interpretation of the wording.

➤ **Be split into sections covering the main points of concern** : Allows for easier interpretation and amendments if required. With the agreement being easier to interpret, it is also more likely to go in your favor if a dispute should go to court.

➤ **Have a provision to set a limit on your liability** : Should there be a situation where all other clauses fail, this provision can be used to make sure that your exposure is limited to what you deem acceptable. This could be limited to the value of the project or just a fraction of what you are being paid, and protects you against the rare but concerning client who hires you with the sole intention of claiming more money than they pay you. At a maximum, the limitation of liability clause should be set to no more than the value of your professional indemnity insurance cover.

➤ **State the responsibilities of the client** : For anything where you are responsible for meeting measureable expectations based on time or quality such as completion dates and assurances of working functionality, there should be a clause to state that delivery to the agreed criteria is dependent on adequate assistance from the client. This avoids situations you are held to account in failing to meet expectations due to the client failing to provide information, content and other resources you need to complete the work. For example, projects will exceed their agreed completion date if you are unable to progress work due to awaiting content or server access from the client.

➤ **Make sure the client pays for work accepted** : Your terms should have a clause to state that live usage of the work you have created for the client signifies its acceptance to the client's satisfaction and therefore any remaining payments under the agreement being due. This protects you against clients who use withholding payments to extend the project specification in order to receive free labor.

➤ **Protect you against third party litigation** : Anything that the client requests you to create or provides for integration with your creation should be the responsibility of the client. This may include provision of imagery, text content or code components that the client doesn't have permission to use. A clause in your terms and conditions to state that the client is responsible for the accuracy, ownership and/or permission to use the content they provide will protect you from copyright and defamation claims from third parties you have no involvement with.

➤ **Distinguish between the immediate project delivery and ongoing maintenance and support** : Clients will often have support requirements long after you have completed the delivery of their software. Having a clause that defines what level of support is provided makes it clear what support requests are acceptable and protects you against situations where you are expected to deliver support that would cost more time than you've been paid for the entire project, or where support requirements expose you to other legal issues. The support clause should clearly describe how long your initial support will last and the detail of activities that the support will cover, with additional support being purchasable under a separate agreement.

> ➤ **Protect against acts of God** : You only need to look at the news during most winters to realize that events such as severe flooding cause havoc. Although unlikely, these events don't just happen to other people and therefore could happen to you at a time critical to completing the client's project. Having a clause in your terms and conditions to state that the agreed timescales and delivery specification exclude occurrences of acts of God will protect you against any claims from the client relating to this.

Defining a specification

The project specification closely ties in with the legalities, expectations and politics. Without clear specifications, you become vulnerable to the type of nonsense that prevents you from developing the type of functionality that is directly relevant to solving the problems that the project looks to address. Spending some time at the beginning of the project to define a clear specification to be made available to everyone working on the project will save a lot more time from being wasted on associated politics relating to changing interpretations and even agendas of other people working on the project.

A clear specification document is a useful asset that can be used to keep the team focused, as well as being a point of reference to deflect any development requests known not to be part of the original agreement.

Creating a specification document

The complexity of the specification should reflect the complexity of the project. The more detailed the specification, the more time will be required to create it. This is not to say that corners should be cut to reduce the time required to create the project specification, but that the time required to create an appropriate specification document should be integrated within the project budget; the more features required by the project, the more detailed the specification document needs to be to describe how those features should be implemented. The complexity of feature requests should never be underestimated, especially when they are described in reference to any of the following words:

> ➤ Easy
> ➤ Simple
> ➤ Only
> ➤ Quick
> ➤ Fast

The use of any of these words by the client or anyone requesting features to be developed typically indicates a combination of the following:

> ➤ A lack of understanding for what is required to create the feature.
> ➤ Limited identification of how the feature is to be created.
> ➤ Unrealistic expectations for delivery timescales.

This type of assumption made by either the client, yourself or anyone else involved in the project poses a high risk of building unrealistic expectations for what can be achieved within the available time and budget. The project specification document should be designed and written in a clear to understand way that allows everyone involved to easily see what is involved, what is to be delivered, the expected timescales and what the limitations are. The following is a structure that could be used for project specifications:

Definitions

Like writing a contract, having a list of definitions used throughout the document helps the reader to make incorrect assumptions such as confusing technical terms such as IP address with IP for intellectual property. This section also serves to protect you against any dispute that may arise from the client claiming that their interpretation of meanings written into the specification being different to how you intended them to be interpreted.

Summary

The purpose of this section is to give a brief description of what the system is to achieve and the level of detail for features to be created. It should provide enough information for the reader to understand what the system is to be without going into specific detail and should be up to three paragraphs in length.

Requirements

This section expands on the summary to give a detailed list of each feature required by the system. The requirement descriptions don't necessarily have to state how they will be created, but should be clearly worded to show what the outcome should be for each feature implemented—and more importantly the limitations of each of the requirements defined. Being specific in stating what the limitations are allows for greater clarity of what has been agreed by closing margins for any assumptions that could be made.

Requirements can be clearly defined using the SMART checklist:

> **Specific**: Wording used should identify exactly what is required without ambiguity that leads to scope for misinterpretation. Similarly, the wording should be created in a way that stops the client from claiming alternative meanings later in the project.

> **Measurable**: Having requirements written in a way that their completion can be measured against will protect you from situations where the client keeps asking for modifications that are beyond the original agreement. Measurability could be worded in the form of specifying the number of acceptable design alterations, or being specific about the amount of data being managed – such as specifying the number of forms or fields to be used.

> ➤ **Achievable**: A requirement for the software is only worth being part of the specification if it is achievable. This could be in terms of available time, available technology or budget – if achievability can't be met for all of these, then the requirement shouldn't be part of the specification.

> ➤ **Realistic**: Although a requirement may be considered achievable, but is it realistic? It could be that the requirement can be achieved within the available time and budget if everything runs at 100% efficiency, but it's not realistic to expect no slippages, especially if you relying for input from a client who has already proven to be unreliable.

> ➤ **Timely**: Like with achievability and being realistic, a specific emphasis should be placed on making sure that there is enough time to fulfill the requirement.

System overview

Unlike the requirements section that describes what the system will do, this section provides details about the different components of the system that will form the ability to provide the defined requirements. Unless the client is highly involved with software development, this section doesn't need to detail everything, but would provide an overview of the main system components—e.g. database(s), programming language, open source components or systems (e.g. Wordpress), etc. The system overview's purpose is to provide some detail about how the system is to be developed and protects you from revelations after the development has started or has been completed such as the client wanting the system to be developed using a different database system or CMS that could lead to a complete rewrite of your code without being paid extra for your time.

Design

Clients can be placed into one of two generic categories when it comes to software development—those who are about visuals and those who are about functionality. For clients who are highly motivated by the visual appeal of the software system they want, having a section to define the design requirements is mandatory.

The design section of the specification isn't meant to provide a final design of the visual components of the software system, but a wireframe in which the final design will be based upon. This is an important part of the specification when dealing with clients who are highly motivated by the visual components due to how visual additions can significantly add to development time. The inclusion of wireframe screen designs allows for the requirements of each screen to be specified at the start of the project where the associated time and costs can be clearly defined, as opposed to new design functionality incrementally being introduced throughout the project that derails your ability to deliver within the agreed timescales and budget. With visually motivated clients more likely to adjust their visual requirements for whatever reason, the design section of your project specification also serves to provide evidence of the original agreement where the project is on a fixed price basis—making it easy to justify additional costs for anything outside of the original design specification.

Timescales

Listing the timescales for the expected delivery of each milestone in the project is required to give the client the ability to estimate when they can start to see the system take shape. This section helps you to avoid being distracted by clients calling you to ask when they can see your work – especially when you are already working on their project when they call! The irony of this situation is that clients perceive they speed up your progress when checking on you like this, but they actually slow your progress. Even worse is when the person is located in the same building and insist on randomly popping in to see you!

It's said that interruptions such as a telephone calls can cost up to 25 minutes of lost productivity for each occurrence due to loss of focus. Those phone calls can add up to hours of additional time invested!

Cost plan

This part of the specification is important for fixed price projects, and is still important as a guideline for projects where you are being paid on a time and materials basis. A good cost plan shows a breakdown for the cost of each component of the system you are developing. Not only does this make it clear what the costs are, but it allows the client to identify how costs can be reduced by eliminating features that aren't so important—this is a good strategy to use for people who attempt to bargain you down on price; instead of offering to sell your time at a lower rate, you use the cost plan to eliminate features that the client can be persuaded to exclude from their requirements.

Feedback

Professional software development isn't just about writing any code to do the job, but more about writing the right code that the buyers of the software demand. There will always be a temptation to save time by making assumptions or to skip the need to have regular meetings with the client so that more time can be invested into writing the code. Although time can be saved from meetings you don't expect to discover new information, it is rare to have meetings with a client where new information isn't discovered – and it is these new pieces of information that can save you many hours from developing features that are no longer required, need alteration, or where their priority has been dropped.

Feedback can be gained using a combination of methods. With projects often suffering from limited time to get the code written, too much time spent on other activities can contribute to deadlines being missed, hence the importance of getting the right balance between time invested in developing the software and efficiently gaining feedback. The following are methods to gain feedback for different types of situation:

Meetings

Nothing beats face to face communication and ensuring that the decision makers are all in the same room to make sure that ideas and opinions can be shared in real time. Providing that all members of the meeting are paying attention, there is no excuse to for people to claim not to be aware of issues raised—furthermore, meetings can be followed up with minutes detailing the topics covered and responsibilities assigned to people.

The downside of meetings is the associated time required from everyone, meaning that too many meetings will become an obstacle to your ability to invest time in developing the system. Time is also required by other people attending the meetings, meaning that too many can also become a disruption to their activities and result in a resistance from people who view the project's meetings as wasting their time. The time cost of a meeting is not only the amount of time taken for the meeting, but also the time for traveling and the remaining time for other activities after the meeting. For example, if people work 9-5 and get back from your meeting at 4:30 p.m., it's likely that the remaining 30 minutes isn't going to be spent productively. Repeat this regularly and you'll find that lots of 30 minutes add up to a lot of hours in lost productivity. Additionally, a meeting requiring you to spend an hour to travel to the client for a one hour meeting means three hours in total, which is nearly half of a full working day.

Some clients may have a culture where there is an over reliance on meetings. This may come from a belief that each meeting contributes to productivity, a "paranoia" to check on your progress, or simply as a way for people to "keep up appearances". Where this occurs, there is a need for you to take control of the frequency of these meetings so that they don't impact on your productivity. The following are some of the more extreme examples where over reliance on meetings will affect your productivity:

> ➤ Being called into four meetings in the same day with the same person about the same project.

> ➤ Being called into meetings that don't require your involvement.

> ➤ Meetings arranged at inefficient times and locations:

>> ➢ A one hour meeting set at 3 p.m. on the other side of the city; when lunch finishes at 2 p.m. and it takes you 30 minutes to travel there, This means you have 30 minutes from 2 p.m. in which there is nothing you can productive get started with code, plus another 30 minutes that you can't productively use from 4:30 p.m.

>> ➢ This type of meeting further impacts productivity when it requires no involvement from you.

> ➤ Requests for meetings on issues that you could resolve in less time required by the meetings.

Focusing on the quality of meetings rather than their quantity will deliver higher quality feedback and less resistance from key members of the project to attend them. For ongoing projects, a meeting each week to identify progress made in the previous week and to identify the focus of the next week is typically adequate, allowing for priorities of each week to be dictated by the acceptance or alteration requests for the features developed in the previous week.

Survey tools

The use of surveys to capture data can be a useful asset when surveys are designed to ask the right questions and where they are distributed to the right people who can be persuaded to take the time to provide answers. Although meetings can be used for the same purpose, surveys have the advantage of allowing participants to provide answers in a format that can be easier to analyze and to be answered in their own time, reducing the risk of bias and forgetting information,

Surveys are only useful when they are designed to capture useful information, so careful consideration should be taken in the selection of its questions. These questions should:

> **Use a mixture of quantitative and qualitative questions:**

>> Quantitative questions are those where answers can be measured to produce statistics—i.e. they are about measuring quantities. These tend to be multiple choice questions where selected options can be analyzed to identify the percentage of people who selected them, but they can also be designed to request numeric information that can be analyzed using Maths, such as to find the average score or age provided.

>> Qualitative questions are those that are answered with detailed information—i.e. they are about providing descriptive information. These questions allow survey participants to write free flowing answers that describe opinions and facts relevant to the question. Because they are free flowing, these answers can't be measured with statistics like quantitative questions, but they are more useful for identifying information of importance that you are initially unaware of.

> **Be clearly worded** - Avoid using jargon or wording that can be misinterpreted— these only increase the risk of inaccurate feedback. Consider getting feedback from other people on how they interpret your questions before distributing the final version of your survey.

> **Have a purpose** - Every question in the survey should allow you to identify something that will influence how the prototypes and final version of the software will be designed and implemented. Some questions should be designed to gain an understanding about the problem(s) that the final software system is intended to solve, whereas other questions should be about the people who will use the system so that you can identify user experience (UX) design requirements that allow the system to become easier and more efficient to use.

Surveys can be used at any time during the project to capture a snapshot of information that provides insight to how the software system can be improved to address the problems it is designed to solve or to become easier for end users to operate. As a minimum, surveys should be considered at the start of the project before any work has started on creating a prototype. Capturing survey based information at this point in the project allows you to identify important factors that will affect how the software should be designed and implemented. Factors for this include time and budget that defines which features are possible, as well as key factors of the problem and the system's intended users that have a direct influence on the feature requirements. Further surveying can be performed throughout the project to support prototyping in ways that identify changes that are required until there are no objections—at which point a production version of the system can be created that matches the prototype specification.

Prototyping

Showing the client a working concept of how the system will function without the need to invest the time to develop the full system is a useful way to gain the type of feedback that clients provide when they use the real system. This use of prototyping also allows you to avoid the risk of wasting time on requested features that are later dropped or significantly altered due to their practicality. In this type of scenario, time is not only saved from writing code that doesn't get used, but also the time required to undo this code—which includes the time to test dependencies.

Prototyping the features you are to develop for the client doesn't have to, and probably shouldn't, involve writing code. Tools such as Microsoft's PowerPoint and Apple's Keynote are ideal for creating concept screen designs using point and click tools. Interactivity can also be simulated with these presentation tools so that the client can see how the system would feel when interacting with it. This allows them to provide you with feedback on subtle functionality changes that would otherwise take a considerable amount of time to adjust how the system may have already been coded by the time you were able to get this feedback using the real system. Notes can be added to presentations that describe any design requirements not obvious from how the presentation has been constructed.

Email

The use of e-mail for defining a specification is a useful means of conducting non-realtime communications that provides time for both parties to review and investigate the implications of each feature proposed for the specification. This consideration is important where there are critical deadlines to be met, or where the project is to be delivered on a fixed budget—underestimating either of these could result in failure for the project.

Additionally, e-mail communications are ideal due to offering the ability to refer back to previous parts of the conversation. This can be advantageous during the development of the software system where anything that is worded vaguely in the final specification needs evidence of what was agreed.

Conference calls

Not all communications are best suited to written forms of communication such as e-mail—largely due to where there is a need for real-time communication, but also that not everyone has the time or skill level to write and read highly detailed written communications. Conference calls can allow fast real-time communications without the need for commitment to travel or have a pre-arranged agenda for the structure of the conversation—although some structure will help to avoid the conversation steering off-track. Although many would argue that conference calls are no replacement for face to face meetings, their real advantage is in allowing shorter conversations to take place at a frequency that would be unfeasible for face to face meetings when travel time is a factor.

In terms of defining a project specification, a few conference calls can go a long way in getting to understand the client. Not just in terms of what they want, but also getting to understand the bigger picture of what they do in order to identify how their requirements may change throughout the project and how their immediate requirements can be expressed in the specification.

Release cycles

It is said that the initial development of a typical software system only accounts for 20% of the total system, meaning that additional enhancements introduced after the first release can account for as much as an additional four times the amount of software development. For projects that are anything other than a simple straightforward system such as a brochure style website, this can become a serious issue because clients without an understanding of software release cycles will want everything in the first release. This can lead to over ambitious expectations, ongoing changes and constant additions to the specification that keep delaying the first release. Ultimately, this risks the system being released too late; whether in terms of the market opportunity already having passed or of the potential to make savings in the client's operations.

How often?

It's a fine balance when deciding how often to release new versions of the software you are being hired to develop. Getting the balance right will allow your client to see the benefits of the system sooner and avoid effort being invested into features that don't get used or provide the type of benefits envisaged by the client; hence highlighting the importance of getting the system into use as quickly as possible. The following are two philosophies that can be adopted for releases of your software projects:

> ➤ **Few and major** : Having small releases provides many benefits for being able to respond quickly to short term requirements as well as for experimenting with features closely related to your business model and identifying how they are used. The monitoring part not only allows you to identify new ideas to improve the software, but also whether these features are in demand; helping you to avoid investing large amounts of time and money on features that don't turn out to be used by your users. The often and small approach is best suited to systems that don't require client side installation, such as web based applications.

> ➤ **Often and small** : Having small releases provides many benefits for being able to respond quickly to short term requirements as well as for experimenting with features closely related to your business model and identifying how they are used; the monitoring part not only allows you to identify new ideas to improve the software, but also whether such features are in demand—and avoid investing large amounts of time and money on features that don't turn out to be used by your users. The often and small approach is best suited to systems that don't require client side installation by the user such as web based applications—users will certainly get annoyed and resist installing updates if they are forced to update their installed apps too regularly.

> Often and small also gives you more leverage for managing the demands of the client, who will typically want to see their features yesterday. Having a release cycle that shows how new features will appear in a short timeframe gives you more negotiation power to stage the introduction of their system, with the features providing the most value to their business model being introduced in the earlier releases. An additional benefit that comes with this strategy is that new feature identifications that benefit the client will create more need for your services to develop them into the software. You just need to make sure that your relationship with the client allows you to be given the extra time and money to make this possible.

Feature order

An important consideration to keep in mind for the management of your software projects is that there is no relationship between how noticeable a feature is and how long a feature takes to develop. This means that at one extreme, there are features that take a long time to develop that go unnoticed, while at the other extreme there are features that get a lot of attention which only take a tiny amount of time to develop. Understanding how to identify where features fit between these two extremes will allow you plan an order for software feature development that avoids/minimizes project management dilemmas relating to politics and business environment influences.

The order for each software feature to be implemented into your software project has two main influential factors for consideration:

> Time

  > How long will it take to develop?

  > When is the optimal time to develop it?

> Impact

  > Who will notice it?

  > How will it be noticed?

  > What outcomes will it produce?

The following is an example template for a chart that can be used to visualize the impact vs time requirements of project tasks:

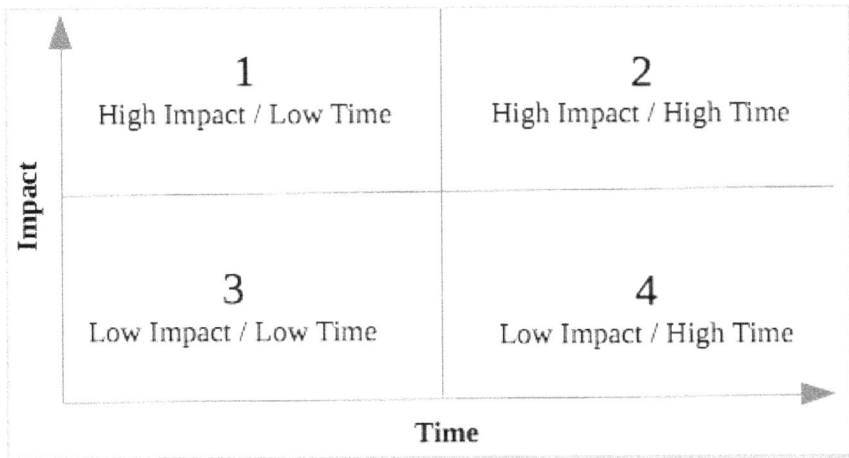

1 High Impact / Low Time	**2** High Impact / High Time
3 Low Impact / Low Time	**4** Low Impact / High Time

(Impact — vertical axis; Time — horizontal axis)

Items can be placed onto this chart according to their expected time requirements and perceived impact. The chart's segment labels are used to help you identify the order of importance to develop each feature—although you may decide to focus completing segments in a different order depending on your specific situation and agenda. The chart segments suggest the following characteristics:

> **High impact/Low time** : Features in this segment are those that produce the highest value outcomes with the least time investment. These are the best value features because they can help you to build a good foundation for the perception of the project's progress—especially if the features are linked to real benefits and not just perceived benefits.

> **High impact/High time** : This segment identifies features that produce the same type of outcomes as those in the high impact/low time segment, but have a higher time cost. The high impact attribute often suggests that these features are a mandatory requirement for the project, with their high time cost making them a necessary evil—especially when it comes to the project's budget; the relationship between time and money meaning their requirement absorbs more of the budget.

> **Low impact/Low time** : The type of feature that can be developed quickly, but that don't have much impact on achieving your agenda. These can be considered as time fillers—the type of task that can be engaged to manage perceptions within project politics, or where there is spare time when awaiting the ability to start development of more important tasks and features.

> **Low impact/High time** : Features in this segment are classed as the least important high risk features. Their high time requirement makes them poor value for time and financial investment due to their low impact return; high time requirements also have a higher risk of being underestimated. Features in this category can be considered for exclusion or placement in the parking list if available time or budget is at risk of being exceeded.

When your software components are broken down to a point where you can understand their influence on development of other components in the software, it becomes a lot more straightforward to understand the time requirements for their development. Placing a value on their impact is an entirely different story because there are multiple perspectives that you can choose from to identify a value for impact, such as:

> Benefit to real users.

>> This perspective focuses on how the feature would be used by real users of the software. The real users of the software are very different to the project owner, who is often the person sponsoring the project with a view to selling it to their customers; or at the very least looking to get people in their organization to use the software. Project owners differ to real users because they can only make judgments based how they perceive the software to be used—while real users actually use the software for real purposes.

> ➢ Priorities for impact values in this perspective focus on allowing the software to produce real use outcomes; ideal for developing your own products and where your performance is being judged by real users or marketers of the software product who are primarily interested being able to market features of interest to buying customers.

➤ Team politics.

> ➢ This perspective is applied to situations where you are working to satisfy people who have hired you to develop the software to match their specification. This type of situation is different to developing software for real users because your progress is measured in terms of the number of items you can tick off the list and what the client's team are reporting to the project owner. It's important to keep in mind that people who don't have experience in writing software are usually unable to distinguish the difference between features and tasks that require a bigger time investment to complete and those that can be completed quickly with minimal effort.

> ➢ Priorities for impact values in this perspective are based between the need to show the quantity of tasks completed and satisfying requests from the team you are working with. Balancing these two agendas will allow you to gain the confidence of the project owner who seeks to see progression in terms of the number of features completed, while on the other hand also gaining satisfaction from those who report their opinions of your progress.

➤ Technical implementation.

> ➢ Unlike the previously mentioned examples, this perspective discards the opinions and requirements of people who are either real users or part of the client's project team, and instead focuses on improving the quality of components implemented for the software. Although this may sound like commercial suicide, there are very good strategic reasons to use this perspective—when time and circumstances allow for it. It should be noted that using this perspective when the time and circumstances are not right will likely lead to more problems than it solves.

> ➢ Priorities for impact values in this perspective focus on activities that provide strategic value to the implementation of the software and not tangible features that users or project owners would be able to see. Strategic advantages that improve the technical implementation quality can include reducing code complexity for better maintainability, developing shared code components to speed up development of future features, and production of documentation that will increase the productivity of other programmers as well as reducing the risk of new bugs being introduced. All of these activities add value to the bigger picture—the main problem being the difficulty to use this approach when there is also a need to keep users and project owners happy, hence the need to carefully manage your project engagement to create time and circumstance opportunities that allow this perspective to become relevant.

The parking list

The parking list is a concept for putting ideas on hold without forgetting them. It's a tool that is handy for features that:

> ➤ Have a risk of delaying the next release of the software beyond a point that is considered to be acceptable.

> ➤ Are difficult to implement or not inline with the business agenda, but involve too much politics to suggest dropping outright—e.g. where an 'ideas' person would be offended by having their idea dropped and who would play team politics to push their ideas through.

> ➤ Need more consideration or refinement before proceeding to develop into the next release.

When used properly, the parking list becomes a valuable asset to use for making sure that the software project stays on track and expectations are kept realistic. It is a great tool for avoiding feature creep where expectations for new features become assumed as part of the original specification, which in turn allows you to educate the client about what the agreed current focus should be without giving the impression that you aren't listening to what they are requesting. The parking list also becomes a valuable tool for planning potential future work in income from the client—the bigger the list grows, the more releases you can develop for them that you can charge for your time to develop.

Creation of the parking list needn't be anything complicated. At its most basic, you could create a document in something like Google Docs that would allow members to add new features to the list—Evernote is also a good tool for this. More advanced projects can make use of dedicated project management software.

Summary

Project management is an activity that will make the difference between the success and failure of your project. Although it may be tempting to jump straight to the technical activities so that results can be produced immediately, a lack of planning and coordination will result in lost productivity and production of work that is irrelevant to the project.

Successful projects require a good foundation to build from, which for software projects includes a maintainable codebase, relevant content/data and the required input from the people who make use of the software. Cutting this effort out of the process can provide an illusion of faster progress at the start of the project, but will result in the project becoming difficult to manage later; where any initial productivity gains will be quickly lost and risk leading the project to failure. The foundation of your project management should make use of both existing processes and resources such as formal processes like DevOps and unit testing that introduce an activity framework that avoid problems common to software projects. Software framework components can also be used to provide your project with the immediate benefit of having a software pattern designed for adaptability—saving you from time required to build and refine this foundation yourself.

After a successful start to your project, you also need to maintain your success. At this point, success becomes heavily dependent on your ability to capture and make use of feedback. This includes monitoring what's happening in relation to time management, activity costs and factors relating to the client; which includes their perception of progress made and changes to their requirements.

If there is anything you should be aware of in project management, it's that change is inevitable. Environment changes are often the main trigger that lead to issues directly affecting the project, whether through availability of skills, costs required to develop the project or the requirements that dictate the specification of the software. Developing your project management strategy to embrace change will allow you to resolve the challenges they pose to your projects.

A final consideration to keep in mind for your project management is that extended time introduces more risk of problems occurring. Whether it be through difficulties in estimating time and budget requirements or through the previously mentioned inevitable change that happens through time, the clear pattern is that time increases the risk of difficulties occurring. You can reduce this risk by eliminating unnecessary time being invested in the project. A good way to achieve this is through the identification of the minimum viable product (MVP), which has the bare minimum features required to achieve the client's ambitions. Especially when working with enthusiastic clients and collaborators, it is easy for a situation to occur where the requirements specification keeps growing with new ideas – or at least where there are a large amount of ideas presented upfront that would too long to develop. This can set the blueprint for a project to become crippled by problems caused from time related changes. Useful tools for managing this type of situation include SMART requirement definitions and the "parking list". When used together, these tools allow you to filter requests that could become problematic to the project, while also avoiding unnecessary politics that can arise from people whose agenda are not primarily in the best interests of the project.

Appendix

Interview 1

Name: Ashley Moore

Role: Web developer

Twitter: @AshMoore_

What are the most notable software related projects that you've worked on?

A visual description tool for road traffic accidents.

What type of technology and software development have you been involved with?

Mostly web using HTML, CSS, JavaScript WordPress and Monkey.

What are the best types of project to work on?

I think it's always a good idea to work on a project which has structure to start with. It's good to be able to imagine what the finished product will look like before you start it. If you know where you're going then it's easier to get there. The road traffic accident project was developed in separate stages of development which adopted this approach of know what something should look like before it was put in to the app.

What approaches would you recommend for developing software?

Object Oriented Programming (OOP) is definitely the best way to go creating maintainable code. This helps to enforce DRY – don't repeat yourself; repeated code causes a lot of problems in software maintenance.

What signs have you learnt that indicate a project may be problematic?

Problems can occur as a result from communication breakdown between individuals working on the team. One instance of this could be a graphic designer who doesn't understand a lot about how functionality works; as a result, they sometimes press on with a design only to find that it doesn't work for the final product.

What strategies do you use to avoid problems and/or keep them under control?

Again, effective communication between the team will always help keep things manageable. If a graphic designer understands a lot about how coding functionality works and what the boundaries are, they can produce a more effective design to suit the purpose of the product.

How do you manage your workflow?

Using a spreadsheet is a great resource for managing your time as well as the current tasks being worked on and who is working on those tasks etc.

What factors do you use to judge credibility of professionals you speak to?

The body language is normally a good sign as it shows how confident they are in the subject they talking about.

What is your definition of a brand?

The brand is something to identify the individual companies and their products. It's a way of encapsulating the products, the reputation and the success of a company.

Are you finding that people's expectations for what is achievable with apps and web apps are growing? Has this caused problems in your projects?

It's no secret that web development technologies are evolving as time goes on and more gates of possibilities are opening for developers, allowing them more flexibility and functionality when developing.

Unfortunately, even with this additional functionality, some people are still using older versions of browsers which so the web app then faces cross browser issues. Clients tend to want everything to work the same on all platforms but this is not always possible.

In your opinion, what differentiates software, apps, web apps and websites?

It all depends on the task at hand really. Websites are great for allowing a user to browse information make purchases, talk to their friends via social media sites etc. Software and apps are better used when the user has a particular task at hand ranging from making lists, checking finances to managing the backing of their websites or playing games and so on.

What makes a good app?

A good app would ideally be usable on a broad range of browser platforms and should also be very user friendly so that it's easy for the user to navigate.

Where do you think the industry is heading?

The mobile platform tends to very popular at the moment for browsing website and using apps. It won't be far off before it will become the normal thing to control almost every device in your house just using your mobile phone.

Interview 2

Name: Bob Pape

Role: Programmer known for ZX Spectrum version of R-Type.

Website: http://bizzley.imbahost.com

My name is Bob Pape and I was, for a period close to sixteen years, a self-employed freelance games programmer. I started in 1987 writing commercial games for the UK home computer market, specifically the ZX Spectrum home computer, and then went on to code for consoles, handheld devices and the PC. For the majority of that time I was represented by an agent, Jacqui Lyons of Marjacq Micro Ltd. who lined up contracts for me, took care of negotiations and (often) chased after outstanding payments I was owed - even when she wasn't due her 15% agency fee of the final amount! Not having to deal with that side of things too much freed me up to concentrate on coding though being a freelancer meant I didn't always have the resources to call on that I would have had I been employed directly by a software development company. As a result I usually had to source my own graphic and music assets from similarly self-employed individuals in the software industry at the time - which meant finding people who were available and could supply what I wanted, arrange contracts with them, work out delivery schedules and of course pay them. To keep track of the money side of things I ran a small daybook that I handed - along with a load of receipts and invoices - to my accountant at the end of the tax year who did her magic and told me how much to pay the Inland Revenue and HMRC, something I would recommend to anyone looking to make money by writing software.

I left the software industry in 2003 when it just wasn't viable to be a freelance coder any more, which means I have had very little involvement with writing games or producing software since. But times have changed and the increasing market for independently produced apps and games on platforms such as Apple and Android means the days of the bedroom coder and small software teams are coming around again. As much as I would like to think that there has been a vast improvement in how people who write games are treated by those who pay them I suspect that a lot of the core problems are still there, so if what follows seems out of date or obsolete then remember the words of philosopher George Santayana - "Those who cannot remember the past are condemned to repeat it."

What are the most notable software related projects that you've worked on?

For those with an interest in retro computing and long memories then I suppose my involvement with various conversions of the R-Type arcade games from IREM is what stands out for most people. Now I really have to qualify that by pointing out we are talking about a very niche group of people here and of software that was written well over twenty five years ago so I always try and remain realistic when talking about 'The Good Old Days' and try and keep things in perspective. Over the course of my software career I wrote thirteen commercial games as well as a number of others games and programs that were either for myself, given away or ended up being cancelled at some stage for various reasons and I'd class only a few of those as being notable, at least to me.

My first commercial release was a conversion of the three-player arcade game RAMPAGE from Bally Midway for the ZX Spectrum and then followed that up with another Spectrum conversion, of the original IREM R-Type arcade game. I've written at length about the gestation and my experience in coding this second game in a freely available e-book so I won't go into too much detail here other than to say it seems to have stood the test of time and even today I get messages from people telling me about their feelings on playing this conversion back in the 1980's.

A few years later I converted the sequel to R-Type for play on Nintendo's original Gameboy handheld console, and a few years after that worked with friend and fellow coder Jas Austin in updating an enhancing both this and his Gameboy conversion of the original R-Type for the new Colour Gameboy machine under the title R-Type DX. I coded two puzzle-based multimedia titles for the PC that were officially licensed by MENSA, the society for members with high IQs, which have had a long life (you can still find them for sale on Amazon) but I doubt if they'll run on modern computer hardware. Unless you're on some kind of royalty deal then you'll have a hard time finding out just how many copies of your game has been sold which is why the two versions I coded of the Sega Megadrive\Genesis game PGA Tour Golf and it's follow up for the Sega Gamegear handheld and Master System console are notable to met. Actually I was on an 'advance of royalty' deal where you're offered an amount based on an assumption of how many copies they think will sell and you only start collecting on the royalties proper once that figure has been reached. It's been a long time now so I don't think I'm giving too much away if I clarify that by saying my deal was that I received $60,000 outright for writing the first PGA Tour Golf game, based on a royalty figure of 50 cents per unit, and once total sales had reached 120,000 then I would be paid for anything over that. If sales didn't go over 120,000 then I'd still keep the $60,000. If I'd gone for a straight no-fee royalty deal then that 50 cents per unit would have been a bit higher but I would have been paid solely on how many units it did sell so (to simplify it a bit) you have to look on it as a gamble on how good a coder you think you are and how well the product will sell as a result. This particular game actually sold 111,000 units in total so I came out slightly ahead of things in the end. For completeness I'll add that you may be offered a non-royalty deal which will usually be higher than advance royalty figure so again you have to decide on how well you think the game will sell in order to come out with the most money.

What type of technology and software development have you been involved with?

Apart from my brief sidestep into PC projects I was mainly involved with the development of 8 bit software, concentrating on the Zilog Z80 processor, which turned out to be a good choice because it and similar processors were used in a lot of the lower end home computers and games consoles around at that time. In the early home computer years there weren't really that many specific game development tools around - and those that were tended to be quite proprietary and relevant to certain games only - so a lot of coders ended up having to write their own. My development schedule for a game usually included a couple of weeks at the start to give me time to put together the sprite, tile, map, level etc. editors that I'd be need to write the game. Only the really big software houses had the luxury of supported in-house development tools as well as libraries of sound drivers, tape loaders, joystick handlers etc. that the rest of us usually had to put together by hand or pay someone else to provide. For most of my games I used a development system called PDS that was a PC-based cross assembler that let you compile and download to a target machine via a parallel interface but for some consoles I'd use hardware specific kits, all of which basically emulated a cartridge plugged into the target machine but let you develop and compile your source code on a connected PC and send it down to the kit quickly and with little fuss. At some point you usually had to plug the real thing into a console which meant programming and burning EPROMS which was done with a SCSI-based writer and a UV box to wipe the chips. For some of my later games I used software emulation of the target machine on the PC rather than hardware, which was easier than having to squint at the small screen of a handheld device all day, but again you always had to try the real thing in a console as you went along which was when you found out how good (or bad) the software emulator you were using really was.

What are the best types of project to work on?

That's easy, the ones where you get paid! Seriously though, there are some basic rules you can follow when deciding on a project, first of which is to decide if you are actually technically competent to code the thing. I found out what my coding strengths and weaknesses were quite quickly and some of those weaknesses were in computer AI and 3D mathematics so I tended to stay away from the types of games that required them in large amounts. I once turned down a soccer game because I knew I wouldn't be able to implement the computer team's A.I. to a level that people wouldn't laugh at so sometimes you have to be realistic about your competence and just walk away rather than have your name linked to a piece of crap that you just couldn't manage properly. Another thing is to have actual enthusiasm for and an interest in the type of project you've taken on rather than just putting the hours in for the money. If you're going to be spending weeks or months writing code for something you don't really care about then that is going to come through in the finished result as well as being an unpleasant experience during development. This sounds as if it would be self-evident but I believe a lot of game coders can remember when writing games stopped being fun and started being hard work. You might want to look at whether the project you've started actually stands a chance of being finished and published, a fate that hits a lot of coders near the end of the life-cycle of the machine they're writing for when someone decides that it would be cheaper to kill it off and cut their losses rather than try and sell it to a shrinking market. I've been involved in a project that suffered this fate as well as another that got pulled for 'political' reasons, and of course companies go bust all the time, but it can really damage your self confidence if something you believe in and have spent months bringing to life never sees the light of day as you view every project after as a gamble. People say you need a good support structure as well and I agree with that, it's too easy to fall into the trap of thinking you can handle and control everything yourself - especially if you've had some success in the past - and that you don't need significant help from others. When you're a one-man-band outfit like I was then you don't have a choice but it's just plain stupid to turn down help and support when it's there for the asking.

What software methodologies do you recommend using for software projects?

One of the things that personal computers did was to break the accepted way of writing software, something that came a bit of a surprise to Atari's American lawyers in 1981 when they sued gaming company On-Line System for distributing Jawbreaker, (what they saw) as a knock-off of their licensed game Pacman. On-Line owner Ken Williams was asked by an Atari lawyer "wasn't it a fact that typically the programmer who's designing these games at least produces a flow chart and then writes out the source code manually prior to punching it in?" and seemed almost incredulous when Williams told him his coders were typically too lazy to make up any sort of flow chart and just started putting routines in wherever they liked in any order. Today most large software projects have more in common with those pre-1980 days than the bedroom coding of the following decades in that everything has to be pretty much pre-planned and locked down before starting, which seeing as a lot of these games resemble movie films in size and complexity is really the only way to do it if you want control over the hundreds or thousands of people responsible for the finished result. Is that a better way of writing software than being spontaneous and adapting to things as you go along? Of course not, nor is it worse, it's just that different sized projects require different approaches in order to get the job done so there's no one way to do things, you use whatever approach you know will work.

I learnt my computer trade on mainframes in the 1970's so I had a lot of the really basic stuff drummed into me right from the start. Of course a lot of that is now obsolete (I no longer need my IBM flowchart template for designing programs) and there have been many books written on this subject alone so my methodology for writing software is quite personal and, while I can say it worked for me, I don't know if it's relevant any more. Taking things from the point of actually having the project green-lighted (and getting to that stage is a whole other story) then I would spend a week or so just walking and talking to myself about what was needed and how I'd do it - which probably got me a lot of odd looks from the neighbors but I found it easier to do this than just jump straight in and start coding. When I was comfortable with the approach I'd use and some of the technical problems sorted I'd sound out those ideas with others connected to the project, mainly my graphic artist and producer, to see if it made sense to them as well. This is where a solid knowledge of the industry you're coding for comes into things because if I'm trying to explain my game mechanics by referring to other past games then it really helps if everyone knows what you're talking about right away and can chip in with suggestions and even reasons why that approach wouldn't work. Just because someone isn't a coder doesn't mean they don't have knowledge and experience of the market you're coding for so it's always worth sounding your ideas out with others who've been around the block a few times.

Once a project was started then my methodology was pretty simple really, code what was needed to reach the next milestone and get paid! Since I was a freelancer my contracts were based around development schedules and payment milestones based on those schedules so it really was as simple as making sure routines X, Y and Z were in and working by a certain date to keep everything running to schedule. I had enough faith\ arrogance in my abilities at the time to lay out and schedule my games at the start of a project and come up with milestones that would cover the complete development of the game and that I knew I could hit, or at least have my excuses ready if things slipped a bit! I was fortunate in my software career never to have gone over the final deadline by any significant amount (and software companies lie when they give you a final completion date anyway) and never really had to work to anybody else's way of thinking. There were a few times that proper Project Management was used to control my games but from my side of the screen I didn't see any advantage, or disadvantage, to this approach and the constant stream of requests as to how I was doing and resultant Gantt charts meant nothing to me. The Basic Rule is you do whatever it takes to get it done.

What signs have you learnt that indicate a project may be problematic?

Before it starts I'd say a project specification that is TOO detailed, where everything is broken down to the n'th degree or timed out to the last hour. You just can't have that micro-control over a large software project and expect to hit every target and it's when you don't, when you start arguing the schedule rather than the code, that's when things get out of control fast. Over confidence at the start is another, it's one thing to be enthusiastic and 110% behind something but when you're reading the project spec. and come across "this is going to be the best game ever!" or "revolutionary software innovation" then someone is going to end up disappointed and someone else (i.e. the coders) are going to get the blame. Some people say to check out a company first or talk to people who've worked for them to get a feel of how things are but that's a purely subjective process, just because someone had a bad experience doesn't necessarily mean that you will, though if everyone is telling you the same negative things about that company then alarm bells should definitely start ringing.

Indications that there may be problems once you've started pretty much fall into the basic business category, they're not specific to software productions (though there can be some) but typical of business practices in general. Not getting paid on time, being given excuses instead of assets, breakdown in communications, loss of key personnel, - you don't have to be long in this or any other business to see the signs that things aren't going to work out. Something more specific to software is the changing of the initial spec. especially if the change is an increase in what has already been agreed. By the time you're dropping deadlines and cutting stuff then your project has gone from 'may be' to 'definitely is' problematic but when someone starts adding things or saying "wouldn't it be great if it did this" then you know that's not going to end in a good way. Now I want to quantify that by saying the resulting problems are not necessarily major ones, it could be something as simple as having to work a weekend when you had other plans, but as you get further into a project and nearer the finish line then any irritant, large, small or even imagined, can be the final straw that sets everything off. Coders working too long hours in the final stages of a project can be tired, stressed and wound up so tight that it takes hardly anything to tip them over let alone adding or changing things to a schedule that was supposed to have been locked down months ago.

What strategies do you use to avoid problems and/or keep them under control?

There's no way to avoid problems completely so the best you can do is try and minimize the damage and make sure you stay on top of things - unfortunately by the time you're aware of a problem then it's already too late. You can't deal with every eventuality, just how do you plan for (say) a colleague who breaks a wrist while playing football and can't type properly for a month, so for that reason it's no good trying to list and counter every problem you think might arise beforehand because you'll never catch them all and you'll be wasting your time planning for eventualities that will never happen. What I tended to do at the start of a project was talk to the people involved and be a bit negative about everything because if I could 'break' things just by talking about them or point out some of the more problematical areas that I saw then at least we had advance warning that we might be in for a rough time or knew what to look out for. This approach can make it seem that you aren't totally behind a project when what you are trying to be is the little boy in the story of the Emperor's New Clothes pointing out what everyone else is too afraid or reticent to say. It's one thing to have high morale during a project but it shouldn't be at the expense of what is really happening.

There will always be problems no matter what approach you use but if the level of problem you encounter is along the lines of running out of coffee or your mouse stops working then that really isn't worth bothering about (but see what I wrote above about minor problems at the end of a project.) We all make mistakes now and again so playing the blame game or trying to find out who was responsible for something going wrong is a bit of a waste of time as well, it makes people feel bad and can seed discontent that will fester so it's just not worth it.....unless this is becoming a regular thing with a person\supplier\piece of software\whatever in which case it's time to cut your losses and find someone or something else that will do the job instead. This is a preventative measure really and you may not be in a position to take it in which case you just have to grit your teeth and be prepared for something similar to happen again. I really only had one strategy when it came to dealing with things that weren't going the way they were supposed to and that was a phrase I picked up from somewhere or other:- "if you can't find the solution, change the problem" which served me well for many years. I don't know where this fits into accepted problem solving techniques or crisis handling but the approach that the way to get around a problem that can't be fixed is to change it to one that can be, though it sounds a bit simplistic, is something that worked for me many times. The tricky part is coming up with alternatives that are both workable and acceptable and this is where you find yourself compromising or doing things you hadn't planned to. It's that triangle you see in all managements books with Cheap, Good and Fast at the corners - you can't change one without affecting the other two.

How do you manage your workflow?

On a large scale, over the years I've tried different ways of working - keeping to office hours, working a certain number of days a week, working only nights etc. and all of them work.....at least for a while. Unfortunately software development is one of those jobs where most of the hours have to be put in towards the end of a project so whatever approach you use gets cast aside as you work all the hours necessary to bring the thing in on time. What you also have is that someone else, usually your Producer, will be trying to get you to meet your schedules no matter what, which is great if everything is going well but falls apart if you're having trouble with code or concepts. Then you'll be 'asked' to do all sorts of things to stay on target and whatever workflow system you had planned will be out the window, which can also happen if there are others involved in the production process. If you are looking for people who will supply you with assets when you actually need them rather than when they feel like it or who will tell you the truth when it comes to future delivery dates then that does require good forward planning.

On a day to day basis then you do have to have some sort of rigidity in place otherwise you end up only coding when you feel like it, which is a sure sign that you've got problems. I prefer to work in the nights: there are less distractions, everything's a lot quieter and what's on the television is usually so bad that you have no choice other than to stay on the computer! When I started coding nothing actually flowed as such, it was all stop-start as I was working out how to do things for the first time and a lot of it was actually trial and error but as I completed more and more games things got a lot smoother and I became more confident in my abilities. That's just me though, there are talented coders who can sit down and come up with what they want with no effort, if you do it long enough you find out what your level of competence is and work to that rather than any particular system. But a lot depends on where you're working and what kind of social life you have (or should that be want?) so if you have family or a relationship to deal with then you've either got to work with that in mind, find a compromise or lock yourself away and suffer the consequences. Game coding is probably suited more to young people because they tend to have less personal and social ties and can work long hours and unusual shift patterns and (generally) the only people being affected are themselves. Once you have a partner or a family and responsibilities then it gets much harder to put in those all-nighters and twenty-four hour sessions and if you insist on doing so then something is going to break and it might not be you.

Do you have any strategy for managing the amount of incoming work you have ñ i.e. to avoid not having any work and to avoid having too much work?

I was lucky in that by my third game I was being represented by Jacqui Lyons at Marjacq who lined up the projects for me so I never had to worry about having too much or too little to do. In the early days of game computing it wasn't unusual to have a coder work on more than one project at a time, if for no other reason than games were much simpler then so it wasn't too much of a stretch, but I always stuck to one game only because I felt I could never do both justice if I was working on two. Actually that's only partially right as I think I felt deep down that I wouldn't be able to keep track in my head of two different projects simultaneously and I wasn't about to take a chance and take more than one on just to find out if I was right or not. I have a recurring dream to this day that I'm working on two games and the unfinished first has been forgotten in the rush to finish the second so there must have been something to it after all! I wish there was actually a strategy to avoid not having any work but until you can actually force people to employ you I don't think it's going to happen. The way you usually got work was based on how good your previous efforts were (as we were always being told, "you're only as good as your last game") but the limited life of early home computers and games consoles meant you had to adapt and shift platforms fairly regularly.

If you were moving to a new machine then somebody had to take a risk with you on that first project which is where personality rather than ability sometimes decided if you got the job or not. Just because you could produce product for home computer X didn't necessarily mean you could do the same for games console Y so it sometimes came down to how well you'd got on with people in the past as it was pretty common then (and perhaps today) in what was a small tight-knit industry for one company to phone up another and have an informal chat about somebody and whether it was safe to employ them or not. Often though one coder usually knew another - or knew of them - so if asked could pass an opinion of what they felt or heard about them and what they thought about their previous games.

What factors do you use to judge credibility of professionals you speak to?

The one that matters to me the most is whether you can work out what they're talking about is based on actual experience or if they they've just briefed themselves on it (or are plain making it up!) I can read a book on Kung Fu but that doesn't make me Bruce Lee so - to give an example - I'm always a bit wary around people who talk about writing and publishing games when they've yet to release anything themselves. This is of course the perennial "those that can, do....those that can't, criticize" that you find in all walks of life and it's not uncommon in the software industry to find people like this in charge of things and passing off their opinions as facts. We're all guilty at times of telling people what they want to hear ("yes of course I can code in FORTRAN, when do I start?") and I think a small amount of stretching the truth is only to be expected if you're publicizing yourself or trying to get a contract. What annoys me though is when you can tell someone really has very little idea of what they're talking about yet is trying to give the impression that they do, I'm usually too polite to call them on it but if it's a subject I do know something about then I like to play the naive innocent, be a bit mischievous and start asking questions about it just to see what they'll do. If I can class 'experts' along with professionals here then that's a group you'll also run up against, they usually DO know everything about a given subject (or at least are highly opinionated about it) yet unlike the real world where expertise in a subject usually implies extensive practical experience it's rare to find the same in the software industry. Really it's all down to how you define the word 'professional' in this context, to me it's a person you believe when they tell you something - a delivery date, a payment, a way of doing things etc. - and credibility is something you gift them with rather than accept from them.

What is your definition of a brand?

An identifiable product. But I think that the idea of brand awareness is often more important to sales and marketing departments than the brand itself, that it's not what you've got to sell but how you sell it that's important, and the sad thing is they're probably right. By that I mean you can pretty much sell anything as long as you can get it to appeal to the buyers somehow and that's where the brand name comes in. You see this in computer game sequels or those that feature characters from previous games as well as in hardware, people are more interested in having the latest branded version rather than what it actually does. There's a really easy way to show this....let's say I've written three successful games featuring "Derek the Singing Wasp" and I write a fourth, exactly the same character, but call him "Norman the Musical Insect" instead. Here Derek is my brand, something people can identify, if I market my game as featuring Norman then what do you think my sales would be compared to a game featuring Derek - same product, same graphics, same marketing spend yet different branding? People buy the brand name not the product.

How has the value of a brand affected the projects you have worked on?

Since brands are usually owned by people who would like to give the impression that they take great care in protecting their good name what we're really talking about here is licensed product. Most of the published software that I wrote was licensed in some way, either as conversions of existing arcade games or by using a trademarked or copyrighted name or title which usually means the license holder gets to have the last say about things. The funny thing is that I hardly ever came across any direct intervention by a license holder to anything I wrote, which I would like to believe was down to my ability to give them exactly what they wanted but was probably more to do with them not caring that much about the finished product. In the early days of computer gaming the hardware was usually so underpowered that no one really expected it to emulate the custom hardware found in arcade cabinets so a company could often get away with murder when they released home computer versions of these games knowing that as long as they had the name and a vague approximation of the gameplay then that would be enough to sell. Later on when consoles meant worldwide sales these license holders got a bit more possessive and protective but again my personal experience was that once they'd made their money licensing the brand they didn't care that much as they knew they weren't going to make any more money from that marketing avenue. What intervention I did suffer was usually along the lines of a suggestion rather than a demand and I always said yes, they were the ones paying me after all and I'd give them whatever they wanted. A company that paid more attention to protecting a brand value was Nintendo - not their brands, that goes without saying - but the knock-on effect of distributing games of other companies that might have put them in a bad light. I think all of us who worked on games from Nintendo had to put up with bug reports from them that spotted (what they thought) were unwholesome and unsavory elements that would have people complaining, usually centered around a High Score table. That you had to take steps to ensure that a player couldn't enter swear words was accepted by us all but to be told (and this actually happened to me) that you had to block a certain word made up of random characters because the letters were the initials of an LA street gang was really ridiculous!

Are you finding that people's expectations for what is achievable with apps and web apps are growing? Has this caused problems in your projects?

As I said at the start I left the software industry in 2003 so my answers to this and the following questions are going to be rather short and lacking in practical knowledge I'm afraid, more opinionated than factual I'm still trying to work out when computer programs died and apps took their place as no one seems to code any more, they 'develop', and long-windedly calling a block of compiled code an 'application' to the wrong people is going to get you labelled as out of touch. The majority of people who use apps are quite happy with what they've got and any expectations are more along the lines of being able to say to their mates "my phone does this better than yours" than having a particular need for something they've been waiting years for. Given a choice between an app that can measure your blood pressure or one that can rate your farts what do you think your average app user is going to download first?

In your opinion, what differentiates software, apps, web apps and websites?

The majority of people who use apps don't care about what's inside them or where they come from as long as they do something, and if that something is useful or entertains them then that's all that matters. With more and more companies offering apps that do the same thing as their websites (Facebook, Twitter etc.) we're seeing the slow migration away from browser-based interaction and sooner or later it will reach a point where the only way to gain access to some sites will be via an app, and then there will be no differentiation because there will be no choice.

What makes a good app?

I didn't want to make this a pedantic answer but it really all does depend on what you mean by 'good'. To some cost is what matters most, for others it's the number of features or speed or security or how addictive it is or what your mates have or the what latest fad is or.....I won't go on.....you get the idea. To me end any app you've installed and then not deleted to free up space is about as 'good' as it gets.

Where do you think the industry is heading?

I think development tools are getting easier to use, more point and click than dealing with the intricacies of opcodes and programming manuals, which means quicker production and better looking results but at the cost of homogenized product I'm sorry to say. As it becomes easier for people to produce software then you're going to see more and more rubbish as well, knock-offs of successful products, apps with incredibly limited appeal, a proliferation of non-approved product and of course a shrinking income for companies as an expanded market invariably means a reduced share. What you won't see is any kind of mass take-up of software development no matter how easy you make it because, simply put, the huge majority don't want to mess around with what goes on inside a computer or phone and are quite happy to just play 3-in-a-row games until their eyes bleed. The power and capabilities of computing hardware is going to keep on improving but the games you play on them will be the same old ones you played on their precursors but with better physics, graphics and hopefully A.I. Someone will show you a new game and tell you how different and revolutionary it is, and they'll probably be right, but there's always a seemingly endless selection of car racing, FPS, dance and sports games being churned out to show you what the market really is all about. I think we've passed a tipping point though and that computer\console gaming is here to stay, which has more to do with the vast amounts of money to be made off of Premium titles than any desire to be creative. Then again that was probably being said by video game companies in the 80's just before it all went wrong. Reports of yearly game revenues dropping from $3.2 billion in 1983 to barely $100 million in 1985 show what can happen when you start to believe you've got the market under control

I think software companies will split into two groups, those that can afford the movie-budget costs needed to put multi-format A-title games together and smaller, looser ones putting out quirky or innovative product and everything in-between will go, a medium sized business won't be able to compete with the quality of big budget releases and won't be able to match the lower overhead and development costs of a small company. There'll be a few left churning out filler and advertising-type material but this will be to a market that's not looking for creativity or originality but what they know is safe and reliable.

I think that companies will need to come up with new revenue models and not concentrate on any particular one as a lot do now, if you're basing your income on In-App Purchases and the government or a group with power decides that too many children are spending Dad's money on virtual tat and start making waves then you better cross your fingers they don't decide that banning it is a good idea as you're going bust! Whatever happens there will be a lot more control over the type of material that can and can't be included in products available from large company app stores. People will start being 'offended' by more and more minor things and those companies that see themselves (or would like others to see them) as responsible, protective, majority-orientated entities will respond by restricting what others, or they, deem to be offensive material. There is nothing new in this, companies like Nintendo and Sega have always controlled what they consider to be offensive material in their games, usually to the baffled incredulity of those of us who produced games for them, but as we become a society less and less tolerant of smaller and smaller things this is going to be echoed in the content of apps and software. Not because these companies have a heart or care but because offended people won't spend money on their products.

What are the biggest differences between being employed by someone and being employed by yourself?

I haven't been self employed for thirteen years now but when I was: working your own hours, setting your own goals, no office politics, not having to haggle If I needed something, very little interference from others, choosing what titles I worked on..... basically everything encompassed by the phrase "being your own boss." If I stick to software then it was really only my first two games where I was employed by someone else, and those who have read my account of those times will know what a mess that all turned out to be! But even with those two games I was pretty much left to do whatever I wanted, neither of them had any sort of advance meetings or guidelines as to how things were to be done I was just given the name of an arcade game and a time limit and expected to come up with something as close to the original as possible. I really hope things today are different as that is no way to run any sort of company and perhaps I was just unlucky enough to choose one that operated that way when I started out and assumed that's how all the others did it. One thing you get as a sit-down-at-the-office-and-work employee though is constant monitoring of how well - or not - you're doing, which you can either view as beneficial or somebody always looking over your shoulder. You also reap the benefits of a regular wage, chances of advancement, the company of like-minded colleagues and no need to go looking for work - if all is well and good. Self employment can be a bit of a gamble, comfortable living when there's plenty of work but less so when times get hard, and you do have to do everything yourself which can be a bit daunting when you realize that a company is spending possibly hundreds of thousands of pounds on production, advertising and marketing of a product that you have pledged to deliver in six months time, fully working and exactly to specification as they require. The Christmas party tends to be a bit of a solitary affair as well.

How did you detect people who may waste your time and how do you deal with them?

Unless you're particularly gifted with some kind of ability to spot timewasters from the off then unfortunately it's all down to experience. If you're just starting out and someone says, for example, that your graphics will be ready in a week then who are you to disbelieve them, but when you've gone through this a few times and you know that it's more likely to be two weeks than one then you know you're being told what they think you want to hear rather than the truth. This also happens with companies looking to employ you, not out of any sort of malice it's just that's the way they work, so you end up putting bids in for projects that you know you won't stand a chance of getting just to stay in their good books and hope they'll think about you when something else comes along. Sometimes it's not the fault of the person you're dealing with, they may be waiting on somebody else to close a deal or supply them before committing to you which is annoying but there's nothing you can do about that except wait along with them. Perhaps I'm naive but I find that people in general don't set out to deliberately waste your time, quite a few of them have a lot of enthusiasm for some idea that to them makes perfect sense - but is obviously unworkable or under funded - and they're looking for someone to listen to them and say yes. I had that once with an amateur author who came to me looking to turn his work into a PC game, to him it was a sure-fire winner but I gently had to explain the realities (and costs) of creating a game and instead came up with a multimedia-type solution that could have been done relatively cheaply instead. I guess that since I wasn't on board with his ideas it meant I was negative about it all as I never heard back from him but I was happy to put some time into it since it obviously meant so much to him.

Interview 3

Name: Jake Birkett

Role: Programmer, owner and founder of Grey Alien Games

Website: http://www.greyaliengames.com

Twitter: @GreyAlien

What are the most notable software related projects that you've worked on?

Back in 2007 I programmed Fairway Solitaire for PC/Mac for Big Fish Games as a contractor and it was very popular. I've made many games over the years and my last hit was Spooky Bonus, a Halloween-themed match-3 game that I shopped in 2013. I'm hoping that my new game, Regency Solitaire, will also be notable :-) I was also part of a team that made My Tribe (a Facebook game) back in 2010 and part of another team that made Eets Munchies (it was in a Humble Bundle and is on Steam), a sequel to Klei Entertainment's original game, Eets.

Before I got into making games in 2005 I spent 9 years making business software for bookshops. At one point the system I designed was the no.1 bookshop system for Windows in the UK and it's still running in places like the Houses of Parliament!

What type of technology and software development have you been involved with?

The bookshop software I made was a multi-user, multi-site, real-time, server/client system called Merlio. It allowed bookshops to run a computerized till system with a barcode scanner and take customer orders and do searches and so on. Then the back office could see the sales live and place supplier orders and receive deliveries onto the system etc. It was pretty vast and complex. We used Delphi to code it.

I've also programmed a game engine called the BlitzMax Game Framework which was on sale for a while until it got bought by Big Fish Games in 2009. I've made a couple more game engines since in different languages but for my own use.

I've shipped 9 commercial downloadable casual games for PC/Mac, ported Titan Attacks to mobile for Puppy Games, overseen several mobile (and console) ports of my games, and made a bunch of free games (both downloadable and online), plus acted as a team member/consultant on some other projects.

What are the best types of project to work on?

Making money from games is *hard*. A lot of programmers find it easier to get a steady job making business software. However, I do find making games very fulfilling and the best projects have been my own IP. I've tracked the revenue from all my projects and I earn the most from my own IP and it's the most fun, so there's little point in doing anything else!

What software methodologies do you recommend using for software projects?

I don't know any formal terms for methodologies as I haven't been trained in them nor researched them. Basically though, I do one of two things: 1) If it's a casual game within a known genre, I'm able to plan out everything in advance in a giant spreadsheet and then execute with only minor plan changes required along the way. I track my progress and reduce scope if need be. 2) if it's a gamejam game (a minigame), I just get coding straight away (make a prototype) to find out what is fun and expand upon the game from there. At some point a To Do list starts to form to keep me on track.

Mostly I work solo so I don't do "Agile development" or anything like that, though I do set myself various milestones and targets. I've shipped multiple seasonal games on time, so I must be getting something right.

What signs have you learnt that indicate a project may be problematic?

Well I think a project can be problematic in several ways: One obvious way is that it's running over budget (I agree fixed prices with artists at the start to avoid that), or over time (I make estimates for all my tasks left to complete and can map that onto realtime to see if I'm on track). Another way is that I may not be motivated to work on a project. Because I work at home and am my own boss, I can easily distract myself if I don't feel like working. I've learned over the years to pick projects that I really want to work on otherwise my motivation suffers badly and that has a big knock on effect to the schedule of course.

What strategies do you use to avoid problems and/or keep them under control?

Well I've kind of answered this in the last question. I make a spreadsheet of all remaining tasks and assign then a time estimate and then keep it updated. I even log my hours on each task to see if my estimates are any good. For my last project I took 50% longer than my estimates so had to descope a few things. As for motivation, I just try to pick projects that are my own IP and where I'm not beholden to anyone else as for some reason that stresses me out.

How do you manage your workflow?

Because I have a giant list of tasks to do, there's always something to do. Depending on what mood I'm in, I may tackle a large complex task (which I then break down into bitesized chunks so that I can feel motivated about my progress) or I pick an easy small task or some kind of polish that has an immediate effect in the game. Basically I just use spreadsheets. I'm sure there are great project management tools out there (I used a few when working at Big Fish Games and with Klei) but I'm personally happy with Excel.

Also, looking at my logs I can see that I clearly go through peaks and troughs of productivity. Not just "the dip" after a project is started but more like monthly oscillations. I wish I didn't, but I do. This is something I'm constantly looking to improve. I've been using RescueTime recently to keep an eye on my productivity and time spent on social media. It's pretty cool, I recommend it.

Do you have any strategy for managing the amount of incoming work you have – i.e. to avoid not having any work and to avoid having too much work?

I've found that I prefer to work on a single project at a time so that I can control the flow of work myself. At times in the past I've been working on more than one project (often one of the projects is my own and the other is for someone else), but have found that stressful and task swapping can lead to a lack of productivity.

I've also decided not to make seasonal games any more as they imposed a huge looming immovable deadline. My last game was non-seasonal, but I did end up spending longer working on it than I'd have liked...

There's never nothing for me to do. Sometimes I slack off and sometimes I crunch.

What factors do you use to judge credibility of professionals you speak to?

Have they shipped games and are they good games? Somebody was giving me advice today on Twitter but they've never shipped a game, so I have to take that with a pinch of salt. They might be right, but it's all "in theory" to them at the moment. When the proverbial hits the fan then maybe they'll have a better idea of what it's really like. Also any fool can ship a crappy mobile game, so game quality is definitely a factor for me as to if I think of someone as "professional" - plus they should be full-time and trying to make a living from it, not a hobbyist giving irrelevant advice. That probably sounds a bit harsh, but tough.

What is your definition of a brand?

I don't think I've got a smart answer to this but in my case it's the type of games I've been making with my trademark care and attention to detail + a bit of humor. Also I use the same logo and sound on the splash screen and on my website/Facebook and I'm called @ greyalien on Twitter etc. I definitely have casual gamer fans who say they love my games and have bought every single one, so something must be going on with regards to brand...

In fact on my wall I have a kinda short list of core values for my company and no.1 is: "Build the Grey Alien Games brand and fan base."

How has the value of a brand affected the projects you have worked on?

Well, when I made Fairway Solitaire for Big Fish Games (I worked with one of their designers and a contract artist they provided), they promoted it on their site and their brand is pretty huge in casual games, so that had a big effect. Years later people still remember that game and mention it.

I haven't made any games for like "brands" like some people might make a Hasbro game or something (though I have been offered work like that several times and turned it down.)

Are you finding that people's expectations for what is achievable with apps and web apps are growing? Has this caused problems in your projects?

This isn't really my area as I make games. However, I have heard clueless customers say things like they think it only takes a couple of days to make a decent game, or maybe a week at the most, whereas the reality is very different of course. Also these days apps like Unity have allowed many more people to make games due to the reduction in specialist skills required (e.g. C++), and whilst that's great, it also means there are more people competing for the same slice of the digital entertainment pie.

In your opinion, what differentiates software, apps, web apps and websites?

I'd say that software runs on desktop machines, apps on mobile, and web apps on websites that do something e.g. project management software, and websites are more like blogs/news etc. That's how I think of it. I kinda dislike apps being used for desktop applications, because I'm snobbish.

What makes a good app?

Does it do what it says it will do? Does it do it well? Does it have a good UX (user experience design)? Is it stable/reliable? Things like that I guess.

Where do you think the industry is heading?

In terms of the game industry, I think that a lot of indie devs will crash and burn soon as the market cannot support so many of them, and also customers are getting a bit jaded with crappy games or games that just plain don't deliver such as Early Access or Kickstarter cons. Many customers are getting fed up of Free to Play (F2P) games, so there may be a big backlash against that business model, but then again, F2P keeps evolving so I guess it'll be around in some form or another. I hope that I can ride it out and keep going with paid games for a good while yet.

What are the biggest differences between being employed by someone and being employed by yourself?

Well, I could probably make a whole blog post about this (and may well have already done so).

Motivation can be an issue if you are your own boss as there's no one to crack the whip (if you aren't doing client work). However, the freedoms it affords are great. I get to take time off whenever I want and go for a walk with my wife or play the guitar, or hang out with my kids (wanting to not be away from my kids so much was a big factor in me going indie in the first place). I can choose exactly what I want to work on, but then I have to make it work - I'm wholly responsible for my own success. There's no safety net of a salary, or paid vacation/sickness, or pension/medical insurance - so if people find that worrisome, working for yourself might be a bit scary.

How do you detect people who may waste your time and how do you deal with them?

Haha, is this question meta? Well hopefully your book will come out and Ill get a mention, though what benefit it may have to me, I'm not sure (just being honest here). But I enjoyed answering the questions and think they'd make a good blog post (which DOES boost my brand and so on).

Well people try to waste my time in so many different ways. For a start there's endless spam from people claiming they can optimize my website, or get me reviews/chart position on mobile, or sell me some kind of monetization service I don't want. These are all insta-binned by me when they appear in my inbox. Then there's the people with a "great idea", who I just shut down pretty quickly as I've got so many of my own I'd never get them all done in 1000 lifetimes. Then there's people who want my advice. I normally offer this because I enjoy it I guess and it sometimes makes me take stock of things as I think through my answers. But sometimes some people keep asking questions and my replies just get shorter.

The other big potential time waste is people coming to me who want me to work on this project or that. Perhaps I should be grateful for such offers but normally they don't appreciate that I'm already doing fine running my own business making my own games and that they'd have to bring something pretty spectacular to the table for me to consider it. If anyone comes to me with a profit share idea, then that's out the door immediately, I need cold hard cash or I won't even consider it. Profit share might be fine if I was a noob, but I'm not and I have a family to feed. I can't rely on someone else doing a great job selling the product, especially if they don't have much at stake.

One of the most useful things I've learned in business over the years is that saying "No" is OK, in fact it's wise. Most things that sound to good to be true are just that, and you can't take on board everything that comes your way, you have to pick and choose the best things for you and your business.

Interview 4

Name: Kate Russell

Role: Technology journalist and presenter of BBC Click.

Website: http://katerussell.co.uk

Twitter: @katerussell

What type of technology and software journalism have you been involved with?

Print, web, TV

What factors make a topic worthy to cover in your journalism/publications?

If someone wants to read about it or I think I have an interesting perspective to offer.

What makes something newsworthy?

If someone wants to read about it!

What factors do you use to judge credibility of professionals you speak to?

Qualifications, experience, previous work, general levels of knowledge on the topic.

What is your definition of a brand?

I don't have one!

What type of brands do you like to reference in your journalism?

I don't. I write about people, places, products of interest to my reader. That is the core driver, not name-checking brands.

Are you finding that people's expectations for what is achievable with apps and web apps are growing?

Yes.

In your opinion, what differentiates software, apps, web apps and websites?

Platform, form & function.. these things are as different as apples and pears.

What makes a good app?

A useful app.

What are the biggest differences between being employed by someone and being employed by yourself?

You have to be motivated & a self-starter. It's always tempting to do anything but work, especially if your office is at home. You need to be able to resist this temptation. You also need to be brave and smart enough to survive the periods when there is little work. They will always come and if you run out of money and have to take a full time job to tide you over then it's increasingly hard to get back to a self-employed status. As a freelancer there is obviously no job security – this stresses some people out, but I actually like the challenge of it. The other big difference is the freedom to plan and execute your own schedule. You can also go shopping on a weekday when everyone else is at work and not feel guilty about it…though if you're anything like me you will end up working on a Saturday to make up for it!

Interview 5

Name: Mark Billen

Role: Freelance journalist and editor – previously editor of Web Designer magazine.

Web: www.markbillen.com

Twitter: @Mark_Billen

What type of technology and software journalism have you been involved with?

During my time as journalist I've tended to focus most on web design related technologies. So in terms of software for a while there was a focus on Adobe's suites, Dreamweaver and Flash predominantly. With the web though and certainly the front-end creative design side of things, it's really more about open standards like HTML, CSS, JavaScript and definitely jQuery these days. With WordPress and the adoption of HTML5 we have seen the browser become much more like a developer environment, whether as a viewer for cloud-based services or via the kinds of debugging tools found within Firefox etc. The beauty of web design in many ways has been that commercial software has never been essential, you just need a text editor and a browser and an idea.

What factors make a topic worthy to cover in your journalism/publications?

Unsurprisingly the business of commercial journalism relies on covering topics that cater to a buzz. Within that you should also seek the kind of credibility whereby you create the next buzz topic and it's your job to be ahead of the curve. So much of today's journalism is about creating content that also fulfills a purpose online, which is an environment that obviously moves so quickly – it's out of date as you click Publish. So you need to be reactive and able to respond with great ideas for covering those trending topics. I think here often the critical thing is being imaginative enough to give people the inside track on those stories they can't get from any other outlet. You tend to find these days that in the hectic swirl of coverage we get a lot of surface information but not much focus or detail. If you can find that new angle or spin you can often almost make new news out of the old.

What makes something newsworthy?

Similarly when something is deemed newsworthy, often the critical factor is that it is new in the sense people haven't necessarily read or heard about it yet. That's the ideal but with such media saturation today this is getting tougher to the point of impossibility. Like I say you have a duty of care to strive for those things that are at the very least in the public's consciousness at that moment in time. Much of this is driven by social media rather than broadcast or print news, so chances are you'll get a wealth of topic or news tip-offs within the community you are trying to reach. Although the crucial thing is in the analysis, opinion, style and investigation your coverage alone can bring to the table.

What factors do you use to judge credibility of professionals you speak to?

I think if you're planning to speak to a certain professional you do your homework on their credibility. Read their website, follow their profiles on Twitter, Facebook and LinkedIn especially for getting a feel for background. It's a good sign if they are a prominent voice in the trade, perhaps a prolific speaker at conferences or a recognized spokesperson of some kind. Many will have been asked to contribute to similar media coverage, perhaps enabling you to put a face to a name from other articles. Like most things it will inevitably come down to trust and to be fair this will depend largely on your publication and the kind of content you produce. For niche stuff people tend to be genuine and so enthusiastic about the work they do that they revel in the opportunity.

You have to also make judgements based on the actual feedback you get and be clued up enough not to be taken in, fooled or exploited. In many ways, certainly as a journalist and editor, you are a filter for information and it's vitally important you are honestly as confident as you can be when putting stuff out there. At the end of the day it will be your credibility that is compromised and not the people you say you've spoken to.

What is your definition of a brand?

My definition of a brand is ultimately a highly recognizable trademark. It is a company name that is sufficiently well known to be in some way thought of as iconic. The brand is a commercial identity that is often reinforced by a pedigree, a history and has fond association within people's minds. You don't always even have to be particularly knowledgeable or keen on a brand product for the most successful brands to penetrate your awareness. Brands tend to command an often unjustified trust and devotion purely through familiarity. They try to make you feel part of something bigger I suppose, but you have to be savvy enough to realize that this doesn't always equate with better.

What type of brands do you like to reference in your journalism?

Personally I like or prefer brands in a journalistic sense that genuinely justify the readers attention. It's ideal for me to know enough about them to believe that they believe in what they are doing before I implicitly recommend them to someone else. Don't insult your audience enough to handle brands in a cynical way. Modern day readers or viewers are far more intelligent than many outlets treat them, so again your credibility will take a nose dive if you unjustly align yourself with brands. Be objective and above all honest, which works both ways – if the brand or brand product is worthy then don't feel embarrassed to praise it. Much of how your audience perceives your agenda will be about the language you use and the overall context of presentation. Take to the time to evaluate what all the elements are pointing to when conveying the message you want to convey.

Are you finding that people's expectations for what is achievable with apps and web apps are growing?

I think consumer expectation of what apps can achieve is healthy but I also think the perception has plateaued somewhat. There's a sense that smartphone apps are so prevalent and integrated into people's lives they are taken for granted. As an early adopter of the iPhone I was impressed by the novelty factor of apps, almost just to collect them without any thought for how useful they were. Subsequently I've decided I only really use two or three at most and those were preloaded into iOS! So for many the browser remains the best mobile app, while ironically in-browser web apps are a rare commodity. HTML5 was meant to underpin development here but of course native language based apps for iOS and Android undeniably lead the way. So web apps really depend so much on developers getting the tools, API's and monetization platforms before expectations can really grow – if they indeed exist at all.

In your opinion, what differentiates software, apps, web apps and websites?

Well software always tended to be a self-contained standalone chunk of executable code, at least in the traditional sense. Software was tied to a platform or a very specific computing environment for it to even run, typically an operating system. So I tend to think of software in those terms, much larger and sophisticated programs. Apps are really just modularized pieces of software, kind of the take away or 'lite' version for modern devices. They have really kicked against the bloated idea of using and buying expensive software, making the experience more streamlined and convenient. They also owe a lot to the way we view websites and smaller more focused bursts of content. Many of them are websites and web services repackaged and optimized for the specific device after all. Lastly, websites to me are still dynamic documents. They are essentially still defined by a markup language owing more to the notion of publishing than building applications.

What makes a good app?

What makes a good app is wholly subjective but technically it comes down to being fit for purpose. Good design in software, apps or websites really is traced back to fundamental principles that can be evaluated for success. Does it do what it says on the tin? (or in this case app store) Is it open to be used in an accessibility sense? Much of these things exist on a subconscious level but chances are that if you keep going back to it on a regular basis then it's doing something right by you. Conversely however, more often or not, it can be the sheer banality of an app that makes it 'good' in an enjoyable way!

Where do you think the industry is heading?

If I could confidently say where the industry is heading I would be doing it and not just writing about it! No but that's always the golden question and tough to predict, which is normally a good sign in a funny way. I think the things I'd like to see develop and spread out are innovations like Microsoft's Kinect. Perversely it doesn't interest me for gaming but for general digital interaction around the home and linking those kinds of systems to all devices, smartphone, tablet and TV etc. I think a bit like Augmented Reality apps have suggested, it's this notion of delivering more natural and pervasive experiences. In the short-term I think innovation here is confined to increasing screen resolution than anything truly revolutionary. Funnily enough I do see the next boom being in the evolution of web-enabled TVs and a more comprehensive app model for home entertainment. There does still seem to be a curious disconnect between the flat screen TV market and the tablet fetish. Surely just a matter of time before Apple wades in here with an iOS television isn't it?

What are the biggest differences between being employed by someone and being employed by yourself?

The biggest difference in working for yourself is that you have to find the work, it tends not to find you. This process becomes a big part of the work of course and you have to be prepared for that. I think also you feel very independent, which has massive benefits, but perhaps you don't get the same feeling of being part of something bigger. That's not a negative and in fact you gain a freedom from that for variety and flexibility. As with anything there are two sides to both coins and I'd only encourage people to do what feels right by them and wish them luck!

Interview 6

Name: Neil Atkinson

Role: Computer games software developer

Website: http://enaysoft.co.uk

What are the most notable software related projects that you've worked on?

Sadly being under NDA I can't disclose that information. But I can say that some of them are household names, so to speak.

What type of technology and software development have you been involved with?

I've worked on PC, game console and mobile platforms. These days it is mostly mobile platforms, sadly.

What are the best types of project to work on?

The best type of projects are ones that don't involve free to play systems.

There is a current trend in the games industry for games to use the free to play business model, which isn't actually free at all because the business model relies on persuading people to pay as possible through the game design mechanics. This takes the emphasis away from creating a product that's meant to be great for the user and instead places the main emphasis on creating a product designed to persuade the user to pay as much money as possible at every opportunity. Everyone stands to lose on these games, with the customer not getting a game that is truly entertaining, and the software developers standing to lose from development and customer support costs if the game's design isn't persuasive enough for people to make enough in app purchases.

What software methodologies do you recommend using for software projects?

Well, this is quite a vague question, but the best is to plan your game and then stick to it and not keep adding things or changing things as progress advances, otherwise the project is certainly not going to be done on time.

What signs have you learnt that indicate a project may be problematic?

Usually when the project starts and there isn't a whole lot to do at the beginning. Often nobody is entirely sure what needs to be done and when a prototype is made, it is changed drastically but instead of starting the project again from scratch, the game is build on top of the prototype, this almost always causes problems throughout the entire development cycle. Prototypes and main game systems should be separate.

What strategies do you use to avoid problems and/or keep them under control?

For me personally time is always an issue. Not that I don't have enough time to do my work, (although that it is usually a problem) but usually that I never know when I might be requested to go outside somewhere to a meeting, or similar. So if I schedule some work for 2 days, it might be 2 days of solid work. Or 2 days of haphazard work between meetings.

Usually I tend to store time, in that if I do finish something early, I just move onto the next part without informing anyone, so that if I do have to go to a meeting and lose some time, it doesn't matter because I am already ahead in my work. If I do happen to announce I have finished early, usually more work just gets given to me.

How do you manage your workflow?

As best I can. Things change all the time, what is important today will not be important tomorrow. As a rule of thumb I try to progress with my work in chunks so I can cleanly leave something and then come back to it later. This also helps if someone is assigned to help me, that way I can easily give them stuff to do without any interruption to my own work. (Usually)

Do you have any strategy for managing the amount of incoming work you have – i.e. to avoid not having any work and to avoid having too much work?

It depends on the project, usually what you do is decided by the planner. If you're the planner as well as the programmer then life is a lot easier.

Sometimes it's a good idea to harass the planners and ask them if what they want is absolutely and 100% what they are asking for. There have been times when I have made something and then they want everything changing. And as you'd expect they want what they requested of me to be done in the same amount of time, thus the work time I just wasted isn't taken into account.

What factors do you use to judge credibility of professionals you speak to?

The way they talk to you. Often programmers are considered to be lazy, this is usually because planners seem to think that work is equal to results. Therefore if you spend a few days making some game engine component, just because you can't show it to them, they assume you haven't been doing anything useful. Credible professionals in my opinion treat their staff as equal, and tend to know how long things will take. If a planner asks you how long it will take you to change a line of text in a game, it's very difficult to take that person seriously when they bark orders at you, for something that isn't your fault.

What is your definition of a brand?

A product that is very (or quite) well known.

How has the value of a brand affected the projects you have worked on?

Oh yes definitely. Which can work both ways. If a game is popular, you know it's going to sell before you even start. This can lead to having extra time longer than usual to have it done well, however certain people might not expect to have to put much effort into the game to make it good, after all it's going to sell by the name right? This is why some high brand name games given to new studios can mess it up.

Are you finding that people's expectations for what is achievable with apps and web apps are growing? Has this caused problems in your projects?

Personally, people are expecting to get awesome apps and for free, and that is slowly becoming the norm. For me, I find this particularly depressing because it means higher risk for software development studios and the need to design apps that focus on providing an incentive to continuously pay rather than to provide features that actually useful and/ or entertaining.

In your opinion, what differentiates software, apps, web apps and websites?

Erm, I have no idea. Their usage? :)

What makes a good app?

Does what it says on the tin.

Where do you think the industry is heading?

The FTP bottleneck is still in full flow, but seems to be slowly lifting thanks to the new console boost. If FTP fades away, which I hope it does, I feel like things will get back to normal. There is only so much time games can be given away in their millions and then make just enough to sustain a company. It's more like gambling that it has ever been.

However, signs also indicate that the market can be split into a few segments when looking at free to play. Whereas the vast majority of gamers can be classed as casual gamers who are attracted to the free to play model common on mobile platforms such as Apple's iOS and Google's Android, hardcore gamers are still attracted to AAA games on platforms such as Sony's Playstation and Nintendo that the traditional upfront game purchase model – with some of these games also taking an influence from casual games by offering downloadable content (DLC) that are offered as a form of in app purchase.

What are the biggest differences between being employed by someone and being employed by yourself?

Job security is a big one. Also, if a problem happens, the company takes the fall. I wouldn't want to be independent anymore. There is no way I would want to manage a hit driven business myself. I was an independent myself for a few years and despite the freedom, I got lonely. Working on other people's games isn't so bad. I get to meet too and talk to similar people. And I now have job security and savings that I didn't currently have. If I made a hit game being independent, for sure I'd be rich. But I'd probably have died of a heart attack from stress before getting there.

www.ingramcontent.com/pod-product-compliance
Lightning Source LLC
Chambersburg PA
CBHW080713220326
41598CB00033B/5406